INTRODUCTION TO GLOBAL POLITICS

BRIEF THIRD EDITION

Steven L. Lamy
University of Southern California

John S. Masker
Temple University

John Baylis
Swansea University

Steve Smith
University of Exeter

Patricia Owens
University of Sussex

New York   Oxford
OXFORD UNIVERSITY PRESS

Oxford University Press is a department of the University of Oxford. It furthers the
University's objective of excellence in research, scholarship, and education by publishing
worldwide.

Oxford New York
Auckland Cape Town Dar es Salaam Hong Kong Karachi
Kuala Lumpur Madrid Melbourne Mexico City Nairobi
New Delhi Shanghai Taipei Toronto

With offices in
Argentina Austria Brazil Chile Czech Republic France Greece
Guatemala Hungary Italy Japan Poland Portugal Singapore South Korea
Switzerland Thailand Turkey Ukraine Vietnam

For titles covered by Section 112 of the US Higher Education Opportunity
Act, please visit www.oup.com/us/he for the latest information about
pricing and alternate formats.

Published by Oxford University Press
198 Madison Avenue, New York, NY 10016
http://www.oup.com

Library of Congress Cataloging-in-Publication Data
Lamy, Steven L.
   Introduction to global politics / Steven L. Lamy, University of Southern California; John
Masker, Temple University; John Baylis, Swansea University; Steve Smith, University of
Exeter; Patricia Owens, University of Sussex. -- Brief Third Edition.
      pages cm
   Includes bibliographical references and index.
   ISBN 978-0-19-939600-9
1. Geopolitics. 2. World politics. 3. International relations. I. Title.
   JC319.L2482 2015
   327--dc23
                                                                    2014017158

Printing number: 9 8 7 6 5 4 3 2 1

Printed in the United States of America
on acid-free paper

To our students and our mentors.

Brief Contents

Contents

Preface xi
About the Authors xxii
Maps of the World xxvii

CHAPTER 2: The Evolution of Global Politics 30

David Armstrong, Michael Cox, Len Scott,
Steven L. Lamy, and John Masker

CHAPTER 3: Theories of Global Politics 67

Tim Dunne, Stephen Hobden, Brian C. Schmidt,
Steve Smith, Richard Wyn Jones, Steven L. Lamy,
and John Masker

PART I: FOUNDATIONS OF GLOBAL POLITICS

CHAPTER 1: Introduction to Global Politics 1

John Baylis, Anthony McGrew, Steve Smith,
Steven L. Lamy, and John Masker

PART II: GLOBAL ACTORS

CHAPTER 4: Making Foreign Policy   108
Steven L. Lamy and John Masker

CHAPTER 5: International Law and Nonstate Actors   145
Devon Curtis, Christian Reus-Smit, Paul Taylor,
Steven L. Lamy, and John Masker

PART III: GLOBAL ISSUES

CHAPTER 6: Global Security, Military
Power, and Terrorism   188

John Baylis, Darryl Howlett, James D. Kiras,
Steven L. Lamy, and John Masker

CHAPTER 7: Human Rights
and Human Security   223

Amitav Acharya, Alex J. Bellamy, Chris Brown,
Nicholas J. Wheeler, Steven L. Lamy,
and John Masker

Preface

WE HAVE DEVELOPED THIS brief third edition of *Introduction to Global Politics* with an increasingly interdependent world in mind. The word *globalization* has become so overplayed that it has not retained much of its original force. And yet there is no unifying topic more important than globalization, no political trend of the same magnitude. Even our everyday decisions—those as seemingly trivial and isolated as what food to eat, what clothes to wear, what books to read, or what movies to see—affect the quality of life of people around us and in distant countries. Meanwhile, decisions made around the world affect our daily life.

Not only is the world changing, becoming more complex and interconnected than ever before, but the nature of this course is also evolving. No matter what it's called—international relations, world politics, or global politics—the course has transformed in recent years, asking us to examine not only relations among countries but also a broader context of global events and issues. In this book, we therefore take a global approach that fosters an awareness of and appreciation for a variety of worldviews. To quote the French writer Marcel Proust, we believe that "the real voyage of discovery consists not in seeking new landscapes but in having new eyes."

Like the comprehensive edition of *Introduction to Global Politics*, this brief third edition offers:

- balanced coverage of the major theoretical perspectives of international relations,
- a thorough examination of global actors, and
- an engaging introduction to global issues such as political economy, conflict, and human rights.

This brief text leads students beyond their existing understanding of global politics and invites them to examine the world by applying foundational concepts to historical and contemporary events, issues, and headlines. We have combined essential concepts with classic and current research, learning aids, and examples that students can relate to. In so doing, we offer a text that encourages the development of critical thinking and imagination that students can take with them as they continue their studies and explore careers.

A GLOBAL APPROACH

So what does it mean to take a "global" view of world politics? By this, we mean two things: First, this book brings together academics from around the world, drawing from a diversity of thought unmatched by other textbooks. Despite the range of views represented here, all of the contributors teach international relations courses, and we agree on emphasizing the challenges we all face as members of a global community. This book thus introduces students not only to the diversity of thinking in our field, but also to its common elements.

Second, we discuss in some detail the various critical actors in global politics. We explore the role of individual nation-states as well as international institutions such as the United Nations, the European Union, and critically important economic institutions, including the World Bank Group and the World Trade Organization. We carefully assess how different groups and individuals have shaped these global institutions, holding different views on how best to govern this world of nearly 200 independent nation-states. We also explore the growing number and significance of nongovernmental actors, both multinational corporations such as Nike and McDonald's and nongovernmental organizations such as Oxfam and Doctors Without Borders.

This text will introduce students to the mainstream theoretical traditions of realism and liberalism and to critical approaches that are often left out of other texts, including constructivism, Marxism, feminism, and utopianism (Chapter 3). Our goal is to introduce students to all relevant voices so they can make an informed choice about how best to both explain and understand our world. We clearly lay out important theories so that they illuminate the actors and issues we discuss, rather than cloud them in further mystery. In short, we hope these pages will help each student develop a more informed worldview.

LEARNING GOALS

An important assumption of this text is that theory matters. Every individual sees the world through theories and uses them to organize, evaluate, and critically review contending positions in controversial policy areas. Unfortunately, many people take positions that lack supporting evidence; they accept a statement or position as true or valid because it fits with their beliefs or reinforces what they believe to be true.

After completing a course using this text, students will know more about the global system, the most important global actors, and the issues that shape the priorities and behavior of states and other actors in that system. This text encourages students to approach global politics in an informed, well-reasoned, and theoretically grounded manner. Overall, the chapters in this brief edition support four core learning objectives:

1. To develop a comprehensive understanding of the various theoretical traditions in global politics and the roles they play.
2. To understand the relationship between theory and policy making or problem solving in global politics.

3. To appreciate the diversity of worldviews and theoretical assumptions that might inform political situations.
4. To develop an understanding of the global system and thereby increase the capacity to act or participate at various levels within it.

In this edition, at the beginning of each chapter we identify specific learning objectives that stem from these overarching goals. The review questions at the end of the chapter check that students have met the learning objectives.

REVIEW QUESTIONS

1. What are the possible connections, both negative and positive, between globalization and environmental change?
2. Why did environmental issues appear on the international agenda, and what were the key turning points?
3. Summarize the consequences of the 1972 UN Conference on the Human Environment and the 1992 UNCED.
4. How would you interpret the meaning of sustainable development?
5. How can regime concepts be applied to the study of international environmental cooperation?

6. Can international trade and environmental protection ever be compatible?
7. Why did the framework convention/control protocol prove useful in the cases of stratospheric ozone depletion and climate change?
8. How does the "tragedy of the commons" story help to illustrate the need for governance of the global commons?
9. Describe the free rider problem in relation to the climate-change regime.
10. Consider the possible security implications of the climate predictions made by the IPCC.

ORGANIZATION

This brief edition includes ten chapters that are organized and color-coded into three parts:

Foundations of Global Politics

Covers the basic concepts, history, and theories of global politics.

Global Actors

Introduces the main actors on the world stage—from states, to intergovernmental organizations, to transnational actors and nongovernmental agencies.

Global Issues

Focuses on issues of crucial importance to the security and prosperity of the people in the world.

Each chapter provides essential information and presents case studies and worldview questions that encourage students to think about issues from contending perspectives.

LEARNING OBJECTIVES

After reading and discussing this chapter, you should be able to:

Define key terms of environmental politics and associated scientific information.

Explain connections between globalization and environmental issues.

Describe the features of environmental protection regimes for climate change, global commons, transboundary pollution, and biodiversity.

Describe the problems associated with regime formation in environmental affairs.

Explain the term *free rider* as it applies to environmental issues.

Describe the role of the UN in the creation of environmental norms.

Explain the connections among economic development, war, and environmental degradations.

FEATURES

The development of critical-thinking skills is an important element of the course. Every chapter provides several active-learning features:

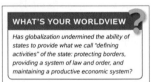

- **Theory in Practice**—These boxes examine real-world scenarios using a variety of theoretical lenses, demonstrating the explanatory power of theories in global politics.
- **Case Studies**—For a more in-depth analysis of a subject, students can turn to these boxed essays that delve into world events. Each Case Study box concludes with a set of discussion questions.
- **What's Your Worldview?**—These short, critical-thinking questions in every chapter challenge students to develop their own, more well-informed ideas about global actors and issues.
- **Thinking About Global Politics**—This feature at the end of each chapter presents in-class activities dealing with real-world political issues. These activities give students the opportunity to develop their critical-thinking skills and apply what they have learned. Each activity includes follow-up questions or writing prompts.
- **Engaging with the World**—These short pieces at the end of each chapter highlight opportunities for students to get involved with organizations working for positive change in the world.

Every part of this text has been developed with today's college student in mind. The book includes a number of integrated study aids—such as lists of key terms and review questions—all of which help students read and retain important information while extending their learning experience. Opposing quotations open every chapter, setting up one possible debate for students to consider while reading. At the end of every chapter, rather than simply summarizing the contents for students, we provide a conclusion that requires students to analyze the various topics and themes of the chapter a bit more critically, placing everything they have learned into a broader context across chapters. Students need to acquire strong critical-thinking skills; they need to learn how to make connections among real-world events they hear about in the news and the ideas they learn about in class—and it is with these goals in mind that we have developed this edition.

Here is one last point with regard to pedagogical features: The photos and figures have been carefully selected to support critical thinking as well; not only do we present a number of maps that offer unique global perspectives on historic events and modern world trends, but also we have incorporated data graphics and compelling photographs to engage students visually. The captions of many of these images include questions for further thought—once again connecting the reader back to the core content of the course, with an interesting prompt or relevant point.

NEW TO THIS EDITION

We have thoroughly updated this brief edition of *Introduction to Global Politics* in light of recent trends and events that are shaping our world, such as the ongoing Arab Spring, the rise of China, and the eurozone crisis. In addition, we have revised for more balanced coverage, and we have strengthened our focus on active learning. In making these revisions, we have taken into account the helpful comments from reviewers as well as our own experience using the first and second editions in our classes.

Chapter-by-Chapter Improvements

Throughout the textbook, figures, tables, maps, timelines, and graphs have been added, replaced, or updated with the latest and most accurate statistics, events, and information.

Chapter 1: Introduction to Global Politics
- Further examination into the growing dynamics of international relations between nation-states such as India and China, and Germany and Russia.
- A brief background and introduction into Rational decision-making (as it pertains to politics and political decision making).

Chapter 2: The Evolution of Global Politics
- A brief list of 2013 world events including: the current depth and status of the global economic crisis, the current depth and status of extreme poverty, the latest in climate politics and its relationship with rich and poor states, the aftermath of the Arab Spring (i.e. Egypt and Syria), the aftermath of the War in Afghanistan, the latest activity from religious extremist movements (i.e. Pakistan, Yemen, and Africa), and the attention or lack thereof paid to Nuclear Weapon Programs in Iran and North Korea.

Chapter 3: Theories of Global Politics
- The latest on the most pertinent international relations matters including, North Korean political and military action, and added examples of Global social movements based on normative ideas like peace, justice, and ecological balance—i.e. Greenpeace's Arctic 30, the World Social Forum, the Global Fund for Women, and a global campaign to end Indian rape culture, and the influence of Kant's Categorical Imperative.

- Results from the 2012 NATO Summit (i.e. exit strategy for Afghanistan, establishment of a new "Smart Defense" initiative, and joint management of weapons, ammunitions, and other security resources).

Chapter 4: Making Foreign Policy
- Further coverage and analysis on the UN Framework Convention on Climate Change.
- Added examples of NGO influence on humanitarian activities—i.e. Action Against Hunger, Doctors Without Borders, and UN resolution sponsored by the French government to prevent further conflict between Christian and Muslim rebel groups.

Chapter 5: International Law and Nonstate Actors
- Updated information to the Forms of INGO Power section, including new information on Information Politics, Symbolic Politics, Leverage Politics, and Accountability Politics.
- Revised *What's Your Worldview?* question boxes that address the complications to international/regional organization as well as the inability to address humanitarian challenges and disintegrating states without this organization.

Chapter 6: Global Security, Military Power, and Terrorism
- Updated information on conflicts taken place in Africa, including the war in the Democratic Republic of Congo where a ceasefire was agreed upon in late 2013, and the new UN peacekeeping mission in the Central African Republic to prevent civil wars and sectarian conflicts that create what the UN calls "pre-genocidal" conditions.
- Added examples of the importance of collective action and reliance on international/regional organization—i.e. NATO-led peacekeeping forcing in Kosovo preventing ethnic violence before a 2012 election, NATO preventing piracy activity off the coast of Somalia, and the Peace and Civil Rights Movement offering alternative strategies and actions to the U.S. and NATO for ending wars like the one in Afghanistan.
- Inclusion of the latest terrorist attacks (i.e. the Boston Marathon Attack) and the controversially expanded role given to American security agencies like the TSA and the NSA.

Chapter 7: Human Rights and Human Security
- Added information on latest human rights crises—i.e. Syria and South Sudan, as well as China who is enforcing regulation and censorship against freedom of press and speech, and those responsible for the Cambodian genocide of the 1970s finally being put to trial.
- Updated information and analysis relating to the yearly Human Security Report and 2013 UN reports.

Chapter 8: Global Economics and Trade
- Added analysis on the current status of global economic interconnection—i.e. the role that governmental intervention has on the economy of their nation-states (free markets included), the potential consequences of the Ukraine-Russia conflict, and a November 2013 report by the OECD that predicts the Greek economy to shrink further, anticipating European Union intervention once again.
- Added concluding thoughts and analysis to Chapter 8.

Chapter 9: Poverty, Development, and Hunger
- Inclusion of the latest global and anti-globalization movements including, the 39th G-8 Summit, the launching of the Big IF campaign to pressure the G-8 countries to increase funding for development and hunger projects, and the movement in Europe known as "Blockupy," which is critical of globalization and institutions that support and promote economic globalization.
- Updated information and analysis in regards to the status of Zimbabwe and their President Robert Mugabe.

Chapter 10: Environmental Issues
- Inclusion of the latest environmental issues including: the Shell oil company drilling in the Arctic, the rising number of carbon emissions emitted on the planet, and the effect climate change is having on living organisms like bees (which are important for sustaining the balance of ecosystems).
- Added information and analysis of the Kyoto Protocol and the results that came from it, and new concluding thoughts and analysis to Chapter 10.

SUPPLEMENTS

Oxford University Press offers instructors and students a comprehensive ancillary package for qualified adopters of *Introduction to Global Politics*.

Companion Website at www.oup.com/he/lamy

This open access companion website includes a number of learning tools to help students study and review key concepts presented in the text including learning objectives, key-concept summaries, quizzes, essay questions, web activities, and web links.

Ancillary Resource Center (ARC)

This convenient, instructor-focused website provides access to all of the up-to-date teaching resources for this text—at any time—while guaranteeing the security of grade-significant resources. In addition, it allows OUP to keep instructors informed when new content becomes available. Register for access and create your individual user account by clicking on the Instructor's Resources link at www.oup.com/he/lamy. Available on the ARC:

- **Instructor's Manual:** The Instructor's Resource Manual includes chapter objectives, a detailed chapter outline, lecture suggestions and activities, discussion questions, video resources, and web resources.
- **Test Item File:** This resource includes nearly 1,000 test items, including multiple-choice, short answer, and essay questions. Questions are identified as factual, conceptual, or applied, and correct answers are keyed to the text pages where the concepts are presented.
- **Computerized Test Bank:** Using the test authoring and management tool Diploma, the computerized test bank that accompanies this text is designed for both novice and advanced users. Diploma enables instructors to create and edit questions, create randomized quizzes and tests with an easy-to-use drag-and-drop tool, publish quizzes and tests to online courses, and print quizzes and tests for paper-based assessments.
- **PowerPoint Presentations:** Each chapter's slide deck includes a succinct chapter outline and incorporates relevant chapter graphics.

Course Cartridges

For qualified adopters, OUP will supply the teaching resources in a course cartridges designed to work with your preferred Online Learning Platform. Please contact your Oxford University Press sales representative at (800) 280-0208.

E-Book

Available through CourseSmart at www.coursesmart.com. CourseSmart's eTextbooks can be read on any browser-enabled computer or mobile device and come with the ability to transfer individual chapters or the entire book offline. Furthermore, CourseSmart was the first to introduce free eTextbook apps for the Android and Apple devices for an even better reading experience.

CNN Videos

Offering recent clips on timely topics, this DVD provides up to 15 films tied to the chapter topics in the text. Each clip is approximately 5–10 minutes in length, offering a great way to launch your lectures. Contact your local OUP sales representative for details.

Now Playing Video Guide

Through documentaries, feature films, and YouTube videos, *Now Playing: Learning Global Politics Through Film* provides video examples of course concepts to demonstrate real-world relevance. Each video is accompanied by a brief summary and 3–5 discussion questions.

Now Playing can be purchased separately or packaged for free with a new copy of this text. Qualified adopters will also receive a Netflix subscription that enables them to show students the films discussed in the book.

The Student Research and Writing Guide for Political Science

This guide provides students with the information and tools necessary to conduct research and write a research paper. This brief guide gives students the basics on how to get started writing a research paper, explains the parts of a research paper, and presents the citation formats found in academic writing. *The Student Research and Writing Guide for Political Science* can be packaged for free with a new copy of this text or purchased separately.

Packaging Options

Adopters of *Introduction to Global Politics* can package **ANY** Oxford University Press book with the text for a 20 percent savings off the total package price. See our many trade and scholarly offerings at www.oup.com, then contact your local Oxford University Press sales representative to request a package ISBN.

- *Introduction to Global Politics: A Reader*, edited by John Masker, offers the best variety of readings, the best coverage of alternative theories, and the best price. Package it with this text and save your students 20 percent!

In addition, the following items can be packaged with the text for FREE:

- *Oxford Pocket World Atlas*, **Sixth Edition:** This full-color atlas is a handy reference for international relations and global politics students.
- **Very Short Introduction Series:** These very brief texts offer succinct Introductions to a variety of topics. Titles include *Terrorism* by Townshend, *Globalization*, Second Edition, by Steger, and *Global Warming* by Maslin, among others.
- *Now Playing* **Video Guide:** Through documentaries, feature films, and YouTube videos, *Now Playing: Learning Global Politics Through Film* provides video examples of course concepts to demonstrate real-world relevance. Each video is accompanied by a brief summary and three to five discussion questions. *Now Playing* can be packaged for free with every new copy of this text. Qualified adopters will also receive a Netflix subscription that enables them to show students the films discussed in the book.
- *The Student Research and Writing Guide for Political Science:* This brief guide provides students with the information and tools necessary to conduct research and write research paper. The guide explains how to get started writing a research paper, describes the parts of a research paper, and presents the citation formats found in academic writing.

Please contact your Oxford University Press Sales Representative at (800) 280-0280 for more information on supplements or packaging options.

ACKNOWLEDGMENTS

The authors thank all members of the Oxford University Press team, in particular Jennifer Carpenter, executive editor, for her tireless sponsorship of this complex project, for her guidance, enthusiasm, and insights; Matt Rohal, editorial assistant, who worked efficiently to research art, prepare manuscripts, write copy, and secure permissions; senior production editor Theresa Stockton, who managed the project with skill and grace; copyeditor Susan Brown, who provided a high polish; and art director Michele Laseau, who updated the book's inviting design for this edition. Beyond the individual authors and editors of this edition, Steve Lamy would like to thank his research assistants Katelyn Masket and Danika Newlee and his students in the School of International Relations at USC.

Likewise, there are many others who are unaffiliated with the authors and editors, who contributed to this new edition's shape and success as well.

We owe a debt of gratitude to the following people, who reviewed the previous two editions and have provided invaluable insight into putting together the past and future editions of this book:

Reviewers for the Brief First Edition

Ali R. Abootalebi
University of Wisconsin, Eau Claire

Nicole Burtchett
Washington State University

Donovan C. Chau
California State University, San Bernardino

Daniel Chong
Rollins College

Michaelene Cox
Illinois State University

Roberto Dominguez
Suffolk University

Joseph J. Foy
University of Wisconsin, Waukesha

Daniel K. Gibran
Tennessee State University

James Michael Greig
University of North Texas

Steven W. Hook
Kent State University

Jeffrey Lewis
Cleveland State University

Fredline M'Cormack-Hale
Seton Hall University

Jessica Peet
University of Florida

Amanda M. Rosen
Webster University

James C. Ross
University of Northern Colorado

Donald H. Roy
Ferris State University

Barbara Salera
Washington State University

Noha Shawki
Illinois State University

M. Scott Solomon
University of South Florida

Jelena Subotic
Georgia State University

Milind Thakar
University of Indianapolis

Glenn Dale Thomas III
University of Memphis

Kimberly Weir
Northern Kentucky University

Min Ye
Coastal Carolina University

Reviewers for the Brief Second Edition

Leah Michelle Graham
University of North Alabama

Eric A. Heinze
University of Oklahoma

Courtney Hillebrecht
University of Nebraska, Lincoln

Paul E. Lenze, Jr.
Northern Arizona University

Andrea Malji
University of Kentucky

Timothy Schorn
University of South Dakota

Jacob Shively
Indiana University

Jelena Subotic
Georgia State University

Richard Tanksley
North Idaho College

Scott Wallace
Indiana University Purdue University Indianapolis

We also owe a debt of gratitude to the following people who reviewed the Comprehensive third edition of this book, which provided helpful wisdom and ingenuity to the development of the Brief third edition:

Reviewers for the Comprehensive Third Edition

Jennifer Bloxom
Colorado State University

Kevin J.S. Duska Jr.
The Ohio State University

John J. Jablowski Jr.
Penn State University

Paul A. Mego
University of Memphis, Lambuth

Alexei Shevchenko
California State University Fullerton

Veronica Ward
University State University

Winn W. Wasson
University of Wisconsin, Washington County

The book would not have been the same without the assistance and insight from these outstanding scholars and teachers. Meanwhile, any errors you might find in the book remain our own. We welcome your feedback and thank you for your support.

Steven L. Lamy
John S. Masker
John Baylis
Steve Smith
Patricia Owens

About the Authors

Amitav Acharya is the UNESCO Chair in Transnational Challenges and Governance and Professor of International Relations at American University, Washington, DC. He has held a number of appointments, including Professor of Global Governance at the University of Bristol, UK; Professor of Political Science at York University, Toronto; Fellow of the Asia Center and the John F. Kennedy School of Government at Harvard University; and Christensen Fellow at St. Catherine's College, Oxford. He is the author of *Rethinking Power, Institutions and Ideas in World Politics* (Routledge 2013); *Whose Ideas Matter? Agency and Power in Asian Regionalism* (Cornell 2009); *Human Security: The Concept and Its Implication* (Zhejiang University Press 2010, in Chinese); and *Promoting Human Security: Ethical, Normative and Educational Frameworks in South-East Asia* (UNESCO, 2007). He is co-editor of *Human Security: From Concept to Practice* (World Scientific 2011). His articles dealing with international relations theory, norm diffusion, comparative regionalism, and Asian security have appeared in *International Organization, World Politics, International Security, and International Studies Quarterly.*

David Armstrong is Emeritus Professor of International Relations at the University of Exeter. His books include *Revolutionary Diplomacy* (California University Press 1977), *The Rise of the International Organization* (Macmillan 1981), *Revolution and World Order* (Clarendon 1993), *International Law and International Relations* (co-authored with Theo Farrell and Hélène Lambert; Cambridge University Press 2007), and *Routledge Handbook of International Law* (editor; Routledge 2009).

John Baylis is Emeritus Professor at Swansea University. Until his retirement in 2008 he was Professor of Politics and International Relations and Pro-Vice-Chancellor at the university. His PhD and DLitt are from the University of Wales. He is the author of more than twenty books, the most recent of which are *The Globalization of World Politics: An Introduction to International Relations* (6th ed. with Steve Smith and Patricia Owens; Oxford University Press 2013), *Strategy in the Contemporary World: An Introduction to Strategic Studies* (4th ed. with James Wirtz and Colin S. Gray; Oxford University Press 2012), and *The United States and Europe: Beyond the Neo-Conservative Divide?* (edited with John Roper; Routledge 2006).

Alex J. Bellamy is Professor of International Relations and Executive Director of the Asia-Pacific Centre for the Responsibility to Protect at The University of Queensland, Australia. His books include *Understanding Peacekeeping* (2nd ed. with Paul D. Williams, 2010), *The Responsibility to Protect: The Global Effort to End Mass Atrocities* (Polity 2009), and *Just Wars: From Cicero to Iraq* (Polity 2007). He is currently writing *Massacres and Morality: Mass Atrocities in an Age of Non-Combatant Immunity* (Oxford University Press) and a book on implementing the Responsibility to Protect (with Sara E. Davies; Routledge).

Chris Brown is Professor of International Relations at the London School of Economics and Political Science and the author of *International Relations Theory: New Normative Approaches* (Columbia 1992), *Understanding International Relations* (Palgrave Macmillan 1997; 4th ed. 2009), *Sovereignty, Rights and Justice* (Polity 2002), and *Practical Judgement in International Political Theory* (Routledge 2010), as well as numerous book chapters and journal articles in the field of international political theory. He edited *Political Restructuring in Europe: Ethical Perspectives* (Routledge 1994) and co-edited (with Terry Nardin and N. J. Rengger) *International Relations in Political Thought: Texts from the Greeks to the First World War* (Cambridge 2002). A former Chair of the British International Studies Association (1998–1999), he was Head of the Department of International Relations at London School of Economics from 2004 to 2007.

Professor **Michael Cox** holds a Chair in International Relations at the London School of Economics and Political Science. He is the author, editor, and co-editor of more than twenty books, including *US Foreign Policy and Democracy Promotion* (Routledge 2013), *US Foreign Policy* (Oxford University Press 2012), *Soft Power and US Foreign Policy* (Routledge 2010), *The Global 1989* (Cambridge University Press 2010), *Twentieth Century International Relations* (eight volumes; Sage 2006), *E. H. Carr: A Critical Appraisal* (Palgrave 2000), *A Farewell to Arms: Beyond the Good Friday Agreement* (2nd ed., Manchester University Press 2006), *American Democracy Promotion* (Oxford University Press 2000), *The Interregnum: Controversies in World Politics, 1989–1999* (Cambridge University Press 1999), and *US Foreign Policy After the Cold War: Superpower Without a Mission?* (Pinter 1995). His work has been translated into several languages, including Japanese, Chinese, Russian, Ukrainian, German, Italian, French, and Spanish. Formerly Chair of the European Consortium for Political Research (2006–2009) and Research Fellow at the Norwegian Nobel Institute in 2002, 2007, and 2011, he is currently Chair of the United States Discussion Group at Chatham House, London, and Co-Director of IDEAS, a Centre for the Study of Strategy and Diplomacy at the LSE.

Devon E. A. Curtis is Lecturer in the Department of Politics and International Studies at the University of Cambridge and a Fellow of Emmanuel College. Her main research interests and publications deal with power-sharing and governance arrangements following conflict, UN peacebuilding, rebel movements in sub-Saharan Africa, and critical perspectives on conflict, peacebuilding, and development. She is the co-editor of *Peacebuilding, Power and Politics in Africa* (Ohio University Press 2012).

Tim Dunne is Professor of International Relations and Director of Research at the Asia-Pacific Centre for the Responsibility to Protect at the University of Queensland. His latest book, co-authored with Ken Booth, is *Terror in Our Time* (Routledge 2012). New editions of two co-edited Oxford University Press books were recently published: *International Relations Theories* (3rd ed. 2013), and *Foreign Policy: Theories, Actors, Cases* (2nd ed. 2012).

Stephen Hobden is Senior Lecturer in International Politics at the University of East London, where he teaches courses on international relations theory and China's changing international role. He is currently working on a research project, together with his colleague Erika Cudworth, on complexity theory and international relations. This has resulted in the publication of a number of articles, together with the book *Posthuman International Relations: Complexity, Ecology and Global Politics* (Zed 2011).

Darryl Howlett is Senior Lecturer in the Division of Politics and International Relations at the University of Southampton. His most recent publications include (with Jeffrey S. Lantis) "Strategic Culture," in *Strategy in the Contemporary World* (John Baylis, James Wirtz, Colin S. Gray, editors; 3rd ed., Oxford University Press 2010) and "Cyber Security and the Critical National Infrastructure," in *Homeland Security in the UK* (Paul Wilkinson, editor; Routledge 2007).

James D. Kiras is Associate Professor at the School of Advanced Air and Space Studies, Maxwell Air Force Base, Alabama, where he has directed the school's course of instruction on irregular warfare for almost a decade. He is also Senior Fellow of the Strategic Studies Division at the Joint Special Operations University, Tampa, Florida, and worked for a number of years in the defense policy, counterterrorism, special operations, and consulting world. Dr. Kiras publishes and lectures on subjects including special operations, irregular warfare, and suicide bombing. His most recent book, co-authored with other contributors, is *Understanding Modern Warfare* (Cambridge University Press 2008). Dr. Kiras's first book was entitled *Special Operations and Strategy: From World War II to the War on Terrorism* (Routledge 2006).

Steven L. Lamy is Professor of International Relations in the School of International Relations at the University of Southern California. He is also the Vice Dean for Academic Programs in the College of Letters, Arts, and Sciences. His latest research is in two areas: religion and international relations funded by a grant from the Luce Foundation and Grotian and Kantian international relations theory.

John S. Masker is Assistant Professor of Political Science at Temple University, where he teaches international relations and political theory. He has had visiting appointments at Williams College, Mount

Holyoke College, and Clark University. Masker has written about nuclear nonproliferation, Russian foreign policy, and US foreign policy.

Anthony McGrew is Professor and Executive Dean of Humanities and Social Sciences at Strathclyde University, Glasgow. He has written extensively on globalization and global governance and is currently working on a project on China and global governance.

Patricia Owens is Reader in the Department of International Relations at the University of Sussex. She was a Fellow at the Radcliffe Institute of Advanced Studies at Harvard University (2012–2013), a Visiting Professor at UCLA, and has held other research fellowships at Oxford, Princeton, UC–Berkeley, and the University of Southern California. She is author of *Between War and Politics: International Relations and the Thought of Hannah Arendt* (Oxford 2007) and co-editor of *European Journal of International Relations*.

Christian Reus-Smit is Professor of International Relations at the European University Institute, Florence. He is author of *American Power and World Order* (Polity Press 2004) and *The Moral Purpose of the State* (Princeton University Press 1999), co-author of *Special Responsibilities: Global Problems and American Power* (Cambridge University Press, 2012), editor of *The Politics of International Law* (Cambridge University Press 2004), and co-editor of *The Oxford Handbook of International Relations* (Oxford University Press 2008), *Resolving International Crises of Legitimacy* (special issue, *International Politics* 2007), and *Between Sovereignty and Global Governance* (Macmillan 1998).

Brian C. Schmidt is Associate Professor of Political Science at Carleton University, Ottawa, Canada. He is the author of *The Political Discourse of Anarchy: A Disciplinary History of International Relations* (SUNY 1998), *Imperialism and Internationalism in the Discipline of International Relations*, co-edited with David Long (SUNY 2005), and *International Relations and the First Great Debate* (Routledge 2012).

Len Scott is Professor of International History and Intelligence Studies at Aberystwyth University. His recent publications include *An International History of the Cuban Missile Crisis: A 50-year Retrospective* (Routledge 2014), co-edited with David Gioe and Christopher Andrew, *The Cuban Missile Crisis and the Threat of Nuclear War: Lessons From History* (Continuum Books 2007), and *Intelligence and International Security: New Perspectives and Agendas* (Routledge 2011), co-edited with R. Gerald Hughes and Martin Alexander.

Sir Steve Smith is Vice Chancellor and Professor of International Relations at the University of Exeter. He has held Professorships of International Relations at the University of Wales, Aberystwyth, and the University of East Anglia, and has also taught at the State University of New York (Albany) and Huddersfield Polytechnic. He was President of the International Studies Association for 2003–2004 and was elected to be an Academician of the Social Sciences (AcSS) in 2000. He was the editor of the prestigious Cambridge University Press/British International Studies Association series from 1986 to 2005. In 1999 he received the Susan Strange Award of the International Studies Association for the person who has most challenged the received wisdom in the profession. He is the author or editor of fifteen books, including (with the late Professor Martin Hollis) *Explaining and Understanding International Relations* (Oxford University Press 1989) and (co-edited with Ken Booth and Marysia Zalewski) *International Theory: Positivism and Beyond* (Cambridge University Press 1995), and some 100 academic papers and chapters in major journals and edited collections. From 2009 to 2011 he was President of Universities UK.

Paul Taylor is Emeritus Professor of International Relations and, until July 2004, was the Director of the European Institute at the London School of Economics, where he specialized in international organization within the European Union and the United Nations system. Most recently he has published *The End of European Integration: Anti-Europeanism Examined* (Routledge 2008), *International Organization in the Age of Globalization* (Continuum 2003; paperback version June 2005), and *The Careless State* (Bloomsbury 2010). He is a graduate of the University College of Wales, Aberystwyth, and the London School of Economics.

The late **Caroline Thomas** was Deputy Vice-Chancellor and Professor of Global Politics at the University of Southampton. She specialized in

North–South relations and published widely on the global politics of security, development, environment, and health.

John Vogler is Professor of International Relations in the School of Politics, International Relations and Environment (SPIRE) at Keele University, UK. He is a member of the ESRC Centre for Climate Change Economics and Policy. His books include *The Global Commons: Environmental and Technological Governance* (John Wiley 2000) and, with Charlotte Bretherton, *The European Union as a Global Actor* (Routledge 2006). He has also edited, with Mark Imber, *The Environment and International Relations* (Routledge 1996) and, with Alan Russell, *The International Politics of Biotechnology* (Manchester University Press 2000).

Nicholas J. Wheeler is Professor of International Relations and Director of the Institute for Conflict, Cooperation, and Security at the University of Birmingham. His publications include (with Ken Booth) *The Security Dilemma: Fear, Cooperation, and Trust in World Politics* (Palgrave Macmillan 2008); (edited with Jean-Marc Coicaud) *National Interest Versus Solidarity: Particular and Universal Ethics in International Life* (United Nations University Press 2008); and (with Ian Clark) *The British Origins of Nuclear Strategy 1945–55* (Oxford University Press 1989). He has also written widely on humanitarian intervention and is the author of *Saving Strangers: Humanitarian Intervention in International Society* (Oxford University Press 2000). He is currently researching a book provisionally entitled *Trusting Rivals: Alternative Paths to Security in the Nuclear Age* as part of a three-year ESRC/AHRC Fellowship on 'The Challenges to Trust-Building in Nuclear Worlds" through RCUK's "Global Uncertainties: Security For All in a Changing World" program. He is co-editor with Professor Christian Reus-Smit of the prestigious Cambridge Series in International Relations.

Ngaire Woods is the Dean of Blavatnik School of Government at Oxford University and Professor of Global Economic Governance; she is the founder and Director of the Global Economic Governance Programme at Oxford University. Her recent books include *Networks of Influence: Developing Countries in a Networked Global Order*, with Leonardo Martinez-Diaz (Oxford University Press 2009); *The Politics of Global Regulation*, with Walter Mattli (Oxford University Press 2009); *The Globalizers: the IMF, the World Bank and Their Borrowers* (Cornell University Press 2006); *Exporting Good Governance: Temptations and Challenges in Canada's Aid Program*, with Jennifer Welsh (Laurier University Press 2007); and *Making Self-Regulation Effective in Developing Countries*, with Dana Brown (Oxford University Press 2007). She has previously published *The Political Economy of Globalization* (Macmillan 2000); *Inequality, Globalization and World Politics*, with Andrew Hurrell (Oxford University Press 1999); *Explaining International Relations Since 1945* (Oxford University Press 1986); and numerous articles on international institutions, globalization, and governance. Ngaire Woods has served as an adviser to the IMF Board, the UNDP's Human Development Report, and the Commonwealth Heads of Government.

Richard Wyn Jones is Professor of Welsh Politics and Director of the Wales Governance Centre at Cardiff University. He has written extensively on Welsh politics, devolution, nationalism, and security studies. His book *Security, Strategy and Critical Theory* (Rienner 1999) is regarded as an important work in the area of critical theory. His most recent books *are Wales Says Yes: The 2011 Referendum and Welsh Devolution* (University of Wales Press 2012, with Roger Scully); (in Welsh) "Y Blaid Ffasgaidd yng Nghymru": Plaid Cymru a'r Cyhuddiad o Ffasgaeth (University of Wales Press 2013), and *The Fascist Party in Wales? Plaid Cymru, Welsh Nationalism and the Accusation of Fascism* (University of Wales Press 2014).

MAPS

OF THE WORLD

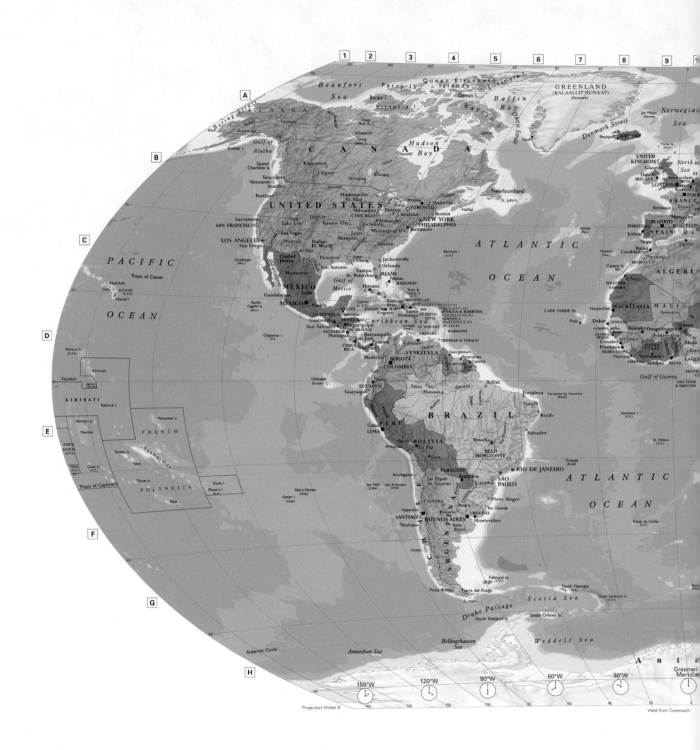

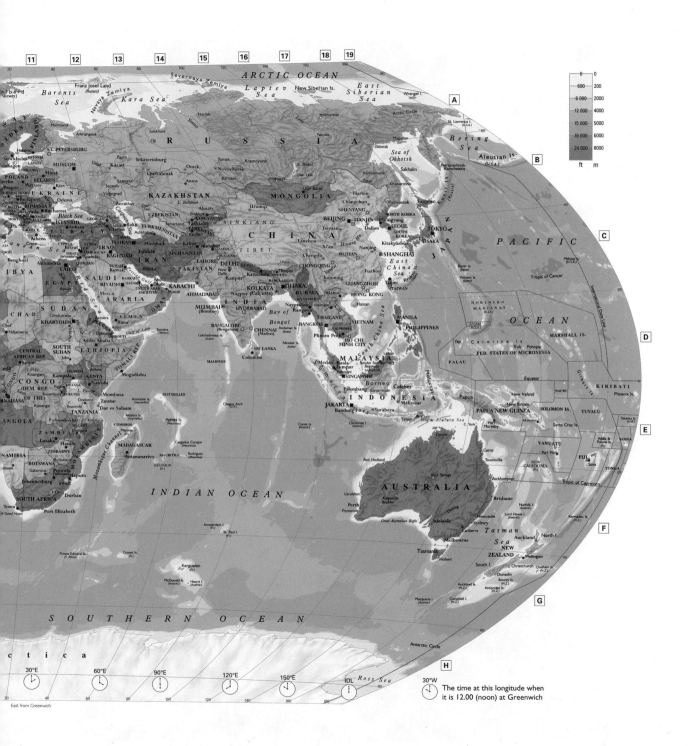

11 **12** **13** **14** **15** **16** **17** **18** **19**

ARCTIC OCEAN

Severnaya Zemlya

Barents Sea   Novaya Zemlya   Kara Sea   Laptev Sea   New Siberian Is.   East Siberian Sea   Wrangel I.

Svalbard (Norway)   Franz Josef Land (Russia)

Nordvik

Arctic Circle

A

R U S S I A

Murmansk   Arkhangelsk   Ob   Salekhard   Yenisey   Norilsk   Lena   Yakutsk   Verkhoyansk   Magadan

Bering Sea

St. Petersburg   Yekaterinburg   Perm   Tomsk   Krasnoyarsk   L. Baikal   Okhotsk   Sea of Okhotsk   Aleutian Is. (U.S.A.)   St. Lawrence I. (U.S.A.)   **B**

MOSCOW   Kazan   Chelyabinsk   Omsk   Novosibirsk   Barnaul   Ulan-Ude   Komsomolsk   Sakhalin   Petropavlovsk-Kamchatsky

Volga   Samara   Saratov   Astrakhan   KAZAKHSTAN   Ulan Bator   Khabarovsk

MONGOLIA   Vladivostok   Sapporo

Almaty   Harbin   Changchun   NORTH KOREA   P A C I F I C   **C**

UZBEKISTAN   KYRGYZSTAN   SINKIANG   Ürümqi   BEIJING   SHENYANG   P'yongyang   SEOUL   SOUTH KOREA   TŌKYŌ   ŌSAKA

TURKMENISTAN   Tashkent   Samarkand   Kabul   C H I N A   TIANJIN   Dalian   Kitakyūshū

Ashkhabad   Mashhad   AFGHANISTAN   Islamabad   Lanzhou   Taiyuan   Xi'an   Hwang   Nanjing   East China Sea   Midway Is. (U.S.A.)

Tehran   Kabul   LAHORE   TIBET   Lhasa   Chengdu   WUHAN   SHANGHAI   Volcano Is. (Japan)   Tropic of Cancer

IRAN   PAKISTAN   DELHI   NEPAL   CHONGQING   Fuzhou   Bonin Is. (Japan)

Esfahan   Shiraz   New Delhi   Kanpur   Katmandu   BHUTAN   Kunming   GUANGZHOU   Taipei   TAIWAN   O C E A N

RIYADH   QATAR   KARACHI   AHMADABAD   I N D I A   Ganges   BANGLADESH   HONG KONG

U.A.E.   Muscat   KOLKATA (Calcutta)   DHAKA   BURMA   Hainan   NORTHERN MARIANAS (U.S.A.)   **D**

SAUDI ARABIA   OMAN   MUMBAI (Bombay)   NAGPUR   HYDERABAD   Naypyidaw   Rangoon   LAOS   Hanoi   GUAM (U.S.A.)   MARSHALL IS.

YEMEN   Bay of Bengal   BANGALORE (Bengaluru)   Lakshadweep Is. (India)   Andaman Is. (India)   THAILAND   VIETNAM   Yap   Caroline Is   Truk   Pohnpei

Aden   Gulf of Aden   Socotra (Yemen)   CHENNAI (Madras)   BANGKOK   CAMBODIA   MANILA   PALAU   FED. STATES OF MICRONESIA   NAURU   KIRIBATI

Mogadishu   SRI LANKA   Nicobar Is. (India)   Phnom Penh   HO CHI MINH CITY   PHILIPPINES   Phoenix Is.

SEYCHELLES   Colombo   MALDIVES   MALAYSIA   Kuala Lumpur   Medan   SINGAPORE   SARAWAK   Borneo   Celebes   Papua   New Ireland   New Britain   SOLOMON IS.   TUVALU

Chagos Arch. (U.K.)   Palembang   Banjarmasin   I N D O N E S I A   Makassar   PAPUA NEW GUINEA

JAKARTA   Bandung   Java   Surabaya   Timor   Arafura Sea   Port Moresby   VANUATU   **E**

Amirante Is. (Seychelles)   Cocos Is. (Austral.)   Christmas I. (Austral.)   C. York   Santa Cruz Is.   Wallis & Futuna Is. (Fr.)   SAMOA

Aldabra Is. (Seychelles)   Cargados Carajos   Darwin   NEW CALEDONIA   FIJI   Suva   TONGA

COMOROS   Mayotte (Fr.)   MADAGASCAR   MAURITIUS   Rodrigues (Mauritius)   Port Hedland   Cairns   Nouméa   Port Vila

Antananarivo   RÉUNION (Fr.)   Alice Springs   Townsville   Norfolk I. (Austral.)   Tropic of Capricorn   **F**

Rockhampton   Kermadec Is. (N.Z.)

I N D I A N   O C E A N   A U S T R A L I A   Brisbane   Lord Howe I. (Austral.)

Geraldton   Kalgoorlie-Boulder   Newcastle   North I.

Perth   Fremantle   Great Australian Bight   Adelaide   Sydney   Auckland

Amsterdam I. (Fr.)   Canberra   Tasman Sea

St. Paul I. (Fr.)   Melbourne   NEW ZEALAND

Tasmania   Wellington   South I.   Chatham Is. (N.Z.)   **G**

Prince Edward Is. (S. Africa)   Crozet Is. (Fr.)   Hobart   Dunedin   Bounty Is. (N.Z.)

Kerguelen (Austral.)   McDonald Is. (Austral.)   Heard I. (Austral.)   Christchurch   Antipodes Is. (N.Z.)

Auckland Is. (N.Z.)   Macquarie I. (Austral.)   Campbell I. (N.Z.)

H

S O U T H E R N   O C E A N

Ross Sea

Antarctica   Antarctic Circle

30°E   **60°E**   **90°E**   **120°E**   **150°E**   **IDL**   **30°W**

East from Greenwich

The time at this longitude when it is 12.00 (noon) at Greenwich

A **B** **C** **D** **E** **F** **G**

ft   m

0   0
600   200
6 000   2000
12 000   4000
15 000   5000
18 000   6000
24 000   8000

AFRICA (partial labels): LIBYA, EGYPT, SUDAN, SOUTH SUDAN, CHAD, CENTRAL AFRICAN REP., ETHIOPIA, SOMALI REP., KENYA, TANZANIA, CONGO (DEM. REP. OF THE), ANGOLA, ZAMBIA, ZIMBABWE, BOTSWANA, NAMIBIA, SOUTH AFRICA, MOZAMBIQUE, MADAGASCAR

Benghazi, Alexandria, CAIRO, Aswan, Mecca, Sana'a, Djibouti, Addis Ababa, KHARTOUM, Omdurman, N'djamena, Bangui, Kisangani, Kampala, UGANDA, RWANDA, BURUNDI, Nairobi, Mombasa, Dar es Salaam, Zanzibar, Dodoma, Lusaka, Harare, Bulawayo, Gaborone, Pretoria, Maputo, Johannesburg, Durban, Port Elizabeth, Cape Town, C. of Good Hope

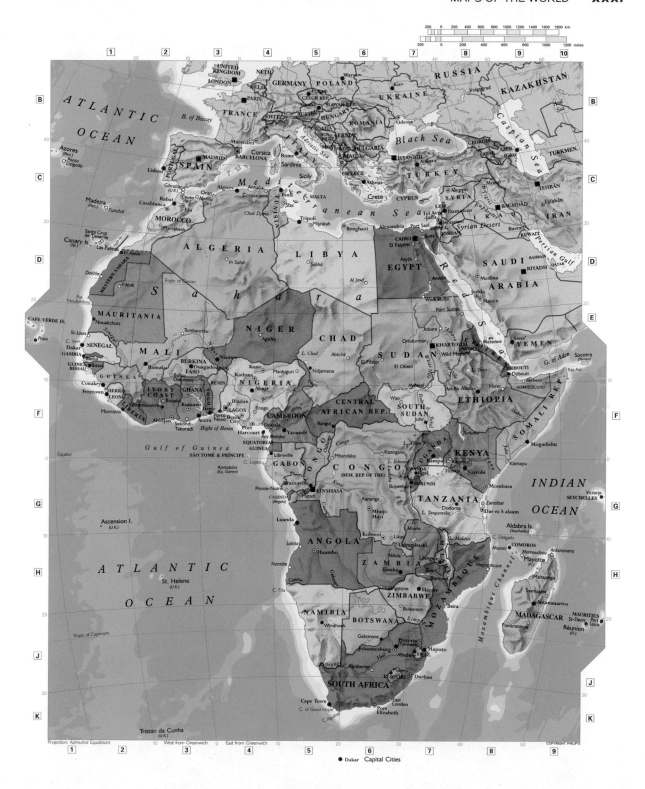

Dakar ● Capital Cities

Projection: Azimuthal Equidistant

COPYRIGHT PHILIP'S

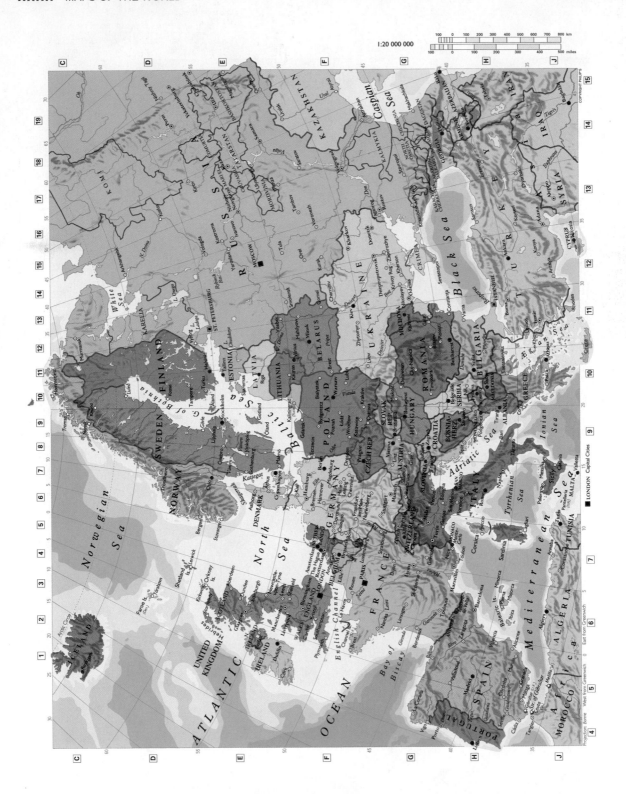

1:35 000 000

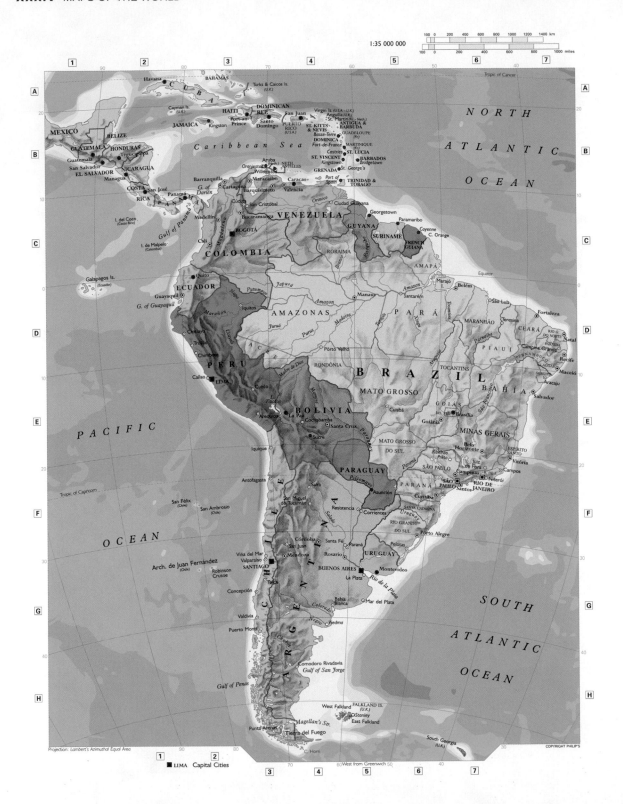

1:35 000 000

Projection: Lambert's Azimuthal Equal Area

■ LIMA Capital Cities

COPYRIGHT PHILIP'S

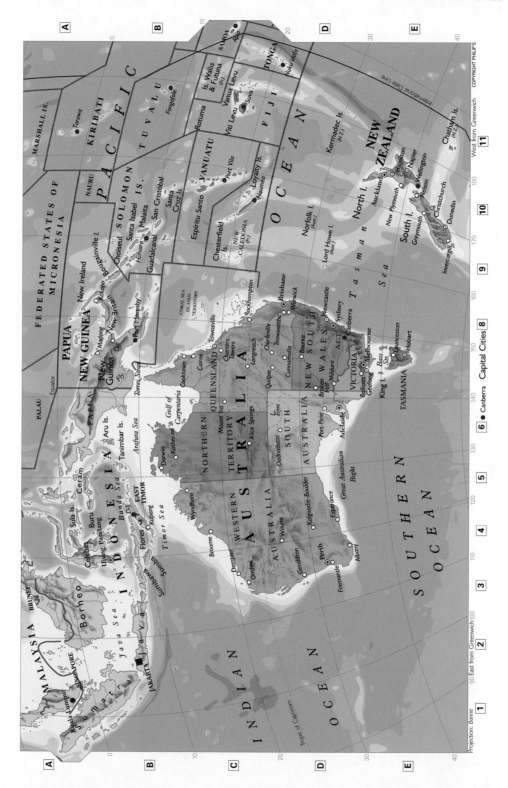

West from Greenwich

International Date Line

NEW ZEALAND

North I.
Auckland
Hamilton
Napier
Wellington
New Plymouth
Nelson
Greymouth
Christchurch
South I.
Dunedin
Invercargill

Chatham Is.
(N.Z.)

Kermadec Is.
(N.Z.)

Norfolk I.
(Aust.)

Lord Howe I.
(Aust.)

T a s m a n   S e a

SAMOA
Apia
Is. Wallis
& Futuna
(Fr.)
TONGA
Nuku'alofa
FIJI
Vanua Levu
Viti Levu
Suva
Rotuma
TUVALU
Fongafale
Loyalty Is.
Nouméa
NEW
CALEDONIA
(Fr.)
Chesterfield
Is.
Espiritu Santo
Port Vila
VANUATU
Santa
Cruz Is.
San Cristóbal
Malaita
Honiara
Guadalcanal
SOLOMON IS.
Santa Isabel
Choiseul

P A C I F I C

O C E A N

KIRIBATI
Tarawa
NAURU

MARSHALL IS.

FEDERATED STATES OF
MICRONESIA

PALAU

Equator

MALAYSIA
Kuala Lumpur
SINGAPORE
BRUNEI
Borneo
Celebes
Sula Is.
Buru
Ujung Pandang
Ceram
Aru Is.
Tanimbar Is.
INDONESIA
Java
Sumatra
JAKARTA
Java Sea
Banda Sea
Flores
Sumbawa
Sumba
Kupang
Dili
EAST
TIMOR
Timor Sea
Arafura Sea

PAPUA
NEW GUINEA
New Ireland
Bougainville I.
New Britain
Kokopo
New
Guinea
(Fr.)
Madang
Lae
Port Moresby
Torres Strait

CORAL SEA
ISLANDS
TERRITORY

Brisbane
Warwick
Rockhampton
Bundaberg
Newcastle
Sydney
Canberra
A.C.T.
Townsville
Charters
Towers
Cairns
Cooktown
Longreach
Charleville
Toowoomba
Bourke
NEW SOUTH
WALES
QUEENSLAND
Mount Isa
Cloncurry
Gulf of
Carpentaria
Katherine
Darwin
Wyndham
Broome
Dampier
Onslow
Wiluna
NORTHERN
TERRITORY
Alice Springs
Oodnadatta
L.
Eyre
SOUTH
AUSTRALIA
Port Pirie
Adelaide
Broken
Hill
Mildura
Geelong
Ballarat
VICTORIA
Melbourne
King I.
Bass
Str.
Launceston
Hobart
TASMANIA
WESTERN
AUSTRALIA
Kalgoorlie-Boulder
Esperance
Great Australian
Bight
Albany
Perth
Fremantle
Geraldton

A U S T R A L I A

INDIAN
OCEAN

SOUTHERN
OCEAN

Tropic of Capricorn

East from Greenwich

Projection: Bonne

Canberra   Capital Cities

Canberra   Capital Cities

Introduction to Global Politics

I am a citizen of the world.

—Diogenes

I am not a citizen of the world . . . I am not even aware that there is a world such that one could be a citizen of it. No one has ever offered me citizenship, or described the naturalization process, or enlisted me in the world's institutional structures, or given me an account of its decision procedures . . . or provided me with a list of the benefits and obligations of citizenship, or shown me the world's calendar and the common celebrations and commemorations of its citizens.

—Michael Walzer

Who will lead the world in this century, in this era of globalization? Will the American Empire come to an end because of its internal economic problems? Will China or India assume the mantle of leadership? Will a new global leader be willing to set aside national interests for the good of the global system? Although both India and China are emerging as major economic players, both have millions of citizens mired in poverty, and each country has significant domestic challenges that could preclude an activist role in global politics. We need to remember that the United States and its alliances have created a global system that has provided opportunities for most countries to prosper. This is not to say, however, that the current system does not struggle with significant global challenges, such as how to help the "bottom billion," the poorest billion people in the world. But will the new superpowers take responsibility for providing the materials and resources needed to manage global problems?

The world is changing, and that change is not only about terrorist networks or the end of the Cold War. Globalization—especially economic globalization—has dramatically reshuffled global power arrangements and

Prime Minister Singh and Premier Li sign an agreement in October 2013 aimed at containing border disputes between their armies. Both countries have aspirations for regional and global leadership.

created new alliances and coalitions with the power to shape our well-being. This is still a world without a central government, but we all depend on the willingness of some states to lead and to manage the institutions essential to controlling the processes of globalization. At the same time, we expect our governments to provide security and opportunities for economic growth, and that is not easily done in this era of globalization. Who will lead is one question, and who can afford to lead might be an even more important question. Still, the global war on terrorism, with tremendous costs in terms of blood and treasure, continues to shape foreign policies of most states. And we know that all nation-states are being dramatically affected by the global economic crisis, which is pinching the wealthy and crushing those without the natural and human resources necessary to compete.

How we react to momentous events like terrorist attacks and the global financial collapse that began in 2008 is linked to how we identify ourselves. Are you a citizen of the world, like Diogenes, or a citizen of a specific place, like Michael Walzer? You might be surprised to know how connected you are to the world. Look at the labels in your clothing. The tag says "Made in Someplace," but have you ever wondered how the pieces of, for example, your sneakers got to the factory where they were assembled? Or how the shoes traveled from that factory in Asia to the store in California, Kansas, or Vermont where you purchased them? Have you ever asked yourself who made your sneakers? How does that person live? How do others in the world view the United States or other wealthy and powerful states? How you are connected goes beyond looking at the goods and services you purchase in a given day. Do you have a passport, and have you traveled internationally? Do you have a Web-capable cell phone, and are you constantly plugged in to Internet applications like Facebook? Are you on Skype talking to friends you met while participating in a study-abroad program? Have you signed up for news alerts from news agencies? Do you also read the international news from foreign sources such as the BBC or Al Jazeera? Do you belong to a global nongovernmental organization (NGO) like Human Rights Watch, Oxfam, or Greenpeace?

All of us have connections to the world that we are not aware of. Other connections we make, like joining a political group or student organization on campus, are more personal and immediate. Yet both types of connections—known and unknown—help shape our identities as individuals in the wider world. The purpose of this book is to help you understand the world of politics that provides those connections. Along the way you will see how interdependent we all are and how our way of life is shaped by forces of globalization.

LEARNING OBJECTIVES

After reading and discussing this chapter, you should be able to:

Describe key global actors and their role in addressing global issues.

Begin to define theories of international relations.

Explain the concept of levels of analysis.

Define the term *globalization*.

Explain academic disagreements about the character of globalization.

This chapter presents an overview of the textbook—the main actors and topics that we will examine. It also introduces the theories that will guide us in our study of global politics. You will learn more about globalization, and you will begin that important journey of discovery by developing new eyes. You will begin to see how different theories construct our world.

Introduction

Probably more than any other events, the global economic crisis and a series of terrorist attacks throughout the world have underscored the significance of globalization. The war in Afghanistan and the particularly controversial invasion of Iraq in 2003, followed by insurgency and civil war, are further clear examples of what it means to call the current era globalized—these events involved international coalitions and transnational violent networks in conflicts that linked events in seemingly unrelated parts of the world. Let us look at how aspects of the **September 11, 2001**, attacks (hereafter 9/11) illustrate the impact of globalization:

- First, 9/11 was an event taking place in one country, the United States, but immediately observed throughout the world: The television pictures of the second plane crashing into the World Trade Center are probably the most widely seen images in television history. Thus, 9/11 was a world event, which had far more of an effect than represented by the number of deaths involved (about 3,000 died in the four attacks that day; on an average day 30,000 children throughout the world die of malnutrition and preventable diseases, although not often in the gaze of television cameras).

- The attacks were carried out by nineteen individuals in the name of a previously shadowy organization known as Al Qaeda. This organization was not a state or formal international body but a loose coalition of committed men based, it is claimed, in more than fifty countries. This was a truly globalized network and not just a traditional organization. Al Qaeda also inspired or directed terrorist attacks in Madrid in 2004 and in London in 2005.

- The attacks were coordinated using some of the most powerful technologies of the globalized world, namely, mobile phones, international bank accounts, and the Internet. Moreover, the key personnel traveled regularly between continents using mass air travel—yet another symbol of globalization.

- The reactions to the events throughout the world were intense, instantaneous, and very mixed: In some Arab

People in New York City gather near Ground Zero, the site of the 9/11 terrorist attacks, to celebrate the news of Osama bin Laden's assassination by US Navy Seals in 2011.

and Muslim countries there was jubilation that the West generally, and the United States specifically, had been hit; in many other countries there was profound shock and an immediate empathy with the United States.

- The attacks were not on ordinary buildings; the Pentagon is the symbol of US military power and hegemony, and the World Trade Center was (as the name implies) an icon of the world financial network and the triumph of capitalism led by the United States and other Western countries.

- It is worth noting that although these were attacks on the United States, many individuals of other nationalities were killed; it is estimated that citizens from about ninety countries were killed in the attacks on the World Trade Center.

- Finally, although there is a lot of disagreement over why Osama bin Laden ordered the attacks, the main reasons seem to have concerned events in yet other parts of the world: Bin Laden himself cited the plight of the Palestinians, as well as the continued support of the United States for the current Saudi regime and the presence of US military personnel on that country's "holy" soil. Therefore, although there are many indicators that the world has become increasingly globalized over the last thirty years, in many ways 9/11 and other Al Qaeda attacks are among the clearest symbols.

Still, globalization can also be seen as one of the causes of these attacks. In many parts of the world dominated by traditional cultures and religious

Russian President Putin and German Chancellor Merkel meet in Moscow. Although they have strong economic ties, Chancellor Merkel was not afraid to criticize the Russian human rights record and Germany has supported the US led opposition to Russia's annexation of Crimea.

communities, fundamentalists see globalization as a Western process bringing popular culture and Western ideas that undermine their core values and beliefs. This "Westoxification" pushed and promoted by globalization is the enemy, and the United States is the leader of this noxious process. Many fundamentalist communities are trying to control, manage, and, if possible, stop the process of globalization. This is possible in totalitarian societies, but it is becoming more difficult as the Internet and global communications spread around the world. The recent upheavals in North Africa and the Middle East—the so-called Arab Spring—were organized using social media. New communication technologies are certainly aiding change agents across the globe; these are transboundary tools that states cannot effectively contain.

Generally, people care most about what is going on at home or in their local communities. We usually elect people to office who promise to provide jobs, fix roads, offer loans for housing, build good schools, and provide quality health care. These promises might get candidates votes, but people in office soon learn that many of the promises cannot be fulfilled without considering the dynamics of the global economy. Leaders are now realizing that to provide for their citizens they must manage the processes of globalization, and this is not a task one country can do alone. Not since the energy crisis of the early 1970s has the world experienced the costs of global interdependence and the vulnerabilities created by globalization.

We all became aware of the breadth and depth of globalization with the economic crisis that began in 2008. The costs of this global financial crisis include unemployment, home foreclosures, bank failures, a collapse in stock markets around the world, and a general anger and dissatisfaction with political leaders for failing to anticipate these problems and respond before the near collapse. Governments must prove that they can regulate global finance and manage the processes of globalization. World leaders have met in a number of settings, including G-20 meetings all over the world. These leaders are now hoping that government spending might stimulate demand and that they can work together to regulate global finance. Further, they hope to direct more funds to countries in the developing world and reform the global institutions that must monitor and manage the forces of globalization.

Currently, fears of a European recession could grow worse if economic rescue plans for Greece and Spain do not work. With Germany in the lead, the European Union (EU) is trying to manage its regional financial crisis and address government debt, high rates of unemployment, and resulting government instability. The entire world is depending on Europe solving this crisis. The United States is particularly concerned because investment in the EU is three times higher than in all of Asia, and EU investment in the United States is around eight times the amount of EU investment in India and China together. About 15 million jobs are linked to the transatlantic economy. Slowly,

Wal-Mart, a global corporation, sells manufactured goods made in China in every store in America, and now they have several supercenters in China. Do you think they are selling American-made goods in these stores?

people throughout the world are realizing that their quality of life is directly tied to the well-being of others in distant lands.

The aim of this book is to provide an overview of global politics in this globalized world. We will therefore begin by introducing you to global politics as distinct from international politics or international relations. We will then expand the discussion to consider globalization. Many scholars think that the contemporary, post–Cold War world is markedly different from previous periods because of the effects of globalization. Is it? What exactly does it mean to say this is an era of globalization? Does it mean that the main features of global politics are any different from those of previous eras? In this introduction we explain how we propose to deal with the concept of globalization, and we offer you some arguments for and against seeing it as an important new development in global politics.

International Relations and Global Politics

Why does the title of this book refer to **global politics** rather than to international politics or **international relations**? These are the traditional names used to describe the kinds of interactions and processes that are the concern of this text. Indeed, you could look at the table of contents of many other introductory books and find a similar listing of main topics, yet often these books would have either "international relations" or "international politics" in their main title. Furthermore, the discipline that studies these issues is nearly always called international relations or international politics.

Our reason for choosing the phrase "global politics" is that we think it is more inclusive than either of the alternative terms. With this phrase, we mean to highlight our interest in the politics and political patterns in the world and not only those between nation-states (as the term international politics implies). Thus, we are interested in relations among organizations that might or might not be states—such as multinational companies, terrorist groups, or **nongovernmental organizations (NGOs)**; these are all known as **transnational actors**. Similarly, the term *international relations* might be too exclusive. Of course, it does represent a widening of our concern from simply the political relations between nation-states, but it still restricts our focus to *inter*-national relations, whereas we think that relations between, say, cities or provinces and other **governments** or international organizations can be equally important. So we prefer to characterize the relations we are interested in as those of "world" politics—or, more specifically, given the powerful influences of globalization, global politics.

However, we do not want such fine distinctions regarding word choice to force you to define politics too narrowly. You will see this issue arising time and time again in the chapters that follow, because many academics want to define politics very widely. One obvious example concerns the relationship between politics and economics; there is clearly an overlap, and a lot of bargaining power goes to the person who can persuade others that the existing distribution of resources is "simply" economic rather than a political issue. So, we want you to think about politics very broadly for the time being. Several features of the contemporary world that you might not have previously thought of as "political" will be described as such in the chapters that follow. Our focus is on the patterns of political relations, defined broadly, that characterize the contemporary world.

Defining *Nation*, *State*, and *Nation-State*

The terms *nation*, *state*, and *nation-state* can be somewhat confusing to newcomers to the field, so we will take a moment to define them here. The two parts of the term *nation-state* derive from different sources. **Nation** derives from the idea that a group of people sharing the same geographic space, the same language, the same culture, and the same history also share a common identity. As most political scientists use the term, *nation* is meant to convey a group identity that is bigger than a family group or tribal unit. **State** has its origins in the Latin language and the legal system of the Roman Empire. At a minimum, political scientists agree that the state is the highest level political structure that makes authoritative decisions within a territorially based political unit. What makes the term confusing for many students in the United States is that the country comprises subunits that are called states. When *nation* and *state* are combined in the pair *nation-state*, we have a term that describes a political unit within which people share an identity. It is important to note that the state is not always coincidental with a nation. Although the state for many political scientists is a set of governing institutions, nation refers to the people who share a history, language, religion, or other cultural attributes. The Flemish in Belgium, the Welsh in the United Kingdom, and the Iroquois of the United States and Canada are examples of nations found within states. Most states,

United State Of America
You Have A New Ally In North Africa
لديكم حليف جديد في شمال أفريقيا

Libyan citizens attending Muslim prayers show their gratitude to the United States, France, and NATO allies who provided valuable air support and intelligence for the fight that ended the authoritarian rule of Muammar Gaddafi in 2011.

even when called nation-states, actually include several nations. As we will see elsewhere in this book, many problems in the modern international system result from nations with historical rivalry that are forced to live within the borders of one state.

The concepts of state and sovereignty are critical to understand if you are a student of international relations, a diplomat, or a political leader. The nation-state—sometimes called a "country" or simply "state"—is the primary unit of analysis in the study of international relations. As we will learn later in this chapter, the Peace of Westphalia in 1648 recognized the state as supreme and the sovereign power within its boundaries. The Westphalian ideal of sovereignty emphasizes the principle of the inviolability of the borders of a state. Furthermore, all states agreed with the idea that it was not acceptable to intervene in the internal affairs of other states. **Sovereignty** is a complex and contested concept in international relations; essentially, it suggests that within a given territory the leaders of a state have absolute and final political authority. However, international relations scholar Manuel Castells (2005) has suggested that the modern nation-state might be adversely affected by globalization in four ways; indeed, all our political institutions are facing the same four crises:

1. States cannot effectively manage global problems unilaterally and thus suffer a *crisis of efficiency*.
2. Policy makers are not always representative of their citizens' interests, and as policy making becomes more global, decisions are made further away from citizens. This is a *crisis of legitimacy*.

3. Citizens are being pulled toward their cultural identity and toward identity and affiliation with NGOs and other civil-society actors. A variety of forces pull them away from citizen identity and have created a *crisis of identity.*
4. Globalization has increased inequality in many states and created a *crisis of equity.*

Castells argues that nation-states must create collaborative networks with NGOs and other nonstate actors to respond effectively to these crises. The nation-state will survive, but states might be forced to share sovereignty with other global actors to provide for their citizens, meet their obligations, and face the issues in the world today.

Global Actors

After we review the history of global politics and present major theories in Chapters 2 and 3, we will take a look at a number of important actors on the world stage. Because states are the most important actors in global politics, we begin our discussion of actors with them in Chapter 4. These are the actors that engage in diplomatic relations, sign the treaties that create the legal foundation for world politics, and go to war.

Increasingly, however, **nonstate actors** are playing important roles globally, and we discuss them in Chapter 5. Some of these actors are international or regional organizations that are composed of states. The United Nations (UN) is the most famous actor in this category; others include the EU, the Organization of American States, the Shanghai Cooperation Organization, and the African Union. **Multinational corporations (MNCs)** are also nonstate actors that have become important players in world politics. These large business organizations can have their headquarters in one country, their design staff in another, and their production facilities in several other countries. The MNCs are important in many ways, but perhaps most significantly because a factory can provide vital jobs in a developing country. Other nonstate actors include NGOs, which have increased in numbers and influence in world politics. NGOs such as Oxfam or World Vision provide expertise for policy makers and provide programs and resources to address global problems like poverty and global health issues. To clarify the difference, some authors call MNCs for-profit nonstate actors and NGOs not-for-profit nonstate actors.

Global Issues

In Chapters 6 through 10, we will turn our focus to global issues. Although we define politics broadly, we can also group the global issues that we will study into two main categories: security (Chapters 6–7) and economy (Chapters 8–10). First, we examine global security and military power, considering the traditional

Aid from international agencies like the World Food Program can help provide immediate relief for starving people. Food aid should be a temporary solution. Ultimately, the world economic system must promote agricultural production in developing states.

responsibility of states to provide for the physical security of their territory. We also consider terrorism, including the various groups that employ this method and the ways in which countries have responded to the threats. Chapter 7 discusses an emerging issue-area of world politics: human rights and human security. Finally, we examine the intersections of world politics and economics—including trade, finance, poverty, development, and environmental issues. Each of these topics overlaps the others, and it's important not to read these chapters merely in a straightforward fashion but also to review the information from previous chapters as you progress through your coursework. Although we have neatly divided these issues for ease of reading, we do not mean to reduce them in their importance or complexity; indeed, throughout, we'll also examine how security issues and economic issues are inextricably linked.

The Origins of Globalization

As we have said, our goal is to offer an overview of world politics in a globalized era. By **globalization**, we mean the process of increasing interconnectedness among societies such that events in one part of the world have effects on peoples and societies far away. A globalized world is one in which political, economic, cultural, and social events become more and more interconnected and also have broader impact. In other words, societies affect one another more and more extensively and deeply. The world seems to be shrinking.

What are some examples of globalization? The World Wide Web is the most graphic example, enabling instant connection to websites around the world. Electronic mail has also transformed communications in ways we could not have envisioned twenty years ago. But these are only the most obvious examples. Others include worldwide television communications, global newspapers, global production of goods (see the Case Study in this chapter), international NGOs, global franchises such as McDonald's and Ikea, the global economy, and global risks such as pollution, global warming, and the AIDS epidemic. We could make a strong case that a new world political system has emerged as a result of globalization.

Having noted this, we want to point out that globalization is not some entirely new phenomenon in world history. Indeed, many argue that it is merely a new name for a long-term process. Our goal here is to provide enough historical context for you to understand the topics we examine throughout this book. We leave it to you to judge whether, in its current manifestation, globalization represents a new phase in world history or merely a continuation of processes that have been around for a long time. We note, however, that there have been several precursors to globalization, as you will see.

Historical Trends: Politics

Many international relations specialists regard the **Peace of Westphalia** that ended the Thirty Years' War in 1648 as the key event ushering in the contemporary international system. The participants of the conference included ambassadors from the Netherlands, Spain, Sweden, France, Austria, and several of the larger German principalities. The accord codified the right of the more than 300 German states that constituted the Holy Roman Empire to conduct their own diplomatic relations—a very clear acknowledgment of their sovereignty. It also granted them "an exact and reciprocal Equality": the first formal acceptance of

The banner reads: "Peace and justice, the people's will" as Sudanese citizens protest outside the Sudanese embassy in Cairo, Egypt, in 2013. Security forces representing the government of Omar al-Bashir had fired on mourners at a funeral for a protester killed during a week of demonstrations.

sovereign equality for a significant number of states. The Peace encapsulated the very idea of a **society of states**, an association of sovereign states based on their common interests, values, and norms. The conference participants very clearly and explicitly took over two rights from the papacy: the rights to (1) confer international legitimacy on individual rulers and states and (2) insist that states observe religious toleration in their internal policies (Armstrong 1993, 30–38). The balance of power was formally incorporated in the **Peace of Utrecht**, which ended the War of the Spanish Succession (1701–1714), when a "just equilibrium of power" was formally declared to be the "best and most solid basis of mutual friendship and durable harmony."

This template for a Westernized international system extended around the globe. European states colonized the world, spreading their political, economic, and social dominance into other societies. As we will see in Chapter 2, after 200 years of this relatively stable expansion, two World Wars (1914–1918 and 1939–1945) would rock the foundations of the Westphalian international order—but they would not overturn it completely. States—including the newly independent former European colonies—were still sovereign over their territories; recourse to war to settle international disputes was still the norm.

After World War II ended, the bipolar international system of the Cold War developed between two superpowers—the USSR and the United States; however, it did not dramatically change the Westphalian international order. The Cold War period was marked by a clear and sharp divide between opposing socioeconomic systems operating by radically different standards, but in terms of the Westphalian order of sovereignty, international law, and occasional war, things had not changed. We could characterize the post–Cold War order (1991 to present), however, as one in which many states were compelled to play by a single set of rules within an increasingly competitive world economy. This is the crucial political change that paved the way for the contemporary globalized system.

Historical Trends: Economics

Karl Marx (1818–1883) argued that economic structures determine political structures (see Chapter 3). However much truth Marx's observation holds, the economic trends we will examine are critical to our overview of globalization. Of course, to understand the economic realities of today's world, we need to know something of these historical trends. At the same time, we need to keep in mind that the economic aspects of globalization seem to mean different things to different theorists. Thus for one school, the hyperglobalists, the trend is in the direction of undermining borders and states—abolishing the Westphalian system. Thomas Friedman (2000) argued that globalization has

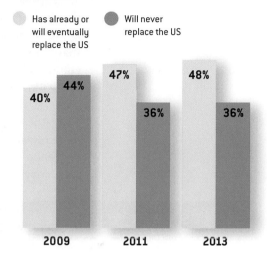

More Say China Has or Will Replace US as the World's Superpower
Percent saying China . . .

○ Has already or will eventually replace the US

● Will never replace the US

Median percent across 39 countries surveyed in 2009 to 2013.

A NEW WORLD LEADER?
Is power shifting to the East?
Source: http://www.pewglobal.org/2013/07/18/chapter-4-global-balance-of-power/

changed world politics forever, giving individuals more tools to influence markets and governments and create networks that challenge the power of states.

Others—the skeptics—take a less cataclysmic view. Globalization, they agree, provides a different context for international relations. But they argue that it is not doing away with the state or destroying the underlying logic of **anarchy**, the absence of central government. Anthony Giddens reminded us that globalization might pull power away from the state, but it might also empower local groups who want to defend their position in this global society. Some writers are even skeptical of whether there is anything especially novel about globalization. **Capitalism**, after all, has always been a global system. Since the sixteenth century, interdependence has been one of capitalism's more obvious features. So why assume that there is much new about the phenomenon simply because academics and publicists talk about it with greater frequency?

WHAT'S YOUR WORLDVIEW

What do you think about globalization? Is it a positive process or negative process?

Such skepticism, however, does not prevent its many critics and equally influential defenders from engaging in an extended and at times heated debate about the impact of globalization on global inequality, climate change, and the more general distribution of power in the international system. What governments tend to say and do also makes very little difference. Globalization, its proponents insist with increasing regularity, is a simple fact of economic life. There is, according to this perspective, no escaping it.

But if there is little meeting of the minds among politicians and academics, there is little doubt of the impact globalization is having on the world economy and in particular on those three core areas of it located in North America, Europe, and East Asia. Here, at least, the theoretical debate about the novelty, existence, and meaning of the phenomenon is being resolved, as this

North Korean troops march in a military parade in Kim Il Sung square in Pyongyang, North Korea. World leaders have not been able to end North Korea's nuclear weapons program and its aggressive behavior in East Asia.

very special triad of economic power (over 80 percent of the world's total) experiences reasonable growth, increased economic interdependence, and massive wealth creation. No doubt the process creates great national uncertainty as firms become ever more internationalized. For example, with the creation of high-speed information technologies, a firm, whether large or small, can have its management offices in one country, its design staff in another, and its production facilities in a third. Many US corporations, encouraged by federal tax code, have led the way in this process. There is also something distinctly unethical about an apparently unregulated economic process that literally makes billions for the few (especially those in the financial sector) while generating insecurity for the many. However, this is a price well worth paying—or so its defenders infer—if there is

Foxconn, a Taiwanese technology company, makes many Apple products. Here, some Chinese universities students holding mock iPads protest the poor safety record of the company. Have you thought about how the person who made your computer, phone, or television is treated as an employee?

to be any semblance of economic progress. In a world where extreme competition rules and money moves at the flick of a switch, there is only one thing worse than being part of this runaway system—and that is not being part of it.

Historical Trends: Religion and Society

Social factors provide the last piece of the background to the contemporary globalized system. How you interact with friends, family, teachers, religious leaders, political officials, and even the music on your MP3 player or the blockbuster movies you saw over the summer are all part of your social world. This social model for the world that we live in today was established shortly after World War II. After 1945, American music, films, television programs, clothing trends, and a host of other social interactions all became components of the phenomenon we call globalization. It would be easy to focus on these material and media cultures that have helped shape the world over the past seventy years. However, perhaps the most important of social trends had their roots further back in time, in the changing role of religion around the world. Therefore, in this section, we will begin by exploring the historical trends that are largely religious in nature, which influenced the past 500 years of the international system, beginning with the events and forces that would lead to increased secularization.

When Martin Luther nailed his Ninety-Five Theses to the door of the cathedral in Wittenburg, Germany, in 1517, he launched more than the **Protestant Reformation**. For the next century, monarchs across Europe found in religion a reason to begin wars allegedly in defense of either Catholicism or

Protestantism. For over a century of war and upheaval, religion provided the justification for conflicts that, most historians agree, were actually about politics and economics. The **Thirty Years' War** (1618–1648) was the last of these religious conflicts in Europe and ostensibly began over a disagreement about the right of political leaders to choose the state religion of their territories. The opponents—including at various times Denmark, France, Austria, Sweden, Spain, and the principalities of the Holy Roman Empire—conducted most of their operations in Germany, killing tens of thousands of soldiers and civilians and devastating cities and farmland.

An important aspect of the Peace of Westphalia was the recognition that political leaders could choose the state's religion. This might seem like a strange concept to many of us who live in the United States, where the Constitution decrees separation of church and state. However, in seventeenth-century Europe, state protection of a specific religious denomination was the rule. Therefore, the gradual diminution of the power of state religions, or "secularization," was an important social trend. Like many such trends, it occurred unevenly across Europe, and it became a component of the concept of human rights that you will learn about in Chapter 7. As we will see in Chapter 4, the amount of secularization in a society is one indicator that political scientists use to describe a state as premodern, modern, or postmodern. Contemporary France is a leader in Europe in enforcing secularization. For example, students may not wear any kind of religious jewelry or religious clothing in a public school. Also, on July 13, 2010, the day before the national holiday Bastille Day, the lower house of the French legislature voted 336 to 1 (with 226 members not voting) to ban the wearing of veils that cover women's faces, a social convention favored by some Muslims. When it entered into force in April 2011, the law imposed a fine of more than $35,000 on any man who forced his wife or daughters to wear the veil.

Secularization has been an uneven social phenomenon within states, too. Religious groups of various denominations might be identified by names such as social conservatives, ultraorthodox, the religious Right, or fundamentalists, but they share a belief that modern technological, globalized society lacks a necessary religious component. At another end of the social spectrum are people who believe that religion has no place in public discourse. This second group shares an idea with the philosopher Thomas Hobbes (1588–1679), who in 1651 wrote that governments should limit divisive opinions based on the demands of "a power Ecclesiasticall" [sic] derived from "a power invisible" (Hobbes 1651, *Leviathan*, Chapter XLII).

However, the contemporary globalized culture is highly secular, and that itself is a source of tension. Critics of the culture contend it is based on the constant press to purchase more and more material products, with marketing specialists who create artificial demands for the latest, newest, most improved telephone, television, automobile, clothing, and on and on. This global consumer culture is the target of many critics including "deep green" ecotopians and some fundamentalist religious communities. These groups object to

THEORY IN PRACTICE

Perception, Continuity, and Change After January 20, 2009

Challenge

The study of global politics depends to a great extent on perception. How we think about the world often determines what we think is important. This habit of mind helps explain how political leaders and opinion makers in the United States were unprepared for the two key events of the late twentieth century: the collapse of the Soviet Union and the rise of militant Islamic fundamentalism. The signs of the two events were in plain sight, if you knew what to look for.

Options

In the case of Islamic fundamentalism, certainly if you lived in a country with a large Muslim population, you would have been aware of the growing appeal of fundamentalist strains of Islam. The Wahabi sect in Saudi Arabia, for instance, forms the basis for society there. Egypt has had problems with violence linked to the Muslim Brotherhood since the time of British colonization. Indeed, the Brotherhood is often blamed for the assassination of President Anwar Sadat. In Afghanistan, the United States itself helped to arm Islamic fundamentalists in their war against the Soviet invasion during the 1980s. The trend was visible every day in public as people rejected European styles of dress: More men grew beards, and more women adopted the clothing styles the fundamentalists preferred.

If North American and European leaders were not ready for the impact of Islamic fundamentalism, how unprepared are people in the rest of the world for trends resulting from the election of Barack Obama as president of the United States? Will there be continuity or change? If we start with what the Bush administration called the "global war on terror," we can see that some things now are the same and some are not. For example, in the early months of 2009 the Obama administration continued to use Predator drone aircrafts to attack people suspected of being Islamic militants in the tribal areas of Pakistan along the Afghanistan border. Pakistani officials objected to such attacks during the Bush years, but President Obama clearly decided that the raids must continue. A major apparent change in US policy could be seen in the fundraising efforts to rebuild Palestinian homes in Gaza. Moreover, as the United States increased the number of its troops in Afghanistan to fight the resurgent Taliban, officials in Washington also quietly expressed their dissatisfaction with the actions of the Karzai government there. Both were major changes from the policy of the Bush administration.

For people outside Western Europe and the United States it is difficult to assess what the appearance of continuity or change in the foreign policy of the United States means. One source of this difficulty is the perception popular in the developing world that the United States is the global hegemonic oppressor. People have been socialized by family members, schools, and political officials to blame the United States and the West for all their sufferings. This is a perception that might not be based in fact, and it could be as incorrect as the perception that all Muslims are terrorists or that Islamic fundamentalism did not pose a threat to Europe and the United States. Perceptions and images are often more powerful than reality.

For Discussion

How can we overcome misperceptions that affect our views of other cultures?

the emphasis on materialism and the undermining of traditional norms and values that goes with Western movies, music, fashion, and art. In Chapter 6, we will see that many analysts contend that the "clash of civilizations," as Samuel P. Huntington (1993) termed it, is the defining conflict of the post–Cold War international system.

The "clash of civilizations" characterization has certainly been fashionable. Nevertheless, there is something distinctly uncompromising about a conflict between those on the one side who support democracy, **pluralism**, individualism, and a separation between state and church and those on the other who preach intolerance and support **theocracy** while calling for armed struggle and **jihad** against the unbeliever. Not that these views are shared by all Muslims. Indeed, these radical views are roundly condemned by the overwhelming majority of Muslim clerics and followers of Islam. Still, as the antagonism has unfolded, there seem to be enough disaffected people in enough societies—including Western ones—to make this aggressive ideology an occasional but potent threat. The way the world in general, and the West in particular, chooses to deal with it is likely to determine the shape of international relations for many years to come.

This very brief summary of key historical trends in globalization introduces the material that we will examine in greater depth later in the book. As we will see in the next section, international relations specialists apply this history in several ways as they seek to create a picture of the world today.

Research Approaches and Levels of Analysis

As curious individuals, we are all interested in understanding the nature of global politics and the behavior of different actors in this global society. Two of the more traditional ways of doing research are the **historical** and **social scientific** approaches. A less traditional method of understanding the world is the approach of **constructivism**.

The Historical Approach

Historians arrive at an understanding of why actions are taken by states, or why events happen, after a careful review of public documents, memoirs, and interviews with key actors. Their goal is to create a thorough description or narrative that helps us understand decisions that were made by key actors during a particular event. The goal is not to understand all wars or all actions by states but to create a history of a particular war or a very thorough description of a country's decision to take a certain policy position.

The Social Scientific Approach: Levels of Analysis

The intellectual interests of social scientists are slightly different. Social scientists want to bring the precision and certainty of the natural sciences to the social world. Uncomfortable with the subjectivity and ambiguity of many historical accounts, social scientists develop hypotheses based on dependent ("Y") and independent ("X") variables (such as "if X, then Y") and then test and confirm these hypotheses or revise and refine them until they are accurate. They seek to explain international relations behavior, predict what others might do in similar situations, and develop a list of policy options or prescriptions for relevant policy makers (Table 1.1). Research, then, is the search for the independent variable. For example,

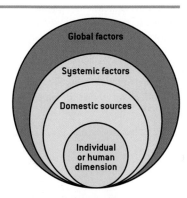

LEVELS OF ANALYSIS.
In the study of global politics, there are four levels of analysis. We make a distinction between *systemic* (or international) factors and *global* factors. What is the argument for this distinction?

Table 1.1 **Decision Makers: Rationality and Politics**

Rational choice: An economic principle that assumes that individuals always make prudent and logical decisions that provide them with the greatest benefit or satisfaction and that are in their highest self-interest.

Bounded rationality: Decision-makers do not always have the ability and information to make a rational decision or one that is optimal. Instead, they first simplify the list of choices available and then apply rationality. By simplifying the list of choices available, the decision-maker is value satisficing instead of value maximizing. Herbert Simon who proposed this model suggested that people are only partly rational and emotions, values, and previous experiences may help shape the decision.

Prospect theory: Involves risk aversion and risk acceptance. Decision makers in an environment of gain will avoid risky options and those in an environment of losses will accept risky options.

Poliheuristic theory: A two-stage analysis; in the first stage decision makers eliminate choices based on cognitive shortcuts and then in the second stage subject these choices to rational processing.

how do we explain a nation-state's allocation of development assistance? We know the amount of development assistance (dependent variable), but we now must find the independent variable that might explain this allocation. Independent variables reside in one of four **levels of analysis**:

1. Individual/human dimension: This level contains the range of variables that can affect leaders' policy choices and implementation strategies. Current research reveals that individuals matter, particularly in the midst of crises, when decisions require secrecy or involve only a few actors, or when time is of the essence. The influence of individuals increases when they have a great deal of latitude to make decisions and when they have expertise in foreign policy.

2. Domestic sources or national attributes: Factors at this level include a state's history, traditions, and political, economic, cultural, and social structures, as well as military power, economic wealth, and demographics, and more permanent elements like geographic location and resource base.

3. Systemic factors: The anarchic nature of international relations might be the most important factor at this level. However, the individual and collective actions states have taken to cope with anarchy via treaties, alliances, and trade conventions—formal contracts created by states in an attempt to provide order—also constitute significant systemic factors. More informal constraints based on traditions, common goals, and shared norms shape state behavior as well. For example, most states respect the sovereignty of all states and follow the rule of international law because they expect others to do the same. This notion of reciprocity is the primary incentive for states to support a rule-based international system. Finally, distribution of power in the system (e.g., bipolar, multipolar) and the nature of order (e.g., balance of power, collective security) are also important systemic factors.

4. Global factors: Often confused with system-level factors, global-level variables challenge notions of boundaries and sovereignty. They derive from

decisions made or actions taken by individuals, states, or nonstate actors, but they are seldom traceable to the actions of any one state or even group of states. A technological innovation—for example, the Internet and the information revolution—that diffuses through the system affecting all, but not belonging to any single actor, is an obvious example. The movement of capital by multinational banks, the broadcasts of CNN, and the revolutionary ideas of religious fundamentalists all represent global factors that shape policy behavior. Natural conditions or events such as earthquakes, environmental degradation, pandemics (e.g., AIDS, SARS, and the flu), and weather patterns also impact foreign policy.

What is exciting about research in our field is that there is always disagreement about which variables explain the most. The strength of any one argument is based on the quality of the empirical evidence collected to support the hypothesis being tested. Because we are not lab scientists, we cannot conduct experiments with control groups to test our propositions. Instead, we look to the work of historians, public policy records, government documents, interviews, budgets, and journalist accounts to gather evidence to confirm or reject hypotheses.

The level chosen as a source for an independent variable depends on the situation you wish to examine, the availability of data or evidence, your research skills and interests, and, finally, your creativity and imagination. Each level is like a drawer in a toolbox; the analytical approaches or variables at each level are the tools that the researcher uses to develop and explore the explanatory power of three kinds of hypotheses: (1) causal hypotheses: if it rains, it will flood; (2) relational hypotheses: if it rains, flooding in certain geological and geographical areas will worsen; and (3) impact hypotheses: if it rains more than *n* amount, the flooding will be particularly severe.

Both Thucydides (ca. 460–ca. 395 BCE) and Immanuel Kant (1724–1804) indirectly discussed levels of analysis in their efforts to explain state behavior. Thucydides focused on the explanatory potential of power capabilities and even suggested that the distribution of power in the international system influenced a state's behavior. Kant referred to the first three levels of analysis when he suggested that nation-states could avoid war by eliminating standing armies, managing the self-interests of rival leaders, and finding ways to provide order in the international system.

The Constructivist Approach

Constructivists, on the other hand, question the underlying assumptions supporting social scientific and historical approaches to understanding international relations. Instead, these scholars postulate that there is no single historical narrative. Rather, the interests of specific actors shape the story, and it is their control of that story that gives them power. No perspective offers the truth, because words, meanings, symbols, and identities are subjective and are used by individuals, groups, and society to gain and maintain power.

Further, constructivists argue that all of us interpret events and global conditions according to our beliefs, interests, values, and goals. We are not free to do anything we want in any given situation; instead, we are handed a menu reflective of dominant interests and goals of powerful groups within a state or in the international system.

These three research approaches—social scientific, historical, and constructivist—help us explain and understand the decisions made by relevant individuals or decision makers in global politics. We will learn in Chapter 4 that foreign policy decisions are shaped by factors or variables that can be found in the levels-of-analysis framework. And in Chapter 3, we will explore in depth some of the more prominent theories of global politics that help us to explain decisions and events, but for now let us turn our attention to thinking more generally about theory and how it can work in our field of study.

Children teach themselves at a Hole-in-the-Wall Learning station in Thimphu, Bhutan. These stations foster collaborative learning among groups of children, including girls, who are often not sent to schools.

Introduction to Theories of Global Politics

The basic problem facing anyone who tries to understand contemporary global politics is that there is so much material to look at; it is difficult to know which things matter and which do not. Where on earth would you start if you wanted to explain the most important political processes? How, for example, would you explain the 9/11 attacks on the United States or the 2003 war in Iraq? Why did Al Qaeda attack the United States? Why did President Bush and Prime Minister Tony Blair authorize the attack on Saddam Hussein's Iraq? Why did President Obama continue the war against the Taliban in Afghanistan and expand it to include Pakistan? Where in the world did the 2008 economic crisis "originate"? Where will it "end"—and when? What policies will global leaders develop to respond to this economic crisis? There are very different answers to questions such as these, and there seems no easy way of arriving at a definitive answer to them. Was the invasion of Iraq motivated by a concern with human rights, with our dependence on oil, with unfinished business from the first Gulf War in 1991, with **imperialism,** with the "war against terrorism"? Whether they are aware of it or not, whenever individuals are faced with such a problem, they have to resort to **theories** to understand the problem and to develop effective responses.

A theory is not simply some grand formal model with hypotheses and assumptions. Rather, a theory is a kind of simplifying device that allows you to decide which facts matter and which do not. A good analogy is sunglasses with different colored lenses; put on the red pair and the world looks red, put on the yellow pair and it looks yellow. The world is not any different, it just looks different. And so it is with theories. Shortly we are going to summarize the main theoretical views that have dominated the study of global politics, so we will get an idea of which "colors" they paint the world. But before we do so, please note that the authors of this book do not think that theory is merely an option. It is not as if you can say that you do not want to bother with a theory and instead all you want to do is to look at the "facts." We believe that this is impossible, because the only way you can decide which of the millions of possible facts to look at is by adhering to some simplifying device that tells you which ones matter the most. We think of theory as such a simplifying device.

You might not even be aware which theory you are using to understand and explain the world around you. It might just be the view of the world that you have inherited from family, a group of friends, or the media. It might just seem common sense to you and not at all anything complicated like a theory. But we fervently believe that all that is happening in such a case is that your theoretical assumptions are implicit rather than explicit, and we prefer to be as explicit as possible when it comes to thinking about global politics.

People have tried to make sense of world politics for centuries, especially since the separate academic discipline of international politics was formed in 1919, when the Department of International Politics was set up at the University of Wales, Aberystwyth. Interestingly, the man who set up that department, a Welsh industrialist named David Davies, saw its purpose as helping to prevent war. By studying international politics scientifically, many scholars believed they could find the causes of the world's main political problems and put forward solutions to help politicians solve them. After the end of World War I, the discipline was marked by such a commitment to change the world. This is known as a **normative orientation,** with the task of academic study being one of making the world a better place. Its opponents characterized this normative position as overly idealistic, in that it had a view of how the world ought to be and focused on means of preventing war and even making war and violence obsolete. It was during the years between World War I and World War II that **idealism** was embraced by a number of antiwar organizations. In its place its opponents preferred an approach they called **realism,** which, rather unsurprisingly, stressed seeing the world as it really is rather than how we would like it to be. And the "real" world as seen by realists is not a very pleasant place; human beings are at best self-interest-oriented and probably much worse. Notions such as the perfectibility of human beings and the possibility of an improvement of world politics seem far-fetched. This debate between idealism and realism has continued to the present day, but it is fair to say that realism has tended to have the upper hand. This is mainly because it appears to accord more with common sense than does idealism, especially when the media bombard us daily with images of how awful humans can be to one another.

Having said this, we would like you to think about whether such a realist view is as neutral as it is commonsensical. After all, if we teach global politics to generations of students and tell them that people are selfish, then doesn't that become common sense? And don't they, when they go off into the media or to work for government departments, or the military, or even when they talk to their children over the dinner table, simply repeat what they have been taught and, if in positions of power, act accordingly? We will leave you to think about this. For now, we would like to keep the issue open and simply point out that we are not convinced that realism is as objective or nonnormative as it is portrayed as being.

International Relations Theories and Globalization

It is true that realism has been the dominant way of explaining world politics in the past nearly 100 years. It is not, however, the only way—and in Chapters 2 and 3 of this book we will examine realism and its four main rivals as theories of world politics: **liberalism**, **Marxism**, and alternative theories like constructivism and **feminism**. These theoretical perspectives have tended to be the main theories used to understand world politics, with constructivism becoming increasingly influential since the mid-1990s. As you will see in later chapters, international relations specialists use many tools in their work, including the increasingly popular "rational choice" method borrowed from economics. In the 1980s, it became common to talk of an **interparadigm debate** among realism, liberalism, Marxism, and constructivism; that is to say that the four major theories (designated **paradigms** by the influential philosopher of natural science Thomas Kuhn) were in competition and that the "truth" about world politics lay in the debate among them. At first glance each seems to be particularly good at explaining certain aspects of world politics, and an obvious temptation would be to try to combine them into some overall account. But this is not the easy option it might seem. The four theories are not so much different views of the same world, but rather four views of different worlds. Let us examine this claim more closely.

Globalization has not ended famine and poverty. Do prosperous countries have an obligation to help people in other lands?

Although it is clear that each of the four broad theoretical traditions focuses on different aspects of world politics (realism on the power relations between states, liberalism on a much wider set of interactions between states and non-state actors, Marxist theory on the patterns of the world economy, and constructivism on the ways in which we can develop different social structures and processes), each is saying more than this. Each view claims that it is picking out the most important features of world politics and that

CASE STUDY : Global Production and the iPod

Take just one component of Apple's iPod Nano: the central microchip provided by the US company PortalPlayer. The core technology of the chip is licensed from the British firm ARM and is modified by PortalPlayer's programmers in California, Washington State, and Hyderabad in India. PortalPlayer then works with microchip design companies in California that send the finished design to a foundry in Taiwan (China) that produces wafers (thin metal disks) imprinted with thousands of chips. The capital costs of these foundries can be more than $2.5 million. These wafers are cut up into individual disks and sent elsewhere in Taiwan to be tested. The chips are then encased in plastic and readied for assembly by Siliconware in Taiwan and Amkor in the Republic of Korea. The finished microchip is warehoused in Hong Kong (China) before being transported to mainland China, where the iPod is assembled.

Working conditions and wages in China are low relative to Western standards. Many workers live in dormitories and work long hours. It is suggested that overtime is compulsory. Nevertheless, wages are higher than the average of the region where the assembly plants are located and allow for substantial transfers to rural areas, helping to reduce rural poverty. PortalPlayer was only established in 1999 but had revenues in excess of $225 million in 2005. Their chief executive officer has argued that the outsourcing to countries such as India and Taiwan of "noncritical aspects of your business" has been crucial to the development of the firm and its innovation: "It allows you to become nimbler and spend R&D dollars on core strengths."

Since the first iPod was launched in 2001, Apple's share price has risen from just over $7 to more than $518. Those who own shares in Apple have benefited immensely from the globalization of the iPod.

For Discussion

1. Many people are what we call economic nationalists—they support policies and practices that help keep jobs in their home country. How much more would you be willing to pay for your iPod if it were made in your country? Is where it's manufactured at all important to you? Why or why not?

2. Some critics of globalization suggest that it allows companies to search for the lowest common denominator, meaning low wages, no labor or safety laws, and no environmental standards. Without these constraints, profits can be quite high. Should consumers consider these factors before buying products? Should there be global standards for wages, worker safety, and protection of the environment? Why or why not?

3. Most global production takes advantage of each country's comparative strengths or assets, and the result is a great product at a good price. Is this not how capitalism should work? Explain.

Sources: C. Joseph, "The iPod's Incredible Journey," Mail on Sunday *(July 15, 2006); "Meet the iPod's 'Intel,'"* Business Trends 32 *(April 2006);* World Bank (2006), Global Economic Prospects 2007: Managing the Next Wave of Globalization *(Washington, DC: World Bank), p. 118.*

it offers a better account than the rival theories. Thus, the four approaches are really in competition with one another; and although you can certainly choose among them, it is not so easy to add bits from one to the others. For example, if you are a Marxist theorist, you think that state behavior is ultimately determined by class forces, forces that the realist does not think affect state behavior. Similarly, constructivism suggests that actors do not face a world that is fixed but rather one that they can in principle change—in direct contrast to the core beliefs of realists and Marxists alike. In other words, these four theories are really versions of what world politics is like rather than partial pictures of it. They do not agree on what world politics is fundamentally all about.

We do not think that any one of these theories has all the answers when it comes to explaining world politics in an era of globalization. In fact, each sees globalization differently. We do not want to tell you which theory seems best, because the purpose of this book is to give you a variety of conceptual lenses. By the end of the book we hope you will work out which of these theories (if any) best explains globalization. We also introduce you to a set of other theories, such as feminism, that many believe are crucial in explaining globalization but that have not yet been dominant in the discipline of international relations. However, we want to reinforce here our earlier comment that theories do not portray "the" truth. In other words, the theories we have mentioned will see globalization differently because they have an a priori view of what is most important in world politics. Therefore, there is not just one view of globalization or one theory that is the best or truest.

Dimensions of Globalization

Our final task in this introductory chapter is to offer a summary of the main arguments for and against globalization as a distinct new phase in world politics. We do not expect you to decide where you stand on the issue at this stage, but we think that we have to give you some of the main arguments so that you can keep them in mind as you read the rest of this book. The main arguments in favor of globalization comprising a new era of world politics are the following:

1. The pace of economic transformation is so great that it has created a new world politics.

2. Communications have fundamentally revolutionized the way we deal with the rest of the world.

3. There is now, more than ever before, a global culture.

4. The world is becoming more homogeneous in some material and ideational areas.

5. Time and space seem to be collapsing.

6. A **global polity** is emerging, with transnational social and political movements and the beginnings of a transfer of allegiance from the state to substate, transnational, and international bodies.

7. A **cosmopolitan culture** is developing as more and more people are beginning to "think globally and act locally."

8. A **risk culture** is emerging because people realize both that the main risks that face them are global and that states are unable to deal with the problems without some form of cooperation.

Antigovernment demonstrators in Moscow, Russia, in 2012. The outcry for human rights and democratic elections is spreading faster than ever before. Has globalization helped promote such movements for reform?

However, just as there are powerful reasons for seeing globalization as a new stage in world politics, often allied to the view that globalization is progressive—that is to say, that it improves the lives of people—there are also arguments that suggest the opposite. Some of the main ones are given briefly here. In later chapters we will return to these arguments.

1. One obvious objection to the globalization thesis is that it is merely a buzzword to denote the latest phase of capitalism.

2. Another obvious objection is that globalization is very uneven in its effects. At times it sounds very much like a Western theory applicable only to a small part of humankind.

3. A related objection is that globalization could well be simply the latest stage of Western imperialism.

4. Critics have also noted that there are people who have much to lose as the world becomes more globalized. This is because it represents the success of liberal capitalism in an economically divided world.

5. We also need to make the straightforward point that not all globalized forces are necessarily good ones.

6. Turning to the so-called **global governance** and **cosmopolitan democracy** aspects of globalization, the main worry here is about responsibility. To whom are the transnational social movements responsible and democratically accountable?

7. Finally, there seems to be a **paradox** at the heart of the globalization thesis. On the one hand, globalization is usually portrayed as the triumph of Western, market-led values. But how do we then explain the tremendous economic success of some national economies that have not adopted many Western values?

For many people, globalization means travel for business and the movement of goods and services. The departure board at a new terminal at Charles de Gaulle airport in Paris will serve 8.5 million passengers a year. Global travel can lead to more awareness but not always understanding of foreign lands and cultures.

We hope that these arguments for and against the dominant way of representing globalization will cause you to think deeply about the utility of the concept in explaining contemporary world politics. The chapters that follow do not take a common stance *for* or *against* globalization. We will end by posing some questions that we would like you to keep in mind as you read the remaining chapters:

- Is globalization a *new* phenomenon in world politics?
- Which theory discussed in this book best explains the effects of globalization?
- Is globalization a positive or a negative development?
- Does globalization make the state obsolete?
- Does globalization make the world more or less democratic?
- Is globalization merely Western imperialism in a new guise?
- Does globalization make war more or less likely?
- Last but not least, what will *your* role be in world politics? How will you choose to identify yourself and participate locally, nationally, and globally?

Conclusion

We hope that this introduction and the chapters that follow help you to answer these questions and that this book as a whole provides you with a good overview of the politics of the contemporary world. We leave you to decide whether or not globalization is a new phase in world politics and whether it is a positive or a negative development.

Returning to both the global economic crisis and 9/11 and its aftermath, we think it important to conclude this chapter by stressing that globalization, clearly, is a very complex phenomenon that is contradictory and difficult to comprehend. Just as the Internet is for most of us a liberating force, so was it the way in which those who planned the 9/11 attacks communicated. Similarly, television can bring live stories right into our living rooms so that we understand more about the world. But on 9/11, television was also a means of communicating a very specific message about the vulnerability of the United States and ultimately a way of constructing the categories within which we reacted. Finally, maybe the most fundamental lesson of 9/11 is that not all people in the world share a view of globalization as a progressive force for positive change in world politics. Those who undertook the attacks were rejecting, in part, the globalization-as-Westernization project. Globalization is therefore not one thing.

How we think about it will reflect not merely the theories we accept, but also our own positions in this globalized world. In this sense, the ultimate paradox of 9/11 is that the answers to questions such as what it was, what it meant, and how to respond to it might themselves be ultimately dependent on the social, cultural, economic, and political spaces we occupy in a globalized world. In other words, world politics suddenly becomes very personal: How does your economic position, your ethnicity, your gender, your culture, or your religion determine what globalization means to you?

Engaging with the **Kiva**

WORLD

So you want to do something about the bottom billion? You want to know more about those who are struggling in our global community and find ways to help them? Get involved with Kiva by becoming a fellow or starting a campus club.

Kiva is a nonprofit organization that lends money to help people around the world start a business and pull themselves out of poverty. More than 600,000 Kiva members have loaned more than $240 million to people without access to traditional banking systems. More than 98 percent of those who received the loans have repaid them! Check out www.kiva.org.

KEY TERMS

Anarchy, p. 14
Capitalism, p. 14
Constructivism, p. 18
Cosmopolitan culture, p. 25
Cosmopolitan democracy, p. 26
Feminism, p. 23
Global governance, p. 26
Globalization, p. 11
Global politics, p. 7
Global polity, p. 25
Governments, p. 8
Historical versus social scientific
    approaches to research, p. 18
Idealism, p. 22
Imperialism, p. 21

International relations, p. 7
Interparadigm debate, p. 23
Jihad, p. 18
Levels of analysis, p. 19
Liberalism, p. 23
Marxism, p. 23
Multinational corporations
    (MNCs), p. 10
Nation, p. 8
Nongovernmental organizations
    (NGOs), p. 8
Nonstate actors, p. 10
Normative orientation, p. 22
Paradigms, p. 23
Paradox, p. 26

Peace of Utrecht, p. 13
Peace of Westphalia, p. 12
Pluralism, p. 17
Protestant Reformation, p. 15
Realism, p. 22
Risk culture, p. 25
September 11, 2001, p. 4
Society of states, p. 13
Sovereign equality, p. 13
Sovereignty, p. 9
State, p. 8
Theocracy, p. 18
Theories, p. 21
Thirty Years' War, p. 16
Transnational actors, p. 8

REVIEW QUESTIONS

1. Is globalization a new phenomenon in world politics?

2. What are the ways in which you are linked to globalization?

3. How do ideas about globalization shape our understanding of the trend?

4. How can different levels of analysis lead to different explanations of the impact of globalization on global politics?

5. Why do theories matter?

6. International relations began as a problem-solving discipline in response to World War I. What are the global problems that now define our field of study?

7. Why did liberal theorists assume the world would become a more stable place after the end of the Cold War, and why did realists disagree with them?

8. If the United States won the Cold War, why did it have such problems defining a grand strategy for itself after 1989 and before 9/11?

9. Has globalization since the Cold War changed the basic character of world politics?

10. How has the "war on terror" changed international politics?

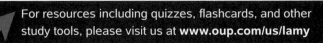

For resources including quizzes, flashcards, and other study tools, please visit us at **www.oup.com/us/lamy**

THINKING ABOUT GLOBAL POLITICS

Why Should I Care?

In this chapter, we have discussed how forces of globalization shape all of our lives. We know that these forces of globalization influence nation-states, but how do they shape your life and the activities of your family and friends? How is your quality of life shaped by global factors that have created a global economy and a global consumer culture? How are your personal choices influenced by the actions of distant actors and economic, political, and cultural conditions pushed by globalization?

PART ONE: YOU AS A GLOBAL CONSUMER

Consider the following questions in small groups with a focus on how you are linked in a web of interdependence that might shape the choices you make. Also, understand that you are making choices in different sectors of global society. It is like playing chess on three or four different chessboards. You are making choices in the economic sector, political sector, and cultural sector. In turn, these choices affect social relations and have profound implications for the natural world or the environmental sector.

1. With the iPod case in mind, consider how many items in your daily *commodity basket* (the sum total of goods and services purchased in a given time frame) are not local and are actually imported from a foreign country.
2. Do you think dependence on foreign goods and services matters? How might your choices influence people in your community and people in distant lands?
3. Individuals, like countries, need to avoid situations where their choices create an unhealthy dependence on foreign goods and services. For example, a country's dependence on oil makes it *vulnerable* to those corporations and countries that supply it. It is okay to be dependent on products, but you hope that this dependency has low political and economic costs. For example, our dependence on oil makes us vulnerable because it is too hard to find a substitute. This is called *vulnerability interdependence*.

But our dependence on good French wine can be replaced by a dependence on good Chilean or Australian wine. The cost of finding an alternative is low; thus, this is called *sensitivity interdependence*. These sensitivity situations are unavoidable in a global economy. Again, considering your lifestyle, are you in the vulnerability or sensitivity category? Is it easy to stay in the sensitivity category?

PART TWO: ASSESSING YOUR POLITICAL CONNECTIONS

1. The entire world changed with the terrorist attacks against the United States, Spain, and the UK. How have global politics changed and how have these changes affected you and your family?
2. Identify four international events that have occurred in the past six months that have had a direct impact on political life in your country. Be specific about how these events have changed the game of domestic politics.
3. What about leadership in this world of global politics? When you consider the impact of globalization and the complex issues we all face as citizens in rich and poor states, what skills and competencies do you think leaders need to possess to be successful in securing the interests of their citizens and providing for world order?

WRITING ASSIGNMENT: THIS IS A QUESTION ABOUT *MORAL INTERDEPENDENCE*

We have become so interdependent economically and politically, but do we recognize our moral responsibility to people who are not our citizens? Do we have any responsibility for the impact of our foreign policy decisions on other countries? For example, in the pursuit of wealth and prosperity, we might trade for oil with authoritarian regimes that oppress their citizens. Are we also culpable? By providing that regime with financial resources, are we contributing to its reign of terror?

CONTRIBUTORS TO CHAPTER 1: *John Baylis, Anthony McGrew, Steve Smith, Steven L. Lamy, and John Masker.*

2 | The Evolution of Global Politics

Those who cannot learn from history are doomed to repeat it.

—*George Santayana*

We learn from history that we learn nothing from history.

—*G. B. Shaw*

I f we were to write a brief list of world events in 2013, it might include the following:

- The global economic crisis has eased for the advanced economies but the recovery may not be sustainable because real risks remain. The eurozone is vulnerable because of its banking system and the polarized domestic political system creates economic risks and uncertainty in the United States. The effects include slowing economic growth in China and India.
- The depth of extreme poverty has fallen by 25 percent in the past thirty years for the developing world as a whole, but most of the drop has happened in China and India. According to the World Bank, those living in extreme poverty in the rest of the developing world are as poor as those in extreme poverty thirty years ago.
- The emergence of a new divide between rich and poor states is related to climate change and *weather weirding*. The typhoon Haiyan ravaged the Philippines and extreme weather events have devastated regions across the world. Yet, in the 2013 Warsaw Climate Change Conference, the world learned that Australia, Japan, and Canada downgraded their efforts at reducing carbon emissions. China and 132 states that belong to the G-77 bloc of developing states criticized the foot dragging by the global rich states and the primary sources of carbon emissions.
- The aftermath of the Arab Spring has not resulted in stable democracies in the Middle East. In Egypt, the military overthrew the elected president, violence and instability continue to thwart efforts at building a

Supporters of Egypt's ousted president Morsi held a demonstration in a suburb of Cairo, Egypt, in September 2013. The Egyptian military government has increased their crackdown on Islamists that support the ousted president.

stable government in Libya, and a civil war has ravaged Syria. The Assad government has used chemical weapons on Syrian citizens and now the world community is involved in a process of containing and destroying those outlawed weapons.

- The United States is coming out of the longest war in its history in Afghanistan, yet instability and violence continue to plague the region and our attempt at state building in Iraq seems to have failed. The United States has increased its use of unmanned drones in Pakistan, Yemen, and many African states.

- Religious extremist movements continue to use violence across the world. Al Shabaab attacked the Westgate shopping center in Nairobi, Kenya, killing seventy. France intervened in Mali to stop jihadi forces and in the Central African Republic to prevent further attacks between Christian and Muslim militias and to protect innocent civilians. Many of these new extremist groups across Africa are financed and trained by Al Qaeda.

- Representatives of the United States, Great Britain, China, France, Germany, Russia, and the European Union negotiated with Iran to limit its nuclear program and to contain the proliferation of nuclear weapons. Meanwhile, no one seems to be watching what North Korea may be doing with its nuclear program.

Add to our list the cycle of violence in Israel and Palestine, which is showing no sign of abating, and the problem of fragile states defined by political crises and economic underdevelopment, which contributes to the poverty and misery of hundreds of millions of people who have no food, shelter, or health care. A child dies from hunger every eleven seconds. Sometimes it's difficult to imagine how things might ever improve; other times it's easy to get caught up in the moment, when something significant or strange occurs on the world stage. Yet each of the current events and enduring conditions listed here stems from a deeper world history, and knowing about these histories takes us a step closer to understanding global politics—past, present, and future.

Perhaps, despite our pessimistic list for 2012, the international system has actually moved in a positive direction. After all, countries that were enemies in 1944—including France, Germany, and Great Britain—are today working together to bring economic prosperity to the world as members of the European Union. The accumulation of human history—political change, economic progress, medical breakthroughs, the lives of ordinary people—are part of the fabric of struggle and cooperation, strife and comity.

Our goal in this chapter is to demonstrate, briefly, how the international system and in some ways the global society has evolved during the past four hundred years. It is, of course, not possible to cover all of international history in one chapter. Therefore, our attention will be primarily on significant political events. In other chapters, we discuss social and economic trends.

Introduction

Kingdoms, empires, city-states, and nation-states have for centuries interacted in the same kinds of patterns that continued after the end of the Thirty Years' War (1618–1648). In China, Africa, India, and ancient Greece, political units of various sizes had engaged in economic relations, exchanged ambassadors, and fought wars. After 1648, we can see the developing template for the international system, now referred to as the "globalized system," that is a theme of this book: Western European arrangements for governance, human rights, and economics that form the basis for the contemporary world. In this chapter we discuss wars and political upheavals. It is a sweeping tale, covering two world wars, the end of European colonization of Africa and Asia, the Cold War and the changes in the international political system that followed its end, and the September 11, 2001, attacks.

World Wars: Modern and Total

Wars on a global scale caused another shock to international society. Although separated by twenty years, World Wars I and II have some similarities beyond mere geography. Changes in military technology shaped the ways in which the combatants fought: Machine guns, airplanes, and submarines all influenced operations. Both wars also featured controversies over the treatment of civilians. Indiscriminate bombing of cities occurred during both wars and reached its nadir with the British and American firebomb air raids on Germany and Japan. Yet one major distinction between the two world wars is worth noting here: The Nazi death camps of World War II were at the time without parallel in human history. Unfortunately, genocide and ethnic cleansing have continued to plague the international system.

For the victorious Allies, the question of how World War I began became a question of how far the Germans and their allies should be held responsible. At the Versailles Palace outside Paris, the victors imposed a statement of German war guilt in Article 231 of the final settlement, primarily to justify the reparations they demanded. Debates among historians about the war's origins focused on political, military, and systemic factors. Some suggested that responsibility for the war was diffuse because its origins lay in complex dynamics of the respective alliances and their military imperatives. One of the more influential postwar interpretations, however, came from the West German historian Fritz Fischer, who, in his

After a rapid German advance into France in August 1914, troops on both sides created extensive networks of defensive trenches. Millions of combatants died.

1967 book *Germany's Aims in the First World War*, argued that German aggression, motivated by the internal political needs of an autocratic elite, was responsible for the war.

However complex or contested the origins of the war were in retrospect, the motivations of those who fought were more explicable. The masses of the belligerent states shared nationalist beliefs and patriotic values. As they marched off to fight, most thought the war would be short, victorious, and, in many cases, glorious. The reality of the European battlefield and the advent of **trench warfare** determined otherwise (see Map 2.1). Defensive military technologies, symbolized by the machine gun, triumphed over the tactics and strategy of attrition, although by November 1918, the Allied offensive finally achieved the rapid advances that helped bring an end to the fighting. It was total war in the sense that whole societies and economies were mobilized: Men were conscripted into armies and women went to work in factories. The western and eastern fronts remained the crucibles of the fighting, although conflict spread to various parts of the globe. Japan, for example, went to war in 1914 as an ally of Britain.

Most important, in response to German aggression on the high seas and domestic public opinion that supported the Allies, the United States entered the war in 1917 under President Woodrow Wilson. His vision of international

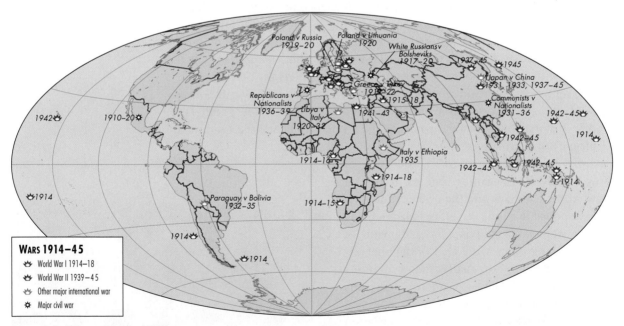

Map 2.1 Wars 1914–1945.

The two world wars were responsible for perhaps more than 80 million deaths. World War I was essentially a European territorial dispute, which, because of extensive European empires, spread as far afield as Africa and Southeast Asia. World War II also started as a European conflict but spread to the Pacific when Japan seized territory. In the interwar period, disputes broke out over territory in South America and East Asia, but elsewhere the reluctance of the colonial powers to become embroiled in territorial disputes maintained an uneasy peace. *Source: Cartography © Philip's.*

society and world order, articulated in his **Fourteen Points**, would drive the agenda of the Paris Peace Conference in 1919. The overthrow of the tsar in February 1917 by what became known as the Provisional Government, and the seizure of power by the Bolsheviks in November 1917, soon led Russia's new leaders to negotiate withdrawal from the war. Germany no longer fought on two fronts but soon faced a new threat, as the resources of the United States were mobilized. With the failure of its last great military offensive in the west in 1918, and with an increasingly effective British naval blockade, Germany agreed to an **armistice**.

The **Treaty of Versailles** failed to tackle what was for some the central problem of European security after 1870: a united and frustrated Germany. The treaty precipitated German revenge by creating new states out of former German and Austrian territories and devising contested borders. For some scholars, the period from 1914 to 1945 represented two acts in a single play, or a thirty-year war. E. H. Carr saw the period from 1919 to 1939 as a twenty-year crisis. The crisis, Carr stated, was caused by an unrealistic and utopian peace treaty that did not address the real causes of the war and would never be supported by the victors. Economic factors were also crucial. The effects of the Great Depression, triggered in part by the Wall Street crash of 1929, weakened the forces of liberal democracy in many areas and strengthened the appeal of communist, fascist, and Nazi parties. It should be noted that from 1873 to 1914 the world economy changed dramatically. Most notably this included the rise of the US and German economies and the decline of Britain. At this time, Japan was beginning to industrialize and India and China were beginning a rapid pace of economic development. What was most significant was the increase in global trade and financial transactions. This growing interdependence of national economies did not result in free trade; instead, protectionist policies increased.

World War I destroyed production facilities in Europe. Britain and France demanded reparations from Germany to pay for their reconstruction. Both the United States and Japan benefited from the war in terms of boosting their industrial production levels. The Great Depression of 1930 and 1931 was not caused by the war. However, the change in the international political system helped bring about the collapse of the trade, finance, and economic management systems.

The effect on German society was particularly significant. All modernized states

On August 6, 1945, the United States dropped an atom bomb on Hiroshima, killing 140,000 and unleashing a weapon system that the world is still trying to control. Now, with the number of nuclear weapons in the world, we can destroy the world as we know it. How can we control these weapons?

suffered mass unemployment, but in Germany, inflation was acute. Economic and political instability provided the ground in which support for the Nazis took root. By 1933, Adolf Hitler had achieved power, and the transformation of the German state began. There remain debates about how far Hitler's ambitions were carefully thought through and how much he seized opportunities. A. J. P. Taylor provided a controversial analysis in his 1961 book *The Origins of the Second World War*, in which he argued that Hitler was no different from other German political leaders. What was different about Germany this time was the particular philosophy of Nazism and ideas of racial supremacy and imperial expansion. British and French attempts to negotiate with Hitler culminated in the Munich agreement of 1938. Hitler's territorial claims over the Sudetenland in Czechoslovakia were accepted as the price for peace, but within months Germany had seized the rest of Czechoslovakia and was preparing for war on Poland. Recent debates about **appeasement** have focused on whether there were realistic alternatives to negotiation, given the lack of military preparedness with which to confront Hitler.

By 1939, the defensive military technologies of the Great War gave way to armored warfare and air power, as the German **blitzkrieg** brought speedy victories over Poland and in the west. Hitler was also drawn into the Balkans and North Africa, in support of his Italian ally, Mussolini. With the invasion of the Soviet Union in June 1941, the scale of fighting and scope of Hitler's aims were apparent. Massive early victories on the eastern front gave way to winter stalemate and the mobilization of Soviet peoples and armies. German treatment of civilian populations and Soviet prisoners of war reflected Nazi ideas of racial supremacy and resulted in the deaths of millions. German anti-Semitism and the development of concentration camps gained new momentum after a decision on the "Final Solution of the Jewish Question" in 1942. The term **Holocaust** entered the political lexicon of the twentieth century as the Nazis attempted the **genocide** of the Jewish people and other minorities, such as the Roma, in Europe.

By 1941, German submarines and American warships were in an undeclared war. The imposition of US economic sanctions on Japan precipitated Japanese military preparations for a surprise attack on the US fleet at Pearl Harbor on December 7, 1941. When Germany and Italy declared war on the United States in support of their Japanese ally, Roosevelt decided to assign priority to the European over the Pacific theater of war. After a combined strategic bombing offensive with the British against German cities, the Allies launched a second front in France, for which the Soviets had been pressing.

Defeat of Germany in May 1945 came before the atomic bomb was ready. In an effort to shorten the war, avoid an invasion of Japan, and push the Japanese government to surrender, the United States dropped the first atomic bomb on Hiroshima on August 6, 1945, and the second on Nagasaki on August 9, 1945. The United States was the first and only state to use these weapons of mass destruction in war. The destruction of the two Japanese cities remains a controversy. Aside from moral objections to attacking civilian populations, the destruction generated fierce debate, particularly among American historians, about why the bomb was dropped.

When World War II ended, the United States and the Soviet Union remained as the two dominant countries in world politics. For some people in the United States, their homeland largely untouched by the destruction of the war, the country seemed poised to take its proper position as world leader. For the leaders of the Soviet Union, the world looked ready for the expansion of the Soviet style of rule. In the next section we examine the process of decolonization of Western European holdings. This process provided both

With the end of the Belgian Congo, the new Democratic Republic of the Congo was embroiled in a civil war. The Russians and Americans supported opposing forces. Here the leader of the pro-Western province of Katanga, Moise Tshombe, greets mercenaries fighting to support his secession from the Congo in 1960.

countries, soon to be called superpowers, many opportunities to expand their influence. American hegemony in the world economy ran from 1938 to 1973 (see also Chapter 8). The United States was willing to commit resources to stabilize the world economy and build global political structures to manage trade, development, and financial affairs.

Legacies and Consequences of European Colonialism

The effects of World War II helped to cause the demise of European imperialism in the twentieth century. More than marking an end of Western European dominance in world politics, the end of imperialism seemed to be the death knell for the European style of managing international relations (see Map 2.2). This change took place against the background of the Cold War, which we discuss in the next section, but it's important first to appreciate the context of decolonization because it reflected, and contributed to, the decreasing importance of Europe as the arbiter of world affairs.

The belief that national self-determination should be a guiding principle in international politics had early marked a transformation of attitudes and values; during the age of imperialism, political status accrued to imperial powers. However, after 1945, imperialism became a term of disgrace. Colonialism of the past and the new UN Charter were increasingly recognized as incompatible, although independence was often slow and sometimes marked by prolonged and armed struggle, especially in many African states. The Cold War also often complicated and hindered the transition to independence.

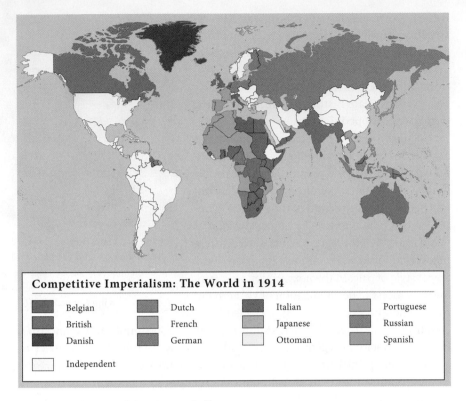

Map 2.2 Competitive Imperialism.

Political, economic, and military factors played various roles in shaping the transfer of power. Different imperial powers and newly emerging independent states had different experiences of withdrawal from empire.

There was no single pattern of decolonization in Africa and Asia, and the paths to independence reflected attitudes of colonial powers, the nature of local nationalist or revolutionary movements, and in some cases the involvement of external states, including the Cold War protagonists. Ethnic and racial factors were also an ingredient in many cases. How far these divisions were created or exacerbated by the imperial powers is an important question in examining the political stability of the newly independent states. Equally important is how capable the new political leaderships in these societies were in tackling their political and economic problems.

In Asia, the relationship between nationalism and revolutionary Marxism was a potent force. In Malaya, the British defeated a communist insurgent movement (1948–1960). In Indochina (1946–1954), the French failed to do likewise. For the Vietnamese, resentment toward centuries of foreign oppression—Chinese, Japanese, and French—soon focused on a new imperialist adversary, the United States. For leaders in Washington, early reluctance to support European imperialism gave way to incremental and covert commitments and then, from 1965, open military and political support of the newly created state of South Vietnam. American leaders and a very influential anticommunist interest community spoke of a domino theory, in which if one state fell to communism, the next would be at risk. Chinese and Soviet support provided additional Cold War contexts. Washington failed, however, to coordinate limited war objectives with an effective political strategy and, once victory was no longer possible, sought to disengage through "peace with honor." The Tet (Vietnamese New Year) offensive of the Vietcong guerrillas in 1968 marked a decisive moment, convincing many Americans that the war would not be won, although it was not until 1973 that American forces finally withdrew, two years before South Vietnam was defeated. Many wars in Asia and Africa started as colonial wars and quickly became proxy wars in the Cold War struggle between the superpowers.

The global trend toward decolonization (see Table 2.1) was a key development in the twentieth century, although one frequently offset by local circumstances. Yet while imperialism withered, other forms of domination or **hegemony** took shape. Simply stated, hegemony means a state has the means and the will to shape and govern the international system. Both the United States and the Soviet Union were vying for global hegemony during the Cold War. The notion of hegemony has been used as a criticism of the behavior of the superpowers, most notably with Soviet hegemony in Eastern Europe and American hegemony in Central America. For both countries this struggle for dominance, regardless of the term used, was the central element of the period we discuss in the next section, the Cold War.

Cold War

The rise of the United States as a global power after 1945 was of paramount importance in international politics. Its conflict with the Soviet Union provided one of the crucial dynamics in world affairs—one that affected, directly or indirectly, every part of the world. In the West, historians have debated with vigor and acrimony which country was responsible for the collapse of the wartime alliance between Moscow and Washington. The rise of the USSR as a global power after 1945 is equally crucial in this period. Relations between Moscow and its Eastern European "allies," with the People's Republic of China, and with revolutionary forces in the third world have been vital issues in world politics, as well as key factors in Soviet–American affairs.

If one feature of the **Cold War** was its **bipolar** structure, another was its highly divided character born out of profoundly opposing views about the best way of organizing society: the Western system of market **capitalism** or the Eastern Bloc's centrally planned economies.

Yet for all its intensity the Cold War was very much a managed conflict in which both sides recognized the limits of what they could do. Certainly, policy makers in the East and the West appeared to accept in private—if not in public—that their rival had legitimate security concerns. The Cold War was

Table 2.1 Principal Acts of European Decolonization, 1945–1980

Country	Colonial State	Year of Independence
India	Britain	1947
Pakistan	Britain	1947
Burma (Myanmar)	Britain	1948
Sri Lanka	Britain	1948
Indonesia	Netherlands	1949
Cambodia	France	1953
Indochina (Vietnam and Laos)	France	1954
Ghana	Britain	1957
Malaya (Malaysia)	Britain	1957
French African colonies*	France	1960
Congo (Zaire)	Belgium	1960
Nigeria	Britain	1960
Sierra Leone	Britain	1961
Tanganyika (Tanzania)	Britain	1961
Uganda	Britain	1962
Algeria	France	1962
Rwanda	Belgium	1962
Kenya	Britain	1963
Guinea-Bissau	Portugal	1974
Mozambique	Portugal	1975
Cape Verde	Portugal	1975
São Tomé	Portugal	1975
Angola	Portugal	1975
Zimbabwe	Britain	1980

*Including Cameroon, Central African Republic, Chad, Gabon, Ivory Coast, Madagascar, Mali, Mauritania, Niger, Senegal, and Upper Volta.

thus fought within a framework of informal rules. This in part helps explain why it remained "cold"—at least in terms of general war between the United States and the Soviet Union, because millions of people died during the period from 1945 to 1990 in what have been called "brushfire" or "proxy" wars in Africa and Asia (see Map 2.3). Indeed, how and why the Cold War remained cold has been the subject of much academic debate. Few, however, would dispute the fact that whatever else might have divided the two superpowers—ideology, economics, and the struggle for global influence—they were in full agreement about one thing: the overriding need to prevent a nuclear war that neither could win without destroying the world and themselves. This, in the end, is why the superpowers acted with such caution for the greater part of the Cold War era. In fact, given the very real fear of outright nuclear war, the shared aim of the two

Did Mao Zedong and Richard Nixon change the balance of Cold War politics when they shook hands in Beijing in 1972?

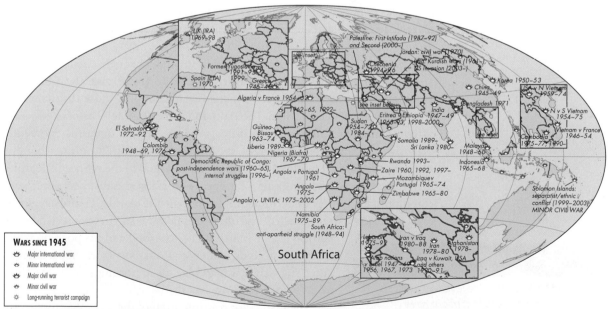

Map 2.3 Wars Since 1945.

As European colonial control was largely destroyed between 1945 and 1970, new nation-states were created. One result was an increase in localized wars, largely arising from boundary disputes, and in civil wars caused by conflicts between different ethnic groups or between those with conflicting religious or political beliefs. Note that many of these wars directly or indirectly involved the United States and the USSR. An estimated 25 million to 30 million people died in these wars, two-thirds of whom were civilians. *Source: Cartography © Philip's and http://www.mesharpe.com/mall/resultsa.asp?Title=Encyclopedia+of+Conflicts+Since+World+War+II%2C+Second+Edition.*

superpowers was not to destroy the other—although a few on both sides occasionally talked in such terms—but rather to contain the other's ambitions while avoiding anything that might lead to dangerous escalation (only once, in 1962, with the Cuban missile crisis, did the two superpowers come close to a nuclear exchange). This, in turn, helps explain another important feature of the Cold War: its stalemated and hence seemingly permanent character.

Some historians date the origins of the Cold War to the Russian Revolution of 1917, although most focus on events between 1945 and 1950. Whether the Cold War was inevitable, whether it was the consequence of mistakes and misperceptions, or whether it reflected the response of courageous Western leaders to aggressive Soviet intent are central questions in debates about the origins and dynamics of the Cold War. Until 1989, these debates have drawn from Western archives and sources and reflect Western assumptions and perceptions. With the end of the Cold War, greater evidence has emerged of Soviet and US motivations and understanding.

Onset of the Cold War

The start of the Cold War in Europe reflected a failure to implement the principles agreed at the 1945 wartime conferences of Yalta and Potsdam. The futures of Germany and various Central and Eastern European countries, notably Poland, were issues of growing tension between the former wartime allies. Reconciling principles of national self-determination with national security was a formidable task. In the West, there was growing feeling that Soviet policy toward Eastern Europe was guided not by historic concern with security, but by ideological expansion. In March 1947, the Truman administration sought to justify limited aid to Turkey and Greece with rhetoric designed to arouse awareness of Soviet ambitions and a declaration that America would support those threatened by Soviet subversion or expansion. The **Truman Doctrine** and the associated policy of **containment** expressed the self-image of the United States as inherently defensive and were underpinned by the **Marshall Plan** for European economic recovery, proclaimed in June 1947, which was essential to the economic rebuilding of Western Europe. In Eastern Europe, democratic socialist and other anti-communist forces were undermined and eliminated as Marxist-Leninist regimes, loyal to Moscow, were installed. The only exception was in Yugoslavia, where the Marxist leader, Marshal Tito, consolidated his position while maintaining independence from Moscow. Subsequently, Tito's Yugoslavia was to play an important role in the third world Nonaligned Movement.

The first major confrontation of the Cold War took place over Berlin in 1948 (see Table 2.2). During the Yalta and Potsdam conferences, Germany and Berlin were divided among the four victorious powers: the United States, the Soviet Union, Great Britain, and France. The former German capital was left deep in the heart of the Soviet zone of occupation

WHAT'S YOUR WORLDVIEW

Why did WWI start? Use levels of analysis to identify the factors that might have contributed to the war. Was it the motivations of individuals, the need for resources at the national level, or the failure of treaties and international organizations?

Table 2.2 Cold War Crises

Years	Crisis	Key Actors
1948–1949	Berlin	USSR/US/UK
1950–1953	Korean Conflict	North Korea/South Korea/US/People's Republic of China
1954–1955	Taiwan Strait	US/People's Republic of China
1961	Berlin	USSR/US/NATO
1962	Cuba	USSR/US/Cuba
1973	Arab–Israeli War	Egypt/Israel/Syria/Jordan/US/USSR
1975	Angola	US/USSR/Cuba/China/South Africa
1979–1992	Afghanistan	USSR/US/Saudi Arabia/Pakistan
1979–1990	Nicaragua–El Salvador	US/USSR/Cuba

(East Berlin), and in June 1948 Stalin sought to resolve its status by severing road and rail communications. West Berlin's population and political autonomy were kept alive by a massive airlift. Stalin ended the blockade in May 1949. The crisis saw the deployment of American long-range bombers in Britain, officially described as "atomic capable," although none was actually armed with nuclear weapons. US military deployment was followed by political commitment enshrined in the **North Atlantic Treaty Organization (NATO)** treaty signed in April 1949. The key article of the treaty—that an attack on one member would be treated as an attack on all—accorded with the principle of collective self-defense enshrined in Article 51 of the UN Charter. In practice, the cornerstone of the alliance was the commitment of the United States to defend Western Europe. In reality, this soon meant the willingness of the United States to use nuclear weapons to deter Soviet "aggression." For the Soviet Union "political encirclement" soon entailed a growing military, and specifically nuclear, threat.

Although the origins of the Cold War were in Europe, events and conflicts in Asia and elsewhere

The US Air Force brings milk to citizens of Berlin during the Soviet road blockade of the city in 1948. This may have been the first time the world saw the true intentions of the Soviet Union and its totalitarian regime.

were also crucial. In 1949, the thirty-year-long Chinese civil war ended in victory for the communists under Mao Zedong. This had a major impact on Asian affairs and on perceptions in both Moscow and Washington. In June 1950, the North Korean attack on South Korea was interpreted as part of a general communist strategy and as a test case for US resolve and the will of the United Nations to withstand aggression. The resulting US and UN commitment, followed in October 1950 by Chinese involvement, led to a war lasting three years, in which more than 3 million people died before prewar borders were restored. North and South Korea themselves remained locked in seemingly perpetual hostility, even after the end of the Cold War.

Conflict, Confrontation, and Compromise

One consequence of the Korean War was the buildup of US forces in Western Europe, lest communist aggression in Asia distract from the real intent in Europe. The idea that communism was a monolithic political entity controlled from Moscow became an enduring American fixation, not shared in London or elsewhere. Western Europeans nevertheless depended on the United States for military security, and this dependence deepened as the Cold War confrontation in Europe was consolidated. The rearmament of the Federal Republic of Germany in 1954 precipitated the creation of the **Warsaw Pact** in 1955. The military buildup continued apace, with unprecedented concentrations of conventional and, moreover, nuclear forces. By the 1960s, there were some 7,000 nuclear weapons in Western Europe alone. NATO deployed nuclear weapons to offset Soviet conventional superiority, but Soviet short-range or "theater nuclear" forces in Europe compensated for overall US nuclear superiority.

The death of Stalin in March 1953 portended significant consequences for the USSR at home and abroad. Stalin's eventual successor, Nikita Khrushchev, strove to modernize Soviet society, and in the process, he helped unleash reformist forces in Eastern Europe. While Poland was controlled, the situation in Hungary threatened Soviet hegemony, and in 1956 the intervention of the Red Army brought bloodshed to the streets of Budapest and international condemnation on Moscow. Soviet intervention coincided with an attack on Egypt by Britain, France, and Israel, precipitated by Colonel Nasser's nationalization of the Suez Canal in a manner that displeased Britain, the former colonial occupier. The French took part in the attack because Nasser's government was providing support to anti-French rebels in Algeria. The British government's actions provoked fierce domestic and international criticism and the most serious rift to date in the "special relationship" between Britain and the United States. President Eisenhower was strongly opposed to the actions of the US allies, and in the face of what were effectively US economic sanctions (a threat to cut off American oil exports to Britain), the British abandoned the operation, as well as their support for the French and Israelis.

Khrushchev's policy toward the West mixed a search for political coexistence with the pursuit of ideological confrontation. Soviet support for

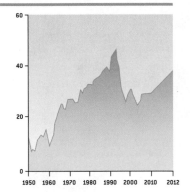

NUMBER OF WARS IN PROGRESS SINCE 1950.

Given what you have read in this chapter, what would you say accounts for these trends— for the increases, spikes, and decreases?

Source: http://armscontrol center.org/issues/nuclear weapons/articles/fact_sheet_ global_nuclear_weapons_ inventories_in_2012/

movements of national liberation aroused fears in the West of a global communist challenge. American commitment to **liberal democracy** and national self-determination was often subordinated to Cold War perspectives, as well as to US economic and political interests. The Cold War saw the growth of large permanent intelligence organizations, whose roles ranged from estimating intentions and capabilities of adversaries to covert intervention in the affairs of other states. Crises over Berlin in 1961 and Cuba in 1962 marked the most dangerous moments of the Cold War. In both, there was a risk of direct military confrontation and, certainly in October 1962, the possibility of nuclear war. How close the world came to Armageddon during the Cuban missile crisis and exactly why peace was preserved remain matters of debate among historians and surviving officials (see Table 2.3).

The events of 1962 were followed by a more stable period of coexistence and competition. Nuclear arsenals, nevertheless, continued to grow. Whether this is best characterized as an **arms race** or whether internal political and bureaucratic pressures drove the growth of nuclear arsenals is open to interpretation. For Washington, commitments to NATO allies also provided pressures and opportunities to develop and deploy their own shorter range ("tactical" and "theater") nuclear weapons. The global nuclear dimension increased with the emergence of other nuclear-weapon states: Britain in 1952, France in 1960, and China in 1964. Growing concern at the spread, or proliferation, of nuclear weapons led to the negotiation of the Nuclear Nonproliferation Treaty in 1968, wherein states that had nuclear weapons committed themselves to halt the arms race, and those who did not possess them promised not to develop them. Despite successes of the Nuclear Nonproliferation Treaty, by 1990 several states had developed or were developing nuclear weapons, notably Israel, India, Pakistan, and apartheid South Africa.

Table 2.3 **Using Levels of Analysis to Explain Why the Cold War Ended**

Level of Analysis	Explanation
Individual	The *belief systems* of significant leaders like President Reagan and General Secretary Gorbachev led them to seek cooperation over conflict.
National	The *economic system* of the Soviet Union could no longer afford to provide domestic services and programs and keep up with the United States in terms of military spending.
	The US government was constrained by increasing costs of Social Security and medical care and sought to reduce military spending.
Systemic	The *distribution of power* in the international system was shifting toward the United States and away from the USSR. Gorbachev and his reformers within the Soviet Union acted to halt this loss of power.
Global	The diffusion of ideas (through travel, education, the media, and popular culture) and the benefits of capitalism and democracy encouraged citizens to push for reforms.

When the Soviet Union dissolved, many of its allies across the world lost their power as well. The pro-Soviet military junta in Ethiopia fell from power in 1991, and statues of Lenin were torn down.

(South Africa later gave up its nuclear weapons program and remains the only state to do so.)

The Rise and Fall of Détente

At the same time that America's commitment in Vietnam was deepening, Soviet–Chinese relations were deteriorating. Indeed, by 1969 the People's Republic of China and the Soviet Union had fought a minor border war over a territorial dispute. Despite (or because of) these tensions, the foundations for what became known as **détente** were laid between the Soviet Union and the United States and for what became known as **rapprochement** between China and the United States. Both terms, long a part of the language of diplomacy, refer to the processes by which countries seek to improve their relations. Détente in Europe had its origins in the *Ostpolitik* of the German chancellor Willy Brandt and resulted in agreements that recognized the peculiar status of Berlin and the sovereignty of East Germany. For his efforts, which finally bore fruit with the end of the Cold War in 1989, Brandt won the Nobel Peace Prize. Soviet–American détente had its roots in mutual recognition of the need to avoid nuclear crises and in the economic and military incentives in avoiding an unconstrained arms race. Both Washington and Moscow also looked toward Beijing when making their bilateral calculations.

In the West, détente was associated with the political leadership of President Richard Nixon and his adviser Henry Kissinger, who were also instrumental in Sino-American rapprochement. This new phase in Soviet–American relations did not mark an end to political conflict, as each side pursued political goals, some of which were increasingly incompatible with the aspirations of the other superpower. Both sides supported friendly regimes and movements and subverted adversaries. All this came as various political upheavals were taking place in the third world (see Table 2.1). The question of how far the superpowers could control their friends, and how far they were entangled by their commitments, was underlined in 1973 when the Arab–Israeli war embroiled both the United States and the Soviet Union in what became a potentially dangerous confrontation. Getting the superpowers involved in the war—whether by design or serendipity—helped create the political conditions for Egyptian–Israeli rapprochement. Diplomatic and strategic relations were transformed as Egypt switched its allegiance from Moscow to Washington. In the short term, Egypt was isolated in the Arab world. For Israel, fear of a war of annihilation fought on two fronts was lifted. Yet continuing political violence and **terrorism**, and the enduring enmity between Israel and other Arab states, proved insurmountable obstacles to a more permanent regional settlement.

In Washington, Soviet support for revolutionary movements in the third world was seen as evidence of duplicity. Some American politicians and academics claim that Moscow's support for revolutionary forces in Ethiopia in 1975 killed détente. Others cite the Soviet role in Angola in 1978. Furthermore, the perception that the USSR was using arms control agreements to gain military advantage was linked to Soviet behavior in the third world. Growing Soviet military superiority was reflected in growing Soviet influence, it was argued. Critics claimed the Strategic Arms Limitation Talks process enabled the Soviets to deploy multiple independently targetable warheads on their large **intercontinental ballistic missiles**, threatening key US forces. The United States faced a "window of vulnerability," critics of détente claimed. The view from Moscow was different, reflecting different assumptions about the scope and purpose of détente and the nature of nuclear deterrence. Other events were also seen to weaken US influence. The overthrow of the shah of Iran in 1979 resulted in the loss of an important Western ally in the region, although the ensuing militant Islamic government was hostile to both superpowers.

December 1979 marked a point of transition in East–West affairs. NATO agreed to deploy land-based Cruise and Pershing II missiles in Europe if negotiations with the Soviets did not reduce what NATO saw as a serious imbalance. Later in the month, Soviet armed forces intervened in Afghanistan to support their revolutionary allies. The USSR was bitterly condemned in the West and in the third world for its actions and soon became committed to a protracted and bloody struggle that many compared to the US war in Vietnam. In Washington, President Carter, who had sought to control arms and reduce tensions with the USSR, hardened his view of the Soviet Union. The first reaction was the Carter Doctrine, which clearly stated that any Soviet attack on countries in the Persian Gulf would be seen as a direct attack on US vital interests. Another result was the Carter administration's decision to boycott the 1980 Summer Olympics in Moscow. Nevertheless, Republicans increasingly used foreign and defense policy to attack the Carter presidency. Perceptions of American weakness abroad permeated domestic politics, and in 1980, Ronald Reagan was elected president. He was committed to a more confrontational approach with the Soviets on arms control, third-world conflicts, and East–West relations in general.

From Détente to a Second Cold War

In the West, critics of détente and arms control, some of whom would later advise the George W. Bush presidential administration, argued in the 1970s and 1980s that the Soviets were acquiring nuclear superiority. Some suggested that the United States should pursue policies and strategies based on the idea that victory in nuclear war was possible. The election of Ronald Reagan in 1980 was a watershed in Soviet–US relations. Ronald Reagan had made it clear during the election campaign that the United States would take a tough stance in its relations with the Soviet Union. In two monumental speeches delivered in March 1983, Reagan stated that the Soviet Union was the "focus of evil in the modern world" and he coined the phrase "evil empire" to describe the USSR. In the second speech, he outlined his idea for a strategic defense against Soviet missiles. One issue that Reagan inherited, and that loomed large in the breakdown of relations between East and West, was nuclear missiles in Europe. NATO's decision to deploy land-based missiles capable of striking Soviet territory precipitated a period of great tension in relations between NATO and the USSR and political friction within NATO.

On arms control, Reagan was disinterested in agreements that would freeze the status quo for the sake of getting agreement, and Soviet and American negotiators proved unable to make progress in talks on long-range and intermediate-range weapons. One particular idea had significant consequences for arms control and for Washington's relations with its allies and its adversaries. The **Strategic Defense Initiative (SDI)**, quickly dubbed "Star Wars," after the new movie, was a research program designed to explore the feasibility of space-based defenses against ballistic missiles. The Soviets appeared to take SDI very seriously and claimed that Reagan's real purpose was to regain the nuclear monopoly of the 1950s. The technological advances claimed by SDI proponents did not materialize, however, and the program was eventually reduced and marginalized, although never fully eliminated from the US defense budget.

The resulting period of tension and confrontation between the superpowers has been described as the second cold war or the end of détente and compared to the early period of confrontation and tension between 1946 and 1953. In Western Europe and the Soviet Union, there was real fear of nuclear war. Much of this was a reaction to the rhetoric and policies of the Reagan administration. American statements on nuclear weapons and military intervention in Grenada in 1983, as well as an air raid against Libya in 1986, were seen as evidence of a new belligerence. Reagan's policy toward Central America and support for the rebel contras in Nicaragua were sources of controversy within the United States and internationally. In 1986, the International Court of Justice found the United States guilty of violating international law by sowing sea mines in Nicaraguan harbors. The Reagan administration ignored this ruling, claiming the International Court of Justice lacked jurisdiction in this situation.

The Reagan administration's use of military power was nonetheless limited: Rhetoric and perception were at variance with reality. Still, the Soviet leadership took Reagan's rhetoric very seriously and might have believed Washington was planning a first strike. In 1983, Soviet air defenses shot down a South Korean civilian airliner in Soviet airspace. The American reaction, and the imminent deployment of US nuclear missiles in Europe, created a climate of great tension in East–West relations.

Throughout the early 1980s, the Soviets were handicapped by a succession of aging political leaders (Brezhnev, Andropov, and Chernenko), whose ill health further

WHAT'S YOUR WORLDVIEW ?

The United States and the USSR fought many proxy wars across the globe, and many current armed conflicts began during the Cold War. Given these facts, is it correct to call the period from 1945 to 1989 a "Cold War"? Some academics call this period World War III. Cold War historian John Lewis Gaddis has called this period the "Long Peace": Is this an accurate description of the Cold War period of tension and conflict?

inhibited Soviet responses to the US challenge and the US threat. This changed dramatically after Mikhail Gorbachev became general secretary of the Soviet Communist Party in 1985, a position that gave him control over the state. Gorbachev's "new thinking" in foreign policy, and his domestic reforms, created a revolution, both in the USSR's foreign relations and within Soviet society. At home, **glasnost** (or openness) and **perestroika** (or restructuring) unleashed nationalist and other forces that, to Gorbachev's dismay, were to destroy the Union of Soviet Socialist Republics.

Gorbachev paved the way for agreements on nuclear and conventional forces that helped ease the tensions that had characterized the early 1980s. In 1987, he traveled to Washington to sign the Intermediate Nuclear Forces Treaty, banning intermediate-range nuclear missiles, including Cruise and Pershing II. This agreement was heralded as a triumph for the Soviet leader, but NATO leaders, including Margaret Thatcher and Ronald Reagan, argued that it was vindication of the policies pursued by NATO since 1979. The Intermediate Nuclear Forces Treaty was concluded more quickly than a new agreement on cutting strategic nuclear weapons, in part because of continuing Soviet opposition to SDI. And it was Reagan's successor, George H. W. Bush, who concluded a **Strategic Arms Reductions Treaty** agreement that reduced long-range nuclear weapons (although only back to the level they had been at in the early 1980s). Gorbachev used agreements on nuclear weapons as a means of building trust and demonstrated the serious and radical nature of his purpose. However, despite similar radical agreements on conventional forces in Europe (culminating in the Paris agreement of 1990), the end of the Cold War marked success in nuclear arms control rather than nuclear disarmament. The histories of the Cold War and of the atomic bomb are very closely connected, but although the Cold War is now over, nuclear weapons are still very much in existence. We discuss the issues surrounding nuclear weapons in Chapter 6.

From the End of the Cold War to the War on Terrorism

The first major global conflict after the Cold War ended was the 1990 Iraqi invasion of neighboring Kuwait. After some attempts to find an Arab solution, the United States led a comprehensive multilateral diplomatic and military effort to punish Saddam Hussein for his actions and to signal to the world that this kind of violation of international law would not stand. The war to liberate Kuwait lasted just forty-two days, and an international coalition of diplomats and military forces helped define the "New World Order" that President George H. W. Bush had talked about since taking office in 1989. The United States wisely included the Soviet Union in its plans and effectively used the UN Security Council to pass more than twelve resolutions condemning the actions of Iraq. What the first President Bush created was a US-led global coalition that was supported by all five permanent members of the Security

Council—a first since the establishment of the UN. The majority of the world was behind this action. The invasion of Kuwait was illegal under international law and the major powers were willing to work together to protect and promote a "rule-based system."

So it was, once again, in 1989 when the last of the "great wars" of the twentieth century—the Cold War—finally wound down. The world in 1990 was full of promise (especially for the victors) but full of potential risk as well. It was also one replete with the sources of further conflict. In fact, looking back now from the perspective of the post-9/11 world, it would appear as if the years following the end of the Cold War were a mere interregnum. This New World Order, as US president George H. W. Bush called it, existed briefly between two eras: one defined by an ongoing struggle between two competing secular ideologies and another shaped by an emerging clash between two conceptions of civilization itself.

The Cold War divided the world for more than forty years, threatened humanity with near destruction, and led to the death of at least 25 million people, mostly in that highly contested zone that came to be referred to during the Cold War as the third world. Yet in spite of these dangers and costs, the Cold War in its central core areas still managed to create a degree of stability that the world had not experienced since the early part of the twentieth century. For this reason, many came to view the bipolar order after 1947 as something that was not merely the expression of a given international reality but something that was desirable and defensible, too. Indeed, as we will see in Chapter 3, some realists seemed to celebrate the superpower relationship on

Civilians as well as the military are targets for landmines and improvised explosive devices. These weapons can have a devastating impact on a society for many years. Should these devices be banned as part of the treaty banning landmines?

the grounds that a world in which there were two balancing powers, each limiting the actions of the other, was likely to be a far more stable world than one in which there were several competing states.

One can thus imagine the enormous shock waves produced by what happened in Eastern Europe in 1989. The world at the time was already undergoing dramatic changes, mainly the result of radical new policies introduced by Soviet leader Mikhail Gorbachev. Many people, of course, hoped that Gorbachev's several reforms would make the world a safer and more humane place. Hardly anybody, though, seriously anticipated the collapse of communism and the destruction of the Berlin Wall. Moreover, few believed that this revolutionary process could be achieved peacefully. Nor had policy makers planned for it, and the intelligence agencies in the West had completely missed the signs of change in the Soviet bloc. It was all rather surprising if not disturbing for those who had thought that this superpower rivalry would never end without some nuclear confrontation. Now world leaders had to remake the world and find ways to integrate former enemies back into the West.

The tasks they confronted certainly seemed very great, ranging from the institutional one of devising new tasks for bodies such as NATO, the **United Nations**, and the **European Union (EU)** to the more economic challenge of facilitating the transition in countries that had had little experience running **market democracies**. Some wondered whether a US-led Atlantic Alliance could survive in an environment where there was no longer a well-defined threat. Certainly, many questioned the need for high military spending, arguing that if the world was now becoming a safer and more integrated place, spending billions on weapons seemed unnecessary.

Globalization: Challenging the International Order?

Some scholars suggested that the Cold War was a conflict between two sets of rule books. If the Cold War period was marked by a clear and sharp divide between opposing socioeconomic systems operating by radically different standards, then the post–Cold War order could readily be characterized as one in which many states were compelled to play by a single set of rules within an increasingly competitive world economy. The question today seems to be which rules to emphasize and who will enforce those rules. The term most frequently used to describe this new order was **globalization**, a notion that had barely been used before 1989 but now came to be employed ever more regularly to define an apparently new system of international relations.

Globalization, however, seemed to mean different things to different theorists. Thus for one school, the hyperglobalists, it was assumed to be undermining borders and states—quite literally abolishing the Westphalian system, which had begun to crystallize more than 330 years ago, as we read about in

Sailors from China's North fleet stand on a guided missile destroyer and a missile frigate at a military port in Qingdao in east China's Shandong province. Japan, Korea, the United States, and India are aware of China's naval buildup and are responding in kind. Will this arms race and resulting *security dilemma* increase the chances for conflict in the region?

Chapter 1. For skeptics or statists, globalization might have weakened the state in some policy areas, but the state remained the locus of governance and the primary actor in the establishment of order and stability. To date, the state has survived and those fighting in the streets of Libya or Egypt are fighting for the control of the state. It might be true that power is shifting away from states in some areas, but states are finding ways to share sovereignty and trade control in some areas that allow them to survive and even prosper.

For scholars of globalization it was a simple fact of economic life. There was no escaping its logic. The only thing one can do (using the oft-repeated words of President Clinton) is to "compete, not retreat." Moreover, if one did not do so, the future for one's own people, and by implication one's state, was bleak. UK Prime Minister Tony Blair agreed and even appeared to use the menace of globalization as a means of attacking those in Europe who would defend old economic ways. In a world of global competition, Blair observed, there was really very little choice. Europe had to either reform or decline. There was no other way.

From Superpower to Hyperpower—US Primacy

If a one-world economy operating under the same set of highly competitive rules was at least one consequence of the end of the Cold War, another was a major resurgence of American self-confidence in a new international system where it seemed to have no serious rival. This was not only a development that few had foretold (in the 1970s and 1980s many analysts believed that the United States was in decline); it was one that many had thought impossible (most realists, in fact, believed that after the Cold War the world would become genuinely multipolar). It was also a situation many feared, on the grounds that an America with no obvious peer competitor would act more assertively and with less restraint. That aside, all of the most obvious indicators by the late 1990s—military, economic, and cultural—seemed to point to only one conclusion: As a result of the Soviet collapse, followed in short order by the economic crisis in Japan and Europe's manifest failure to manage the conflict in the former Yugoslavia, the United States by the turn of the century had been transformed from a mere superpower (its designation hitherto) to what French Foreign Minister Hubert Vedrine in 1998 termed a **hyperpower**. Former Secretary of State Madeleine Albright might have also agreed, in her own way, with this assessment, although she used more diplomatic language—she called the United States "the indispensable power" in global politics.

This claim to unilateral privilege was linked to a particularly bleak view of the world shared by many, although not all, US policy makers. The Cold War might have been over, they agreed: America might have emerged triumphant. But this was no reason to be complacent. To repeat a phrase often used at the time, although the "dragon" in the form of the USSR had been slain, there were still many "vipers and snakes" lurking in the long grass. Among the three most dangerous and pernicious of these were various "rogue states" (Iran, Iraq, North Korea, Libya, and Cuba), the constant threat of nuclear proliferation (made all the more likely by the disintegration of the USSR and the unfolding nuclear arms race between Pakistan and India), and the threat of religious fundamentalists and ideological extremists (all

In 2000 Al Qaeda attacked the USS *Cole* using a motorboat containing a large bomb. Why did the leaders of the United States and other Western democracies ignore the growing threat of Islamic militants prior to September 11, 2001?

the more virulent now because of the fallout from the last great battlefield of the Cold War in Afghanistan). Indeed, long before 9/11, the dangers posed by radical Islamism were very well known to US intelligence, beginning with the bombing of the US Marine barracks in Beirut, Lebanon, in October 1983 that caused the deaths of almost 300 American personnel. The devastating bombing of the World Trade Center in 1993 and the US embassies in Tanzania and Kenya five years later, as well as the audacious attack on the USS *Cole* in 2000, all pointed to a new form of terrorism that could be neither deterred nor easily defeated by conventional means.

Yet in spite of these several threats, there was no clear indication that the United States was eager during the 1990s to project its power with any serious purpose. The United States might have possessed vast capabilities, but there appeared to be no real desire, in a post–Cold War environment, to expend American blood and treasure in foreign adventures. The desire sank even further following the debacle in Somalia in 1993: The death of eighteen US soldiers there created its own kind of syndrome that made any more US forays abroad extremely unlikely. The United States after the Cold War was thus a most curious hegemon. On the one hand, its power seemed to be unrivaled (and was); on the other, it seemed to have very little idea about how to use this power other than to bomb the occasional "rogue" state when deemed necessary (as in the former Yugoslavia), while supporting diplomatic solutions to most problems when need be (as in the cases of the Middle East and North Korea). The end of the Cold War and the disappearance of the Soviet threat might have rendered the international system more secure and the United States more powerful, but it also made the United States a very reluctant warrior. In a very important sense, the United States during the 1990s remained a superpower without a mission.

Europe in the New World System

If for the United States the most pressing post–Cold War problem was how to develop a coherent global policy in a world where there was no single major threat to its interests, then for Europeans the main issue was how to manage the new enlarged space that had been created as a result of the events in 1989. Indeed, although more triumphant Americans would continue to proclaim that it was they who had actually won the Cold War in Europe, it was Europeans who were the real beneficiaries of what had taken place in the late 1980s. There were sound reasons for thinking this way. A continent that had once been divided was now whole again. Germany had been peacefully united. The states of Eastern Europe had achieved one of the most important of international rights: the right of self-determination. The threat of war with potentially devastating consequences for Europe had been eliminated. Naturally, the transition from one order to another was not going to happen without certain costs, borne most notably by those who would now have to face up to life under competitive capitalism. Nor was the collapse of communism in some countries an entirely bloodless affair, as events in the former Yugoslavia (1990–1999) revealed only too tragically. With that said, a post–Cold War Europe still had much to look forward to.

Many in Europe debated the region's future, but policy makers themselves were confronted with the more concrete issue of how to bring the "East" back into the "West," a process that went under the general heading of enlargement. In terms of policy outcome, the strategy scored some notable successes. Indeed, by 2007 the EU had grown to twenty-seven members, and NATO one less at twenty-six, with most of the new members coming from the former Soviet bloc. The two bodies also changed their club-like character in the process, much to the consternation of some people in the original member states, who found the entrants from the former Soviet bloc to be as much trouble as asset. In fact, according to critics—both politicians and academics—enlargement had proceeded so rapidly that the essential meaning of both organizations had been lost. The EU, it was now argued by some, had been so keen to enlarge that it had lost the will to integrate. NATO, meanwhile, could no longer be regarded as a serious military organization with an integrated command structure. One significant aspect of this was the "out of area" problem that limited NATO activities to Europe itself. This would change after September 11, 2001. Still, it was difficult not to be impressed by the capacity of NATO and the EU in their new roles. These institutions had helped shape part of Europe during the Cold War and were now being employed to help manage the relatively successful (although never easy) transition from one kind of European order to another. For those who had earlier disparaged the part institutions might play in preventing **anarchy** in Europe, the important roles played by the EU and NATO seemed to prove that institutions were essential.

Europe, it was generally recognized, remained what it had effectively been since the end of World War II: a work in progress. The problem was that nobody could quite agree when—if ever—this work would be completed and where—if anywhere—the EU would end. Some analysts remained remarkably upbeat. The EU's capacity for dealing with the consequences of the end of the Cold War, its successful introduction of a single currency (the euro, in January 2002), and its ability to bring in new members all pointed to one obvious conclusion: The EU's future was assured. A few even speculated that the new twenty-first century would itself be European rather than American. Many, however, were more skeptical. After a decade-long period of expansion and experimentation, Europe, they believed, had reached a dead end. It was more divided than united over basic constitutional ends, and it faced several challenges—economic, cultural, and political—to which there seemed to be no easy answers. Indeed, according to some commentators, European leaders not only confronted older issues that remained unsolved, but also faced a host of new ones (e.g., Turkish membership of the EU, how to integrate its 13 million Muslim citizens, rising economic competition from China) to which they had no ready-made solutions. Europe, by the beginning of the twenty-first century, might have been well aware of where it was coming from, but it had no blueprint for where it wanted to go to. In some ways, Europe had "lost the plot."

Civilians escorted by Kenyan police and soldiers escape the Westgate mall in Narobi, Kenya, that was attacked by Al Shabaab, a radical Islamic group supported by Al Qaeda. The terrorists targeted Kenya for sending peacekeeping troops to Somalia.

Russia: From Yeltsin to Putin

One of the many problems facing the new Europe after the Cold War was how to define its relationship with post-communist Russia, a country confronting several degrees of stress after 1991 as it began to transform itself from a Marxist superpower with a planned economy to a democratic country that was liberal and market oriented. As even the most confident of Europeans accepted, none of this was going to be easy for a state that had had the same system for nearly three-quarters of a century. And so it proved during the 1990s, an especially painful decade during which Russia lost its ability to effectively challenge the United States and was instead a declining power with diminishing economic and ideological assets. Nor was there much in the way of economic compensation. On the contrary, as a result of its speedy adoption of Western-style privatization, Russia experienced something close to a 1930s-style economic depression, with industrial production plummeting, living standards sinking, and whole regions once devoted to Cold War military production experiencing free fall.

President Boris Yeltsin's foreign policy, meanwhile, did little to reassure many Russians. Indeed, his decision to get close to Russia's old capitalist enemies gave the distinct impression that he was selling out to the West. This made him a

WHAT'S YOUR WORLDVIEW ?

With the end of the Cold War, many analysts talked optimistically about a "peace dividend"—that is, a chance to shift spending from military to social programs like education, health, and job training. However, in the 1990s, the United States did not cut military spending and shift funding to domestic priorities. Why do you think this happened? Do you think US leaders feared a return of an authoritarian Soviet state, or did they anticipate the need for a strong military to support their hegemonic position?

CASE STUDY : Russia and Realism

Background

The year 2009 began quite cold for millions of people in Europe. Western Europeans shivered while the governments of Russia and Ukraine squabbled over the price of natural gas that Gazprom, the Russian state monopoly, charged Ukraine for its supply of this prime heating fuel. Because Ukrainian Prime Minister Yulia Timoshenko's government refused to meet Russia's price, Gazprom closed the valves on all the pipelines routed through that country and, by extension, on all of its Western European customers.

The Case

On the face of it, this crisis was a simple business dispute about supply and demand. Russian-owned Gazprom actually offered its product to Ukraine for less than it charged its other European customers—under the late-2008 proposal from Gazprom, Ukraine would pay $250 for each 1,000 cubic meters of gas, whereas other Europeans had to pay more than $500 for the same amount. Timoshenko's government complained that this was an unjustified increase. Gazprom's reaction to this rejection was a counteroffer of $418 per unit.

Realist theory provides a clear explanation for this dispute: Both countries are former Soviet republics and this dispute is part of the end of that empire. Nationalists in both Moscow and Kiev, goes this argument, were using the price of natural gas in an attempt to satisfy domestic political pressures in a game of international power politics. For many Russian, the implosion of the USSR was a humiliation. Instead of being the leaders of the country, Russians were forced to negotiate with other nationalities such as the Chechens, with whom Russia fought two wars in the 1990s, and the Ukrainians. By shutting off the heat for millions in Europe, Russia could show that it still mattered in international politics. For Ukrainians, supplies of natural gas were yet another unwanted example of how Russians were trying to continue their hated hegemony over the former Soviet republics. By standing up to the Russian giant, Ukraine's leaders were asserting the Ukrainian nationalist agenda.

Outcome

In the end, Russia won. The terms of the new ten-year contract promised to supply Ukraine gas at a starting price of $360 per 1,000 cubic meters for the first quarter of 2009. For many Russians, this is a satisfying result. Fifteen years ago, as the program of economic shock therapy faltered, Russian leaders had to ask the International Monetary Fund and World Bank for loans in exchange for radical restructuring of the economy. One ultranationalist politician called it a humiliation and "paying for the sausages." With its vital natural gas, Russia now held the cards, and it was the European leaders who had to ask for help.

For Discussion

1. How might the Russian government react if petroleum products from Azerbaijan, a former Soviet republic, become more readily available to Western Europe and Ukraine?
2. Power is often defined in terms of material or tangible resources and intangible assets such as the values and way of life that define a society. What power does Russia have in this situation? Now that Putin is the president again, will Russia likely continue to use its material resources to enhance its power and influence?
3. Can you think of other recent cases in which a resource-rich state has used its assets as a lever in its dealings with another state?

hero to many outside Russia. However, to many ordinary Russians it seemed as if he (like his predecessor Gorbachev) was conceding everything and getting very little in return. Nationalists and old communists, still present in significant numbers, were especially scathing. Yeltsin and his team, they argued, had not only given away Russia's assets at "discount prices" to a new class of **oligarchs**, but also was trying to turn Russia into a Western dependency. In short, he was not standing up for Russia's national interest.

Whether his successor Vladimir Putin, a former official in the KGB, had a clear vision for Russia when he took over the presidency matters less than the fact that, having assumed office, he began to stake out very different positions. These included a greater authoritarianism and nationalism at home, a much clearer recognition that the interests of Russia and those of the West would not always be one and the same, and what turned into a persistent drive to bring the Russian economy—and Russia's huge natural resources—back under state control. This did not lead to a turning back of the clock to Soviet times. What it did mean, though, was that the West's leaders could no longer regard the country as a potential strategic partner. Certainly, Western governments could not assume that Russia would forever be in a state of decline. The West must instead confront a state with almost unlimited supplies of oil and gas and with a leadership determined to defend Russia's interests and to restore Russia to a position of global leadership.

Still, the West had less to fear now than it had during the Cold War proper. Economic reform had made Russia dependent on the West (although some Western countries, like Germany, were dependent on Russia for their energy requirements). Furthermore, the official political ideology did not in any way challenge Western institutions or values. The world had changed forever since 1991. Nor was Russia the power it had once been during Soviet times. Indeed, not only was it unable to prevent some of its former republics from either signing up to former enemy institutions like NATO or moving more openly into the Western camp, but also, by 2007, it was effectively encircled by the three Baltic republics to the northwest, an increasingly pro-Western Ukraine to the south, and Georgia in the Caucasus. Adding to its potential woes was the fact that many of its more loyal, regional allies ran highly repressive and potentially unstable governments: Belorussia, Turkmenistan, and Azerbaijan, for example.

Many in the United States and a few in Europe were compelled to conclude that although Russia might have changed in several positive ways since the collapse of the USSR in 1991, it remained historic Russia with an authoritarian outlook, a disregard for human rights, and an inclination toward

The "stare down" at the G-8 summit in Northern Ireland between the leaders of two powerful states may reveal the deep divisions between President Obama and President Putin over the conflict in Syria and the negotiations over Iran's nuclear weapons. Now one might add the serious disagreement over Russian policy toward Ukraine.

empire. A new future might have beckoned, but the heavy hand of the past continued to influence relations between Russia and the West.

East Asia: Primed for Rivalry?

If perceived lessons from history continue to play a crucial role in shaping modern Western images of post-Soviet Russia, then the past also plays a part in defining the international relations of East Asia—and a most bloody past it has been. The time following World War II was punctuated by several devastating wars (in China, Korea, and Vietnam), revolutionary insurgencies (in the Philippines, Malaya, and Indonesia), authoritarian rule (nearly everywhere), and revolutionary extremism (most tragically in Cambodia). The contrast with the postwar European experience could not have been more pronounced. In fact, scholars of international relations have been much taken with the comparison, pointing out that whereas Europe managed to form a new liberal security community during the Cold War, East Asia did not. In part this was the result of the formation of the EU and the creation of NATO (organizations that had no equivalents in Asia). But it was also because Germany managed to effect a serious reconciliation with its immediate neighbors whereas Japan (for largely internal reasons) did not. The end of the Cold War in Europe transformed the continent dramatically, but this was much less true in East Asia, where powerful communist parties continued to rule—in China, North Korea,

North Korea's young leader, Kim Jong-un, has promised to improve the quality of life for citizens in his country, but economic change has been replaced with an acceleration of its military plans to attack the US allies in Asia. Should the world be concerned?

and Vietnam—and at least two outstanding territorial disputes (one less important one between Japan and Russia and a potentially far more dangerous one between China and Taiwan) continued to threaten the security of the region.

For all these reasons, East Asia, far from being primed for peace, was still ripe for new rivalries. Europe's very bloody past between 1914 and 1945, went the argument, could easily turn into Asia's future. This was not a view shared by every commentator, however. In fact, as events unfolded, this uncompromisingly tough-minded realist perspective came under sustained criticism. Critics did not deny the possibility of future disturbances: How could they, given Korean division, North Korea's nuclear weapons program, and China's claim to Taiwan? But several factors did suggest that the region was not quite the powder keg some thought it to be.

The first and most important factor was the great economic success experienced by the region itself. The sources of this have been much debated, with some people suggesting that the underlying reasons were cultural, others that it was directly economic (cheap labor plus plentiful capital), and a few that it was the by-product of the application of a nonliberal model of development employing the strong state to drive through rapid economic development from above. Some have also argued that the United States played a crucial role by opening its market to East Asian goods while providing the region with critical security on the cheap. Whatever the cause, or combination of causes, the simple fact remains that East Asia by the end of the twentieth century had become the third-largest powerhouse in the global economy, accounting for nearly 25 percent of world **gross domestic product**.

Second, although many states in East Asia might have had powerful memories of past conflicts, these were beginning to be overridden in the 1990s by a growth in regional trade and investment. Indeed, although East Asia carried much historical baggage (some of this deliberately exploited by political elites in search of legitimacy), economic pressures and material self-interest appeared to be driving countries in the region together rather than apart. The process of East Asian economic integration was not quick—the **Association of Southeast Asian Nations** was only formed in 1967. Nor was integration accompanied by the formation of anything like the EU. However, once regionalism began to take off during the 1990s, it showed no signs of slowing down.

A third reason for optimism lay with Japan. Here, in spite of an apparent inability to unambiguously apologize for past misdeeds and atrocities—a failure that cost it dearly in terms of **soft power** influence in the region—its policies could hardly be characterized as disturbing. On the contrary, having adopted its famous peace constitution in the 1950s and renounced the possibility of ever acquiring nuclear weapons (Japan was one of the strongest upholders of the original 1968 Nonproliferation Treaty), Japan demonstrated no interest in upsetting its neighbors by acting in anything other than a benign manner. Furthermore, by spreading its considerable largesse in the form of aid and large-scale investment, it went some of the way in fostering better international relations in the region.

Even its old rival China was a significant beneficiary, and by 2003 more than 5,000 Japanese companies were operating on the Chinese mainland.

This leads us, then, to China itself. Much has been written about "rising China," especially by analysts who argue—in classical realist fashion—that when new powerful states emerge onto the international stage, they are bound to disturb the existing balance of power. China looks benign now, they agree. It will look different in a few years' time—once it has risen. Again, though, there might be more cause for guarded optimism than pessimism, largely because China itself has adopted policies (both economic and military) the clear purpose of which is to reassure its neighbors that it can rise peacefully and thus effectively prove the realists wrong. It has also translated policy into action by supporting regional integration, exporting its considerable capital to other countries in East Asia, and working as a responsible party rather than a spoiler inside regional multilateral institutions. Certainly, such policies are beginning to bear fruit, with once-skeptical neighbors—even possibly Japan—increasingly viewing China as a benevolent instrument of economic development rather than a threat.

In the end, however, all strategic roads in China (and in East Asia as a whole) lead to the one state whose presence in the region remains critical: the United States of America. Although theoretically opposed to a unipolar world in which there is only one significant global player, the new Chinese leadership has pursued a most cautious policy toward the United States. No doubt some Americans will continue to be wary of a state run by the Communist Party, whose human rights record can hardly be described as exemplary. However, so long as China continues to act in a cooperative fashion, there is a good chance that relations will continue to prosper. There is no guaranteeing the long-term outcome. With growth rates around 10 percent per year, with its apparently insatiable demand for overseas raw materials, and with enormous dollar reserves at its disposal, China has already changed the terms of the debate about the future of international politics. Of course, it remains to be seen what lasting effects the global economic crisis will have on China; and for some time to come, China could well remain what one observer has called a "colossus with feet of clay," overly dependent on foreign investment and still militarily light years behind the United States. But even such a colossus presents a set of challenges that did not exist in the much simpler days of the Cold War. Indeed, one of the great ironies of international history might be that China as a rising capitalist power playing by the rules of the market might turn out to be more of a problem for the West than China the communist power, in those far-off days when it denounced the imperialists across the ocean and called on Asians to drive Americans out of the region.

The War on Terrorism: From 9/11 to Iraq and Afghanistan

The end of the Cold War marked one of the great turning points of the late twentieth century, but 9/11 was a reminder that the resulting international order did not find ready acceptance everywhere. Osama bin Laden was no doubt motivated by far more than a dislike for globalization and American primacy. As many analysts have pointed out, bin Laden's vision was one that pointed back to a golden age of Islam rather than forward to something modern. That said, his method of attacking the United States using four planes, his use of video to communicate with followers, his employment of the global financial system to fund operations, and his primary goal of driving the United States out of the Middle East could hardly be described as medieval. He represented a very modern threat, one that could not be dealt with by the kind of traditional means developed during the Cold War. As the administration of George W. Bush constantly reiterated, this new danger meant that old strategies, such as containment and deterrence, were no longer relevant. If this was the beginning of a "new global war on terrorism," as some seemed to argue at the time, then it was one unlikely to be fought using policies and methods learned between 1947 and 1989.

The new threat environment provided the United States with a fixed point of reference for organizing its international affairs. It built close relations with the many states—Russia, India, Pakistan, and China perhaps being the most important—that were now prepared to join it in waging a global war against terror. After the 9/11 attacks, Bush administration officials felt compelled to act more assertively abroad. Some of Bush's more conservative supporters believed that one of the reasons for the attack on the United States in the first place was that it had not been assertive enough in the 1990s. Finally, policy makers in the Bush administration seemed to abandon the defense of the status quo in the Middle East. The events of 9/11, they argued, had changed the original formula whereby the United States turned a blind eye to autocratic regimes that existed in the region, in exchange for cheap oil and stability.

Yet Iraq had not been involved in 9/11; the regime itself was secular; and it shared the same goal as the United States in at least one respect—that of seeking to contain the geopolitical ambitions of Islamic Iran. For all these reasons, different analysts have identified different factors to explain the war, ranging from the ideological influence exercised by the neoconservatives on President Bush, to America's close relationship with Israel, and to America's desire to control Iraq's oil. We are still left with more questions than easy answers. The most credible might be that the United States went to war partly because it thought it would win fairly easily, partly

WHAT'S YOUR WORLDVIEW

Both China and India are gaining power and influence in global affairs. Both countries are members of the G-20, and both have strong economies that were not devastated by the recent economic crisis. These two states are also increasing their military spending, including the expansion of their naval power. Some experts argue that this is only the beginning of a shift of global power toward Asia. What do you think? Is this a real challenge to other major powers or just a rebalancing of the world?

THEORY IN PRACTICE

The Iraq War and Its Origins

Challenge

International relations, as a field, has always been concerned with the origins of wars. Long-term changes in the balance of power, fear of encirclement, and imperial ambition—not to mention misperception and ideology—have all been employed at one time or another to explain why states engage in military action. Levels of analysis discussed in Chapters 1 and 4 offer the student of international relations a variety of plausible explanations for why a state goes to war. The Iraq War presents a useful, and possibly difficult, test case for various theories of war origins. It should be noted that the war was costly in both blood and treasure. The total cost from 2003 through 2011 was $801.9 billion. US military deaths from March 2003 through July 2010 totaled 4,421, and the number of civilian deaths from 2003 through 2012 was approximately 119,157.

Options

Several competing explanations have been advanced so far to explain the US decision to go to war against Iraq in 2003. These include, among others, the official argument that Iraq represented a serious and potentially rising threat to a critically important region; the more materialist thesis that the United States was determined to secure direct control of Iraq's massive reserves of oil; and the popular claim that the war was the product of pressures arising from within the United States itself—here identified as the Israel lobby, the ideologically inclined neoconservatives, and their various supporters on the Christian Right. The student of world politics, however, is still left with a number of unanswered questions. First, would the war have happened without the quite unexpected election of George W. Bush in late 2000 and the influence of Vice President Dick Cheney and his neoconservative foreign policy advisors? In other words, did the president and vice president make a huge difference to the decision taken? Second, could Bush have then led the United States into war without the profound shock created by the equally unexpected attack of 9/11? Considered this way, wasn't the war largely the by-product of fear and insecurity? Third, what role did British Prime Minister Tony Blair play? Indeed, was this a war made possible by an alliance with a major European power like the United Kingdom? Fourth, would it have been feasible at all if various American writers and policy makers had not thought the United States so powerful that it could more or less do anything in the world? To what extent, in other words, did the notion of the "unipolar moment" contribute to the final decision to go to war? Furthermore, were the intellectual grounds for the war not also laid by those during the post–Cold War period who thought it wise to promote democracy and encouraged others to intervene in the internal affairs of sovereign states for humanitarian purposes? Finally, to what extent could one argue that the Iraq War was in the US national interest; and if it was, then why did so many realists oppose the war?

For Discussion

1. Why do you think wars start? Use levels of analysis to identify potential causes.
2. If we know the causes of war in the past, why is it so hard to prevent new wars?
3. The Iraq War is considered a war of choice. Iraq did not attack the United States, and the reasons for going to war were somewhat suspect. When all of us are aware of the costs of war, why do our leaders continue to make this dangerous choice?
4. During the 2007 surge in US forces in Iraq to counter the increase in antigovernment and religiously linked sectarian attacks, American troops were often caught in a crossfire. Did the increase in troops succeed?

because it got its intelligence wrong, and partly because some political leaders thought—rather unwisely—that building a new regime in Iraq would be just as easy as getting rid of the old one.

It was clear by 2009 that this "war of choice" in Iraq was a strategic blunder that neither delivered stable democracy to Iraq nor inspired others in the region to undertake serious political reform. It has also had the doubly dangerous consequence of disturbing the whole of the Middle East while making it possible for Iran to gain even greater influence in the region than it had before. In fact, by undermining the old regime in Iraq, the United States has effectively created a vacuum into which an increasingly self-confident Iranian regime has marched. Finally, as a result of their action in Iraq, the United States and its allies have provided radical Islamists around the world with a rallying point that they appear to have exploited with some skill. The bombings of transit systems in Madrid (2004) and London (2005) were no doubt the result of many factors; however, few now believe they were entirely unconnected to what had been happening in the Middle East since 2003.

After the 9/11 attacks, Al Qaeda was given sanctuary by the Taliban government in Afghanistan. The United States immediately demanded that the leaders of this terrorist network be turned over to the United States for trial. The Taliban refused, and on October 7, 2001, the US military invaded Afghanistan, destroyed Al Qaeda's terrorist training camps, and overthrew the Taliban-controlled government. NATO members invoked Article 5 and came to the aid of the United States.

Currently, NATO maintains the International Security Assistance Force, which consists of 130,000 troops at a cost of about $100 billion a year. Since 2009, the United States has moved away from a counterinsurgency policy that put an emphasis on protecting civilians, providing services, and nation building toward more direct military action: increasing airstrikes in both Afghanistan and Pakistan, the use of drones for surveillance and attacks on suspected terrorist leaders, a dramatic increase in covert operations, and the use of special forces surprise attacks on terrorist camps in the tribal regions that extend into Pakistan. Clearly, the United States and its allies have decided that the stick is more effective than the carrot, and the decision has been made to use lethal force to drive the Taliban to the negotiating table.

In crisis situations, the beliefs of decision makers matter the most. What other factors might have shaped the decision to pursue and eventually eliminate Osama bin Laden?

With the successful covert operation that resulted in the killing of Osama bin Laden in 2011, many citizens in NATO countries were wondering why their men and women continued to fight and die for a corrupt and ineffective government in Afghanistan. Suicide bombers continued to kill civilians who cooperated with the United States and the Afghan government, and the Taliban increased their attacks and found refuge in tribal mountain regions that extend into Pakistan. One of the most dangerous terrorists groups, the Haqqani network, is based in Pakistan and funded by the Pakistani intelligence agency, the Inter-Services Intelligence directorate. The Afghanistan government claims that the directorate has supported a fivefold increase in insurgent attacks since 2006.

The United States and Pakistan are allies, but they have different interests in Afghanistan. The United States hopes that when it withdraws, Afghanistan will be a relatively stable, prosperous, and democratic state that is no longer an incubator for terrorists. Pakistan does not want a strong Afghanistan that might be governed by ethnic Tajiks, who are traditionally allies of India, Pakistan's rival in the region. We must remember that India and Pakistan are rivals in this region and both have nuclear weapons. When the United States and NATO withdraw, peace and stability in this region might not yet be achieved.

Conclusion

In this chapter we have seen some of the trends and events that created the contemporary globalized system. War (both "hot" and "cold"), revolutions, colonization, and its collapse—each had a role in the evolution of international society. The irony might be found in this fact: Religion played a role in both 1648 and 2001. The signatories of the Peace of Westphalia wanted to remove religion from European international politics. Members of Al Qaeda want to bring religion back into global politics.

The Peace of Westphalia in the seventeenth century created an international system in Europe that many people at the time believed would make for more orderly politics on the continent. In the same way, the end of the Cold War in the twentieth century seemed to promise a more peaceful world. But as we have seen in this chapter, these hopes went unfulfilled. The effects of revolutions, wars, and European imperialism have revealed the hollow nature of the European international system. Moreover, during the Cold War—while much of the attention of politicians and academics in the developed world was focused on the US–USSR confrontation—other wars, economic trends, and social movements around the world were too often ignored. As a result, the euphoria in Western Europe and the United States that followed the end of the Soviet Union soon gave way to a new set of challenges and threats. And many of the "new" challenges were actually quite old, such as the persistence of poverty in underdeveloped nations. We explore these issues in depth later in Chapters 6 and 9. But first, in Chapter 3, we examine theories that we can use to approach these issues more thoughtfully, helping us better understand and explain our ever-changing political world.

Engaging with the WORLD

Give Peace a Chance

Interested in working for peace? Many groups are committed to this initiative and offer ways to get involved.

One is the Quaker religious community, whose peace testimony states that their "opposition to all forms of violence imposes responsibility to seek alternative responses to conflict and injustice." Visit http://friendspeaceteams.org/

Another is the Ecumenical Accompaniment Program in Palestine and Israel, a peace project of the World Council of Churches. Volunteers monitor and report violations of human rights and international law and work with Palestinian and Israeli peace activists to promote nonviolent responses to the problems in this region. Check out www.eappi.org.

KEY TERMS

Anarchy, p. 54
Appeasement, p. 36
Armistice, p. 35
Arms race, p. 45
Association of Southeast Asian
  Nations, p. 59
Bipolar, p. 39
Blitzkrieg, p. 36
Capitalism, p. 39
Cold War, p. 39
Containment, p. 42
Détente, p. 46
European Union (EU), p. 51
Fourteen Points, p. 35

Genocide, p. 36
Glasnost, p. 49
Globalization, p. 51
Gross domestic product, p. 59
Hegemony, p. 39
Holocaust, p. 36
Hyperpower, p. 52
Intercontinental ballistic
  missiles, p. 47
Liberal democracy, p. 45
Market democracies, p. 51
Marshall Plan, p. 42
North Atlantic Treaty Organization
  (NATO), p. 43

Oligarchs, p. 56
Ostpolitik, p. 46
Perestroika, p. 49
Rapprochement, p. 46
Soft power, p. 59
Strategic Arms Reductions
  Treaty, p. 49
Strategic Defense Initiative (SDI), p. 48
Terrorism, p. 46
Treaty of Versailles, p. 35
Trench warfare, p. 34
Truman Doctrine, p. 42
United Nations, p. 51
Warsaw Pact, p. 44

REVIEW QUESTIONS

1. Was nineteenth-century European international society merely a means of legitimizing imperialism?

2. How did the method by which European colonies in Africa and Asia gained their independence determine their post-independence internal politics?

3. Why did the United States become involved in wars in Asia after 1950? Illustrate your answer by reference to either the Korean War or the Vietnam War.

4. How have scholars of international relations attempted to explain the end of the Cold War?

5. Why did liberal theorists assume the world would become a more stable place after the end of the Cold War, and why did realists disagree with them?

6. If the United States won the Cold War, why did it have such problems defining a grand strategy for itself after 1989 and before 9/11?

7. Has globalization since the Cold War changed the basic character of world politics?

8. How successfully has Europe adapted to the challenges facing it since the end of the Cold War?

9. How has the "war on terror" changed international politics?

For resources including quizzes, flashcards, and other study tools, please visit us at **www.oup.com/us/lamy**

THINKING ABOUT GLOBAL POLITICS

Understanding and Resolving International Conflicts

INTRODUCTION

In this exercise, you will be asked to analyze several conflict situations from the perspective of different state and nonstate actors or players directly or indirectly involved in a given conflict. First, we ask you to explore the causes of this conflict, and second, we ask you to consider possible ways of managing or resolving the conflict. You might have to do some research to find answers to our questions. This is a great opportunity to explore the wide variety of sources on the Web and in your university or college library.

PROCEDURE

This is a cooperative learning exercise. In groups of three or four, begin by reviewing the list of Cold War conflicts in this chapter and the list of conflicts in Figure 7.2 in Chapter 7.

1. Review the list of Cold War conflicts and identify those that might still be going on. Identify those that have ended. How did they end? What were the reasons these conflicts were resolved?
2. Now, look at the list of conflicts from 1946 to 2009. Pay particular attention to those conflicts that began after the end of the Cold War and respond to the following questions:
   a. Who is involved in this conflict? Primary actors? Secondary actors?
   b. What do these actors claim are the causes of the conflict?
   c. What other factors serve to accentuate the conflict and increase its lethality?
3. In Chapter 1 and Chapter 4, we introduce you to levels of analysis: tools for explaining decision making and the behavior of states in the international system. Because war and conflict are a constant in the international system, we can use levels to explain why wars begin and how they might end. With your cooperative learning team, come up with plausible explanations for the start of each conflict. Was it caused by the leader's desire for power (level 1), the state's need for oil (level 2), or the fear of a neighbor's military buildup or the security dilemma (level 3)? Now, share your list of plausible explanations with the rest of the class. See if you can reach an agreement on the most frequent reasons why countries go to war. Are there any patterns that develop? You might also check your ideas with the work of historians or official records on the war. If we know why countries go to war, can we anticipate and even prevent future wars?
4. Now, with some understanding of why wars begin, let's review several examples of peacemaking efforts. There are many examples of conflicts that have ended peacefully. Select at least two of these conflicts and identify the factors that helped all the parties reach an acceptable peace. For example, was one party defeated and forced to accept a peace agreement, like Japan and Germany in World War II, or was peace achieved because a third party offered mediation and assistance, like Norway did to help reach a peace agreement in Sri Lanka?

WRITING ASSIGNMENT

What has this exercise taught you about the difficulties of preventing future wars and the problems associated with peacemaking? Do you think peace, defined as an absence of war, is a utopian dream? Must we live in a world where all we can hope to do is manage conflict and prevent systemic war?

CONTRIBUTORS TO CHAPTER 2: *David Armstrong, Michael Cox, Len Scott, Steven L. Lamy, and John Masker.*

A nation's survival is its first and ultimate responsibility; it cannot be compromised or put to risk.

—*Henry Kissinger*

Though it be true that democratic government will make wars less likely, it will not eliminate all causes of conflict between nations, and if the enormous sacrifices of this war are not to be made in vain, not merely must democracy triumph in individual states, but in the society of states as well.

—*Woodrow Wilson*

Theory is always *for* someone, and *for* some purpose.

—*Robert W. Cox*

There are several "states of concern" for the leading world powers. North Korea may present one of the most difficult problems for those concerned with national security and the control of nuclear weapons. A quick review of recent North Korean actions suggests that no state seems to be able to control this intransigent state and its leaders.

In May 2009, North Korea, the last Stalinist state in the international system, test-fired six missiles after detonating a nuclear device several days before. South Korean spy satellites captured images that showed the North Koreans moving missiles to launch pads close to the demilitarized zone. One of the suspected missiles is the type that is capable of reaching US territory.

Robert Gates, who was US Secretary of Defense at the time, stated that these nuclear tests and missile launches were a direct threat to US national security. He was adamant in stating that the United States would not accept North Korea as a nuclear state. Meanwhile, the armed attacks on South Korea by the North have continued. In March 2010, a North Korean torpedo sank the *Cheonan*, a South Korean warship, killing forty-six people. In November 2010, a North Korean artillery barrage hit the island of Yeonpyeong in South Korean territory. These

A South Korean military officer displays fragments of shells that North Korea fired at a South Korean island in November 2010. The South reacted with calls for more troops on potential targets, and North Korea stridently warned South Korea about any military provocations. Are we headed for a nuclear showdown in this region? Did the December 2012 South Korean elections defuse the tensions?

attacks heightened immediate concerns in South Korea, Japan, and other East Asian states. In November of 2013—the three-year anniversary of the North Korean shelling of the South Korean border island of Yeonpyeong—the North Korean regime threatened to turn South Korea's presidential office into a "sea of fire." In the same month, the North Korean government restarted a nuclear reactor that is capable of producing plutonium for bombs. The United States does not fear an attack by North Korea, but does worry that North Korea will sell its technology to terrorist networks or other states interested in attacking the United States. The North Korean government is in direct violation of international rules and has rejected attempts by the International Atomic Energy Agency—the international agency in charge of controlling the proliferation of nuclear arms—to inspect their nuclear sites and prevent the production of weapons-grade nuclear material.

From the realist perspective, negotiations and diplomacy have costs as well as benefits. Realists believe one must always negotiate from strength and be prepared to act with force or the threat of force when dealing with rogue states that have no intention of following international rules. Realists claim that the basic flaw of liberal thinking is that North Korea can be talked out of these weapons. The power, prestige, and influence of the United States and liberal institutions like the International Atomic Energy Agency are being undermined by North Korea. Realists argue that the major powers must put pressure on North Korea by choking off its ability to export and import weapons and military equipment, cut off all access to financial resources, and pressure China to rein in its North Korean ally. Liberal thinkers, on the other hand, still hold out hope for arms-control talks and the promise that North Korean leaders will want to end their intransigence and join the international community of nation-states.

As we discuss in this chapter, both realism and liberalism are effective theories by which we can more closely examine interactions among states. Both have become important in the study of international relations at universities around the world. Yet both have their limitations as well. The basis for both theories is a very different understanding about human nature, the goal of a state's policy, and the nature of the international system. In addition, there are alternative or critical theories that bring up other questions: about the connections between the owners of the means of production or the business leaders and the political leaders and about the role of the state. These critical theorists question the viability of the past and present international system and ask us to consider our traditional assumptions about global politics.

Introduction

In Chapter 1, we asked you to consider your personal worldview, or perspective on international events, which can result from your citizenship, personal identity, and other factors. In this chapter we begin to present the concept of

LEARNING OBJECTIVES

After reading and discussing this chapter, you should be able to:

Define the term "theory" and give examples.

Describe the historical origins of the realist, liberal, Marxist, constructivist, and feminist schools of thought.

Name key theorists of the five schools of thought.

Explain the relation among the levels of analysis and the different variants of the five schools of thought.

Explain the benefits and shortcomings of the different variants of the five schools of thought for the study of international relations.

theory. By **theory** we mean a set of propositions that help us to understand events. Like pairs of sunglasses that can block different amounts of sunlight, a theory can limit what we see or, like magnifying glasses, help us to see things better.

Theories of international relations help explain how political leaders view and understand the world. We do not mean that a leader one day announces, "I am a realist," or "I am a liberal," and then follows a recipe for foreign policy. Instead, theories provide a lens through which to view political actions and explain these actions and other events. Theories can also help predict future actions on the basis of what has occurred in the past. But we must keep in mind that the theories we use—like sunglasses—might also restrict what we think.

There are many contending theories of global politics. Of these, realism and liberalism have the deepest historical roots, and they gained dominance in the study of international relations during the twentieth century. The basis for both theories is a very different understanding about human nature, the role of the state and its foreign policy goals, and the nature of the international system. Schools of thought devoted to realism, liberalism, and their offshoots are considered mainstream or traditional. Both theories have become important in the study of international relations at universities around the world. Yet both have limitations that have led to the development of alternative theories.

As we shall see, both realism and liberalism are useful theories for explaining and understanding the behavior of states in the international system. But these traditional theories are not as effective in helping us understand some of the transformative actors and issues in today's globalized world, such as NGOs, transnational networks, the importance of economic structures, and minority voices that have been marginalized over the years. The second part of this chapter explores a number of alternative theories that have recently become part of the international relations discourse, in part as a response to the shortcomings of realism and liberalism but also in reaction to a different set of stimuli. These alternative approaches include Marxism, constructivism, and feminist theory, each of which can provide important ideas to understand trends and events in global politics and globalization in ways that realism and liberalism cannot.

What Is Realism?

Over the centuries, various world leaders have sought to create international rules to make life more stable and predictable by decreasing outbreaks of violent aggression. European nations signed two treaties that we now know as the Peace of Westphalia (1648), which established a principle that still governs international relations: sovereignty. Signatories agreed that only a legitimate government could exercise control over its citizens and territory, could act independently and flexibly in its relations with other states, and could craft its own strategies and policies aimed at securing perceived national interests. By inference, no state could interfere in the domestic affairs of any other state.

Of course, the principle of sovereignty applied more to the continent of Europe and less to societies anywhere else on earth; nevertheless, sovereignty was—and still is today—a critically important concept.

By declaring some regions of the world to be sovereign and agreeing that sovereign states could not legally interfere with the internal business of other sovereign states, political leaders *thought* they had solved the problem of foreign wars. However, this attempt to eliminate war failed early and often: Within a year of the Peace of Westphalia, England invaded Ireland; within four years, the English and the Dutch were at war; within six years, Russia and Poland were at war; and so it went.

With this reality in mind, it is relatively easy to understand why the earliest perspective on international relations, referred to as **realism**, is based on the following three assumptions:

- States are the only actors in international relations that matter.
- A policy maker's primary responsibility is to create, maintain, and increase national **power**—the means available to a state to secure its national interests—at all costs.
- No central authority stands above the state. The anarchic nature of the international system is an essential assumption for realist thinkers and, in fact, for most liberal thinkers and even some critical-approach thinkers.

The world perceived by realists is lawless, competitive, and uncertain. In fact, one influential philosopher who helped to define realism, Thomas Hobbes, published this pessimistic observation about life in his political treatise *Leviathan*: "The life of man is solitary, poor, nasty, brutish and short." The only way to avoid misery and anarchy, according to Hobbes, was to have a strong ruler of a strong state impose order and provide protection from external attack (Hobbes 1651).

The Essential Realism

In later sections we will see how realism can be regarded as a broad theoretical umbrella, covering a variety of perspectives, each with its own leading authors and texts. Despite the numerous denominations, keep in mind that, essentially, all realists subscribe to the following three S's: statism, survival, *and* self-help. Let's discuss these three essential elements in more detail and also examine some of realism's shortcomings.

Statism

For realists, the state is the main actor and sovereignty is its distinguishing trait. The meaning

With the military a powerful political actor in both India and Pakistan, will nationalism and leaders who embrace realist views of the world lead the region and world to war?

of the sovereign state is inextricably bound up with the use of force. In terms of its internal dimension, to illustrate this relationship between violence and the state we need look no further than Max Weber's famous definition of the state as "the monopoly of the legitimate use of physical force within a given territory" (M. J. Smith 1986, 23). Within this territorial space, **sovereignty** means that the state has supreme authority to make and enforce laws. This is the basis of the unwritten contract between individuals and the state. According to Hobbes, for example, we trade our liberty in return for a guarantee of security. Once security has been established, **civil society** can begin. But in the absence of security, people are in the state of nature, where there can be no business, no art, no culture, and no society. The first move, then, for the realist is to organize power domestically. Only after power has been organized can community begin.

> ## WHAT'S YOUR WORLDVIEW
>
> *Do you think that Hobbes's pessimism about life applies to our society in the twenty-first century? Have we advanced at all since the seventeenth century?*

The first move of the state is to organize power domestically and maintain law and order, and the second is to accumulate power internationally. It is one thing to say that international politics is a struggle for power, but this merely begs the question of what realists mean by power. Hans Morgenthau offers the following definition of power: "Man's control over the minds and actions of other men" ([1948] 1955, 26). There are two important points that realists make about the elusive concept of power. First, power is a relational concept; one does not exercise power in a vacuum but in relation to another entity. Second, power is a relative concept; calculations need to be made not only about one's own power capabilities but also about the power that other states possess. Yet the task of accurately assessing the power of states is infinitely complex. Too often, power calculations are reduced to counting the number of troops, tanks, aircraft, and naval ships a country possesses, in the frequently mistaken belief that this translates into the ability to get other actors to do something they would not otherwise do.

Survival

The second principle that unites realists is the assertion that in international politics the preeminent goal is survival. Although there is an ambiguity in the works of the realists as to whether the accumulation of power is an end in itself, one would think that there is no dissenting from the argument that the ultimate concern of states is for security. Survival is held to be a precondition for attaining all other goals, whether these involve conquest or merely independence.

Niccolo Machiavelli tried to make a science out of his reflections on state survival. His short and engaging book, *The Prince*, was written with the explicit intention of codifying a set of maxims that would enable leaders to maintain their hold on power. In important respects, we find two related Machiavellian themes recurring in the writings of modern realists, both of which derive from the idea that the realm of international politics requires different moral and political rules from those that apply in domestic politics.

Why is the US military prison at Guantánamo Bay, Cuba, still holding prisoners? These protestors were taking part in a demonstration in front of the White House and reminding President Obama of his campaign promise to close the prison and stop torture.

The task of understanding what realists believe is the true nature of international politics, and the need to protect the state at all costs (even if this might mean the sacrifice of one's own citizens) places a heavy burden on the shoulders of state leaders. In the words of Henry Kissinger, the academic realist who became secretary of state during the Nixon presidency, "a nation's survival is its first and ultimate responsibility; it cannot be compromised or put to risk" (1977, 204). Their guide must be an **ethic of responsibility**, an idea suggested by Max Weber: the careful weighing of consequences and the realization that individual acts of an immoral kind might have to be undertaken for the greater good.

The principal difficulty with the realist formulation of an "ethics of responsibility" is that, although it instructs leaders to consider the consequences of their actions, it does not provide a guide for how state leaders should weigh the consequences (M. J. Smith 1986, 51).

Not only does realism provide an alternative moral code for state leaders, proponents claim, but also it suggests a wider objection to the whole enterprise of bringing ethics into international politics. Starting from the assumption that each state has its own particular values and beliefs, realists argue that the state is the supreme good and there can be no community beyond borders. This moral relativism has generated a substantial body of criticism, particularly from liberal theorists who endorse the notion of universal human rights.

Self-Help

Kenneth Waltz's *Theory of International Politics* (1979) brought to the realist tradition a deeper understanding of the international system itself. Unlike

Multipolar system

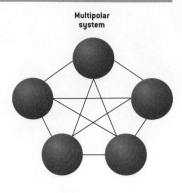

Bipolar

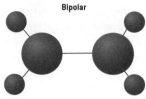

Unipolar (Hegemony)

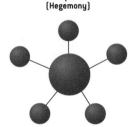

POWER, POLITICS, AND POLARITY.

Which of these power arrangements best represents the world today? What about the world of the early twentieth century? The nineteenth century? How does theory help us understand these global power dynamics?

many other realists, Waltz argued that international politics is not unique because of the regularity of war and conflict, because this is also familiar in domestic politics. The key difference between domestic and international orders lies in their structure. In the domestic polity, citizens usually do not have to defend themselves. In the international system, there is no higher authority, no global police officer, to prevent and counter the use of force. Security can therefore only be realized through self-help. In an anarchic structure, "self-help is necessarily the principle of action" (Waltz 1979, 111). But in the course of providing for one's own security, the state in question will automatically be fueling the insecurity of other states.

The term given to this spiral of insecurity is the **security dilemma**. This suggests that one state's quest for security is often another state's source of insecurity. States find it very difficult to trust one another and often view the intentions of others in a negative light. Thus the military preparations of one state are likely to be matched by neighboring states.

In a self-help system, "structural realists" argue that the balance of power will emerge even in the absence of a conscious policy to maintain it (i.e., prudent statecraft). Waltz argues that balances of power result irrespective of the intentions of any particular state. In an **anarchic system** populated by states with leaders who seek to perpetuate themselves, alliances will be formed that seek to check and balance the power against threatening states. Classical realists, however, are more likely to emphasize the crucial role state leaders and diplomats play in maintaining the balance of power. In other words, the balance of power is not natural or inevitable; the leaders of states construct it.

Historically, realists have illustrated the lack of trust among states by reference to the parable of the "stag hunt." In *Man, the State and War*, Kenneth Waltz revisits Rousseau's parable:

Assume that five men who have acquired a rudimentary ability to speak and to understand each other happen to come together at a time when all of them suffer from hunger. The hunger of each will be satisfied by the fifth part of a stag, so they "agree" to cooperate in a project to trap one. But also the hunger of any one of them will be satisfied by a hare, so, as a hare comes within reach, one of them grabs it. The defector obtains the means of satisfying his hunger but in doing so permits the stag to escape. His immediate interest prevails over consideration for his fellows. (1959, 167–168)

Waltz argues that the metaphor of the stag hunt provides a basis for understanding the problem of coordinating the interests of the individual versus the interests of the common good and the payoff between short-term interests and long-term interests. In the self-help system of international politics, the logic of self-interest mitigates against the provision of collective goods, such as "security" or "free trade." Thus, the question is not whether all will be better off through cooperation, but rather who will likely gain more than another. Because of this concern with relative-gains issues, realists argue that cooperation is difficult to achieve in a self-help system.

One Realism or Many?

So far in this chapter we have treated the realist lens as if it were a unified set of beliefs and propositions; it is, however, not at all that way, as both the model's supporters and its critics have pointed out. Next, we will outline key differences between two versions, classical realism and structural realism, or neorealism (Table 3.1).

Classical Realism

The **classical realism** lineage begins with Thucydides' representation of power politics as a law of human behavior. The classical realists argued that the drive for power and the will to dominate are the fundamental aspects of human nature. The behavior of the state as a self-seeking egoist is understood to be merely a reflection of the characteristics of the people who comprise the state. Therefore, it is human nature that explains why international politics is necessarily power politics. This reduction of realism to a condition of human nature is one that frequently reappears in the leading works of the doctrine, most famously in the work of the most famous proponent of postwar realism, Hans J. Morgenthau.

Another distinguishing characteristic of classical realism is its adherents' belief in the primordial character of power and ethics. Classical realism is fundamentally about the struggle for belonging, a struggle that is often violent. Patriotic virtue is required for communities to survive in this historic battle between good and evil, a virtue that long predates the emergence of sovereignty-based notions of community in the mid-seventeenth century.

How is a leader supposed to act in a world animated by such malevolent forces? The answer given by Machiavelli is that all obligations and treaties with other states must be disregarded if the security of the community is under threat. Moreover, imperial expansion is legitimate because it is a means of gaining greater security. Other classical realists, however, advocate a more temperate understanding of moral conduct. Mid-twentieth-century realists such as Butterfield, Carr, Morgenthau, and Wolfers believed that wise leadership and the pursuit of the national interest in ways that are compatible with

A critical element of power is the possession of natural resources like oil and natural gas. Russia's gas monopoly, Gazprom, provides vital energy supplies to all of Europe, as this control room map suggests. Does this powerful monopoly give Russian political leaders some influence in European politics?

Table 3.1 Classical and Structural Realisms

Type of Realism	Key Thinkers	Key Texts	Big Idea
Classical realism (human nature)	Thucydides (ca. 430–406 BCE)	*The Peloponnesian War*	International politics is driven by an endless struggle for power that has its roots in human nature. Justice, law, and society either have no place or are circumscribed.
	Machiavelli (1532)	*The Prince*	Political realism recognizes that principles are subordinated to policies; the ultimate skill of the state leader is to accept, and adapt to, the changing power-political configurations in global politics.
	Morgenthau (1948)	*Politics Among Nations*	Politics is governed by laws that are created by human nature. The mechanism we use to understand international politics is the concept of interests defined in terms of power.
Structural realism, or neorealism (international system)	Rousseau (ca. 1750)	*The State of War*	It is not human nature but the anarchical system that fosters fear, jealousy, suspicion, and insecurity.
	Waltz (1979)	*Theory of International Politics*	Anarchy causes logic of self-help, in which states seek to maximize their security. The most stable distribution of power in the system is bipolarity.
	Mearsheimer (2001)	*The Tragedy of Great Power Politics*	The anarchical, self-help system compels states to maximize their relative power position.

international order could mitigate anarchy. Taking their lead from Thucydides, they recognized that acting purely on the basis of power and self-interest, without any consideration of moral and ethical principles, frequently results in self-defeating policies.

WHAT'S YOUR WORLDVIEW

In our global system with new technologies, relatively easy opportunities for travel, and transnational terrorist networks willing to use weapons of mass destruction to challenge nation-states, can any state guarantee security for its citizens?

Structural Realism, or Neorealism

Proponents of **structural realism**, sometimes called **neorealism**, agree that international politics is essentially a struggle for power, but they do not endorse the classical-realist assumption that this is a result of human nature. Instead, structural realists attribute security competition and interstate conflict to the lack of an overarching authority above states and the relative distribution of power in the international system.

Kenneth Waltz, the best known structural realist, defines the structure of the international system in terms of three

CASE STUDY | The Melian Dialogue— Realism and the Preparation for War   **3.1**

Background

Thucydides, the former Athenian general and historian, wrote that the history of the Peloponnesian War was "not an essay which is to win applause of the moment, but a possession of all time." Most realists find references to all of their core beliefs in this important document. The Melians were citizens of the Isle of Melos, which was a colony of Sparta. The Melians would not submit to the Athenians, as many of the other islands had. Athens was a dominant sea power, and Sparta was more of a land power. At first Melos tried neutrality, but Athens attacked and plundered the territory and then sent envoys to negotiate. A short excerpt from the dialogue appears below (Thucydides [1954] 1972, 401–407). Note that the symbol [. . .] indicates one or more line breaks from the original text.

The Case

ATHENIANS: Then we on our side will use no fine phrases saying, for example, that we have a right to our empire because we defeated the Persians**.** [. . .] you know as well as we do that, when these matters are discussed by practical people, the standard of justice depends on the equality of power to compel and that in fact the strong do what they have the power to do and the weak accept what they have to accept.

MELIANS: [. . .] You should not destroy a principle that is to the general good of all men—namely, that in the case of all who fall into danger there should be such a thing as fair play and just dealing [. . .]

ATHENIANS: This is no fair fight, with honor on one side and shame on the other. It is rather a question of saving your lives and not resisting those who are far too strong for you.

MELIANS: It is difficult . . . for us to oppose your power and fortune. [. . .] Nevertheless we trust that the gods will give us fortune as good as yours [. . .]

ATHENIANS: Our opinion of the gods and our knowledge of men lead us to conclude that it is a general and necessary law of nature to rule whatever one can. This is not a law that we made ourselves, nor were we the first to act upon it when it was made. We found it already in existence, and we shall leave it to exist forever among those who come after us. We are merely acting in accordance with it, and we know that you or anybody else with the same power as ours would be acting in precisely the same way. [. . .] You seem to forget that if one follows one's self-interest one wants to be safe, whereas the path of justice and honor involves one in danger. [. . .] This is the safe rule—to stand up to one's equals, to behave with deference to one's superiors, and to treat one's inferiors with moderation.

MELIANS: Our decision, Athenians, is just the same as it was at first. We are not prepared to give up in a short moment the liberty which our city has enjoyed from its foundation for 700 years.

ATHENIANS: [. . .] You seem to us [. . .] to see uncertainties as realities, simply because you would like them to be so.

For Discussion

1. What assumptions about the international system and the nature of power are obvious in this discussion?

2. Thucydides is credited with the statement "The strong do what they will and the weak do what they must." Do you think this still applies to global politics today?

---

elements—organizing principle, differentiation of units, and distribution of capabilities. He identifies two different organizing principles: anarchy, which corresponds to the decentralized realm of international politics, and hierarchy, which is the basis of domestic order. He argues that the units of the international system are functionally similar sovereign states; hence unit-level variation is irrelevant in explaining international outcomes. It is the third tier, the distribution of capabilities across units, that is, according to Waltz, of fundamental importance to understanding crucial international outcomes.

For structural realists, the relative distribution of power in the international system is the key independent variable to understanding important international outcomes such as war and peace, alliance politics, and the balance of power. Many structural realists are interested in providing a rank ordering of states so as to be able to differentiate and count the number of great powers that exist at any particular point in time. The number of great powers, in turn, determines the structure of the international system.

How does the international distribution of power affect the behavior of states, particularly their power-seeking behavior? The possibility that any state may use force to advance its interests results in all states being worried about their survival. According to Waltz, power is a means to the end of security. In a significant passage, Waltz writes, "because power is a possibly useful means, sensible statesmen try to have an appropriate amount of it." He adds, "in crucial situations, however, the ultimate concern of states is not for power but for security" (Waltz 1989, 40). In other words, rather than being *power* maximizers, states, according to Waltz, are *security* maximizers. Waltz argues that power maximization often proves to be dysfunctional because it triggers a counterbalancing coalition of states.

John Mearsheimer's theory of **offensive realism**, which is another variant of structural realism, offers a different account of the power dynamics within the anarchic system. Although sharing many of the basic assumptions of Waltz's structural-realist theory, frequently termed **defensive realism**, Mearsheimer differs from Waltz in describing the behavior of states. Most fundamentally, "offensive realism parts company with defensive realism over the question of how much power states want" (Mearsheimer 2001, 21). According to Mearsheimer, the structure of the international system compels states to maximize their relative power position. Under anarchy, he agrees that self-help is the basic principle of action. Yet he also argues that not only do all

NATO leaders attending the 2012 Summit in Chicago discussed a wide range of topics, including an exit strategy for Afghanistan and the establishment of a new "Smart Defense" initiative that includes pooling and sharing resources for the production of weapons and the joint management of weapons, ammunitions, and other security resources.

states possess some offensive military capability, but also there is a great deal of uncertainty about the intentions of other states. Mearsheimer concludes that there are no satisfied or status quo states; rather, all states are continuously searching for opportunities to gain power at the expense of other states. Contrary to Waltz, Mearsheimer argues that states recognize that the best path to peace is to accumulate more power than anyone else.

It is perhaps a mistake to understand theoretical traditions as a single stream of thought, handed down neatly from one generation of theorists to another. Instead, we encourage you to think of living traditions like realism as the embodiment of both continuities and conflicts. In the next section, we examine liberalism, another tradition within the field of international relations theory. We will see that realism and liberalism share certain assumptions but disagree strongly about others.

WHAT'S YOUR WORLDVIEW

Which of the assumptions of realism make the most sense to you? Do you think most world leaders embrace a realist worldview?

What Is Liberalism?

Just as realism derives from the observations and interpretations of political "realities," so does liberalism. The seeds of a liberal perspective had been sown in the wake of the fifteenth century's so-called Age of Discovery, which fostered the rampant expansion of global commerce as states, explorer entrepreneurs, and trading companies became involved in the business of exchanging goods and services. Commerce across political and cultural boundaries was never just a matter of private individuals swapping one commodity for another (otherwise known as *barter*) or for money. To engage in commerce, these pioneer global traders had to negotiate the terms of trade, they had to abide by new and different cultural norms and legal systems, and they had to bargain with political leaders to gain and maintain market access. In other words, trade formed linkages that transcended political, social, cultural, and economic boundaries.

As trade expanded to include the exchange of a wider variety of commodities from all over the world, so did the linkages. Over time, a complex web of connections evolved, along with the multitude of formal and informal agreements needed to facilitate commerce. As economic and social interactions crossed political boundaries with increasing frequency,

New security challenges involve protecting vulnerable populations and providing basic human needs. These Kenyan children lost their parents to HIV; 69 percent of global HIV victims are in sub-Saharan Africa. Radical liberals would support more funding for these types of programs and less funding for neoliberal infrastructure projects—people, not buildings, should be the priority.

trade and immigration patterns rendered realist guidelines decreasingly useful to policy makers. It was no longer so easy to engage in unilateral actions without experiencing economic repercussions, as World War I emphatically demonstrated.

As World War II came to an end, key decision makers in the United States experienced their own transformation: They now recognized that the United States needed to be an active player on the world scene. They also saw that the United States had the financial and military power to enforce a new world order based on its political and economic visions. Moreover, they realized that, in a world where sovereignty remained the reigning principle, decisions affecting two or more states required the participation of all affected stakeholders and the backing of the rule of law. Embedded in this **multilateralist** approach to global governance is a principle of political liberalism, namely that the "governed" (in this case, states) should have a say in the development of those rules, norms, and principles by which they will be governed. And so, as they endeavored to avoid an even more calamitous World War III, the political leaders of the United States and its allies created a whole host of international governmental organizations including the UN and the Bretton Woods economic institutions, to manage global relations in key political and economic arenas. The mandates of these international governmental organizations were informed by **liberal internationalism**, a combination of the following:

- Democratic values (political liberalism)
- Free-trade markets (economic liberalism)
- Multilateral cooperation (multilateralism)
- A rule-based international society that respects sovereignty and human rights.

We discuss these principles further as we define the boundaries of liberal thinking and begin to understand how neoliberalism—and radical liberalism—has since evolved its own set of arguments from the liberal tradition.

Defining Liberalism

In essence, liberalism argues for human rights, parliamentary democracy, and free trade—while also maintaining that all such goals must begin *within a state*. The early European liberals thought that reforms within one's own country would be the first step in a long process, a process that could eventually extend to world affairs. The belief in the possibility of progress is one identifier of a liberal approach to politics (Clark 1989, 49–66), but there are other general propositions that define the broad tradition of liberalism.

Perhaps the appropriate way to begin this discussion is with a four-dimensional definition (Doyle 1997, 207). First, all citizens are equal before the law and possess certain basic rights to education, access to a free press, and religious toleration. Second, the legislative assembly of the state possesses only the authority invested in it by the people, whose basic rights it may not abuse. Third, a key dimension of the liberty of the individual is the right to own property, including productive forces. Fourth, liberalism contends that the most effective system of economic exchange is one that is largely market driven and not subordinate to bureaucratic regulation and control, either domestically or internationally. When these propositions are taken together, we see a stark contrast between liberal values of individualism, tolerance, freedom, and constitutionalism and realism's conservatism, which places a higher value on order and authority and is willing to sacrifice the liberty of the individual for the stability of the community.

Although in the past many writers have tended to view liberalism as a theory of domestic government, what is becoming increasingly apparent is the explicit connection between liberalism as a domestic political and economic theory and liberalism as an international theory. Properly conceived, liberal thought on a global scale embodies a domestic political and economic system operating at the international level. Like individuals, states have different characteristics—some are bellicose and war prone, others are tolerant and peaceful: In short, the identity of the state determines its outward orientation. Liberals see a further parallel between individuals and sovereign states. Although the character of states might differ, all states in a global society are accorded certain "natural" rights, such as the generalized right to nonintervention in their domestic affairs. Historically, liberals have agreed with realists that war is a recurring feature of the anarchic states system. But unlike realists, they do not identify **anarchy** as the cause of war. How, then, do liberals explain war? Certain strands of liberalism see the causes of war located in **imperialism**, others in the failure of the balance of power, and still others in the problem of undemocratic regimes.

Unlike what we learned about realism, liberalism is at its heart a doctrine of change, reform, and belief in progress. As can be seen from a critical appraisal of the fourfold definition just presented, liberalism pulls in two directions: Its commitment to freedom in the economic and social spheres leans in the direction of a minimalist role for governing institutions, whereas the democratic political culture required for basic freedoms to be safeguarded requires robust and interventionist institutions. This has variously been interpreted as a tension between different liberal goals and more broadly as a sign of rival and incompatible conceptions of liberalism.

Emanuele Kant.

One of the founders of the English School, Martin Wight, introduced three theoretical traditions: Machiavellian (realists), Grotian (liberal reformers), and Kantian (radical liberals or idealists). Many of the critical theorists embrace Kantian ideas such as the possibility of peace and the universal values of human rights, justice, and the categorical imperative. In foreign policy, the categorical imperative means that states act according to the principle that a state's actions should be the maxim by which all states base their actions.

WHAT'S YOUR WORLDVIEW

Liberal internationalism emerged as a dominant perspective after the two world wars. After these conflicts, most states wanted to return to a rule-based system that promotes democracy and free trade. Yet, historically, this view does not last. What are some possible reasons for the failure of liberal-internationalism thinking to prevail?

Liberal theory holds that networks of cooperation involving citizens in a variety of occupations exist to help strengthen state-to-state ties. Here, Bill Gates speaks during a session at the 2012 World Economic Forum in Davos, Switzerland. As government funds dry up in the global economic crisis, wealthy individuals and their foundations might play a greater role in global politics.

The Essential Liberalism

Immanuel Kant and Jeremy Bentham were two of the leading liberals of the **Enlightenment**. Both were reacting to the barbarity of international relations, or what Kant graphically described as "the lawless state of savagery," at a time when domestic politics was at the cusp of a new age of rights, citizenship, and constitutionalism. Their abhorrence of the lawless savagery led them individually to elaborate plans for "perpetual peace." Although written over two centuries ago, these manifestos contain the seeds of core liberal ideas, in particular the belief that reason could deliver freedom and justice in international relations.

Kant's claim that liberal states are peaceful in their international relations with other liberal states was revived in the 1980s. In a much-cited article, Michael Doyle argued that liberal states have created a "separate peace" (1986, 1151). According to Doyle, there are two elements to the Kantian legacy: restraint among liberal states and "international imprudence" in relations with nonliberal states.

This central plank of liberal internationalist thought has been called the **democratic peace thesis**. Although the empirical evidence seems to support this thesis, it is important to bear in mind the limitations of the argument. In the first instance, for the theory to be compelling, believers in the thesis need to provide an explanation as to why war has become unthinkable between liberal states. Kant had argued that if the decision to use force was taken by the people, rather than by the prince, then the frequency of conflicts would be drastically reduced. Democratic or liberal states tend not to go to war with other liberal or democratic states, but they *will* go to war with nonliberal or undemocratic states. Historical evidence supports this point. Thus, Kant's idea that democratic states will not go to war cannot be supported.

Two centuries after Kant first called for a "pacific federation," the validity of the idea that democracies are more pacific continues to attract a great deal of scholarly interest. The claim has also found its way into the public discourse of Western states' foreign policy, appearing in speeches made by US presidents as diverse as Ronald Reagan, Bill Clinton, George W. Bush, and Barack Obama. Less crusading voices within the liberal tradition believe that a legal and institutional framework must be established that includes states with different cultures and traditions. At the end of the eighteenth century, Jeremy Bentham advocated such a belief in the power of law to solve the problem of war. "Establish a common tribunal" and "the necessity for war no longer follows from a difference of opinion" (Luard 1992, 416). Like many liberal thinkers after him, Bentham showed that federal states such as the German Diet, the

American Confederation, and the Swiss League were able to transform their identity from one based on conflicting interests to a more peaceful federation. As Bentham famously argued, "between the interests of nations there is nowhere any real conflict."

Because liberal politics and capitalism are intimately linked, many writers believe, with Adam Smith, that the elimination of tariffs, duties, and other restrictions on imports would be a vital step in dissemination of liberalism's program. For example, Richard Cobden's belief that **free trade** would create a more peaceful world order is a core idea of nineteenth-century liberalism. Cobden, a British politician and public intellectual, was the leader of the liberal Manchester School that supported free trade in agricultural products. Trade brings mutual gains to all the players, irrespective of their size or the nature of their economies. But there was never an admission that free trade among countries at different stages of development would lead to relations of dominance and subservience. Indeed, since World War II, this is one of the problems that both the General Agreement on Tariffs and Trade and its successor, the World Trade Organization, have faced.

Like free trade, the idea of a "natural harmony of interests" in international political and economic relations came under challenge in the early part of the twentieth century. From the turn of the century, the contradictions within European civilization, of progress and exemplarism on the one hand and the harnessing of industrial power for military purposes on the other, could no longer be contained. Europe stumbled into a horrific war, which killed 15 million people. The war not only brought an end to three **empires** but also was a contributing factor to the Russian Revolution of 1917.

World War I shifted liberal thinking toward a recognition that peace is not a natural condition, but one that must be constructed. Perhaps the most famous advocate of an international authority for the management of international relations was Woodrow Wilson. According to this US president, peace could only be secured with the creation of an international organization to regulate the international anarchy. Just as peace had to be enforced in domestic society, the international domain had to have a system of regulation for coping with disputes and an international force that could be mobilized if nonviolent conflict resolution failed. In this sense, more than any other strand of liberalism, idealism rests on the idea that we can replicate the liberalism we know domestically at the international level (Suganami 1989, 94–113).

In his famous "Fourteen Points" address to Congress in January 1918, Wilson argued that "a general association of nations must be formed" to preserve the coming peace—the League of Nations was to be that general association. For the League to be effective, it had to have the military power to deter aggression and, when necessary, to use a preponderance of power to enforce its will. This was the idea behind the **collective security** system that was central to the League of Nations. Collective security refers to an arrangement where "each state in the system accepts that the security of one is the concern of all, and agrees to join in a collective response to aggression" (Roberts and

US president Woodrow Wilson, a liberal internationalist, thought that the key to international security was an international organization, the League of Nations. Why did the league fail?

Kingsbury 1993, 30). It can be contrasted with an alliance system of security, where a number of states join together, usually as a response to a specific external threat (sometimes known as collective defense). In the case of the League of Nations, Article 16 of the League's charter noted the obligation that, in the event of war, all member states must cease normal relations with the offending state, impose sanctions, and, if necessary, commit their armed forces to the disposal of the League Council should the use of force be required to restore the status quo. The League's constitution also called for the self-determination of all nation-states, another founding characteristic of liberal-idealist thinking on international relations.

Although the organization was able to be a mediator to relatively minor disputes, the overall experience of the League of Nations as a peacekeeper was a failure. Whereas the moral rhetoric at the creation of the League was decidedly liberal and idealist, in practice states remained imprisoned by self-interest in the style of realism. There is no better example of this than the United States' decision not to join the institution it had created. With the Soviet Union initially outside the system for ideological reasons, the League of Nations quickly became little more than a debating society for the member states. Hitler's decision in March 1936 to reoccupy the Rhineland, a designated demilitarized zone according to the terms of the Treaty of Versailles, effectively ended the League.

According to the realist's version of the history of the discipline of international relations, the collapse of the League of Nations dealt a near-fatal blow to liberal idealism. There is no doubt that the language of liberalism after 1945 was more pragmatic: How could anyone living in the shadow of the Holocaust be optimistic? Yet familiar core ideas of liberalism—belief in the benefits of progress, free trade, and respect for human rights—remained. Even as World War II raged, key political leaders in Europe and North America recognized the need to replace the League with another international institution with responsibility for international peace and security. Only this time, in the case of the UN, there was an awareness of the need for a consensus between the great powers for enforcement action to be taken. The framers of the UN Charter therefore included a provision (Article 27) allowing any of the five permanent members of the Security Council the power of veto. This revision constituted an important modification to the classical model of collective security (A. Roberts 1996, 315). With the ideological polarity of the Cold War, the UN procedures for collective security were stillborn (because either of the superpowers and their allies would veto any action proposed by the other). It was not until the end of the Cold War that a collective security system was put into operation, following the invasion of Kuwait by Iraq on August 2, 1990.

Academic interest in the positive benefits from transnational cooperation informed a new generation of scholars (particularly in the United States) in the 1960s and 1970s. Their argument was not simply about the mutual gains from trade, but that other **transnational nonstate actors** were beginning to challenge the dominance of sovereign states. World politics, according to pluralists (as they are often called, using a term from the study of domestic politics), was no longer an exclusive arena for states, as it had been for the first 300 years of the Westphalian states system. The inability of the United States to win the Vietnam War—not simply an academic pursuit—provided the impetus to this research, for that conflict seemed to challenge realism's central claims about power determining outcomes in international politics. In one of the central texts of this genre, Robert Keohane and Joseph Nye (1972) argued that the centrality of other actors, such as interest groups, transnational corporations (e.g., Shell Oil or AIG), and NGOs, like Oxfam or Human Rights Watch, had to be taken into consideration. They also asserted that military power had a declining utility in international politics. The overriding image of international relations was one of a cobweb of diverse actors linked through multiple channels of interaction.

Although the phenomenon of transnationalism was an important addition to the international relations theorists' vocabulary, it remained underdeveloped as a theoretical concept. Perhaps the most important contribution of **pluralism** was its elaboration of **interdependence**. Because of the expansion of capitalism and the emergence of a global culture, pluralists recognized a growing interconnectedness in which "changes in one part of the system have direct and indirect consequences for the rest of the system" (Little 1996, 77). Absolute state autonomy, so keenly entrenched in the minds of state leaders, was being circumscribed by interdependence. Such a development brought with it enhanced potential for cooperation as well as increased levels of vulnerability.

In the course of their engagement with Waltz and other neorealists, early pluralists modified their position. Neoliberals, as they came to be known, conceded that the core assumptions of neorealism were indeed correct: the anarchic international structure, the centrality of states, and a view of decision making that emphasized strategic or rational-choice approaches to social scientific inquiry. At the heart of **rational choice** is the idea that decision makers will always act as value maximizers and thus a state's actions are based on rational calculations in which policy options are assessed and valued. The final policy choices are based on a strategy of maximizing benefits and minimizing costs. In what became the most important difference between neorealists and neoliberals, the latter argued that actors would enter into cooperative agreements if the gains were evenly shared. Neorealists dispute this hypothesis, saying that what matters is a question not so much of mutual gains as of **relative gains**: In other words, a neorealist (or structural-realist) state has to be sure that it has more to gain than its rivals from a particular bargain or regime.

Neoliberalism

There are two important arguments that set **neoliberalism** apart from democratic-peace liberalism and the liberal idealists of the interwar period. First, academic inquiry should be guided by a commitment to a scientific approach to theory building. Whatever deeply held personal values scholars maintain, their task must be to observe regularities, formulate hypotheses as to why that relationship holds, and subject these to critical scrutiny. This separation of fact and value puts neoliberals on the positivist or social scientific research side of the methodological divide. Second, writers such as Keohane are critical of what they consider the naive assumption of nineteenth-century liberals that commerce breeds peace. A free-trade system, according to Keohane, provides incentives for cooperation but does not guarantee it. Here he is making an important distinction between cooperation and harmony. "Co-operation is not automatic," Keohane argues, "but requires planning and negotiation" (1989b, 11).

Neoliberal institutionalism (or institutional theory) shares many of the assumptions of neorealism; however, its adherents claim that neorealists focus excessively on conflict and competition and minimize the chances for cooperation, even in an anarchic international system. Currently, neoliberal institutionalists are focusing their research on issues of global governance and the creation and maintenance of institutions associated with managing the processes of globalization.

For neoliberal institutionalists, the focus on mutual interests extends beyond trade and development issues. With the end of the Cold War, states were forced to address new security concerns like the threat of terrorism, the proliferation of weapons of mass destruction, and an increasing number of internal conflicts that threatened regional and global security. Graham Allison (2000) states that one of the consequences of the globalization of security concerns like terrorism, drug trafficking, and pandemics like HIV/AIDS is the realization that threats to any country's security cannot be addressed unilaterally. Successful responses to security threats require the creation of regional and global regimes that promote cooperation among states and the coordination of policy responses to these new security threats.

The neoliberal-institutional perspective is more relevant in issue areas where states have mutual interests. For example, most world leaders believe that we will all benefit from an open trade system, and many support trade rules that protect the environment. Institutions have been created to manage international behavior in both areas. The neoliberal view might have less relevance in areas in which states have no mutual interests.

The appointment of Senator John Kerry as the new US Secretary of State suggests that the Obama administration's foreign policy is likely to remain pragmatic and liberal internationalist. How important is continuity in foreign policy?

Thus, cooperation in military or national-security areas, where someone's gain is perceived as someone else's loss (a zero-sum perspective), might be more difficult to achieve.

Liberalism in Practice: Globalization

When applying liberal ideas to international relations today, we find two clusters of responses to the problems and possibilities posed by globalization. Before outlining these responses, let's quickly recall the definition of liberalism set out at greater length earlier, the four components being *juridical equality*, *democracy*, *liberty*, and the *free market*. As we see next, these same values can be pursued by very different political strategies.

The first response we'll address is that of the **liberalism of privilege** (Richardson 1997, 18). According to this perspective, the problems of globalization need to be addressed by a combination of strong democratic states in the core of the international system, robust regimes, and open markets and institutions. For an example of the working out of such a strategy in practice, we need to look no further than the success of the liberal hegemony of the post-1945 era. G. John Ikenberry is an articulate defender of this liberal order. In the aftermath of World War II, the United States took the opportunity to embed certain fundamental liberal principles into the rules and institutions of international society. Most important, and contrary to realist thinking, the leaders of the United States chose to forfeit short-run gains in return for a durable settlement that benefited all the world's states.

> ## WHAT'S YOUR WORLDVIEW
>
> *The new liberal order has left many countries and their people in poverty and in conflict. Consider the young people in Tunisia who were jobless and hopeless and sought change. Are there ways to create programs that give capitalism a human face? What do you think could be done to address global poverty and instability in some states?*

Let us accept for a moment that the neoliberal argument is basically correct: The post-1945 international order has been successful and durable because US hegemony has been of a liberal character. The logic of this position is one of institutional conservatism, meaning that to respond effectively to global economic and security problems, there is no alternative to working within the existing institutional structure. At the other end of the spectrum, the current order is seen by many critics of the liberal international order as highly unresponsive to the needs of weaker states and peoples. According to the United Nations Development Programme, the resulting global inequality is "grotesque." One statistic is particularly graphic: The richest 20 percent of the world's population holds three-quarters of the income; the poorest 20 percent receives only 1.5 percent.

Given that liberalism has produced such unequal gains for the West and the rest, it is not surprising that the hegemonic power has become obsessed with the question of preserving and extending its control of institutions, markets, and resources, just as realists predicted it would. When this hegemonic liberal order comes under challenge, as it did on 9/11, the response is uncompromising. It is notable in this respect that President George W. Bush mobilized the language of liberalism against Al Qaeda, the Taliban, and also

Iraq. He referred to the 2003 war against Iraq as "freedom's war," and the term *liberation* is frequently used by defenders of Operation Iraqi Freedom.

This strategy of preserving and extending liberal institutions is open to a number of criticisms. For the sake of simplicity, these will be gathered up into an alternative to the liberalism that is seen to benefit only a few states and individuals that we will call **radical liberalism.** An objection made by proponents of radical liberalism concerns the understanding of liberalism embodied in the neoliberal defense of contemporary international institutions. The liberal character of those institutions is assumed rather than subjected to critical scrutiny. As a result, the incoherence of the purposes underpinning these institutions is often overlooked. The kind of economic liberalization advocated by Western financial institutions, particularly in economically impoverished countries, frequently comes into conflict with the norms of democracy and human rights. Three examples illustrate this dilemma.

First, the more the West becomes involved in the organization of developing states' political and economic infrastructure, the less those states are able to be accountable to their domestic constituencies, thereby cutting through the link between the government and the people that is so central to modern liberal forms of representative democracy (Hurrell and Woods 1995, 463). Second, to qualify for Western aid and loans, states are often required to meet harsh economic criteria requiring cuts in many welfare programs. The example of the poorest children in parts of Africa having to pay for primary school education (Booth and Dunne 1999, 310)—which is their right according to the Universal Declaration of Human Rights—is a stark reminder of the fact that economic liberty and political equality are frequently opposed. Third, the inflexible response of the International Monetary Fund (IMF), World Bank, and other international financial institutions to various crises in the world economy has contributed to a backlash against liberalism. Richard Falk puts this dilemma starkly: There is, he argues, a tension between "the ethical imperatives of the global neighborhood and the dynamics of economic globalization" (Falk 1995a, 573). Radical liberals argue that the hegemonic institutional order has fallen prey to the neoliberal consensus, which minimizes the role of the public sector in providing for welfare and elevates the market as the appropriate mechanism for allocating resources, investment, and employment opportunities.

If we take the area of political economy, the power exerted by the West and its international financial institutions perpetuates structural inequality. A good example here is the issue of free trade, which the West has pushed in areas where it gains from an open policy (e.g., in manufactured goods and financial services) but resisted in areas in which it stands to lose (agriculture and textiles). At a deeper level, radical liberals worry that *all* statist models of governance are undemocratic because elites are notoriously self-serving.

Radical liberals place great importance on the civilizing capacity of global society. The rule of law and the democratization of international institutions are a core component of the liberal project, but it is also vital that citizens' networks are broadened and deepened to monitor and cajole these institutions. These groups form a linkage among individuals, states, and global institutions. It is easy to portray radical-liberal thinking as utopian, but we should not forget the many achievements of global civil society so far. The evolution of international humanitarian law, and the extent to which these laws are complied with, is largely the result of the millions of individuals who are active supporters of human rights groups like Amnesty International and Human Rights Watch (Falk 1995b, 164). Similarly, global protest movements have been responsible for the heightened sensitivity to environmental degradation everywhere.

Alternative Theories

Although realism and liberalism remain the dominant, mainstream approaches to global political theory, several other approaches have gained credibility in academic circles and in some policy communities. These provide an increasingly diverse set of ideas for understanding international relations (Table 3.2). How and why did these alternative approaches develop?

The World Social Forum was held in Tunisia in 2013. While Davos, Switzerland, brings together the rich and famous in an economic summit, the World Social Forum brings together representatives from the poor, the marginalized, and those who seek peace and global equality by ending war and closing the gap that separates rich and poor. These two goals help to define the field of international relations.

• First, a resurgence of liberalism, in the form of neoliberal institutionalism, challenged realism's dominance.
• Second, the shift from a bipolar world to a more multilateral or nonpolar world (see Chapters 4 and 5) paved the way for new approaches, as did the forces of "globalization." Whatever the explanatory power of realism, it did not help us understand many important economic, sociological, and cultural issues, such as the rise of **nonstate actors**, race and gender politics, transnational social movements, and the impact of information technology.
• Third, major developments in other academic disciplines in the social sciences and philosophy attacked the underlying methodological assumption of realism, which is known as **positivism.** This is the idea that political scientists can conduct research following the scientific method that guides the physical sciences, such as physics, chemistry, and biology. In its place, social scientists in other fields proposed a host of alternative ways of thinking, and the academic field of international relations simply caught up. Since then, international relations scholars have proposed many alternative approaches as more relevant to world politics in the twenty-first century.

In this chapter we examine the three most influential alternatives to realism and liberalism.

Table 3.2 Alternative International Relations Theories at the Beginning of the Twenty-First Century

	Central Idea	View of International System	Key Authors
Marxist: Dependency school	Global capitalist system eliminates harmony of interests of workers.	Core–periphery relationship. Unfair terms of international trade. Underdevelopment in periphery.	Prebisch, Frank, Cardoso, O'Donnell
Marxism: World-system	Expansion of European capitalist system. Systems have life cycle, new ones develop.	Hegemonic powers. Core–periphery–semiperiphery relationship. Exploitation on a global scale, semiperiphery elites benefit.	Wallerstein, Chase-Dunn
Constructivism	Seeks to understand change. Ideas are social creations. Relationships result from historical processes. Ideas can evolve, replace older ways of thinking.	A process. Result of hegemonic ideas. Can change as result of evolving ideas.	Onuf, Walker, Wendt
Liberal feminism	Change women's subordinate position in existing political systems.	Improve women's representation in international nongovernment organizations (INGOs). End gender bias in INGOs and NGOs.	Caprioli, Enloe, Elshtain, Tickner, Tobias
Socialist and Marxist feminism	Ideas about gender relations impact economic relations.	States encourage gendered division of labor.	Chin, Hennessy, Ingraham, Whitworth
Standpoint feminism	Ideas about gender are social constructs.	Ideas about gender shape international system.	Hartsock, Prügl, Zalewski
Postmodern feminism	Perceptions of gender determine positions on gender. Dichotomized language.	Distinctions like order–anarchy, public–private, developed–underdeveloped linked to gender.	Fausto-Sterling, Hooper, Kinsella, Longino
Postcolonial feminism	Effects of colonial experience on gender identity.	Challenges Western portrayals of third-world women. Globalization perpetuates colonial-era gender-based exploitation.	Mohanty, Spivak

We turn our attention first to Marxism, the oldest of the challengers to the teachings of realism and liberalism. Although the Communist Party state of the Soviet Union is gone and never reached the goal of a pure Marxist state, and the authoritarian Chinese Communist Party permits a form of capitalism in China, the central ideas of Marxism can still help us understand the inequality that characterizes the globalized economy.

The Essential Marxism

One might ask, why spend time on Marxism, when the Soviet Union collapsed? Most socialists or Marxists have two very convincing answers. First, the Soviet Union never provided a model of the ideal socialist or Marxist state. Michael Harrington (1989, 79), an American socialist, describes Soviet socialism as follows:

> [Soviet] Socialism was a bureaucratically controlled and planned economy that carried out the function of primitive accumulation and thus achieved rapid modernization. The state owned the means of production, which made some people think it must be socialist; but the party and the bureaucracy owned the state by virtue of a dictatorial monopoly of political power.

Harrington called the Soviet system a moral disaster for socialism. It was a totalitarian state and not an ideal Marxist state.

A second reason is globalization. Marx (1967, 83–84) described how increasing interdependence will inevitably create a single global market and a global consumer culture:

> The bourgeoisie has through its exploitation of the world market given a cosmopolitan character to production and consumption in every country. . . . All old-established national industries have been destroyed or are daily being destroyed. They are dislodged by new industries, whose introduction becomes a life and death question for all civilized nations, by industries that no longer work up indigenous raw material, but raw material drawn from the remotest zones; industries whose products are consumed, not only at home, but in every quarter of the globe.

A global economy shifts the key elements of Marxist thought from the domestic level to the global level.

A Marxist interpretation of world politics has been influential since the mid-1800s. In his inaugural address to the Working Men's International Association in London in 1864, Karl Marx told his audience that history had "taught the working classes the duty to master [for] themselves the mysteries of international politics."

Marx was an enormously prolific writer whose ideas developed and changed over time.

The founders of "scientific socialism," Karl Marx and Friedrich Engels, sit together in a park that was once in communist-controlled East Berlin. Can you think of ways in which socialist ideas still influence politics in your country?

It is not surprising that his legacy has been open to numerous interpretations. In addition, real-world developments have led to the revision of his ideas in the light of experience. A variety of schools of thought have emerged that claim Marx as a direct inspiration or whose work can be linked to Marx's legacy.

All the theorists discussed in this section share with Marx the view that the social, political, and economic world should be analyzed as a totality. The academic division of the social world into different areas of inquiry—history, philosophy, economics, political science, sociology, international relations, and so on—is both arbitrary and unhelpful. None can be understood without knowledge of the others: The social world has to be studied as a whole. Given the scale and complexity of the social world, this requirement clearly makes great demands of the analyst. Nonetheless, for Marxist theorists, the disciplinary boundaries that characterize the contemporary social sciences need to be transcended if we are to generate a proper understanding of the dynamics of world politics.

WHAT'S YOUR WORLDVIEW ?

Has globalization increased worker exploitation and therefore the likelihood of workers around the world uniting for change, if not revolution, according to Marxist political thought? How would realists and liberals respond to a Marxist prescription?

Another key element of Marxist thought, which serves further to underline this concern with interconnection and context, is the materialist conception of history. The central contention here is that processes of historical change are ultimately a reflection of the economic development of society. That is, economic development is effectively the motor of history. The central dynamic that Marx identifies is tension between the means of production and relations of production that together form the **economic base** of a given society.

As the means of production develop, for example through technological advancement, previous relations of production become outmoded, which restricts the most effective utilization of the new productive capacity. This, in turn, leads to a process of social change whereby relations of production are transformed to better accommodate the new configuration of means. For example, computer-driven machines for manufacturing might replace auto factory workers, or because of the labor costs their jobs might be sent to a country where labor and production costs are lower. Workers, but fewer of them, are still needed, and most of those must be retrained to repair computers or develop software and no longer make car doors. In other words, developments in the economic base act as a catalyst for the broader transformation of society as a whole. This is because, as Marx argued, "the mode of production of material life conditions the social, political and intellectual life process in general." Thus the legal, political, and cultural institutions and practices of a given society reflect and reinforce—in a more or less mediated form—the pattern of power and control in the economy. It follows logically, therefore, that change in the economic base ultimately leads to change in the "legal and political **superstructure**."

And so, as you might have guessed by now, **class** plays a key role in Marxist analysis. Marx defines class as "social relations between the producers, and the conditions under which they exchange their activities and share in the total act of production" (Marx and Engels 1848). For most Americans, class is simply a way of designating an individual's position within the income distribution of a society. We talk about upper, middle, and lower income classes, and these represent income groups in our society. For Marxists, your income does not determine your class. Instead, your class is defined by your position within the hierarchy of production. In contrast to liberals, who believe that there is an essential harmony of interest between various social groups, Marxists hold that society is systemically prone to class conflict.

The Marxist perspective on globalization seeks to describe the ways inequality affects the lives of millions of people. Marx and his co-author Friedrich Engels predicted that capitalism would spread around the world and then, and only then, would the proletariat become aware of their exploitation as workers, alienation from their government, and estrangement from society ruled by the bourgeoisie. In this situation, globalization might be the catalyst for awareness and eventual transformation. As we see in the data presented in Table 3.3, for example, despite the wealth generated in the global economy in the ten years prior to the economic depression of 2008 through 2011, that

Table 3.3 Indicators of World Inequality

Worldwide, more than 1.2 billion people live on less than $1 per day.

In 1990 the average American was 38 times richer than the average Tanzanian. By 2005 this had risen to 61 times richer.

More than 1.1 billion people lack access to clean water.

Average incomes in more than 50 developing countries are now at a lower level than they were in 1990. In 21 countries a larger proportion of the people are hungry. In 14 countries a higher proportion of children are dying before reaching the age of 5, and in 34 countries life expectancy has decreased.

Tariffs on manufactured goods from the developing world are four times higher than those on manufactured goods from other Organization for Economic Cooperation and Development (OECD) countries.

One-sixth of the world's adults are illiterate (two-thirds of the world's illiterates are women).

In the developed world, subsidies to agricultural producers are six times higher than overseas development aid.

More than 10 million children die every year from easily preventable diseases.

A child born in Zambia today is less likely to live past the age of 30 than a child born in 1840 in England.

In Africa only one child in three completes primary education.

In sub-Saharan Africa a woman is 100 times more likely to die in childbirth than women in high-income OECD countries.

African countries pay out $40 million every day on debt repayment.

Sources: World Bank, UNDP, Jubilee Research.

World-system theorists proposed that goods, such as boots made in Vietnam, are made in the periphery for sale in the core. Is there evidence to suggest that globalization will increase the division between rich and poor or reduce the gap between core and periphery?

prosperity did not improve the living conditions of most of the world's population.

It is important to emphasize that the essential elements of Marxist thought, all too briefly discussed in this section, are also essentially contested. That is, they are subject to much discussion and disagreement even among those contemporary writers who have been influenced by Marxist writings. The work of the more contemporary Marxists, for example, draws far more directly on Marx's original ideas than does the work of the critical theorists. Indeed, the critical theorists would probably be more comfortable being viewed as post-Marxists than as straightforward Marxists. But even for them, as the very term *post-Marxism* suggests, the ideas of Marx remain a basic point of departure.

World-System Theory

The origins of contemporary world-system theory can be traced back to the first systematic attempt to apply the ideas of Marx to the international sphere; that is, to the critique of imperialism advanced by a number of thinkers at the start of the twentieth century (see Brewer 1990). The most well-known and influential work to emerge from this debate is the pamphlet written by Lenin, published in 1917, called *Imperialism: The Highest Stage of Capitalism*. Lenin accepted much of Marx's basic thesis but argued that the character of capitalism had changed since Marx published the first volume of *Capital* in 1867 (Marx 1992). Capitalism had entered a new stage—its highest and final stage—with the development of **monopoly capitalism**. Under monopoly capitalism, a two-tier structure had developed within the world economy: a dominant core exploiting a less developed periphery. With the development of a core and periphery, there was no longer an automatic harmony of interests among all workers. The bourgeoisie in the core states could use profits derived from exploiting the periphery to improve the lot of their own proletariat. In other words, the capitalists of the core could pacify their own working class through the further exploitation of the periphery.

To outline the key features of world-system theory, we begin with the work of perhaps its most prominent protagonist, Immanuel Wallerstein. For Wallerstein, history has been marked by the rise and demise of a series of world systems. The modern world system emerged in Europe at around the turn of the sixteenth century. It subsequently expanded to encompass the entire globe. The driving force behind this

CASE STUDY
The Power of Ideas: Politics and Neoliberalism
3.2

Background

A very good example of the hegemonic power of the United States, many Marxists would argue, is the success that it has had in getting neoliberal policies accepted as the norm throughout the world.

The Case

The set of policies most closely associated with the neoliberal project (in particular, reduction of state spending, currency devaluation, privatization, and the promotion of free markets) are, revealingly, known as the **Washington Consensus**. Many would argue that these are "commonsense" policies and that those third-world countries that have adopted them have merely realized that such economic policies best reflect their interests. However, Marxists would argue that an analysis of the self-interest of the hegemon, and the use of coercive power, provide a more convincing explanation of why such policies have been adopted.

The adoption of neoliberal policies by third-world countries has had a number of implications. Spending on health and education has been reduced, they have been forced to rely more on the export of raw materials, and their markets have been saturated with manufactured goods from the industrialized world. It does not take a conspiracy theorist to suggest that these neoliberal policies are in the interests of capitalists in the developed world. There are three main areas where the adoption of neoliberal policies in the third world is in the direct interest of the developed world. First there is the area of free trade. We need not enter into arguments about the benefits of free trade, but it is clear that it will always be in the interest of the hegemon to promote free trade—this is because, assuming it is the most efficient producer, its goods will be the cheapest anywhere in the world. It is only if countries put up barriers to trade, to protect their own production, that the hegemon's products will be more expensive than theirs. Second, there is the area of raw materials. If third-world countries are going to compete in a free trade situation, the usual result is that they become more reliant on the export of raw materials (because their industrial products cannot compete in a free trade situation with those of the developed world). Again this is in the interest of the hegemon because increases in the supply of raw material exports mean that the price falls. Additionally, where third-world countries have devalued their

currency as part of a neoliberal package, the price of their exported raw materials goes down. Finally, when third-world governments have privatized industries, investors from North America and Europe have frequently been able to snap up airlines, telecommunications companies, and oil industries at bargain prices. Duncan Green (1995) gives an eloquent description of the impacts of neoliberalism on Latin American countries.

If neoliberal policies appear to have such negative results for third-world countries, why have they been so widely adopted? This is where the coercive element comes in. Through the 1970s and 1980s and continuing to today there has been a major debt crisis between the third world and the West. This debt crisis came about primarily as a result of excessive and unwise lending by Western banks. Third-world countries were unable to pay off the interest on these debts, let alone the debt itself. They turned to the major global financial institutions, such as the IMF, for assistance. Although the IMF is a part of the UN system, it is heavily controlled by Western countries, in particular the United States. For example, the United States has 18 percent of the votes, whereas Mozambique has only 0.07 percent. In total, the ten most industrialized countries have over 50 percent of the votes.

Outcome

For third-world countries, the price of getting assistance was that they would implement neoliberal policies. Only once these were implemented, and only on condition that the policies were maintained, would the IMF agree to provide aid to continue with debt repayment.

Hence Marxists would argue that a deeper analysis of the adoption of neoliberal policies is required. Such an analysis would suggest that the global acceptance of neoliberalism is very much in the interests of the developed world and has involved a large degree of coercion. That such policies seem "natural" and "commonsense" is an indication of the hegemonic power of the United States.

For Discussion

China's economic policies are based on state control of the economy. All capitalist activities serve the interests of the nation-state. This system, called the Beijing Consensus, is seen as a challenge to the dominance of the neoliberal Washington Consensus. Will China's economic success encourage other nation-states to take more control over their economies?

seemingly relentless process of expansion and incorporation has been capitalism, defined by Wallerstein as "a system of production for sale in a market for profit and appropriation of this profit on the basis of individual or collective ownership" (1979, 66). Within the context of this system, all the institutions of the social world are continually being created and re-created. Furthermore, and crucially, it is not only the elements within the system that change. The system itself is historically bounded. It had a beginning, has a middle, and will have an end.

In terms of the geography of the modern world system, in addition to a core–periphery distinction, Wallerstein identified an intermediate "semiperiphery." According to Wallerstein, the semiperipheral zone displays certain features characteristic of the core and others characteristic of the periphery. Although dominated by core economic interests, the semiperiphery has its own relatively vibrant indigenously owned industrial base. Because of this hybrid nature, the semiperiphery plays important economic and political roles within the modern world system. In particular, it provides a source of labor that counteracts any upward pressure on wages in the core and also provides a new home for those industries that can no longer function profitably in the core (e.g., car assembly and textiles). The semiperiphery also plays a vital role in stabilizing the world political structure.

Constructivism

Most writers who call themselves **constructivists** argue that our actions and words make society—and society, in turn, shapes our actions and words. This is a direct challenge to the strategic or rational-choice thinkers who believe that our interests are primarily material and can be objectively determined and evaluated. Rational-choice scholars assume that all states and their leaders are "value maximizers."

In contrast, constructivists believe that we construct rules that first identify for us the key players (i.e., who has agency) in a given situation, recognizing that no one actor in the international system is an agent in all policy situations; then those rules instruct, direct, and commit actors to take certain actions. For example, realist rules during the Cold War dictated that all states were subservient to and would follow the lead of the United States or the USSR. However, actual practice does not always comply with the rules: Frequently states found areas where these superpowers had little interest—for example, development or peacekeeping—and established a niche to serve their interests. The George W. Bush administration tried to assert a similar pattern of hegemonic rules after the attacks of September 11, 2001, with phrases like "coalition of the willing" and "You are either with us or you are with the terrorists."

Over time, rules and practices can form a stable pattern that serves the interests of key agents. These patterns become "institutions." The Cold War, described earlier, was a twentieth-century institution, and the global economy is a good example of a twenty-first-century institution. Its rules and practices are based on neoliberal free market capitalism that best serves the interests of corporations, global economic institutions, and the wealthy states. The wealthy states' power in the system is based on both material factors (e.g., control of resources) and discursive power (power based on knowledge and the control of language and ideas within a society).

Constructivists argue that the international system is defined by socially constructed realities, and therefore, to understand the system, one must focus on shared rules, practices, meanings, identities, and norms. These factors define the interests, identities, preferences, and actions of each state in the system. By emphasizing the social construction of reality we also are questioning what is frequently taken for granted.

Constructivists assert that ideas shape how we view the world. Tony Benn was a longtime member of parliament and political leader of the most socialist wing of the Labor Party. He spent his life promoting progressive causes. He served as the president of "Stop the War Coalition." What would constructivists say about his worldview, given his practices?

This raises several issues. One is a concern with the origins of those social constructs that now appear to us as natural and are now part of our social vocabulary. After all, the notion of sovereignty did not always exist, as we have learned in Chapter 1; it was a product of historical forces and human interactions that generated new distinctions regarding where political authority resided. Also, the category of weapons of mass destruction is a modern invention. Although individuals have been forced to flee their homes throughout the course of human history, the political and legal category of refugees is only a century old. To understand the origins of these concepts requires attention to the interplay between existing ideas and institutions, the political calculations by leaders who had ulterior motives, and morally minded actors who were attempting to improve humanity.

Constructivists also examine how actors make their activities meaningful. Following Max Weber's insight that "we are cultural beings with the capacity and the will to take a deliberate attitude toward the world and to lend it *significance*" (1949, 81), constructivists attempt to recover the meanings that actors give to their practices and to the objects they create. Constructivists argue that culture, rather than private belief, informs the meanings people give to their action. Sometimes constructivists have presumed that such meanings derive from a hardened culture. But because culture is fractured and society comprises different interpretations of what is meaningful activity, scholars need to consider these cultural fault lines; to pinpoint or fix any precise meaning is largely a political and temporary accomplishment—it is not to discover some transcendent truth.

Some of the most important debates in world politics are about how to define particular activities. Development, human rights, security, humanitarian intervention, sovereignty—topics that we discuss in later chapters—are important, orienting concepts that can have any number of meanings. States and nonstate actors have rival interpretations of the meanings of these concepts and will fight to try to have collectively accepted their preferred meaning.

Indeed, the fact that these meanings are fixed through politics, and that once these meanings are fixed they have consequences for the ability of people to determine their fates, suggests an alternative way of thinking about power. Most international relations theorists treat power as the ability of one state to compel another state to do what it otherwise would not and tend to focus on the material technologies, such as military firepower and economic statecraft, that have this persuasive effect. Constructivists have offered two important additions to this view of power. The forces of power go beyond **material**: They also can be **ideational** or discursive. Ideational power is more than control over meaning—it is also the acceptance of ideas or a way of life. The notion that *your* way of thinking is "the norm" is but one example of ideational power.

Consider the issue of **legitimacy**. States, including great powers, crave legitimacy—the belief that they are acting according to, and pursuing, the values of the broader international community. There is a direct relationship between state legitimacy and the costs associated with a course of action: The greater the legitimacy, the easier time state leaders will have convincing others to cooperate with their policies. The lesser the legitimacy, the more costly the action. This means, then, that even great powers will frequently feel the need to alter their policies to be viewed as legitimate—or bear the consequences. Further evidence of the constraining power of legitimacy is offered by the tactic of "naming and shaming" by human rights activists. For example, Iran's release of a US reporter in 2009, who was charged with spying, shows how the international media and NGOs dedicated to promoting and protecting press freedoms can be influential in changing government policy.

Global social movements based on *normative ideas* such as peace, justice, and ecological balance, drive groups like Greenpeace to protest against drilling in the fragile Arctic region. Thirty activists protesting the drilling by the Russian energy company were arrested and held by the Russian government. The Arctic 30 were released in November after a global campaign by other governments and global social movements representing human rights groups, advocates of international law, and environmentalists.

Other scholars look for points of connection and evaluate the relative strengths of each approach to see when they might be combined to enrich our understanding of the world. One possibility is strategic social construction (Finnemore and Sikkink 1998). Actors attempt to change the norms that subsequently guide and constitute state identities and interests. Human rights activists, for instance, try to encourage compliance with human rights norms not only by naming and shaming those who violate these norms, but also by encouraging states to identify with these norms because it is the right thing to do.

Another possibility is to consider the relationship between the normative structure and strategic behavior. Some use constructivism to elucidate how identity shapes the state's interests and then turn to rational choice for understanding strategic behavior. In this view, the American identity shapes national interests, and then the structure of the international system informs its strategies for pursuing those interests. Yet some scholars go further and argue that the cultural context shapes not only identities and interests of actors, but also the very strategies they can use as they pursue their interests. In other words, although "game" metaphors are most closely associated with **game theory** and rational choice, some constructivists also argue that the normative structure shapes important features of the game, including the identity of the players and the strategies that are appropriate.

How does constructivism help us understand how and why things change? Proponents of constructivism scolded structural-realist and neoliberal-institutionalist scholars for their failure to explain contemporary global transformations. The Peace of Westphalia, for instance, helped to establish sovereignty and the norm of noninterference, but in recent decades various processes have worked against the principle of noninterference and suggested that state sovereignty is conditional on how states treat their populations. **World orders** are created and sustained not only by great-power preferences, but also by changing understandings of what constitutes a legitimate **international order**. Until World War II, the idea of a world organized around empires was not illegitimate—but now it is.

WHAT'S YOUR WORLDVIEW

How would your view of the wars in Iraq and Afghanistan change if you analyzed the wars based on the role of women and the impact of war on women in all the societies involved?

Feminist Theory

Often misunderstood as an attack on males, feminist theory provides useful tools with which to analyze a range of political events and policy decisions. In this section we offer an overview of five main types of feminist theory, which have become common since the mid-1980s—liberal, socialist/Marxist, standpoint, postmodern, and postcolonial. Although this section is titled "Feminist Theory," the heading is both deliberate and misleading. It is deliberate in that it focuses on the socially constructed roles that "women" occupy in world politics. It is misleading because this question has to be understood—as we noted in the previous section—in the context of the construction of differences between women and men and contingent understandings of masculinity and femininity. In other words, the focus could more accurately be on gender rather than on women, because the very categories of women and men, and the concepts of masculinity and femininity, are highly contested in much feminist research. Similarly, distinctions such as liberal and socialist are slightly misleading, because, as we discuss in more detail later, these categories do not exactly correspond to the diverse thinking of feminist scholars, especially in contemporary work, in which elements from each "type" are often integrated.

The term *gender* usually refers to the social construction of the difference between "men" and "women." Although it is a complex concept, here is one way to think of it: Biology determines your sex; gender is determined by a mix of social and cultural norms, as well as your own sense of identity. Some of the theories covered in this section assume natural and biological (e.g., sex) differences between men and women. Some of the approaches do not. What all of the most interesting work in this field does, however, is analyze how gender both *affects* world politics and *is an effect of* world politics. As with all theoretical traditions, there are different shades of feminism that combine with some of the more traditional theoretical ideas in global politics. We discuss five forms, or varieties, of feminist thinking.

Feminist theory in international relations originally grew from work on the politics of development and peace research. But by the late 1980s a first wave of feminism, **liberal feminism**, was more forcefully posing this question: Where are the women in world politics? The meaning of "liberal" in this context is decidedly not the same as that discussed earlier in the chapter. This definition is more in line with traditional views of liberalism that put equal and nondiscriminatory liberty at the center of the international debate.

In the context of feminism, the term *liberal* starts from the notion that the key units of society are individuals, that these individuals are biologically determined as either men or women, and that these individuals possess specific rights and are equal. Thus, one strong argument of liberal feminism is that all rights should be granted to women equally with men. Here we can see how the state is gendered insofar as rights, such as voting rights, right to possess property, and so on, have been predicated solely on the experiences and expectations of men—and, typically, a certain ethnic or racial class of men. Thus, taking women seriously made a difference to the standard view of world politics. Liberal feminists look at the ways in which women are excluded from power and prevented from playing a full part in political activity. They examine how women have been restricted to roles critically important for the functioning of things but not usually deemed important for theories of world politics.

A second strand of feminist theory is socialist/Marxist feminism, with its insistence on the role of material and primarily economic forces in determining the lives of women. This approach is also sometimes known as materialist feminism (Hennessy and Ingraham 1997).

Feminist thinkers ask "where are the women?" as a means to understand power relationships. In places like Saudi Arabia, women are not even allowed to drive cars. Here a woman uses a loophole in the law to drive a dune buggy. What factors might cause a state to limit the rights and privileges available to women?

For Marxist feminism, the cause of women's inequality is to be found in the capitalist system; overthrowing capitalism is the necessary route for the achievement of the equal treatment of women (Sargent 1981). Socialist feminism, noting that the oppression of women occurred in precapitalist societies and continues in capitalist societies, differs from Marxist feminism in that it introduces a second central material cause in determining women's unequal treatment, namely, the patriarchal system of male dominance (Braun 1987; Gottlieb 1989). According to Marxist feminists, then, capitalism is the primary oppressor; for socialist feminists it is capitalism plus patriarchy. For socialist/Marxist feminists the focus of a theory of world politics would be on the patterns by which the world capitalist system and the patriarchal system of power lead to women being systematically disadvantaged compared to men. The approach, therefore, has much in common with postcolonial feminism, which is discussed later in this section. Both are especially insightful when it comes to looking at the nature of the world economy and its differential advantages and disadvantages that apply to women. But postcolonial feminism, as we will see, criticizes socialist/Marxist feminism for presuming the "sameness" of patriarchy throughout the world and across time.

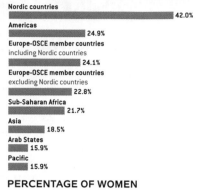

Nordic countries — 42.0%
Americas — 24.9%
Europe-OSCE member countries including Nordic countries — 24.1%
Europe-OSCE member countries excluding Nordic countries — 22.8%
Sub-Saharan Africa — 21.7%
Asia — 18.5%
Arab States — 15.9%
Pacific — 15.9%

PERCENTAGE OF WOMEN LEGISLATORS IN SELECTED COUNTRIES, 2012.
What does this graph suggest about the feminist movement worldwide? Do you find these percentages as expected or surprising?

The third version of feminist theory we discuss is standpoint feminism (Zalewski 1993; Hartsock 1998). This variant emerged out of socialist feminism and the idea of a particular class system. The goal was to try to think about how women as a class might be able to envision politics from a perspective denied to those who benefited from the subordination of women. Drawing on socialist-feminist interpretations of structure, standpoint feminism began to identify how the subordination of women, as a particular class, by virtue of their sex rather than economic standing (although the two are seen as related), possessed a unique perspective—or standpoint—on world politics as a result of their subordination. This first insight was later developed to consider also how the knowledge, concepts, and categories of world politics were predicated on a norm of masculine behavior and masculine experiences and therefore represented not a universal standard, but a highly specific, particular standard.

The fourth version is postmodern feminism, which develops the work of poststructuralism (especially that of Michel Foucault and Jacques Derrida) to analyze specifically the concept of gender. Essentially, postmodern feminism criticizes the basic distinction

Women in India strike against what they call a rape culture. In early 2013, a woman was gang raped on a bus and later died. The government was reluctant to punish the men guilty of this crime and a global campaign to protect women and end the crime of rape began. These women are protesting the more recent rape of a photojournalist.

THEORY IN PRACTICE

Reimaging War

Challenge

Realism is often called the dominant, traditional, or mainstream theory of international relations. As we have seen in this book, this means that the central assumptions of realism—anarchy, a self-help world, an enduring struggle for power—provide the framework for academic discussions of all aspects of the discipline. Foreign policy makers in all countries use the vocabulary of realism. However, unlike in the academic world, where an essay on political theory only receives a grade, in the world of political leaders a political theory can impact the lives of millions of people. What if politicians used one of the other theoretical perspectives, like constructivism or feminism?

Let's begin with what the former Bush administration in the United States called the "global war on terror." We see territory-based political units—countries in the customary Westphalian style of sovereign states—trying to defeat attacks from nonstate actors: terrorist organizations claiming their legitimacy from religious texts. This is not only an armed struggle; in terms of political theories it is a confrontation between two kinds of theories, explanatory and constitutive. Leaders in Western Europe and the United States use the former when they look at the world; the followers of Islamic fundamentalist leaders employ the latter as they seek to create a new world with their ideas. This dichotomy in perspectives has practical policy implications. The US leaders of the Bush administration, in line with the teaching of realism, believed that if they attacked terrorist strongholds and leaders around the world, they could defeat the terrorists. Islamists who employ terror as a means of conflict are equally convinced that the deaths of individual people will not kill the idea of re-creating the caliphate and, with it, the rule of Islamic law.

Options

The alternative theories we have studied offer another take on events and ideas surrounding this global war on terror. They would begin by pointing to the overall lack of success in the attempt to eliminate terrorists. Indiscriminate attacks by remotely piloted aircraft have killed people who were Muslims but not necessarily members of terrorist organizations. However, as news reports tell us, attacks on wedding ceremonies mistakenly believed by US mission planners to be Islamist cell meetings have created more anger directed against the United States and its interests around the world. A gendered perspective on the global war on terror would contend that the methods the Bush administration adopted are stereotypically masculinist: Instead of seeking to open a dialogue with the Islamists, the United States followed a realist path, focusing on its own view of national security, and launched a military attack. The same set of alternative-theory lenses can help us to understand events leading up to the 2003 US-led invasion of Iraq and the occupation of the country. Rejecting the consensus-building approach that his father (the former president) adopted prior to the 1991 Iraq War, George W. Bush made it clear early on that the invasion would happen whether or not UN arms-control inspectors (permitted by Saddam Hussein's government) found the banned nuclear, biological, and chemical weapons. Adopting the realist perspective, the Bush administration seemed convinced that Al Qaeda planned the September 11, 2001, attacks with active material assistance from the Iraq government. The Americans were apparently convinced that such a coordinated event was beyond the capabilities of a nonstate actor operating out of Afghanistan. The Bush foreign policy team labeled critics of their strategy as "not tough enough," "soft on terrorism," or "weak on security," all terms that attract the attention of advocates of the gendered perspective.

For Discussion

Perspective matters in the arena of public policy. Many pessimists tend to gravitate to the realist lens. They see a dangerous world in which war is always about to happen and their allies of today might desert them tomorrow. This is not to say that the alternative theories of international relations are not pessimistic; for instance, some advocates of the gendered perspective see disheartening patterns of sexualized language to describe wars. And yet, if we do not try to use a range of theories to understand events, we might miss opportunities to learn or to make better policy choices. Certainly both the global war on terror and the belief that Iraq had nuclear, biological, and chemical weapons demonstrate what can happen if leaders act on faulty assumptions.

between **sex and gender** that earlier feminist theories found so useful in think-ing about the roles of men and women in world politics and in analyzing the gendered concepts of world politics itself. This distinction between sex and gender was useful because it allowed feminists to argue that the position of women and men in the world was not natural but highly contingent and depen-dent on the meaning given to biological differences. Yet, although extremely useful, the acceptance of the sex–gender distinction retained the binary opposi-tion of male–female and presumed that, whereas gender was constructed, sex was wholly natural. However, as a number of scholars demonstrated, what we understood sex to be, what biological differences were, was heavily influenced by our understanding of gender—that is, that sex was constructed as gender (Fox-Keller 1985; Haraway 1989, 1991; Longino 1990; Fausto-Sterling 1992, 2000).

The final form of feminism to mention is postcolonial feminism. Postco-lonial feminists work at the intersection of class, race, and gender on a global scale. They especially analyze the gendered effects of transnational culture and the unequal division of labor in the global political economy. From this perspective, it is not good enough to simply demand (as liberal feminists do) that men and women should have equal rights in a Western-style democracy. Such a move ignores the way in which poor women of color in the global South or developing world remain subordinated by the global economic system—a system that liberal feminists were slow to challenge. In other words, the concerns and interests of feminists in the West and those in the rest of the world might not, therefore, so easily fit together. Postcolonial fem-inists are also critical of Western, privileged academic intellectuals (men and women) who claim to be able to "speak for" the oppressed, a form of cultural imperialism with important material effects. Perhaps the most influential postcolonial feminist scholar in this vein is Gayatri Spivak, who combines Marxism and feminism to interpret imperialism, past and present, and ongo-ing struggles for decolonization. In an influential essay, "Can the Subaltern Speak?," Spivak (1988) acknowledged the ambiguity of her own position in a privileged Western university and argued that elite scholars should be wary of homogenizing the "subaltern" and trying to speak for them in their "true" voice (what she calls a form of "epistemic violence"). The term *subaltern* refers to subordinated groups and in this instance to underprivileged women in the global South. In not recognizing the heterogeneity of experience and opin-ion of these diverse women, goes the argument, seemingly benevolent and well-meaning academics are at once patronizing in their desire to redeem them and unwittingly complicit in new forms of colonialism.

Conclusion

In the past fifteen to twenty years the dominance of the realism and liberalism theories within mainstream scholarly thinking has changed dramatically in two ways. First, there has been a lively academic debate between advocates of structural realism, or neorealism, and advocates of neoliberalism, exposing

Table 3.4 Some Models of the International System

	Realist	Liberal, Institutionalist	Marxist	Constructivist, Feminist
Primary unit	State	States, NGOs, MNCs, transnational corporations	State	Various
International system is . . .	Anarchic	Self-interestedly cooperative	Based on capitalist exploitation	Various: sum of ideas, a fiction, gendered
Leaders are . . .	Rational	Rational	Capitalists	Biased

shortcomings of both approaches. The second change has been the steadily growing intellectual appeal of a range of new approaches developed to understand world politics. These new perspectives reflect a transformed world. The most obvious failure was the inability for either of the mainstream theories—realism or liberalism—to predict the end of the Cold War. As the bipolarity of the international system dramatically disappeared, so too did the explanatory power of the theory that most relied on it.

Although the proponents of the alternative theories presented in this chapter seek to challenge the conventionally dominant theories of international relations, their work does more than that. In addition to offering new critical ways in which to view the field, the alternative theories, if combined with aspects of realism and liberalism, give us a richer understanding of international processes (as summarized in Table 3.4). We can see, for example, that war might result not only from countries' struggle for material power but also from the power of ideas or constructed notions of a proper masculine role in society.

In the coming chapters we will learn about contemporary issues and globalization. As you read, think of the various theories as glasses to help you to see the central problem of each issue. You should be open to multiple interpretations of events, while remembering that no one theory can explain everything, because by accepting a single theory as your basis for understanding and explaining world politics, you are excluding other perspectives that might also be valid.

 Engaging with the WORLD

Global Fund for Women

The Global Fund for Women is a publicly supported, nonprofit grant-making foundation that advances women's human rights by funding women-led organizations worldwide. We provide general operating support grants to organizations working at the local, regional, and national levels to enable women and girls to reach their potential and live free of discrimination and violence. Internship opportunities are designed for undergraduate and graduate students to provide first-hand experience with an international grant-making foundation on global women's rights.

Summer Internship Duration: We host student interns generally from June to August for unpaid assignments of up to forty hours/week. The number of internship positions available will be determined every spring according to team needs. Any opportunities will be posted on our website.

Special Internship Programs: The organization also serves as a hosting agency for other formal internship programs from educational institutions that provide funding to student programs related to philanthropy.

KEY TERMS

Anarchic system, p. 74
Anarchy, p. 81
Civil society, p. 72
Class, p. 93
Classical realism, p. 75
Collective security, p. 83
Constructivists, p. 96
Defensive realism, p. 78
Democratic peace thesis, p. 82
Economic base, p. 92
Empire, p. 83
Enlightenment, p. 82
Ethic of responsibility, p. 73
Feminist theory, p. 100
Free trade, p. 83
Game theory, p. 99

Ideational (sources of power), p. 98
Imperialism, p. 81
Interdependence, p. 85
International order, p. 99
Legitimacy, p. 98
Liberal feminism, p. 100
Liberal internationalism, p. 80
Liberalism of privilege, p. 87
Material (sources of power), p. 98
Monopoly capitalism, p. 94
Multilateralist, p. 80
Neoliberalism, p. 86
Nonstate actors, p. 89
Offensive realism, p. 78
Pluralism, p. 85
Positivism, p. 89

Power, p. 71
Radical liberalism, p. 88
Rational choice, p. 85
Realism, p. 71
Relative gains, p. 85
Security dilemma, p. 74
Sex and gender, p. 103
Sovereignty, p. 72
Structural realism
    (neorealism), p. 76
Superstructure, p. 92
Theory, p. 70
Transnational nonstate actors, p. 85
Washington Consensus, p. 95
World orders, p. 99

REVIEW QUESTIONS

1. How does the Melian dialogue (see Case Study 3.1) represent key concepts such as self-interest, the balance of power, alliances, capabilities, empires, and justice?

2. Is realism anything more than the ideology of powerful, satisfied states?

3. How would a realist explain the war on terrorism?

4. Can realism help us to understand the globalization of world politics?

5. Should liberal states promote their values abroad? Is force a legitimate instrument in securing this goal?

6. Are democratic-peace theorists right, but for the wrong reasons?

7. Are liberal values and institutions in the contemporary international system as deeply embedded as neoliberals claim?

8. Why have alternative theoretical approaches to realism become more popular in recent years?

9. How would you explain the continuing vitality of Marxist thought in a post–Cold War world?

10. How did Lenin's approach to international relations differ from that of Marx?

11. What is Wallerstein's notion of a semiperiphery? Why might it be useful?

12. What is the core concept of constructivism?

13. What do you think are the core issues for the study of global change, and how does constructivism help you address those issues? Alternatively, how does a constructivist framework help you identify new issues that you had not previously considered?

14. Feminists define gender as a social construction. What does this mean? What kinds of questions does international relations feminism try to answer using gender as a category of analysis?

15. Which variant of feminist theory, or any combination of them, seems to capture most accurately what Enloe calls "gender makes the world go around"?

THINKING ABOUT GLOBAL POLITICS

A Summit on Global Problems

GOAL

This analytical exercise provides an opportunity for you to explore alternative views of global problems. By conducting careful research, you will gain an understanding of how theories shape policy priorities. What might realists, liberal institutionalists, or Marxists think about what issues are most important?

EXPECTATIONS

In this exercise, you will work with your team members to research, synthesize, and apply basic data, as well as compare values and assumptions about how the world works. Based on your research and analysis, you and your team will also be expected to write concise policy recommendations. Your professor can decide how best to divide the classroom into eight (or however many) teams to represent a number of diverse countries.

SCENARIO

You have been asked to participate in a significant international event: a summit conference aimed at identifying and then proposing solutions to global problems. These problems threaten our international stability and influence or affect most citizens in the world.

The agenda for this conference will be decided by eight nation-states, and the agenda will decide what issues are discussed—and in what order. The nation-states are the United States, India, France, Brazil, Russia, Norway, Saudi Arabia, and China.

PROCEDURE

This is a cooperative learning project. With your team, choose which one of these countries you will represent. Then, as a team, you should complete the following tasks:

1. Using academic journals and the official websites of countries, NGOs, and foreign policy think tanks, find answers to the following questions: What are your nation-state's policy priorities and what worldview prevails? What position has your country supported in economic, political, military, and sociocultural policy issue areas?
2. Once you know something about your country, consider which theories of international relations are consistent with your country's past and present policy priorities. Are the leaders of your country realists, liberals, Marxists, feminists, or something else?
3. As a group representing your country and its worldview**, develop an agenda of policy issues that you would like the summit to address. For example, you might include human rights issues, war and violence, and global poverty. Consider the order in which you would want these issues to be addressed and why.
4. Be prepared to explain the causes of these problems and suggest effective policy responses that are consistent with your country's interests and priorities.

DISCUSSION

After preliminary work with your country team, the entire group of eight nation-states will come together with the purpose of developing a specific agenda. Only six items may appear on the final agenda for the global conference. In this eight-nation-state preliminary summit, you are to do the following:

1. Present your country's suggestions to the groups of eight nation-states.
2. Evaluate and critically review the agenda items presented by the other seven countries.
3. After your discussion of each state's list, the entire class should try to reach consensus on only six policy problems for the upcoming summit. The method of selecting these issues is left to the class and your professor. The goal is to reach agreement on six issues; however, this might not be possible.

Continued

THINKING ABOUT GLOBAL POLITICS *continued*

FOLLOW-UP

1. Were you able to reach consensus on six items? Why or why not?
2. Were some issues more acceptable than others?
3. Did your national interest prevent acceptance of some issues?
4. Are there some global problems that are better left to a few powerful and influential states? Why? Which states?

**A worldview represents basic values and assumptions people use to describe the world around them. An individual uses his or her worldview to identify problems and evaluate and analyze policies aimed at responding to these problems. Also, from worldviews emerge theories that we use to explain issues and events. For example, a Marxist would most likely explain persistent inequality by focusing on the failures of capitalism.

CONTRIBUTORS TO CHAPTER 3: *Tim Dunne, Stephen Hobden, Brian C. Schmidt, Steve Smith, Richard Wyn Jones, Steven L. Lamy, and John Masker.*

Statecraft is the strategy of power. Power is the capacity to direct the decisions and actions of others. Power derives from strength and will.

—*Charles Freeman*

It is possible to achieve goals only by persuasion, eloquence, threats and—if need be—intimidation.

—*Abba Eban*

S mall states are not usually seen as leaders in global politics. At times, they might play a major role in a regional organization or as part of a coalition in an international organization, but they rarely lead major global policy debates. Global factors affect both small and large states, however, and therefore play a role in shaping the foreign policy of all states. Here, Naderey Sano, the Filipino delegate to the 2013 UN Framework Convention on Climate Change, is asking the world to create and implement policies that will address the dangers presented by global climate change. The Philippines was recently devastated by Typhoon Haiyan. Climate change cannot be blamed for a specific weather event but the melting of Arctic ice, increases in CO_2 levels, and the warming of the oceans have contributed to unusual and severe weather events. Sea level is projected to rise three feet by the end of the century—and that would be the end of this sovereign state with its own culture, language, and history. Other states in the Pacific face similar challenges. Citizens in Papua New Guinea and the Solomon Islands have been forced to flee their homes because of rising tides, and Tuvalu, Kiribati, and the Marshall Islands might vanish entirely within the next fifty years.

Climate change, a global phenomenon, is shaping the foreign policy priorities of many small developing states like the Philippines and Vietnam, as well as Asian middle powers like Japan and South Korea and even European middle powers like Sweden, Norway, and the Kingdom of Denmark.

Philippine Climate Commissioner Naderev Sano, at the UN Framework Convention on Climate Change in Warsaw, asks the world to consider the destruction from Typhoon Haiyan on the Philippines and the possible impact of climate change. Like many vulnerable developing states, countries like the Philippines are trying to shape the final agreement so it includes funds for emissions control and for dealing with the damage from climate change. The developing and developed states remain divided on the policy solutions.

The Pacific Small Island Developing States was established in 2007 as an informal group of eleven island countries. They list their first challenge as climate change and they use the forums of the UN to promote their national and regional interests. Ambassador Marlene Moses of Nauru suggested that these eleven states share vulnerabilities such as their size and remoteness and that their "low-lying nature exposes them to adverse effects of climate change," which has a major impact on national security. Since 2009, the UN Assembly has recognized the link between climate change and global security. Most states put military and economic security ahead of environmental policies that might address the causes of climate change. The small states of the Pacific, the European members of the Arctic Council, and the participants in the 2013 African Climate Conference hope to convince the rest of the world that global consumerism is altering the earth's climate and threatening human survival, especially in vulnerable states.

As we will see in this chapter, there may be both concrete and abstract limits to what one person can accomplish in foreign policy. We discuss the methods that political leaders around the world use in pursuit of their foreign policy goals, including promoting and securing what they see as the national interests of their countries. All countries in the post–Cold War world—rich and poor, large and small, democratic and authoritarian—operate within the same set of limits and possibilities in the domestic and international arenas.

After reading and discussing this chapter, you will know something about how the foreign policy process works and how citizens and their leaders manage to articulate, promote, and eventually secure their national interests in this global setting. You will also have a better understanding of what tools and strategies small, middle, and great powers use to secure material interests and promote values and norms that fit with their ideational goals. Finally, you will have a second look at levels of analysis, categories of analytical tools that students and scholars in our field use to explain the foreign policy of all states.

Introduction

Each of the theories that we examined in Chapter 3 described the behavior of an actor called the state or nation-state. As you will recall from Chapter 1, there is a lot of disagreement in international relations theory about what we mean by "the state." But for this chapter we need to begin by accepting that the state exists and that it is the most important actor in the contemporary globalized international system, so that we can better understand the relationship among nations and states, nationalism and national interests, and globalization and global politics. Only then will we be able to discuss the process by which this system of states interacts: We call this process **foreign policy**.

We begin this chapter with a brief discussion of the state, nationalism, and national interests, and then we define foreign policy and explore the tools of **statecraft** used by governments to secure and promote their national interests. We also explore the growing importance of soft power in the post–Cold War era, which is defined more by globalization and global challenges. We see how, in global politics, foreign policy actors will often pursue different goals simultaneously because foreign policy connects domestic politics and international relations. For example, a leader might advocate human rights policy to satisfy domestic interest groups but maintain trade relations with an authoritarian state because of the need for natural resources.

In the next section of the chapter we offer an analytical framework of the foreign policy process, providing an overview of how foreign policy is made in most states. We then present a brief overview of levels of analysis and the study of foreign policy behavior. Here we learn to explain why states make certain choices over others. In the final section of the chapter, we review foreign policy styles and traditions across great, middle, and small states around the world.

States and Nationalism

To understand the relationships among states, nationalism, and national interests, we must first remember these points:

1. From about the mid-seventeenth century, an order of sovereign, territorial states known as the Westphalian system developed in Europe.
2. The rise of nationalism from the late eighteenth century nationalized this state order, later extending beyond Europe until the whole world was organized as a series of nation-states (see Table 4.1). International relations were relations between nation-states.

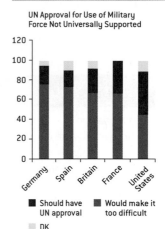

UN Approval for Use of Military Force Not Universally Supported

■ Should have UN approval   ■ Would make it too difficult

□ DK

VIEWS ON MULTILATERALISM AND INTERVENTION.
Is the era of unilateralism over?
*Source: http://www.pewresearch
.org/fact-tank/2013/08/30/
un-approval-bcforc-using-
military-force-lacks-widespread-
global-agreement/*

Table 4.1 **The Development of a World of Nation-States**

Date	Rough Number of Nation(al) States*
1500	4 (England, France, Spain, and Portugal)
1800	6 (Britain, France, Holland, United States, Spain, and Portugal)
1900	30 (including Belgium, Germany, Italy, Serbia, Romania, Greece, Brazil, Argentina, Japan, and Canada)
1923	45 members of the League of Nations
1945	51 states established the UN
1950	60 members of UN
1960	99 members of UN
1970	127 members of UN
2009	192 members of UN
2011	193 members of UN (196 countries worldwide)

*Before 1923 this is an estimate based on historical judgment. Thereafter it is based on membership of the League of Nations and the UN.

3. Globalization may undermine this political order by eroding sovereign territorial power and by creating competing identities and multiple loyalties.

It should be noted that even in undemocratic or authoritarian states, domestic interests such as those favored by military leaders, government bureaucrats, and business leaders shape both domestic and foreign policy. Citizens might not have as much to say about what their leaders decide to do in the international system, but bureaucratic agencies and elites do have a voice. Consider how the Chinese business community has worked to open up the communist regime in that country. The leaders of a state might often seem to be like Janus, the Roman god of doors and beginnings, who had two aspects—one facing inward and the other outward. But as we will see in the next section, the foreign policy process is essentially that—the act of balancing domestic and international factors.

What Is Foreign Policy?

Foreign policy is the articulation of national interests and the means chosen to secure those interests, both material and ideational, in the international arena. **Material interests** could be trade agreements, energy resources, and even control over strategic territory. **Ideational interests** include the promotion of values, norms, and policy ideas that enhance the security and prosperity of a nation-state. The national interests of any state are shaped by individuals (especially political leaders or elites), interest groups, geographic position, traditions, norms, and values that are part of a country's political culture. International events and the actions of both friends and enemies can also influence a country's national interests.

Do governments matter? Belgium, a state made up of three nations—Flemish, French, and German regions—was without a national government from June 2010 until December 2011. Here citizens march in Brussels in 2011 in support of national unity, drawing attention to Belgium's record-breaking length of time without a government.

CASE STUDY : Refugees

Background

Who is a refugee? As refugees, can they be called citizens of any country? Why does this category matter, and how has it changed? How do refugee issues challenge those making foreign policy? There are many ways to categorize people who leave their homes, including migrants, temporary workers, displaced peoples, and refugees.

The Case

Prior to the twentieth century, refugee as a legal category did not exist, and it was not until World War I that states recognized people as refugees and gave them rights. Who was a refugee? Although many were displaced by World War I, Western states limited their compassion to Russians who were fleeing the Bolsheviks (it was easier to accuse a rival state of persecuting its people); only they were entitled to assistance from states and the new refugee agency, the High Commissioner for Refugees. However, the High Commissioner took his mandate and the category and began to apply it to others in Europe who also had fled their country and needed assistance. Although states frequently permitted him to expand into other regions and provide more assistance, states also pushed back and refused to give international recognition or assistance to many in need—most notably when Jews were fleeing Nazi Germany. After World War II, and as a consequence of mass displacement, states reexamined who could be called refugees and what assistance they could receive. Because Western states were worried about having obligations to millions of people around the world, they defined a refugee as an individual "outside the country of his origin owing to a well-founded fear of persecution" as a consequence of events that occurred in Europe before 1951. In other words, their definition excluded those outside Europe who were displaced because of war or natural disasters because of events after 1951. Objecting to this arbitrary definition that excluded so many, the new refugee agency, the UN High Commissioner for Refugees, working with aid agencies and permissive states, seized on events outside Europe and argued that there was no principled reason to deny to them what was given to Europeans. Over time the

political meaning of *refugee* came to include anyone who was forced to flee his or her home and crossed an international border, and eventually states changed the international legal meaning to reflect the new political realities.

In the contemporary era of Rwanda, Darfur, and Bosnia after the Cold War, we are likely to call someone a refugee if he or she is forced to flee home because of manmade circumstances, without having to cross an international border. To capture the idea of those who flee but are still in their homeland, we use the term *internally displaced peoples*. Indeed, the concept of refugees has expanded impressively over the past 100 years, and the result is that there are millions of people who are now entitled to forms of assistance that are a matter of life and death. Watching this world tragedy unfold has led many states to support the human-security movement and the October 2005 UN resolution on the responsibility to protect (see Chapter 7).

Outcome

One reason why states wanted to differentiate "statutory" refugees from internally displaced peoples is because they have little interest in extending their international legal obligations to millions of people and do not want to become too involved in the domestic affairs of states. For example, in the early 1990s refugees fleeing the civil war in Yugoslavia flooded into Germany. However, the German government was already paying for the reunification with East Germany and could not afford to support more refugees at the time. Therefore, because of domestic political reasons, the German government had to look to other states for a solution to a foreign policy problem. The German government chose to lobby for intervention by the EU, NATO, and the UN.

For Discussion

1. Do states have a responsibility to accept political refugees?
2. Should states intervene in other states to alleviate refugee crises?
3. Should domestic political considerations—such as electoral politics—shape the foreign refugee policy of a state?

When discussing national interests, the most important questions are these: Which interests are national? Why these interests over others? Who determines these interests? So far in this book, we have learned that different theoretical views provide different perspectives on both issues and policies. For realists, **national interests** are relatively unchangeable over time. Hans Morgenthau argues that a state's national interest is the pursuit of power and that power, once acquired, is used to secure material aims, protect social and physical quality of life, and promote specific ideological or normative goals. However, neoclassical realists believe that domestic political interests also shape foreign policy, and thus a state's priorities could change. As we saw in Chapter 3, realists like Morgenthau believe in a state-centric international system in which states act as a single coherent actor that pursues national interests in a rational manner. Here, rational means selecting a policy path that maximizes benefits for the state and minimizes risks. Morgenthau and his disciples considered "national interest as the pursuit of power" the essence of politics.

For realists, the principal national interest is national security, or maintaining the integrity of a country's territory and its economic, political, and cultural institutions. Morgenthau argued that to understand foreign policy one has to understand the "political and cultural context within which foreign policy is formulated" and that interests and ideas shape foreign policy actions and priorities. He quotes the noted scholar Max Weber to make his point: "Interests (material and ideal), not ideas, dominate directly the actions of men. Yet the 'images of the world' created by these ideas have very often served as switches determining the tracks on which the dynamism of interests kept actions moving" (1960, 9).

The objectives of foreign policy, according to many realists, must be defined in terms of material national interests and must be supported by adequate power. Military power is the dominant coin of the realm, from a realist

To enhance their prestige and global image, leaders of nation-states try to secure the sponsorship of major global conferences and cultural and sporting events. Brazil will be sponsoring the 2014 World Cup and the 2016 Olympics. Unfortunately, security is a critical element for these events and no host country can afford to allow a major terrorist attack. Brazilian Federal Police like those outside Maracana Stadium will provide law and order, safety, and security for people coming to these events.

view; however, in this era of globalization the tools of statecraft have changed in both their utility and their efficacy. All the major states today, for instance, have substantial armed forces, yet all states face the potential of attacks by terrorist groups, and a strong military is not always an effective deterrent.

Robert Pastor (1999) argues that a state's leaders rank their foreign policy goals from *vital* or *essential* to *desirable*. From his realist view, Pastor ranks national interests as follows:

1. National security that includes the defense of borders and the prevention of external influence over domestic affairs.
2. The pursuit of economic interests and securing vital resources.
3. The defense of a country's traditions and values and the promotion of its ideals in the international system.
4. The implicit and explicit effort to make the world more like itself.

Moreover, as we learned in Chapter 3, proponents of the liberal perspective on international relations believe that a state's power is not measured by force alone. Liberals might define national interest in terms of maintaining rule of law in the international system and empowering international institutions and regimes that promote global governance in policy areas such as economic development and global finance. Liberal internationalists like the former Canadian foreign minister Lloyd Axworthy (2003, 5) have taken bold steps to reform the international system and shift foreign policy priorities from narrow national interests to a much more universal focus on human security and human interests. Axworthy described a goal that many liberal middle powers have embraced:

> We propose a way of seeing the world and tackling global issues that derives from serving individual human needs, not just those of the nation-state or powerful economic interests.

Liberal internationalism in this case has evolved to embrace a more Kantian or normative view of national priorities and interests.

Constructivists, meanwhile, believe that state interests and foreign policy goals are "defined in the context of internationally held norms and understandings about what is good and appropriate" (Finnemore 1996, 2). This normative context changes over time, and this helps us understand shifts in foreign policy behavior and interests promoted by national leaders. For example, with the end of the Cold War, many states returned to their own traditions and values as guideposts for foreign policy; and the more internationalist context supported this shift away from ideological conflict to engagement and cooperation.

Marxists, on the other hand, believe that foreign policy is generally controlled by economic and political elites who also control power at home. National interests are determined by the wealthy and powerful, not the average citizen. This leads to conclusions that wars are fought primarily for economic reasons and that the goal of a country's development-assistance programs is to make poor countries dependent on the donor state and to ensure that the developing regions of the world are kept in the position of providing cheap labor, cheap resources, and a welcome place for foreign investors.

What Do We Expect From Foreign Policy?

National interests are usually related to what we, as citizens, expect from our governments. At the basic level we want the state to protect our borders, provide internal security, and support and maintain a means of exchange or a marketplace. This is the point at which domestic and international policy distinctions begin to blur. Foreign policy and domestic policies are clearly interdependent in this global age. Most foreign policy experts believe citizens expect their state's foreign policy to deliver in seven areas (Hill 2003, 44–45):

1. Protecting citizens living or traveling in a foreign country.
2. Projecting an image or identity in the international system that enhances a state's prestige and makes that state's values, beliefs, and traditions attractive to other states in the international system.
3. Maintaining the status quo in terms of providing stability and protecting citizens against external threats.
4. Advancing prosperity and providing the ways and means for accumulating wealth.

Failed States Index

	Factors Contributing to the State's Fragility
Somalia	Jihadist terrorism, piracy, poverty, food insecurity
Congo, D.R.	Civil war, massive human rights abuses, disease, mass rape and torture
Sudan	Civil war, authoritarian government, terrorism, poverty, overdependence on oil
South Sudan	Poverty, corruption, food shortages, armed conflict, human rights abuses
Chad	Poverty, influx of refugees, radicalized youth population, tribal/religious conflicts
Yemen	Jihadist terrorism, human rights abuses, external interference, poverty, disease, lack of food and clean water
Afghanistan	Violent protests, assassinations by Taliban, external interference, drug trade
Haiti	Corruption, forced evictions, poverty, crime, continued inability to cope with effects of natural disasters
Central African Republic	Natural disasters, inadequate infrastructure, terrorism, violent protests, governmental coups
Zimbabwe	Economic collapse, humans rights abuses, political instability and corruption
Iraq	Destroyed infrastructure, terrorism, ethnic conflict, external interference

Source: http://ffp.statesindex.org/rankings-2013-sortable.

5. Assisting leaders in making decisions about whether to intervene in a global crisis or get involved in an alliance or international institution.
6. Providing support for international negotiations aimed at creating and maintaining a stable world order.
7. Working toward protecting the global commons (e.g., oceans) and providing global public goods (e.g., clean air).

These foreign policy goals are influenced and shaped by a variety of internal and external actors and structures. Globalization has pushed domestic and foreign policy processes into a complex and interconnected relationship. Domestic societies are more exposed to external or international developments, and foreign policies both shape and are shaped by domestic developments. In capitols across the world, foreign policy leaders talk about policy issues that are transnational in nature, like migration, poverty, environmental challenges, and trade. In crafting government policies to slow global warming, for example, political leaders must contend with the demands of business and industry groups and those of concerned citizens at home—not to mention those demands that leaders, corporations, and citizens of other states bring to negotiations. These leaders also understand how domestic interests often prevent the realization of foreign policy goals. One of the most difficult issues for foreign policy leaders is how to make bold foreign policy decisions without alienating a powerful domestic group that might influence the next election. For example, the leaders of the world know that genocide took place in Rwanda and Darfur, and yet few states were willing to intervene in the area to stop the killing. Most recently, the major powers of the world watched as Colonel Gaddafi of Libya slaughtered opposition forces. Humanitarian intervention presents a difficult policy choice for most leaders. After weeks of debate and dithering, the UN Security Council voted 10–0 to authorize "all necessary methods" to protect civilians. This resulted in the establishment of a "no-fly zone" over Libya and other military actions in defense of the civilian population. Five states abstained from this resolution, which suggests that it is difficult to convince domestic groups to sacrifice blood and treasure for people from distant lands.

Now that we've covered some foundational aspects of what foreign policy is, and what we expect from it, we turn to a discussion about how foreign policy is accomplished; we examine the strategies and tools that states might use to secure their goals and meet their priorities in the international system.

> **WHAT'S YOUR WORLDVIEW**
>
> *Who do you think determines a country's foreign policy priorities? Who do you think should determine a country's foreign policy priorities? What are your country's top foreign policy interests, and are they what you would expect them to be?*

Foreign Policy Strategies and Tools

The organized statements of goals and beliefs that political leaders formulate, and the methods they intend to employ to achieve those goals, are called foreign policy strategies. For the political leaders of a state, a foreign policy doctrine provides a sextant, or, in current technology, a GPS system, that leaders use to chart policy strategies and determine national priorities. The doctrine guides decisions, such as where to invest critical resources to secure both long- and short-term goals. Like most countries, the United States has had one dominant strategy for protecting national interests—a combination of military, economic, and diplomatic resources aimed at protecting our homeland and maintaining an open global economy. During the Cold War, the strategy developed a global reach and was identified with the presidents at the time. The Truman, Nixon, and Reagan doctrines were all aimed at either containing or confronting communist expansion. The Carter Doctrine was aimed at protecting US interests in the Middle East, and the recent Bush Doctrine included policies aimed at confronting extremist groups that use terrorism and the states that support them. Unilateralism and preemptive war were also core principles in the Bush Doctrine.

Most states have coherent foreign policy strategies to attain both material and ideal goals. For example, after emerging from apartheid and exclusive white rule in the late 1980s, the new South African state has developed a foreign policy that promotes human rights across the world and supports an African Renaissance. For China, the 2008 Summer Olympics was a symbolic announcement of its leadership status in world affairs. South Africa's sponsorship of the World Cup soccer matches in 2010 signaled to the world that South Africa is capable of leading an economic, political, and cultural resurgence of African states. Similarly, after years of rule by military dictators, Chilean democratic leaders have decided that an activist foreign policy based on the theme of "diplomacy for development" will help them overcome their structural constraints of size and geographic location and allow them to develop a niche as a regional leader and an honest broker in international affairs.

All countries have three kinds of foreign policy tools from which to choose: sticks, carrots, and sermons. Sticks refer to threats, carrots to inducements, and sermons to what diplomats might call *moral suasion*. We could also add the power that comes with having a positive image or reputation in the international system. Being an "honest broker" or a moral leader seeking to help resolve regional conflicts can also become a source of power in the international world. Norway, for example, took the lead to resolve the Middle East conflict and the conflict in Sri Lanka. Norwegian leaders are supported in these endeavors because Norwegian citizens see it as their responsibility to the global community. Norwegian nationalism includes a strong sense of internationalism. It is important to remember that, because of differences in resources, population, and level of economic development, some countries might not be able to use some or all of the options we discuss next.

Sticks, or Threats

In the international system of the realist perspective that influences many political leaders, states must secure their interests by military power. Because there is no common power or central government and no agreement on rules governing the system, some countries use force or the threat of force to secure their interest and gain more power and influence in the international system. Other military tools include military aid or assistance, sharing intelligence, alliances, military research, and technological innovations.

Sometimes the decision to deploy a weapon system can be a stick for diplomats to use. The G. W. Bush administration supported the development and deployment of a ballistic missile defense system in Eastern Europe to defend Europe against missiles from Iran or terrorist groups in the Middle East. Perhaps fearing growing US power and influence in the region, the Russian government saw the installation of such a defense system as a menace to Russia's security needs. In response, the Obama administration offered the Russians a carrot by declining to build the missile defense system.

The use of foreign policy sticks is not limited to leaders who have adopted the realist perspective on global politics. Liberals also recognize the importance of military tools of statecraft. Woodrow Wilson did not shy away from using America's military resources to help end World War I. However, he called for a collective security arrangement with the League of Nations. Wilson also supported arms-control treaties and pushed for more rules of war. Even today, progressive-liberal states like Canada, the Netherlands, and Denmark are active members of NATO and have willingly deployed their armed forces in Iraq and Afghanistan. Many middle and small powers are active participants in peacekeeping forces in conflict regions around the world. Collective humanitarian interventions and peacekeeping are military tools that are becoming more important in areas where states have failed to provide basic security or are disintegrating. The UN has some seventeen current peacekeeping operations, eight in Africa alone.

In addition to military inducements, states can also employ economic sticks. This type of influence can include product or **economic sanctions**, boycotts, arms embargoes, and punitive tariffs. Sanctions are used to both alter domestic politics and influence the foreign policy behavior of a target state. In the war on terrorism, the United States froze bank and investment assets from Afghanistan and Iraq as well as several Islamic charity organizations. Blocking access to multilateral lending institutions such as the World Bank and investment restrictions have become major tools in attempts to influence state behavior at home and abroad. Monetary sanctions involving the buying and selling of large quantities of a target state's currency to manipulate its exchange rate and create an economic crisis are another economic tool. Additionally, restrictions on travel and business are often used to force change in a society.

The best example of an effective sanction effort was the global, cultural, political, and

Twenty-six Cuban doctors set up a field hospital in central Chile to treat earthquake survivors. Cuban medical teams offer high-quality care to those in need all around the world. Why do you think the United States continues to restrict travel to and trade with Cuba? Could it be all about votes in Florida?

economic boycott of South Africa during its apartheid regime. Currently, the United States is working with other members of the UN Security Council to punish North Korea for its production and testing of nuclear weapons. Similarly, the UN has initiated sanctions against Iran for its refusal to submit to inspections by the International Atomic Energy Agency. Economic tools need not be all negative. States often use the promise of material assistance to reach a desired goal.

Carrots, or Inducements

Most of the wealthy states in the international system are donor states, or those states that give a significant amount of development assistance or aid to less wealthy or poor states. For donor states, development assistance is a means of pursuing foreign policy objectives. There are at least five forms of foreign assistance:

1. *Project aid* provides a grant or loan to a country or an NGO for a specific project.
2. *Program aid* is given to a government to create certain policy conditions in the recipient country, such as opening a market or supporting balance of payments.
3. *Technical assistance* provides a country with equipment or technicians in a given policy area.
4. *Humanitarian* or *disaster assistance* provides states funds for food, materials, and medicine and other basic supplies.
5. *Military* or *security aid* is often given to allies or partners in programs like the war on terrorism or to those participating in UN peacekeeping activities.

As we discuss more fully in Chapter 9, aid is given for a variety of purposes, but even when giving humanitarian aid most states will tie their aid to national interests such as security, economic growth, or prestige. Food aid helps the hungry, but it also helps farmers in the donor state who sell their crops and cattle to the government. Even the most generous states use this economic tool to serve some of their own domestic interests. Assistance programs include the sharing of expertise and technology. Giving humanitarian assistance might also enhance a state's prestige and its image in the international system. Christine Ingebritsen and colleagues (2006, 283) argue that the small countries of Scandinavia, consistently major donors, have played a pivotal role in promoting global social justice and strengthening norms of ethical behavior (see Chapter 9). These small and middle powers have used carrots such as development assistance, trade agreements, and other nonforce resources to encourage peaceful resolution of conflict, promote multilateralism, and work toward a more equitable distribution of global wealth. A typical Nordic aid program might include funding for public health and education, environmental protection, promotion of human rights and democracy, and family planning. The Nordic countries also give a high percentage of their aid to multilateral organizations and NGOs working in developing regions of the world (see Figure 4.1). About 40 percent of the United Nations Children's Fund (UNICEF) budget comes from Nordic countries, and organizations like Oxfam and Save the Children receive funds from Nordic governments.

Development assistance or aid programs in the United States are administered by the US Agency for International Development (USAID). Under the Clinton administration, USAID goals were trimmed from thirty to five. These reflected the neoliberal goals of the administration for the enlargement of democratic and capitalist states:

1. Provision of human relief
2. Stabilization of population growth
3. Promotion of democracy
4. Environmental protection
5. Economic growth

These goals changed slightly with the Bush administration. Namely, a focus was placed on preventing HIV/AIDS, and family planning programs were no longer supported.

Other economic tools include trade agreements, the provision of loans, and the sharing of development or trade experts. Countries give economic resources in two main methods: directly to another country, in what are called bilateral agreements, or indirectly, through global institutions like the World Bank, the IMF, and a variety of regional development banks like the Asian Development Bank. World Bank aid in the developing world can finance a range of projects, such as rural electrification or creating an export-driven agricultural market.

Rank Country	Economic Aid (billion $)
1. United States	23.53
2. United Kingdom	12.46
3. Japan	11.19
4. France	10.6
5. Germany	10.44
6. Netherlands	5.45
7. United Arab Emirates	5.2
8. Sweden	3.95
9. Canada	3.9
10. Spain	3.81

Figure 4.1 Top Ten Foreign Aid Donors, 2011.
Do you see a pattern among the countries that are on this list? What motivates these states to give such large amounts of aid?

Sermons: Diplomatic Messaging and the Use of the Media

Military and economic sticks address material interests. Sermons address ideal interests. These might include *demarches*, or simple warnings, directives, or position statements sent to governments as a form of moral suasion. A charismatic leader giving a speech to the world can be a powerful diplomatic tool. President Obama's speech on June 4, 2009, given in Cairo, Egypt, addressed a global audience and was a clear attempt to convince the Muslim world that the US policy toward Islam was going to change. Minutes after its completion, the US government had it on the Internet in several languages. Time will tell whether this particular speech will succeed; as a kind of public diplomacy it is an effective use of modern media and global communications to serve political purposes.

Diplomacy plays a critical role in the preservation of peace and world order. Many experts consider diplomacy a lost art, arguing that advanced communications, summit meetings, the increasing importance of international and regional organizations, and the demands of a global media industry all undermine the often secret aspects of diplomatic messaging or bargaining. Specialists assert that diplomacy performs four important functions:

1. Communication between actors
2. Negotiation
3. Participation in regional and international organizations
4. Promotion of trade and other economic interests

Diplomats today must deal with a host of new global challenges that require cooperation among state and nonstate actors. Diplomatic meetings aimed at addressing global challenges like climate change, terrorism, organized crime, human rights, and international investments are becoming major sources of power for countries with basic knowledge, scientific expertise, and the means to implement the policies. The role states play in the development

Table 4.2 The Five Largest Importers of Major Conventional Weapons and Their Major Suppliers, 2008–2012

Importer	Share of International Arms Imports (%)		Main Suppliers (Share of Importer's Total Imports), 2008–2012		
	2008–2012	2003–2007	1st	2nd	3rd
India	12	9	Russia (79%)	United Kingdom (6%)	Uzbekistan (4%)
China	6	12	Russia (69%)	France (13%)	Ukraine (10%)
Pakistan	5	2	China (50%)	United States (27%)	Sweden (5%)
South Korea	5	5	United States (77%)	Germany (15%)	France (5%)
Singapore	4	1	United States (44%)	France (30%)	Germany (11%)

of global regimes is an important source of power in this era of globalization. Small and middle powers tend to value the role of diplomacy and use some of their most qualified foreign policy experts in diplomatic roles.

Public diplomacy is fast becoming an important foreign policy tool. In the past this form of diplomacy might have been called propaganda, but today it involves telling the world about the positive characteristics of your society. These educational, cultural, and informational programs are also an important source of power. Countries can provide funds for educational exchanges of students, faculty, and diplomats. The US Fulbright Program, for example, sends students and scholars from the United States around the world and brings foreign scholars to the United States. Concerts, book tours, movies, and art exhibits are all part of a country's efforts to promote its values and cultural attributes. During the Cold War, the US Information Agency sponsored tours of jazz bands to the Soviet Union and other communist countries.

Media sources are also ways to promote a state's interests and make a state attractive to others. For example, the BBC and the Voice of America provide global radio programs that attract listeners and learners across the world, and during the Cold War, Radio Moscow provided a Soviet perspective on news events.

Finally, in a world of nuclear weapons and internal wars that kill both civilians and soldiers, **coercive diplomacy** has become a valuable foreign policy tool because "it seeks to persuade an opponent to cease his aggression" rather than going to war (George 1991, 5). In 1990, the first Bush administration used a strategy of coercive diplomacy in an attempt to get Saddam Hussein to leave Kuwait. The Bush administration made a clear demand, or *ultimatum*, that the Iraqi government ignored. The administration then took a variety of steps that involved the buildup of forces, economic sanctions, and diplomatic maneuvers in the UN. This strategy of gradually turning the screw was aimed at getting Iraq to see how costly a war with the United States and a coalition of forces representing some thirty-six countries would be. In this case, coercive diplomacy failed because Iraq did not back down, and the US-led coalition destroyed the Iraqi military with the blessings of the UN and most of the world community.

Soft and Hard Power in Foreign Policy

One way to understand the methods of foreign policy making is to think of both carrots and sticks as **hard power** tools. However, these inducements and threats are only part of the diplomatic process in the international system. Harvard professor and former Clinton administration official Joseph Nye introduced the concept of **soft power**, or the ability to "shape the preferences of others" (2004, 5–15). Soft power, as Nye presented the concept, tries to co-opt people and countries rather than to simply threaten or coerce them. Political leaders can use soft power to encourage cooperation and to shape what other states want in the international system. A country's culture and ideology are important sources of soft power.

Nye asserts that the soft power of any country is based on three sources: (1) its culture, (2) its political values, and (3) its foreign policy. If a country's

SREBRENICA: nooit vergeten!

"Never forget Srebrenica" is the message on this poster as a Dutch activist participates in a 2007 memorial in The Hague to the victims of Europe's worse massacre since World War II. The failure of Dutch troops to protect Bosnian Muslims in the designated safe area of Srebrenica still haunts the people of the Netherlands, and this event shapes the foreign policy of the country today.

culture is attractive to others, it can be a source of power. Similarly, if a country's political values—like democracy and respect for human rights—are attractive to other citizens and other states, then that country can gain power and influence in the international system. Finally, a country with a moral foreign policy can also have power and influence in the international system. From this view, the United States might have lost its international standing because of its use of torture and prisoner abuse in Iraq and secret prisons around the world; when the United States lost moral credibility, its foreign policy activities were more likely to be seen as unethical by most of the global community. Nye suggests that if a country promotes values that other states want, leadership will cost less.

Soft power is not merely the same as influence. After all, influence can also rest on the hard power of threats or payments. Soft power is more than just persuasion or the ability to move people by arguments, although that is an important part of it. It is also the ability to attract, and attraction often leads to acquiescence. Simply put, in behavioral terms soft power is *attractive power*.

Both hard- and soft-power tools will be an important part of any future leader's foreign policy doctrine and policy agenda. In this **nonpolar world** (Hass 2008), where no one state or group of states controls all power and authority and where power and influence are distributed among a variety of state and nonstate actors, it will be harder to control these actors and even harder to build multilateral alliances to respond to global challenges. With no clear concentration of power in many policy areas, the number of threats and vulnerabilities is likely to increase, and states will need to work harder to maintain order and stability. Most experts predict that all states and transnational actors will need to combine resources to address the most significant global problems the world faces. The entire global effort aimed at addressing climate change, for example, will require major collective action. Globalization might not have changed enduring national interests such as the search for security and prosperity, but it has certainly changed how states pursue these interests.

Explaining Foreign Policy: Levels of Analysis

As a student of foreign policy, you might be interested in finding answers to puzzles or unexpected actions by a state. Why did North Korea's leaders decide to develop nuclear weapons? Why do Nordic governments give so much development assistance? Why did China increase its defense budget 12.7 percent and announce that it was building its first stealth jet, renewing concerns around the world? These are complex issues, but there are some explanations that are better than others. Foreign policy analysis is the search for factors or variables that explain the most about a state's behavior. Scholars doing research in this area are interested in questions like the following: Why do states behave in a certain way? What factors explain a state's behavior? Why do leaders pick one option over another? If a state spends a significant amount of money on its military, what factors explain that choice?

Although there are always questions about "agency," or which actors actually make foreign policy, foreign policy analysis offers plausible explanations for foreign policy behavior. We say "plausible explanations" because this is not an exact science: The social scientist trying to explain foreign policy puzzles can never replicate the certainty of the natural scientist working in the lab and controlling all the variables. Yet if the social scientist can identify factors that shape foreign policy, it might help us better understand the foreign policy process and even predict how states might behave in similar situations. In this section, we discuss one such approach to the agency question: levels of analysis.

Earlier, we discussed how some research in international relations attempts to replicate the research methods and assumptions of the natural sciences. The idea here is that one can develop theories, test them by gathering evidence, and find useful explanations for the decisions made by leaders. Foreign policy analysis, a subfield of international relations, puts the individual at the center of decision making.

Most studies of decision making begin with the assumption that all decision makers act rationally or always act to maximize benefits and minimize costs. In his classic study of decision making in a crisis situation, *Essence of Decision*, Graham Allison (1971) introduces three models, or analytical tools, for explaining decision making. The first, the rational-actor model, provides a useful example of using rationality. The other two models, organizational behavior and bureaucratic politics, are second-level, or domestic-level, tools. Unfortunately, some foreign policy decision makers cannot meet the requirements of rationality. For example, it might not be possible for policy makers to

LEVELS OF ANALYSIS IN FOREIGN POLICY.
Many factors influence foreign policy. As a scholar one must consider each level when trying to explain the behavior of nation-states.

know all of their options and assign values to those options. They might lack access to information that is essential to selecting policies that result in value maximization. Thus, other factors, like a decision maker's belief system, the political structure of a state, or the distribution of power in the international system, might influence the range of choices and the eventual policy choice.

Most texts suggest that there are three levels of analysis: the **individual level of analysis**, or the human dimension, the **national level of analysis**, or domestic factors, and the **systemic level of analysis**, or the nature of the international system. A number of scholars have added a fourth level that focuses on global conditions or factors (see Table 4.3). Discussions about the importance of globalization and technological innovations like the Internet suggest that these are potentially factors that influence decisions made by national leaders.

Individual Factors, or the Human Dimension

We assume that all leaders are rational actors (i.e., always selecting a policy path that maximizes benefits and minimizes costs), but other factors like beliefs, personality factors, images, and perceptions also shape decision making.

Table 4.3 Using Levels of Analysis to Explain Foreign Policy Decisions

Level of Analysis	Explanation Types
Individual	• Bounded rationality/cybernetics • Biological explanations • Motivation/personality • Perception/images • Belief systems/information processing
National	• Power capabilities • Domestic politics: finding coalitions for policy and support for retaining power • Decision-making styles and structures: bureaucratic politics and organizational behavior • Size and resource base • Geographic factors • Political structure • Economic system • Political culture
Systemic	• Level of anarchy or order • Distribution of power • Obligations, treaties, alliances • Regimes or governing arrangements
Global	• Global social movements • Environmental conditions and challenges • Media and popular cultural forces • Decisions by transnational nonstate actors such as transnational enterprises and international NGOs • Ideas, values, and norms that transcend culture and time

Foreign policy research suggests that these other factors or filters are most important in a crisis situation, a decision requiring secrecy and thus involving few actors, or a decision demanding a quick response. This level is also important when a leader is given a great deal of latitude to make a decision and when the decision maker has an interest or expertise in foreign policy.

To act rationally, leaders must be able to know all of their options, be capable of assigning values to these options, and have enough information to select the higher valued options. Scholars who use these other idiosyncratic factors like *belief systems* or *personality types* to explain behavior do not believe any decision maker can be rational all of the time. Most decision makers operate in an environment of uncertainty with imperfect information. Many leaders talk about "going with their gut" when they are making decisions in crises, but they are usually relying on previous experience (e.g., analogical reasoning) or their worldview (e.g., realism or liberalism). Leaders filter information based on their worldviews and generally seek programs that fit with these beliefs. Former British Prime Minister Margaret Thatcher, with a strong realist belief system, convinced George H. W. Bush to take the 1990 Iraqi invasion of Kuwait seriously and respond militarily. She also decided to use force rather than diplomacy to take back the Falkland Islands after the Argentine invasion in 1982.

Domestic Factors, or National Attributes

At the domestic or national level, researchers look at a country's history, traditions, and its political, economic, cultural, and social structures. Changing elements such as military power, economic wealth, and demographic factors shape policy. More permanent elements like geographic location and resource base also matter in this set of factors.

A powerful variable in many democratic societies is domestic politics, or electoral calculations. Politicians often find that they are unable to achieve their desired goals because of the demands of the election cycle. A further complication is the role of bureaucracies in the policy process. Unelected civil servants can influence outcomes that the politicians want. Examples of this are found in the range of academic work, beginning with Graham Allison's *The Essence of Decision*. In his exploration of crisis decision making within the Kennedy administration, Allison found that **standard operating procedures (SOPs)**, or the way things are usually done in an organization, employed by governmental agencies, as well as the inherent goal of all bureaucrats to gain more power and influence in the decision-making process, are major determinants of foreign policy behavior. Large organizations employ SOPs to respond to a range of events. For instance, when a natural disaster like a hurricane or earthquake happens, agencies have plans ready to provide the correct kind of assistance. Normally, a state's agencies of all kinds—military, intelligence, foreign affairs—have SOPs ready for every foreseeable eventuality. Bureaucratic politics, Allison's third model, suggests that within every government, bureaucratic agencies compete with each other for control over resources and policy. The result of this competition is eventually the policy.

Systemic Factors

The anarchic nature of the international system might be the most important factor at this level. As we have seen in this book, however, countries take individual and collective actions to cope with the lack of global central authority. Thus treaties, alliances, and trade conventions, which states agree to abide by, are seen as systemic constraints. These are formal contracts created by states in an attempt to provide order in the system.

A country's behavior is also shaped by more informal constraints based on traditions, common goals, and shared norms. For example, most states respect the sovereignty of all states, and most follow the rule of international law. These laws cannot be enforced, but states abide by them because they expect others to do the same. This notion of **reciprocity** is the primary incentive for states to support a rule-based international system. The distribution of power in the system (e.g., bipolar, multipolar, or nonpolar) and the nature of order (e.g., balance of power, collective security) are also important system-level factors. Neorealists believe that the lack of a common power or a central government at the global level is the defining element of international relations, and a state's foreign policy is primarily aimed at survival in this anarchic system. This anarchic condition of the system is described by Kenneth Waltz (1959, 238):

> Each state pursues its own interests, however defined, in ways it judges best. Force is a means of achieving the external ends of states because there exists no consistent, reliable process of reconciling the conflicts of interest that inevitably arise among similar units in a condition of anarchy.

No good deed goes unpunished! Norway has taken the lead in trying to end conflicts in the Middle East with the Oslo Accords and in the Sri Lankan civil war. In Sri Lanka in 2009 pro-government forces demonstrate against the Norwegians for not punishing pro-Tamil demonstrators.

Liberals, on the other hand, believe that anarchy forces states to create rules and develop regimes or governing arrangements aimed at encouraging cooperation and multilateralism. Today, many liberals are focused on more effective global governance across policy areas. As the world has learned with the very recent global economic crisis, rules and regulations that govern all markets are indeed essential.

Global Factors

These are often confused with system-level factors. Simply stated, the difference is that global factors are not necessarily created by states, whereas systemic factors are. Global-level variables can be the outcome of decisions made by individuals, interest groups, states, or nonstate actors. They could also be the results of natural conditions. These factors cannot be traced to the actions of any one state or even group of states. In fact, they usually challenge the ideas of boundaries and sovereignty.

The Internet and resulting information revolution, multinational broadcasts, and revolutionary ideas all represent global factors that might shape policy behavior. The process of globalization promotes such factors. Consider, for example, what role social media played in the unrest and eventual "revolutions" in Tunisia and Egypt. Social media such as Twitter and Facebook are tools that allow opposition groups to promote participation, organize allies, recruit new followers, and train these same people.

Environmental factors such as pollution, pandemics, and weather patterns could also have a global impact on foreign policy. Conditions such as global warming and drought might lead to new alliances or to conflicts over the control of critical resources. As writers such as Peter Gleik and Michael Klare have shown, there is a very real possibility of "water wars" in the Middle East and Africa. These conditions might be the result of actions taken by specific national or transnational actors, but the effects are felt globally.

We should remember that by explaining foreign policy we might be able to predict what states would do in a given situation. Likewise, we can use previous decisions as analogues and make suggestions or prescriptions for future foreign policy.

The Foreign Policy Process

So far we have examined the explanations and influences of foreign policy, answering questions of "why" and "what for"; in this section, we get down to the nuts and bolts and look at the process of "how" foreign policy comes about.

You might be surprised to learn that the foreign policy–making apparatus of most democratic countries is basically the same. Political systems tend to divide the responsibility for decision making among members of the executive branch, which carries out the policies, and the deliberative or legislative branch, which sets spending priorities and guidelines for the executive to follow. Deliberative bodies often have a responsibility to oversee the actions of the executive branch. Both branches of government might subdivide responsibility further into geographic regions, economic sectors, or military affairs. In addition to the formal governmental actors with legal authority, there are also any number of individuals and groups outside the formal government structure that might influence the policy process. The actors that make up this informal sector vary by issue area, but they can include business groups, religious groups, news media, and private citizens.

As we suggested earlier in the chapter, even authoritarian or totalitarian states have decision-making processes in which government ministries debate issues and work with private interests to promote specific policy positions. Leaders rarely act alone and create a foreign policy that adheres specifically to their own interests. For example, military leaders and various bureaucrats within North Korea and Iran support their countries' policies of defiance directed at the United States and the international community.

Four Phases of Foreign Policy Making

The study of foreign policy making assumes that governmental officials with the legal authority to act do so in a logical manner. Political scientists call this the *rational-actor model* of foreign policy making. Proponents of this model assert that a government's foreign policy officials are able to (1) define a problem, (2) develop responses to the problem, (3) act on one or more of the responses, and then (4) evaluate the effectiveness of the policy. In the following sections, we discuss these four phases in more depth.

Phase One: Initiation or Articulation

Issues are often first articulated or otherwise promoted by media and interest groups attempting to influence the policy–making process. Information about a foreign policy issue is disseminated, and as public awareness of an issue increases, this informed public may pressure elected officials to either act on the issue or, in some cases, stay clear of the problem.

Both internal (or formal) and external (or informal) actors may push a particular position and pressure political leaders to take action. For example, in the case of the ongoing conflict and genocide in Darfur, NGOs using the Internet have been providing the public with information about the atrocities. These same NGOs have initiated further global-awareness campaigns with celebrities and notable public leaders that have attracted the attention of major media outlets and many elected officials who recognize the importance of the issue for either moral reasons or more pragmatic electoral calculations.

Individuals and research institutes (often called think tanks) can initiate a debate about a foreign policy issue. Once public awareness increases, attentive members of the public might pressure a government to act. A natural disaster or an unexpected tragedy or crisis might also inspire some official reaction from governments. For example, in general the US public is not very supportive of increasing foreign aid, but if a flood or earthquake devastates an area, US citizens generally want the government to supply emergency aid.

Technologies such as the Internet and cell phones may actually contribute to the democratization of foreign policy. Today, citizens in industrialized states have an opportunity to be better informed than ever before, and they are presented with a variety of options to become actively involved in a particular issue area. Citizen involvement also now transcends borders: Global or transnational social movements have mobilized citizens to work to end hunger, forgive debt, and end the use of certain weapons. These campaigns have been successful in their efforts to persuade governments to use official foreign policy tools to address their concerns. For example, Bono, the lead singer from the musical group U2, spent time with the late senator Jesse Helms and other members of Congress as a representative of the Jubilee movement that urged wealthy states to forgive the debts of poor states. Other celebrities have joined members of the domestic Christian Coalition to increase awareness of the issues surrounding poverty and third-world debt and to lobby both the executive branch of government and members of Congress.

Global and domestic actors also have an impact on policy makers in authoritarian or nondemocratic states. China continues to be a favorite target for human rights groups, and they have had some impact on Chinese domestic policies. Tragically, many of these NGOs have had no impact on policy makers in failed states like Zimbabwe or extremist states like Sudan, Somalia, and Libya.

Phase Two: The Formulation of Foreign Policy

The **formulation phase of policy making** involves the actual creation of an official government policy. Internal and external actors—individuals, interest groups, corporations, and foreign governments—initiate policy debates and put pressure on policy makers to act. The formulation phase is when parliaments, executive offices, ministries, and bureaucratic agencies work to develop an effective foreign policy. For example, this is the point when relevant agencies within a government discuss the idea to forgive the debt of third-world countries. The legislative branches debate the cost and benefits of forgiving debt, and specialists in various financial departments provide the essential information for the final policy position.

Specialists inside and outside of government provide the essential information for policy makers. Often, in the policy–making process, the original intention of the policy is loaded with other priorities that might help the politician get reelected or might help a bureaucracy gain more power and more resources. In noncrisis situations, foreign policy is formulated much like domestic policy. It is a complex process involving legislatures, executive agencies, ministries and departments, and a wide variety of interest communities.

In crisis situations, foreign policy is made by a smaller group of individuals and agencies. Since the end of World War I, in the United States and many other Western democracies, the executive branch or cabinet has taken over the

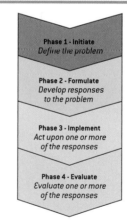

A TYPICAL DECISION-MAKING PROCESS.
What do we mean by "rational actor"? What about this model suggests rationality? Of course this graphic is a simplification. Can you draw a more complex process model, or flowchart, based on what you have read so far? What other steps or loops would your model represent?

Middle powers like Canada play an important role in humanitarian activities across the world. As leaders of the human security movement, Canada works frequently with NGOs to respond to natural disasters and long-term human crises. Here, Canadian armed forces help an NGO, *Action Against Hunger*, deliver food aid in the Philippines after the November 2013 typhoon.

foreign policy process. Foreign ministries, defense departments, and special advisors to the prime minister or president are usually charged with responding to crises. In the administration of George W. Bush, decisions about the war in Iraq were made by a group of advisors scattered in the National Security Council, the vice president's office, and the Defense Department—while the State Department was often left out or its ideas were dismissed by the president's inner circle.

Although in most democracies elected members of legislatures serve on committees with foreign policy oversight, most of these committees react to policy plans formulated by the head of government and that person's advisors. Most legislative bodies do have budget responsibilities and can use this power to support or change foreign policy priorities. However, shrewd leaders who appeal to the public for support of their foreign policy actions can neutralize the legislature's power of the purse. For example, few members of the US Congress challenged funding for military actions or aid programs for an important ally for fear of being called antimilitary or unpatriotic. Generally, when dealing in areas of foreign policy the old adage applies: "Partisanship ends at the water's edge." After 9/11, it was very easy for the Bush administration to get congressional support for any program that could be framed as part of the global war on terror. Prime Minister Blair had the same advantages after the July 2005 attacks in Britain. US presidents since the end of World War II used the Cold War and the containment of communism around the world as justifications for financing an expansionary foreign policy. Hundreds of anticommunist organizations, the defense industries, and many ethnic communities, such as Polish and Hungarian Americans, kept pressure on US leaders to never ease up on the Soviet Union.

Phase Three: Foreign Policy Implementation

Once a policy is decided in a legislature or in a department or ministry, it is usually assigned to policy actors in a ministry or department and other affiliated actors in the field. These actors are expected to implement the policy.

For example, if the US Congress passes a bill allocating funds for development assistance or foreign aid, the money is sent to the most appropriate agency, in this case, USAID, which receives the funds and distributes them to its various field offices. The money is then given to development projects that might have been organized by local governments, NGOs, and development agencies from other countries. It is not unusual for countries to form coalitions with local communities, NGOs, and other aid agencies. Funds are not always spent on intended projects, and they are often not spent at all. Corruption, project delays, new priorities, and leadership changes often get in the way of intended consequences. US agencies intending to reduce poverty in developing countries must deal with a variety of factors that might delay a program or prevent it from reaching its goals.

Phase Four: Foreign Policy Evaluation

Policy evaluation is the final step in the process, and it is rare that this step occurs. Although the review provision might be built into the program, the administrators of the policy might have a personal interest in keeping the program active. The media might focus their attention on the policy outcomes if the policy program was a success or a failure. All interested parties will have a position and will try to influence future decisions in this policy area. Often, the very public and private actors involved in the previous phases of the policy process will be involved in the evaluation of policy outcomes.

Most legislatures conduct public hearings related to major foreign policy expenditures. These hearings can become particularly important if a policy program has failed or had a major impact on a society. Consider, for instance, the Iraq Study Group's hearings on the Iraq War or congressional committee hearings on the future of NATO or US trade policy toward China. Congress tends to use every opportunity to evaluate the foreign policy activities of a particular administration. In some political systems, like the UK and Canada, the prime minister must face the parliamentary opposition during a legislative session called *question time*. This is a form of evaluation that generally attracts a great deal of public attention and comments from opposition politicians.

Another form of evaluation that usually triggers policy actions is comprehensive studies done by universities, think tanks, research institutions, and NGOs. Human Rights Watch, Greenpeace, the International Crisis Group, the International Committee of the Red Cross, and hundreds of other interest groups provide policy makers with comprehensive studies on just about every foreign policy issue area (see Chapter 5 for more on NGOs). To illustrate, in 2007 the International Committee of the Red Cross released a report on the "treatment of high value detainees" being held by the Central Intelligence Agency. This report could have a major impact on future decisions about how to treat individuals taken prisoner in the war on terrorism.

Foreign Policy Styles and Traditions

Now that we have considered the many moving parts of foreign policy, let's take a step back and consider the bigger picture, how it all works together—that is, the various styles and traditions of foreign policy, as well as the various ways in which great powers, middle powers, and weak states might differ in their approaches.

Analysts of foreign policy behavior often assert that factors such as the geographic size of a country, its resource base, and its population can determine the kind of foreign policy—or style—that a country will undertake. A **foreign policy style** is often the result of the ways in which the country deals with other

THEORY IN PRACTICE

China, the United States, and Korea: When Great Powers' Interests Collide

The Challenge

International relations specialists often use the language of physics to describe or explain the behaviors of states. This is useful for heuristic purposes and because it helps us also to predict future actions. However, as the case of China, the United States, and Korea seems to tell us, we should always remember that prophecy is definitely not a science.

Options

China and the United States first clashed in the Korean Peninsula in the early 1950s during the Korean conflict. When that war ended in a stalemate in 1953, each outside power continued to support its wartime allies, supplying military aid and economic development assistance. Although the last Chinese troops left the Democratic People's Republic of Korea (DPRK) not long after the armistice that ended the fighting, the United States continues to this day to station troops and military hardware in the Republic of Korea (ROK), as the southern portion of the peninsula is called.

Application

Over the past fifty years, China and the United States have behaved as physics might predict: Each has sought to maintain the power balance, not letting its ally (some might say "client state") do too much to upset that balance. From the US perspective, this has meant encouraging South Korean restraint in the

US Vice President Joe Biden spoke in South Korea about the US rejection of China's self-declared "air defense identification zone" in the East China Sea. Biden reaffirmed the US commitment to allies like South Korea, Japan, and Taiwan. These countries and others in the region will likely come into conflict with China over this expanded air defense identification zone. China reserves the right to deny access to any aircraft.

face of frequent provocations by the DPRK, which have included assassinations of ROK diplomats; raids across the demilitarized zone that divides the peninsula; the seizure of the *Pueblo*, a US Navy intelligence-gathering ship; the development of a nuclear-weapons program; and a guiding doctrine that promises reunification of the country by force.

How does China perceive the situation? The realist school of thought gives us one way to analyze the confrontation. In this case China, a rising economic and military power, does not like to have its status challenged in what it contends is its own regional sphere of influence. This pattern

began in October 1950, when Chinese "volunteers"—eventually over a million soldiers—offered their services to the DPRK in its struggle with the "capitalist forces" led by the United States. With each event that the United States and the ROK called a "provocation," the Chinese government publically supported its own Korean ally. It could be that privately the Chinese leaders urged North Korean restraint, but the world press only saw a united front.

As noted earlier, prophecy is an inexact science. Still, it was a safe bet to say that China would take the side of North Korea after a South Korean warship, *Cheonan*, sank in

Continued

disputed waters on March 26, 2010, killing nearly half of the ship's company. A subsequent investigation of the ship revealed that it was the victim of a torpedo attack, most likely of a kind that DPRK submarines carry. North Korea denied any responsibility and demanded the right to examine the salvaged ship.

Throughout that spring and into summer 2010, South Korea and the United States conducted joint military exercises, some in the very spot where *Cheonan* sank. Chinese government officials and press reports denounced these activities as provocative and promised to conduct their own joint maneuvers with North Korea. Chinese foreign ministry personnel also stepped up their criticism of the United States for supporting Taiwan and for open talks with Vietnam over nuclear energy technology. China has a long history of interactions with both states and justifiably sees both as being in China's regional sphere of interest.

What if a country from outside the region began to exert its military influence in waters near South or Central America? How would the US government react? This is a frequent theme in Chinese government statements and press commentary essays: China sees itself as a country that now has a global set of interests and has a legitimate right to be heard. And what happens if another world power, perhaps the United States, denies that right? Some international relations theories might refer us to the Peloponnesian War and Thucydides' account of the reasons for that war. However, the past is often a bad mirror for seeing the present. As for prophecy—well, we will just have to wait to see what unfolds in the Korean Peninsula.

For Discussion

1. How would you use levels of analysis to explain North Korea's actions and the United States and China's response?

2. Analysts of the DPRK government often describe the leaders as "unpredictable." Does this characterization undercut the precise language of international relations as physics? Why?

3. What policy recommendations would you make to US leaders to resolve DPRK–ROK tensions?

members of the international community. When this style continues over a long period of time, we call it a **foreign policy tradition**. Both the foreign policy style and the tradition include a common set of public assumptions about the role of the state in the international system. A tradition includes national beliefs about how the world works and what leaders must do to secure their national interests. Styles and traditions promote different foreign policy strategies, and each suggests different sets of policy priorities. In this section we discuss some aspects of foreign policy style and foreign policy tradition.

Great Powers, Middle Powers, and Small States

The foreign policy of all states is aimed at securing national interests and responding to the needs, values, and interests of their citizens. All states seek a role, or *niche*, in the international system. James Rosenau (1981) suggested that all states develop a strategy for adapting to the conditions created by the international system. Smaller states with limited resources and little capacity to influence other powers by unilateral actions are likely to select an **acquiescent strategy**. This strategy suggests they will adapt their interests to fit with the interests of larger and more powerful regional or global leaders.

Consider, for example, the role of "client states" and alliances during the Cold War. These states followed the lead of the United States or the USSR and

A UN resolution sponsored by the French government authorized an increase in French and African Union troops attempting to prevent further violence between Christian and Muslim groups in the Central African Republic. The entire population is suffering from the violence. Fragile or failed states may present the biggest foreign policy challenges for global institutions like the UN and for the major powers.

were rewarded with the promise of security and prosperity in the form of aid, military assistance, and trade agreements. Those states that were once global leaders and even hegemonic powers at times seek policies aimed at preserving their power and status in the international system. This **preservative strategy** is employed by countries like the UK and France. Preservative policies include taking a leadership role in international and regional organizations, identifying issues that need attention, and taking the lead in responding to these challenges. The UK's efforts to lead the debt-relief campaign and France's role in the Middle East peace talks are examples of this behavior.

The most powerful states seek to retain and possibly increase their power and authority by adopting a **promotive foreign policy**. The United States and the Soviet Union promoted their views, values, and interests after World War II as they competed for the hearts and minds of all citizens around the globe. Each superpower created an alliance structure that divided the world into two armed camps with the capacity to destroy the world as we know it. After the Cold War, the US leaders talked about establishing a new world order that served the interests of the United States and its allies. Some experts talked about the unipolar moment, a time when the United States could promote its values, traditions, and interests to create a peaceful and prosperous world.

There are always states that believe that the existing international system is unfair, oppressive, violent, and alienating. These states seek to transform the international system by promoting an **intransigent foreign policy**. These states do not accept the "rules of the game," and they mobilize their resources to challenge the great powers in the international system. During the 1960s and 1970s, leaders of the Nonaligned Movement—namely, Cuba, Pakistan, India, and Indonesia—pushed intransigent policy programs challenging the dominant rules of the game. Today, North Korea and Iran are challenging great-power rules, namely, the rules that restrict the number of states with nuclear weapons.

To a certain extent, these four **adaptation strategies** describe the foreign policies of states today. The assertion that the choice of strategy is linked to a given country's size or influence has been, at times, the center of significant debate among academics. Although it is clear that countries choose a foreign policy strategy because of their resources and needs, it is not always the case that size determines a particular policy option. A brief overview of what we might expect from great, middle, and small powers follows. States are constantly adapting to changes in the international system and to the domestic factors that might limit a state's ability to act in the system or, conversely, provide opportunities for more active participation.

Great-Power Foreign Policy

Most of the research about **great power** politics and foreign policy is shaped by traditional realist assumptions about world politics and as a result tends to ignore cases that contradict the academic goal of a parsimonious theory. It is also, as we learned in Chapter 3, an arguably bleak perspective, because it sees enemies everywhere. For example, John Mearsheimer (2001, 29–32), an influential realist scholar, contends that great powers always seek to maximize their share of world power and all great powers seek hegemony in the international system.

When President Barack Obama addressed the UN General Assembly in New York in 2009, he spoke of a world in which states had eliminated the threat nuclear weapons pose to world peace. Has what you learned in this chapter convinced you that this is likely or unlikely? Why?

For all great powers, survival is the primary goal. These states all think strategically about how to survive in a system in which all states are potential threats. More specifically, the goals of great powers include advancing the economic and political interests of their people and maintaining the rules and institutions in the international system that serve their interests. The United States and its allies created the primary institutions of global governance after World War II. The only significant challenge to that system was advanced by the Soviet Union. Some have called the Cold War a war about whose rule book would be followed. With the end of the Cold War, there is now only one rule book, and the current battle is over which rules to apply and how to apply them. Those countries invited to the G-8 and G-20 meetings are all great global powers and great regional powers. They are meeting to debate about the best way to respond to the current economic crisis, and what they decide will affect the entire world.

Mistrust and uncertainty force states to act always in accordance with their own self-interest. Mearsheimer (2001, 33) suggests that great powers act "selfishly in a self-help world." This means the foreign policies of great powers are focused on gaining power and authority in the military world and beyond. Great powers seek to lead in all policy sectors. The dominant currency is military power, and all great powers must respond to the **security dilemma**. Without any form of central authority in the international system, states must seek security through military power and security alliances. Because all states are potential threats, foreign policy for great powers might be described as a "ceaseless competition" for security, power, and authority in all policy sectors.

Middle-Power Foreign Policy

Relying again on realist assumptions and definitions, a scholar might focus on national attributes such as land area, resource base, population, and military capabilities to distinguish **middle powers** from small or weak states and great powers. However, in a world where power and influence are no longer solely defined in terms of physical attributes and military strength, a state's behavior or experience in various policy situations might provide better insights into how that state sees itself and how others see its role in the international system. Most middle powers are liberal states with social democratic political systems and economies based on trade. This means their survival and prosperity depend on global stability and order. These states seek incremental reform by extending a liberal world order, which they see as the most effective way to achieve both human and national security. Canada, Australia, and the Nordic countries are great examples of active middle powers.

In describing the importance of a "behavioral" measure of middle powers, Cooper, Higgott, and Nossal (1993) describe their attributes as follows:

A. *Catalysts*: States that provide resources and expertise to take leadership roles in global initiatives.

B. *Facilitators*: States that play active roles in setting agendas in global policy discussions and building coalitions for collaborative responses.

C. *Managers*: Middle powers that support institution building at the international level and encourage support for existing international organizations and multinational activities.

The same authors quote Gareth Evans, a former Australian minister for foreign affairs and trade, in describing a concept called **niche diplomacy**. This form of middle-power activism "involves concentrating resources in specific areas best able to generate returns worth having, rather than trying to cover the field" (Cooper et al. 1993, 25–26).

The middle powers, because of their position and past roles in international affairs, have very distinctive interests in the future order. Middle powers are activists in international and regional forums, and they are confirmed multilateralists in most issue areas. They actively support an equitable and pluralistic rule-based system. They are, for the most part, trading states and thus favor a relatively open and stable world market. Because stability is so important to them, most middle powers see themselves as global problem solvers, mediators, and moderators in international disputes (Holbraad 1984; Wood 1998). Middle powers usually play a leadership role in regional organizations (e.g., the EU) and in functionally specific institutions such as the World Health Organization and the Development Assistance Committee of the OECD.

A third view of middle powers places an emphasis on the **normative orientation** of this group of states. Although subject to much criticism, the image of middle powers as potentially more wise and virtuous than other states is usually promoted by national leaders and progressive interest groups to gain domestic support for international activism and to enhance the reputation of their states in the international community. This image of global

Bilateral and multilateral diplomacy is a critical aspect of foreign policy in this complex world. EU High Representative Catherine Ashton played a key role in negotiations with Iran's foreign minister, Mohammad Javad Zarif. The negotiations also involved the United States, China, France, Britain, Russia, and Germany. The final agreement reached in November 2013 was a foreign policy achievement for the EU.

moral leaders, bridging the gap between rich and poor communities, fits well with the egalitarian social democratic values of most Western middle powers. Robert Cox (1989, 834–835) argues that the traditional normative aims of middle powers, namely, greater social equity and more diffusion of power in the system, might give them more leverage as principled problem solvers in continuing economic and political challenges faced by all states in the system today.

The middle powers could play a critical role as the catalysts of problem-solving initiatives or the managers of regimes initiated by greater powers with less interest for internationalism and little domestic support for egalitarian goals and values.

Small-State Foreign Policy

Researchers agree that small states are defined by a small land mass, gross national product, and population. In addition, they usually do not have large military forces or the resources to have a significant impact on global politics. However, if they act in concert with other states, it is possible for small states to have an impact on the system. For example, the like-minded states that played a pivotal role in the formation of the International Criminal Court included a coalition of small and middle powers.

Small states can also identify a niche and develop expertise in a given policy area. Most wealthy small states, like Belgium and New Zealand, often focus their foreign policy on trade and economic issues. They will also participate in regional organizations and at times take leadership roles in crisis situations. New Zealand, along with Australia and the island state of Vanuatu, took the lead to create a nuclear-free zone in the Pacific in 1985. The Reagan administration's response to this action demonstrates the limits to small-state actions: When the New Zealand Labour government banned nuclear-capable US Navy ships from its harbors, the United States terminated security cooperation with the country. Belgium is one of the most active members of the EU, NATO, and every other regional and international organization. Because of its colonial past, it has worked with many African states in development and peacekeeping activities.

It should be stated that with the end of the Cold War and the intensity of forces of globalization there has been a change in the valuation of states' capacities and their potential influence in the international system. After all, military power might not be as important as policy expertise or technology in this new world where new security challenges include climate change, pandemics, poverty, and cyberwarfare. Foreign policy in a nonpolar world is less constrained by the structure of the system and allows for more flexibility and independence. Globalization has also increased the number of opportunities for citizen participation, and technology like the Internet makes it much easier to organize for a specific cause or policy position and to promote a small state's national interest in the global community.

Some small states have taken on the role of norm entrepreneurs in the international system. Christine Ingebritsen and colleagues (2006, 275) describe this role:

> Thus, Scandinavia, a group of militarily weak, economically dependent small states, pursues "social power" by acting as a norm entrepreneur in the international community. In three policy areas (the environment, international security, and global welfare), Scandinavia has acted to promote a particular view of the good society.

Other attributes of small-state foreign policy include the following (Henderson, Jackson, and Kennaway 1980, 3–5):

- Most small states have limited financial and human resources and thus have to decide carefully when and where to participate. Generally, this means a limited global role and a focus on their geographic region and the interests of their own citizens.
- With limited resources (their citizens), most small states focus on economic and trade issues.
- Small states generally take an active role in regional and international organizations. Multilateralism is a preferred strategy, and small states consider it the best way to secure their interests.
- Small states can play critical roles in alliances and in global policy regimes. Many of these states have resources and expertise, and they seek roles as global problem solvers in policy areas of importance to their domestic population.

As the space between domestic and foreign policy sectors blurs or even disappears, domestic politics and the interests of citizens play a greater role in shaping foreign policy. In both small and middle powers, what citizens expect from states at home has a significant influence on how these states behave internationally.

Conclusion

In this chapter we provided an overview of the primary issues and actors in the foreign policy process. We saw that many variables shape the world of diplomacy in the contemporary international system: material needs, ideas, and people themselves. The rational-actor model offers one way to understand the policy-making process. We also learned about different styles and traditions in foreign policy. In the following chapters we turn to specific topics that comprise the critical challenges in the international system; for example, we will see how globalization is undermining the autonomy of the nation-state. International and regional organizations like the UN and the EU, NGOs, and MNCs are all gaining power and influence in some of the core policy areas that were once the sole responsibility of nation-states. This trend is an important factor shaping relations in the contemporary world that we examine in depth in the next chapters.

Engaging with the

The Otesha Project

The Otesha Project organizes bike tours in Canada and the UK, educating young people about the environmental dangers of our global consumer society. These bike tours last two months, and the participants stop in small towns and cities, visiting schools and community organizations where they educate people about the environment and about our responsibility to protect it. Otesha is a word in Swahili that means *reason to dream*! Visit the Otesha Project at http://www.otesha.ca/.

KEY TERMS

Acquiescent strategy, p. 135
Adaptation strategies, p. 137
Coercive diplomacy, p. 123
Diplomacy, p. 122
Economic sanctions, p. 119
Foreign policy, p. 110
Foreign policy style, p. 133
Foreign policy tradition, p. 135
Formulation phase of policy making, p. 131
Great power, p. 137

Hard power, p. 123
Ideational interests, p. 112
Individual level of analysis, p. 126
Intransigent foreign policy, p. 136
Material interests, p. 112
Middle powers, p. 138
National interests, p. 114
National level of analysis, p. 126
Niche diplomacy, p. 139
Nonpolar world, p. 124
Normative orientation, p. 139

Preservative strategy, p. 136
Promotive foreign policy, p. 136
Public diplomacy, p. 123
Reciprocity, p. 128
Security dilemma, p. 138
Soft power, p. 123
Standard operating procedures (SOPs), p. 127
Statecraft, p. 111
Systemic level of analysis, p. 126

REVIEW QUESTIONS

1. What are the ways in which personal characteristics can affect outcomes in the rational-actor model?

2. What are the four levels of analysis? How are they used to explain the behavior of states?

3. How do bureaucracies influence the foreign policy process?

4. Do "small states" have any power and influence in the international system?

5. "Contemporary globalization erodes nation-state sovereignty but does *not* undermine nationalism." Discuss.

6. Who are the actors in creating foreign policy? What are the phases?

7. What is a foreign policy doctrine?

8. Do you think the foreign policy process is shifting away from the state?

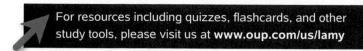

For resources including quizzes, flashcards, and other study tools, please visit us at **www.oup.com/us/lamy**

THINKING ABOUT GLOBAL POLITICS

Designing a New World Order

BACKGROUND

The significant changes in the political and economic landscape in Europe and the former Soviet Union, the unprecedented collective response to Iraqi aggression in Kuwait, and the puzzling failure of the major powers to respond effectively to aggression in Somalia, Rwanda, and the former Yugoslavia suggest that it might be time for the rule-making actors in the international system to establish a new set of standards and rules of behavior in *a new world order.* This new system of explicit and implicit rules and structures will replace the East–West Cold War "bipolarity," or the "balance of nuclear terror." Many leaders, including former presidents the first Bush and Clinton, have frequently invoked the concept of "new world order" as a justification for foreign policy decisions. However, there does not seem to be any consensus in the United States or in other nation-states about the structure of this new world order. Some world leaders have called for a series of discussions about the future of world politics in an effort to prevent US hegemony and avoid drifting toward a new era of competition and anarchy. They want to know their role in this new system. Who will be the new rule makers? How will order be maintained? What are the rules? What are the new security challenges? These are some of the questions leaders are asking.

EXPECTATIONS

In this small-group discussion exercise, you will explore various world-order models, review how changes in the structure of the system might influence or shape foreign policies of states, and then make a case for a new US global strategy and a new world order.

PROCEDURE

1. Review the options presented in the "World-Order Models" section that follows. You might want to review historical periods when these systems were in operation (not all systems of order presented here have been implemented).

2. With reference to a traditional realist's three system-level challenges and constraints—order, anarchy, and the security dilemma—which world-order system would you find most effective for US interests? What about the interests of other major powers (e.g., Japan, Germany, Russia, and Great Britain)? What about the concerns of developing states or the South?

3. Discuss the nature of foreign policy under each system structure. For example, how would the foreign policy of major, middle, and small powers be influenced if the system moved from bipolarity to hegemony? Review each possible system structure and its influence on foreign policy.

WORLD-ORDER MODELS

One-country rule: One country governs the rest of the world, controlling all resources, industry, and trade. The superpower determines the national interest of all other nations and the interest of the world—all are defined in terms of the superpower's interests.

Bipolar: Two superpowers have divided the world. Each controls a large group of countries and controls the resources, industry, and trade within its bloc. Relations between the two blocs are determined by the superpowers to serve their own interests.

Polycentrism: Each country has its own government and controls its own resources, industry, and trade. There are no international organizations or alliances—every country operates in its own interest.

Continued

Regionalism: Countries located in the same part of the world have formed regional governments that control resources, industry, and trade within each region. Relations between regions are governed by regional interests.

World law: All nations of the world have established a world authority that makes laws against international violence and has agencies to enforce these laws, keep the peace, and resolve conflicts. Individual nations control their own resources, industry, internal security, and trade. The world authority acts only to prevent the use of violence in relations between nations.

Some other order: Draw your own model of an international system. Specify how international relations, trade, and security are handled in your model. Why is your model better than any of the other models?

DISCUSSION AND FOLLOW-UP

If time permits, in small groups, discuss what you think will be the major issues facing the world's leaders in the next ten years. Then try to reach consensus on a system structure (i.e., world-order model) that you feel will create an international environment that will enable states to constructively and effectively respond to these issues.

CONTRIBUTORS TO CHAPTER 4: *Steven L. Lamy and John Masker.*

Only in a universal union of states can the property and rights of states become settled and a true state of peace come into being.

—*Immanuel Kant*

This is an ungoverned world. The UN has no autonomous power; it is what its members want it to be, and usually its members don't want it to be anything much . . . When it is said that it is better if things are done multilaterally, too often this means accepting the lowest common denominator.

—*Stanley Hoffmann*

Peace was the final prize Alfred Nobel mentioned in his will, which established five Nobel Prizes. The first peace prize went to two people: Henry Dunant, who founded the International Committee of the Red Cross, and Frederic Passy, a leading pacifist, in 1901. Clearly, the Nobel committee was signaling to the world that transnational organizations like the Red Cross might provide the way forward in meeting humanitarian challenges, whether natural disasters or human-made crises.

In 2012, the committee awarded the peace prize to the EU. It credited the EU with contributing to Franco-German reconciliation; promoting and then supporting the transition from dictatorship to democracy in Portugal, Spain, and Greece in the 1970s; and contributing to the political transformation and economic prosperity of the countries that were once part of the Soviet bloc.

The EU is currently struggling with an economic crisis, and austerity programs in both Greece and Spain have led to unrest. The selection committee nevertheless urged the members of the EU and its supporters across the world to not forget its sixty years of success. Further, the prize committee warned the EU leadership to not allow this model for creating a multilateral community to disintegrate

In 2012, the EU received the Nobel Peace Prize under European Commission president Jose Manuel Barroso for promoting peace in Europe and as a global actor around the world. What kind of worldview do you think the leaders of the EU have?

because its existence guards against the rise of extreme nationalism in Europe. One way to peace is to support more regional cooperation and the building of regional institutions such as this. As far back as 1971, Professor Joseph Nye called this process *peace in parts* as he imagined a world of European Unions linked together to promote the rule of law and encourage **multilateralism** and cooperation.

Introduction

Leaders in all countries face the challenge of managing the processes of globalization. States seek to create international institutions and laws that enable them to secure their national interests in a more globalized society. **Global governance** describes the formal and informal processes and institutions that guide and control the activities of both state and nonstate actors in the international system; global governance does not mean the creation of a world government. After all, this governance is not always led by states, nor is it always led by international organizations that are created by states.

Indeed, multinational corporations and even NGOs create rules and regulations to govern behavior in some policy areas. For example, banks will set up informal rules for exchanging currencies, and NGOs have set up ethical rules for fundraising and intervention in crisis regions. As demonstrated by the work of Elinor Ostrom, 2009 Nobel Prize winner in economics, sometimes private, nongovernmental groups can do a better job of creating rules for governing a shared resource. In this case the state is the primary actor but not the only one in global governance.

In this complex and increasingly global system, states are working with international and regional organizations like the UN and the EU and **nonstate actors** like Oxfam, Save the Children, and Amnesty International through diplomacy, international law, and regimes or international governing arrangements to solve common regional and global problems. Cary Coglianese (2000, 299–301) suggests that international organizations and international law are critical in responding to three types of problems:

1. Coordinating global linkages: In this area, rules and laws are critical for managing the exchanges of information, products, services, money, and finance and even for managing collective responses to criminal activity.

2. Responding to common problems: The global community faces common problems like global warming, poverty, human rights abuses, refugees, and pandemics, all of which require some form of coordination and collective policy response.

3. Protecting core values: Institutions and laws are essential for protecting and promoting core values like equality, liberty, democracy, and justice across the world.

LEARNING OBJECTIVES

After reading and discussing this chapter, you should be able to:

Identify the principal organs of the UN.

Explain key differences between the League of Nations and the UN.

Discuss the evolution of UN peacekeeping operations since 1950.

Explain the arguments for reforming the UN organs and operations.

Describe the development of the EU and its integration process.

Give examples of how various types of nongovernmental actors influence global politics.

The problems listed here and others increase with globalization. States will undoubtedly become more dependent on international and regional institutions like the UN or the African Union to promote international and regional cooperation in these critical areas. The global system has institutions capable of coordinating responses to global crises, but successful responses depend on voluntary compliance by both state and nonstate actors. If global actors consider the laws, regimes, and institutions to be fair and legitimate, they will be more likely to comply. Here we mean international laws, or the body of legal standards, procedures, and institutions that govern the interactions of sovereign states. A **regime** is a governing arrangement that guides states as well as transnational actors and institutions (described in detail in the next section); it is a set of rules, norms, and practices that shape behavior of all actors in a given issue area. **International law** is an international institution.

Regionalism has become a pervasive feature of international affairs. According to the World Trade Organization (WTO), by July 2005 only one WTO member—Mongolia—was not party to any regional trade agreement, and a total of 489 such agreements had been ratified. Regional peacekeeping forces have become active in some parts of the world. Regionalism has in the past decades become one of the forces challenging the traditional centrality of states in international relations.

That challenge comes from two directions. The word *region* and its derivatives denote one distinguishable part of some larger geographical area. Yet they are used in different ways. On the one hand, regions are territories within

The UN General Assembly has seen memorable speeches from world leaders. How well has the international organization translated rhetorical flourishes into concrete programs?

a state, occasionally crossing state borders. On the other, regions are particular areas of the world, covering a number of different sovereign states. We focus on this latter description of regionalism in our discussion.

In this chapter, we discuss four linked topics:

- First we introduce the basics of international law that provide a framework for the interactions of states, international and regional actors, and nonstate actors in global politics.
- Next we turn to the UN, the largest international organization with a mandate to prevent future world wars and protect human rights.
- We then discuss the concept of regional integration, with a focus on the EU, the most successful and comprehensive regional organization.
- In the final section we explore the wide variety of nonstate actors and the increasingly important role these actors are playing in global politics.

International Law

In this section we consider the practice of modern international law and the debates surrounding its nature and efficacy. For our purposes, there is one central question: What is the relationship between international law and international politics? If the power and interests of states are what matters, as we discussed in Chapter 4, then international law is either a servant of the powerful or an irrelevant curiosity. And yet—if international law does *not* matter, then why do states and other actors devote so much effort to negotiating new legal regimes and augmenting existing ones? Why does so much international debate revolve around the legality of state behavior, the applicability of legal rules, and the legal obligations incumbent on states? And why is compliance with international law so high, even by domestic standards?

Our starting point, therefore, should be made clear: International law is best understood as a core international institution—a set of norms, rules, and practices created by states and other actors to facilitate diverse social goals, from order and coexistence to justice and human development. It is an institution with distinctive historical roots, and understanding these roots is essential to grasping its unique institutional features.

International Order and Institutions

Realists portray international relations as a struggle for power, a realm in which states are "continuously preparing for, actively involved in, or recovering from organized violence in the form of war" (Morgenthau 1985, 52). Although war has certainly been a recurrent feature of international life, it is a crude and deeply dysfunctional way for states to ensure their security or realize their interests. Because of this, states have devoted as much, if not more, effort to liberating themselves from the condition of war than to embroiling themselves in violent conflict. Creating some modicum of international order has been an abiding common interest of most states most of the time (Bull 1977, 8).

To achieve international order, states have created international institutions. People often confuse institutions and organizations, incorrectly using the two terms interchangeably. **International institutions** are commonly defined as complexes of norms, rules, and practices that "prescribe behavioral roles, constrain activity, and shape expectations" (Keohane 1989a, 3). **International organizations**, like the UN, are physical entities that have staffs, head offices, and letterheads. International institutions can exist without any organizational structure—the 1997 Ottawa Convention banning landmines is an institution, but there is no head office. Many institutions have organizational dimensions, however. The WTO (formerly the General Agreement on Tariffs and Trade) is an institution with a very strong organizational structure. Whereas institutions can exist without an organizational dimension, international organizations cannot exist without an institutional framework. Their very existence presupposes a set of norms, rules, and principles that empower them to act and that they are charged to uphold. If states had never negotiated the Charter of the UN, the organization could not exist, let alone function.

In modern international society, states have created three levels of institutions:

• There are deep constitutional institutions, such as the principle of sovereignty, which define the terms of legitimate statehood.

• States have also created fundamental institutions, like international law and multilateralism, which provide the basic rules and practices that shape how states solve cooperation and coordination problems. These are the institutional norms, techniques, and structures that states and other actors invoke and employ when they have common ends they want to achieve or clashing interests they want to contain.

• Last, states have developed issue-specific institutions or regimes, such as the Treaty on the Nonproliferation of Nuclear Weapons, which enact fundamental institutional practices in particular realms of interstate relations. The treaty is a concrete expression of the practices of international law and multilateralism in the field of arms control.

We are concerned here with the middle-level, fundamental institutions. These are "the elementary rules of practice that states formulate to solve the coordination and collaboration problems associated with coexistence under anarchy" (Reus-Smit 1999, 14). In modern international society, a range of such institutions exist, including international law, multilateralism, bilateralism, diplomacy, and management by the great powers. Since the middle of the nineteenth century, however, the first two (international law and multilateralism) have provided the basic framework for international cooperation and the pursuit of order.

How do states develop international law? Why do states follow international law if there is no international government to enforce these laws? Why is international law not given a higher priority in the study of international relations? These are important questions that might help us understand the development of international law as an international institution.

The principal mechanism modern states employ to legislate international law is **multilateral diplomacy**, which is commonly defined as cooperation among three or more states based on, or with a view to formulating, reciprocally binding rules of conduct. It is a norm of the modern international legal system that states are obliged to observe legal rules because they have consented to those rules. A state that has not consented to the rules of a particular legal treaty is not bound by those rules. The only exception to this concerns rules of customary international law, and even then, implied or tacit consent plays an important role in the determination of which rules have customary status.

With the world trapped in a seemingly endless economic crisis, French lawyer and financial expert Christine Lagarde took over as Managing Director of the International Monetary Fund in 2011. How important are global institutions as we search for solutions to this crisis?

In many historical periods, and in many social and cultural settings, the political and legal realms have been entwined. For instance, the absolutist conception of sovereignty bound the two realms together in the figure of the sovereign. In the modern era, by contrast, the political and legal realms are thought to be radically different, with their own logics and institutional settings. Domestically, this view informs ideas about the constitutional separation of powers; internationally, it has encouraged the view that international politics and law are separate spheres of social action. This has not only affected how the academic disciplines of international relations and law have evolved, but also how state practice has evolved.

Realists generally believe that international law should serve the interests of the powerful states. This perspective has led to criticisms of international law and of international organizations like the UN, which protects the interests of major powers by focusing decision-making power in the Security Council. As we discuss, some non-Western states argue that many of these laws do not account for their interests, traditions, and values.

Criticisms of International Law

From one perspective, international law is easily cast as a Western, even imperial, institution. As we have seen, its roots lie in the European intellectual movements of the sixteenth and seventeenth centuries. Ideas propagated at that time drew a clear distinction between international laws that were appropriate among Christian peoples and those that should govern how Christians related to peoples in the Muslim world, the Americas, and, later, Asia. The former were based on assumptions of the inherent equality of Christian peoples and the latter on the inherent superiority of Christians over non-Christians.

Further evidence of this Western bias can be found in the "standard of civilization" that European powers codified in international law during the nineteenth century (Gong 1984). According to this standard, non-Western polities were granted sovereign recognition only if they exhibited certain domestic political characteristics and only if they were willing and able to participate in the prevailing diplomatic practices. The standard was heavily biased toward Western political and legal institutions as the accepted model. On the basis of the standard, European powers divided the world's peoples into "civilized," "barbarian," and "savage" societies, a division they used to justify various degrees of Western authority.

Many claim that Western bias still characterizes the international legal order. Critics point to the Anglo-European dominance of major legal institutions, most notably the UN Security Council, and international human rights law, which they argue imposes a set of Western values about the rights of the individual on non-Western societies where such ideas are alien. According to this argument, Western powers use their privileged position on the Security Council to intervene in the domestic politics of weak, developing countries.

There is truth in these criticisms. However, the nature and role of international law in contemporary world politics are more complex than they first appear. To begin with, at the heart of the modern international legal system lies a set of customary norms that uphold the legal equality of all sovereign states, as well as their rights to self-determination and nonintervention. Non-Western states have been the most vigorous proponents and defenders of these cardinal legal norms. Second, non-Western peoples were more centrally involved in the development of the international human rights regime than is commonly acknowledged. The Universal Declaration of Human Rights (1948) was the product of a deliberate and systematic process of intercultural dialogue, a dialogue involving representatives of all of the world's major cultures (Glendon 2002). The International Covenant on Civil and Political Rights (1966), which is often portrayed as a reflection of Western values, was shaped in critical ways by newly independent postcolonial states (Reus-Smit 2001). What's more, international human rights law has been an important resource in the struggles of many subject peoples against repressive governments and against institutions such as colonialism.

From International to Supranational Law?

So long as international law was designed primarily to facilitate international order—to protect the negative liberties (i.e., freedom from outside interference) of sovereign states—it remained a limited, if essential, institution. In recent decades, however, states have sought to move beyond the simple pursuit of international order, toward the objective of global governance, and international law has begun to change in fascinating ways.

First, although states are "still at the heart of the international legal system" (Higgins 1994, 39), individuals, groups, and organizations are increasingly recognized as subjects of international law. An expansive body of international human rights law has developed, supported by evolving mechanisms of enforcement. Examples of enforcement include the war crimes tribunals (discussed later in this chapter) for Rwanda and the former Yugoslavia, the creation of a new International Criminal Court (ICC), and the fourteen cases the ICC is pursuing against war criminals such as the leaders of the Lord's Resistance Army.

Second, nonstate actors are also becoming important *agents* in the international legal process. Although such actors cannot formally enact international law, and their practices do not contribute to the development of customary international law, they often play a crucial role in the following:

- Shaping the normative environment in which states codify specific legal rules.
- Providing information to national governments that encourages the redefinition of state interests and the convergence of policies across states.
- Drafting international treaties and conventions (the first of which was the 1864 Geneva Convention, drafted by the International Committee of the Red Cross; Finnemore 1996).

Third, the rules, norms, and principles of international law are no longer confined to maintaining international order, narrowly defined. Recent decisions by the UN Security Council have treated gross violations of human rights by sovereign states as threats to global peace and security, thus legitimating action under Chapter VII of the UN Charter. (Examples include the international intervention in East Timor in 1999 and, more recently, the authorization of measures to protect civilians in Libya in 2011.) In doing so, the Security Council implies that international order is dependent on the maintenance of at least minimum standards of global justice.

Because of these changes, international law might be gradually transforming into a system of supranational law. States are no longer the only subjects and agents of international law, and it has expanded into global regulation, with a scope encompassing issues of justice as well as order.

This desire to promote a rule-based global society that would protect human rights and prevent war led world leaders to create the UN in 1945. We now take a step back in time and turn to a discussion of this important international institution.

The United Nations

The **United Nations** has the unique status of being the largest international organization, or what some call a **supranational global organization**, and the only one that has a universal focus. Other supranational organizations with more specific responsibilities include the World Bank, the IMF, and the WTO. The states that make up the UN created a group of international institutions, which include the central system located in New York; the Specialized Agencies, such as the WHO and the International Labor Organization; and the Programmes and Funds, such as the United Nations Children's Fund (UNICEF) and the United Nations Development Programme. When created more than half a century ago in the aftermath of World War II, the UN reflected the hope for a just and peaceful global community.

The UN is the only global institution with legitimacy that derives from universal membership and a mandate that encompasses security, economic and social development, and, more specifically, the protection of human rights and the environment. Yet the UN was created by states for states, and questions about the meaning of **state sovereignty** and the limits of UN action remain key issues.

Since the founding of the UN, its activities have expanded to address conditions within states, and it has improved its capacity in economic and social work. Threats to global security addressed by the UN now include interstate conflict and threats by nonstate actors, as well as political, economic, and

San Francisco was the scene of the signing of the Charter of the UN in 1945. Has the time come to revise the document and reform the UN?

social conditions within states. In 2005, the UN established the **Responsibility to Protect Resolution (R2P)**, asserting the moral obligation for states to intervene in other states that violate human rights.

Despite the expanding scope of UN activities, however, there are some questions about the relevance and effectiveness of the UN. The failure of the United States and the UK to get clear UN Security Council authorization for the war in Iraq in 2003 led to well-publicized criticism of the UN and a crisis in international relations. Yet the troubled aftermath of the invasion and persistent questions about the legitimacy of a war that was not sanctioned by the UN show that the UN has acquired important moral status in international society.

After describing the history and main organs of the UN, this section looks at the changing role of the UN in addressing matters of peace and security and then matters of economic and social development. We also focus on how the UN's role has evolved in response to changes in the global political context and on some of the problems that it still faces.

A Brief History of the UN and Its Principal Organs

The UN was established on October 24, 1945, by fifty-one countries as a result of initiatives taken by the governments of the states that had led the war against Italy, Germany, and Japan. As early as 1939, American and British diplomats were discussing the need for a more effective international organization like the UN. It was intended to be a **collective security** organization, an arrangement where "each state in the system accepts that the security of one is the concern of all, and agrees to join in a collective response to aggression" (A. Roberts and Kingsbury 1993, 30). Unfortunately, as we will see later in this chapter, the Cold War bipolar international system undermined the effectiveness of the UN in security affairs.

By 2011, 193 states were members of the UN—nearly every state in the world. Notable exceptions include Western Sahara and Kosovo (neither of which is recognized as a self-governing territory), Taiwan (which is not recognized as a separate territory from China), and Palestine and Vatican City (both of which enjoy nonmember observer status). When joining, member states agreed to accept the obligations of the **United Nations Charter**, an international treaty that set out basic principles of international relations. According to the Charter, the UN had four purposes: to maintain international peace and security, to develop friendly relations among nations, to cooperate in solving international problems and in promoting respect for human rights, and to be a center for harmonizing the actions of nations. At the UN, all the member states—large and small, rich and poor, with differing political views and social systems—had a voice and a vote in this process. Interestingly, although the UN was clearly created as a grouping of states, the Charter referred to the needs and interests of peoples as well as those of states (go to www.oup.com/us/lamy to read more on the UN Charter).

GROWTH IN UN MEMBERSHIP.
There are 196 countries in the world and 193 are members of the UN. If the UN Security Council continues to block effective action like preventing mass atrocities in Darfur and punishing the Syrian government for using chemical weapons, do you think countries will quit the UN?

In many ways, the UN was set up to correct the problems of its predecessor, the **League of Nations**. The League of Nations had been established after World War I and was intended to make future wars impossible, but it lacked effective power. There was no clear division of responsibility between the main executive committee (the League Council) and the League Assembly, which included all member states. Both the League Assembly and the League Council could only make recommendations, not binding resolutions, and these recommendations had to be unanimous. Any government was free to reject any recommendation. Furthermore, there was no mechanism for coordinating military or economic actions against miscreant states. Key states, such as the United States, were not members of the League. By World War II, the League had already failed to address a number of acts of aggression.

The structure of the UN was intended to avoid some of the problems faced by the League of Nations. The UN has six main organs: the Security Council, the General Assembly, the Secretariat, the Economic and Social Council, the Trusteeship Council, and the International Court of Justice (see Figure 5.1).

The Security Council

The **UN Security Council** was given the main responsibility for maintaining international peace and security. It was made up initially of eleven states and then, after 1965, of fifteen states. It includes five permanent members (sometimes called the P-5), namely, the United States, Britain, France, Russia (previously the Soviet Union)—the victors in World War II—and China, as well as ten nonpermanent members. (China was represented by Nationalist China and not the People's Republic of China.) In contrast to the League of Nations, the UN recognized great-power prerogatives in the Security Council, offering each of the P-5 a **veto power** over all Security Council decisions. The convention emerged that abstention by a permanent member is not regarded as a veto. Unlike with the League, the decisions of the Security Council are binding and must only be passed by a majority of nine of the fifteen members. However, if one permanent member dissents, the resolution does not pass.

The five permanent members of the Security Council were seen as the major powers when the UN was founded. They were granted a veto on the view that if the great powers were not given a privileged position, the UN would not work. This recognition of a state's influence being proportional to its size and political and military power stems from the realist notion that power determines who rules in the international system. Indeed, this tension between the recognition of power politics through the Security Council veto and the universal ideals underlying the UN is a defining feature of the organization. There have been widespread and frequent calls for the reform of the Security Council, but this is very difficult. In both theoretical and policy terms, the inability to reform the Security Council shows the limits of a collective security system and liberal thinking that suggests all states are equal.

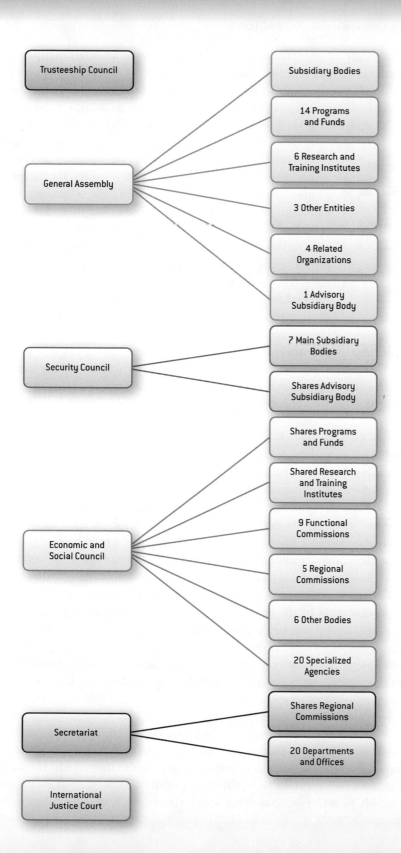

Figure 5.1 The Structure of the UN.

When the Security Council considers a threat to international peace, it first explores ways to settle the dispute peacefully under the terms of Chapter VI of the UN Charter. It might suggest principles for a settlement or mediation. In the event of fighting, the Security Council tries to secure a cease-fire. It might send a peacekeeping mission to help the parties maintain the truce and to keep opposing forces apart (see the discussion of peacekeeping later in this chapter). The Council can also take measures to enforce its decisions under Chapter VII of the Charter. It can, for instance, impose **economic sanctions** or order an arms embargo. (See Chapter 4 for a discussion of these foreign policy tools.) On rare occasions, the Security Council has authorized member states to use all necessary means, including collective military action, to see that its decisions are carried out. The Council also makes recommendations to the General Assembly on the appointment of a new secretary-general and on the admission of new members to the UN.

WHAT'S YOUR WORLDVIEW

The leaders of many states demand respect for their national sovereignty. How might that hurt the chance of success for any international or regional organization? How might that influence the future of the UN and other international and regional organizations?

The General Assembly

The recognition of power politics through veto power in the Security Council can be contrasted with the universal principles underlying the other organs of the UN. All UN member states are represented in the **UN General Assembly**—a "parliament of nations"—which meets to consider the world's most pressing problems. Each member state has one vote. A two-thirds majority in the General Assembly is required for decisions on key issues such as international peace and security, the admission of new members, and the UN budget. A simple majority is required for other matters. However, the decisions reached by the General Assembly only have the status of recommendations, rather than binding decisions. One of the few exceptions is the General Assembly's Fifth Committee, which makes decisions on the budget that are binding on members.

The General Assembly can consider any matter within the scope of the UN Charter. Recent topics discussed by the General Assembly include the impact of globalization on societies, the role of diamonds in fueling conflict, international cooperation in the peaceful uses of outer space, peacekeeping operations, sustainable development, and international migration. Because General Assembly resolutions are nonbinding, they cannot force action by any state, but the Assembly's recommendations are important indications of world opinion and represent the moral authority of the community of nation-states.

The Secretariat

The **UN Secretariat** carries out the substantive and administrative work of the UN as directed by the General Assembly, the Security Council, and the other organs. It is led by the secretary-general, who provides overall administrative guidance. In December 2006, Ban Ki-moon from South Korea was sworn in as the eighth secretary-general. The Secretariat consists of departments and offices with a total staff of 8,900 under the regular budget and a nearly equal number under special funding.

On the recommendation of the other bodies, the Secretariat also carries out a number of research functions and some quasi-management functions. Yet the role of the Secretariat remains primarily bureaucratic, and it lacks the political power of, for instance, the Commission of the EU. The one exception to this is the power of the secretary-general, under Article 99 of the Charter, to bring situations that are likely to lead to a breakdown of international peace and security to the attention of the Security Council. This article was the legal basis for the remarkable expansion of the diplomatic role of the secretary-general, compared with its League predecessor. The secretary-general is empowered to become involved in a large range of areas that can be loosely interpreted as threats to peace, including economic and social problems and humanitarian crises.

The Economic and Social Council

The **UN Economic and Social Council (ECOSOC)**, under the overall authority of the General Assembly, is intended to coordinate the economic and social work of the UN and the UN family of organizations. It also consults with NGOs, thereby maintaining a vital link between the UN and civil society. ECOSOC's subsidiary bodies include functional commissions, such as the Commission on the Status of Women; regional commissions, such as the Economic Commission for Africa; and other bodies.

Whereas the League of Nations attributed responsibility for economic and social questions to the League Assembly, the Charter of the UN established ECOSOC to oversee economic and social institutions. ECOSOC does not have necessary management powers, however; it can only issue recommendations and receive reports. In consequence, the UN's economic and social organizations have continually searched for better ways of achieving effective management.

> **WHAT'S YOUR WORLDVIEW**
>
> *With nation-states reluctant to send their own forces into harm's way and no real international force, how will the UN and other global institutions respond to humanitarian challenges and disintegrating states?*

The Trusteeship Council

When the UN was created, the **UN Trusteeship Council** was established to provide international supervision for eleven Trust Territories administered by seven member states and to ensure that adequate steps were taken to prepare the territories for self-government or independence. By 1994, all Trust Territories had attained self-government or independence, either as separate states or by joining neighboring independent countries. The last to do so was the Trust Territory of the Pacific Islands, Palau, which had been previously administered by the United States under special rules with the UN called a strategic trust. Its work completed, the Trusteeship Council now consists of the five permanent members of the Security Council. It has amended its rules of procedure to allow it to meet when necessary.

The home of the ICJ in The Hague, Netherlands, was built with donations from member states and private donors.

The International Court of Justice

The **International Court of Justice (ICJ)** is the main judicial organ of the UN. Consisting of fifteen judges elected jointly by the General Assembly and the Security Council, the Court decides disputes between countries. Participation by states in a proceeding is voluntary, but if a state agrees to participate, it is obligated to comply with the Court's decision. The Court also provides advisory opinions to other UN organs and specialized agencies on request. Only states may bring cases before the ICJ. If people who live in one state want to bring a suit against another state, they must get their home state to file the suit.

Three factors reduce the effectiveness of the ICJ:

• First, the competence, or jurisdiction, of the Court is limited, as already noted, to cases that states bring against states. The Court's statutory jurisdiction extends to anything related to a state's undertakings by signing the UN Charter and any matter related to a ratified treaty. If a state is not a signatory, there can be no recourse to the good offices of the ICJ. In addition, if the UN itself is a party to the case, at least one state party of the ICJ must be an applicant as well. This happened with the South-West Africa cases of the 1970s.

- A second factor that reduces the ICJ's effectiveness is the question of compulsory jurisdiction. States that are party to the ICJ statute are not bound by compulsory jurisdiction unless they agree to it; this is the "option clause" problem. For example, in the *Aerial Incident of July 27, 1955 (Israel v. Bulgaria)* the court found that Bulgaria was not liable for damages because its compulsory jurisdiction option had expired.

- A third factor—the state reservations—limits the effectiveness of the ICJ and follows from the option-clause problems, because not only may a state let its compulsory jurisdiction lapse, but also it can refuse to accept the ICJ jurisdiction if the state claims that its own existing national law covers the issue before the courts. This occurred, for example, in a 1957 case in which Norway sued France over a debt owed to Norwegian investors. France claimed that its domestic legal system had jurisdiction in the matter, and Norway lost.

In Chapter 7, we discuss the ICC, an independent international organization that is not part of the UN.

Maintenance of International Peace and Security

Political context has shaped the performance of the UN in questions of peace and security. Clearly, changes in international society since the UN was founded in 1945 have had an impact on the UN system. The Cold War between the United States and the Soviet Union hampered the functioning of the UN Security Council, because the veto could be used whenever the major interests of the United States or Soviet Union were threatened. From 1945 to 1990, 193 substantive vetoes were invoked in the Security Council, compared with only 19 substantive vetoes from 1990 to 2007. Furthermore, although the UN Charter provided for a standing army to be set up by agreement between the Security Council and consenting states, the East–West Cold War rivalry made this impossible to implement. The result was that the UN Security Council could not function in the way in which the UN founders had expected.

Because member states could not agree on the arrangements laid out in Chapter VII of the Charter, especially with regard to setting up a UN army, a series of improvisations followed to address matters of peace and security:

- First, the UN established a procedure under which the Security Council agreed to a mandate for an agent to act on its behalf. This occurred in the Korean conflict in 1950 and the Gulf War in 1990, when action was undertaken principally by the United States and its allies.

- Second, the UN has engaged in classical peacekeeping, which involves establishing a UN force under UN command to be placed between disputing parties after a cease-fire. Such a force uses its weapons only in self-defense, is established with the consent of the host state, and does not include forces from the major powers. The first instance of this was in 1956, when a UN force was sent to Egypt to facilitate the exodus of the British and French forces from the Suez Canal area and then to stand between Egyptian and Israeli forces. Since the Suez crisis, there have been a number of classical peacekeeping missions, for instance, at the Green Line in Cyprus, in the Golan Heights, and after the decade-long Iraq–Iran War. The primary drawback to this kind of peacekeeping operation is that it is not effective if the war parties do not want peace. Such operations can also be difficult to conclude.

- Third, a new kind of peacekeeping, sometimes called multidimensional peacekeeping or **peace enforcement**, emerged after the Cold War. These missions are more likely to use force for humanitarian ends when order has collapsed within states. A key problem has been that the peacekeepers have found it increasingly difficult to maintain a neutral position and have been targeted by belligerents. Examples include the intervention in Somalia in the early 1990s and intervention in the former Yugoslavia in the mid-1990s. In both cases, until the EU, NATO, or the United States was directly involved in the operations, peace was elusive. Even after the US intervention in 1993 in Somalia, sadly best known for the "Black Hawk Down" incident, the country remains a failed state, characterized by clan-based violence.

In the early 1990s, after the end of the Cold War, the UN agenda for peace and security expanded quickly. The secretary-general at the time, Boutros Boutros-Ghali, outlined a more ambitious role for the UN in his seminal report, *An Agenda for Peace* (1992). The report described interconnected roles for the UN to maintain peace and security in the post–Cold War context. These included four main kinds of activities: (1) **preventive diplomacy**, which involves confidence-building measures, fact finding, and preventive deployment of UN authorized forces; (2) **peacemaking**, designed to bring hostile parties to agreement, essentially through peaceful means; (3) **peacekeeping**, the deployment of a UN presence in the field with the consent of all parties (this refers to classical peacekeeping); and (4) **postconflict peace building**, which ideally will develop the social, political, and economic infrastructure to prevent further violence and to consolidate peace. However, when all peaceful means have failed, peace enforcement authorized under Chapter VII of the Charter might be necessary, and it may occur without the consent of the parties in conflict.

The governments of Norway and Denmark agreed to transport chemical weapons out of Syria. The plan for destroying these weapons was a joint project of the Organization for the Prohibition of Chemical Weapons and the UN. This is a great example of multilateral cooperation at the national and international levels.

UN peacekeeping went through a rapid expansion in the early 1990s. In 1994, UN peacekeeping operations involved nearly 80,000 military personnel around the world, seven times the figure for 1990 (Pugh 2001, 115). In February 2010, the total number of peacekeeping personnel (military and police) in the UN's fifteen ongoing peacekeeping operations was just over 100,000 (UN 2011).

Increased Attention to Conditions Within States

The new peacekeeping was the product of a greater preparedness to intervene within states. An increasing number of people believed that the international community, working through the UN, should address individual political and civil rights, as well as the right to basic provisions like food, water, health care, and accommodation. Under this view, violations of individuals' rights were a major cause of disturbances in relations between states: A lack of internal justice risked international disorder. The UN reinforced this new perception that pursuing justice for individuals, or ensuring **human security**, was an aspect of national interest. (We discuss human security in Chapter 7.)

In some states, contributions to activities such as peacekeeping were defended in terms of national interest. States such as Canada and Norway could justify their contributions to peacekeeping as a "moral" course of action, but these contributions also served their national interests by enhancing their status in the international community. The Japanese also responded to moral pressure founded in national interest when they contributed substantially to defraying the cost of British involvement in the 1990–1991 Gulf War. This act can be explained in terms of the synthesis of morality and interest. For some states, a good reputation in the UN had become an important national goal.

These actions reflected an increasing concern with questions of justice for individuals and conditions within states. Yet in the past, the UN had helped to promote the traditional view of the primacy of international order between states over justice for individuals, so the new focus on individual rights was a significant change. What accounts for this change? We offer two reasons:

- First, the international environment had changed. The Cold War standoff between the East and the West had meant that member states did not want to question the conditions of the sovereignty of states.
- Second, some analysts made strong arguments that challenged the privileging of statehood over justice during the process of decolonization. Charles Beitz was one of the first, concluding that statehood should not be unconditional and that the situation of individuals after independence demanded attention (Beitz 1979). Michael Walzer (1977) and Terry Nardin (1983) produced arguments leading to similar conclusions: States were conditional entities in that their right to exist should be dependent on a criterion of performance. Such writings helped alter the moral content of diplomacy.

The new relationship between order and justice was, therefore, a product of particular circumstances. After the Cold War, the international community began to sense that threats to international peace and security did not emanate only from aggression between states. Rather, global peace was also threatened by civil conflict (including refugee flows and regional instability), humanitarian emergencies, violations of global standards of human rights, and other conditions such as poverty and inequality.

More recently, other types of non-state-based threats, such as terrorism and the proliferation of small arms and weapons of mass destruction, have had an increasingly prominent place on the UN security agenda. Partly in response to the terrorist attacks in the United States in 2001, as well as the impasse reached in the UN Security Council over Iraq in 2003, then Secretary-General Kofi Annan named a high-level panel to examine the major threats and challenges to global peace. The final report, *A More Secure World: Our Shared Responsibility* (UN 2004), emphasized the interconnected nature of security threats and presented development, security, and human rights as mutually reinforcing. Many of the report's recommendations were not implemented, but some were, notably the establishment of a new UN Peacebuilding Commission.

The UN Peacebuilding Commission was established in December 2005 as an advisory subsidiary body of the General Assembly and the Security Council. It was proposed first by the secretary-general's High-Level Panel on Threats, Challenges, and Change in December 2004 and again in the secretary-general's report *In Larger Freedom* in March 2005 (UN 2005). This panel and report argued that existing UN mechanisms were insufficient in responding to the particular needs of states emerging from conflict. Many countries, such as Liberia, Haiti, and Somalia in the 1990s, had signed peace agreements and hosted UN peacekeeping missions but reverted to violent conflict. The Peacebuilding Commission aims to provide targeted support to countries in the volatile postconflict phase to prevent the recurrence of conflict. It proposes integrated strategies and priorities for postconflict recovery to improve coordination among the myriad of actors involved in postconflict activities. The establishment of the Peacebuilding Commission is indicative of a growing trend at the UN to coordinate security and development programming.

Intervention Within States

As the international community more clearly understood issues of peace and security to include human security and justice, it expected the UN to take on a stronger role in maintaining standards for individuals within states. One difficulty in carrying out this new task was that it seemed to run against the doctrine of nonintervention. **Intervention** was traditionally defined as a deliberate incursion into a state, without its consent, by some outside agency

THEORY IN PRACTICE

Neoconservatives and the UN

The Challenge

For analysts from the realist school of thought, states exist in an anarchic, self-help world, looking to their own power resources for national security. This was the perspective of the neoconservatives who dominated the administration of US President George W. Bush. They subscribed to a strain of realist thinking that is best called hegemonist; that is, they believed the United States should use its power solely to secure its interests in the world. They were realists with idealistic tendencies, seeking to remake the world through promoting by force, if necessary, freedom, democracy, and free enterprise.

Paul Wolfowitz, an important voice in the neoconservative camp, wrote that global leadership was all about "demonstrating that your friends will be protected and taken care of, that your enemies will be punished, and those who refuse to support you will live to regret having done so."* Although it would be wrong to assume that all realist thinkers and policy makers are opposed to international organizations such as the UN, most are wary of any organizations that prevent them from securing their national interests. The belief is that alliances should be only short-term events because allies might desert you in a crisis.

For some realists, such as the Bush neoconservatives, committing security to a collective security organization is even worse than an alliance because, in a worst-case situation, the alliance might gang up on your country. Even in the best-case situation, it would be a bad idea to submit your military forces to foreign leadership.

Options

In its early years, before the wave of decolonization in Africa and Asia, the UN's US-based realist critics did not have the ear of the country's political leadership. Presidents Truman and Eisenhower both found a way around the USSR's Security Council veto by working through the General Assembly, a body that at the time was very friendly to the United States and its goals. However, with the end of European control of Africa and Asia, the General Assembly changed. The body frequently passed resolutions condemning the United States and its allies. One result was a growing movement to end US involvement in the UN, especially among the key foreign policy advisers to President Reagan.

Application

In the 1980s, political realists saw no tangible benefit for the United States to remain active in the UN once the leaders in Washington could no longer count on a UN rubber stamp for US policies. For a number of years, the United States did not pay its dues to the UN.

This rejection of UN-style multilateralism revived with the George W. Bush presidency, beginning in 2001. In a controversial recess appointment, Bush chose John Bolton to be the US ambassador to the UN in 2005. This appointment came as a surprise because Bolton was a staunch opponent of multilateral organizations such as the UN. The Bush foreign policy advisers were against the peacekeeping operation in the former Yugoslavia. In her criticism of Clinton administration foreign policy, National Security Adviser Condoleezza Rice said the United States would not send its troops to countries for nation building. More important, the Bush administration did not want to have its hands tied when dealing with Iraq and its alleged store of nuclear, chemical, and biological weapons. President Bush and his top advisers believed that sanctions—an important weapon in the UN's moral-suasion arsenal—would never force Iraq to disarm and that only force could do so. The irony is that, after the 2003 invasion, the US's own weapons inspectors could find no evidence that Iraq had any of the banned weapons.

For Discussion

1. What might be a Marxist criticism of the UN and its operations?
2. Is there any way to overcome realists' belief of international anarchy and the impossibility of global governance?
3. Some utopians believe that a world government would end war and provide answers to other global challenges. Do you agree or disagree? Why or why not?
4. Do the five permanent members of the Security Council have too much power over the operations of the organization? Why or why not?

*Paul Wolfowitz, "Remembering the future," *National Interest* 59 (Spring 2000), p. 41.

to change the functioning, policies, and goals of its government and achieve effects that favor the intervening agency (Vincent 1974).

The founders of the UN viewed sovereignty as central to the system of states. States were equal members of international society and were equal with regard to international law. Sovereignty also implied that states recognized no higher authority than themselves and no superior jurisdiction. Intervention in the traditional sense was in opposition to the principles of international society, and it could only be tolerated as an exception to the rule.

By the 1990s, some believed that there should be a return to an earlier period when intervention was justified, but that a wider range of instruments should be used. Supporters of this idea insisted on a key role for the UN in granting a license to intervene. They pointed out that the UN Charter did not assert merely the rights of states, but also the rights of peoples: Statehood could be interpreted as being conditional on respect for such rights. There was ample evidence in the UN Charter to justify the view that extreme transgressions of human rights could be a justification for intervention by the international community.

Yet there have been only a few occasions where a UN resolution justified intervention because of gross infringements of human rights. The justification of NATO's intervention in Kosovo in 1999 represented a break from the past in that it included a clear humanitarian element. Kosovo was arguably the first occasion in which international forces were used in defiance of a sovereign state to protect humanitarian standards. NATO launched the air campaign in March 1999 in Kosovo against the Republic of Yugoslavia without a mandate from the Security Council because Russia had declared that it would veto such action. Nonetheless, NATO states noted that by intervening to stop ethnic cleansing and crimes against humanity in Kosovo they were acting in accordance with the principles of the UN Charter.

The Iraq War in 2003 was another case, although the legality of intervention under existing Security Council resolutions is contested. The US action against Afghanistan in 2001 is an exceptional case in which the UN Security Council acknowledged the right of a state that had been attacked—referring to the events of 9/11 in the United States—to respond in its own defense.

The difficulty in relaxing the principle of nonintervention should not be underestimated. For instance, the UN was reluctant to send troops to Rwanda, Bosnia, Kosovo, and Sudan to respond to acts of ethnic cleansing and genocide. More recently, the UN took several weeks to decide to intervene to protect civilians in Libya in 2011, and they have yet to decide how best to protect civilians in Syria's civil war. Some fear a slippery slope whereby a relaxation of the nonintervention principle by the UN will lead to military action by individual states without UN approval. There are significant numbers of non-UN actors, including regional organizations, involved in peace operations, and several states are suspicious of what appears to be the granting of a license to intervene in their affairs.

An increasing readiness by the UN to intervene within states to promote internal justice for individuals would indicate a movement toward global governance and away from unconditional sovereignty. There have been some signs of movement in this direction, but principles of state sovereignty and nonintervention remain important. There is no clear consensus on these points. There is still some support for the view that Article 2(7) of the UN Charter should be interpreted strictly: There can be no intervention within a state without the express consent of the government of that state. Others believe that intervention within a country to promote human rights is only justifiable on the basis of a threat to international peace and security. Evidence of a threat to international peace and security could be the appearance of significant numbers of refugees or the judgment that other states might intervene militarily. Some liberal internationalists argue that this condition is flexible enough to justify intervention to defend human rights whenever possible.

Overall, then, the UN's record on the maintenance of international peace and security has been mixed. There has been a stronger assertion of the responsibility of international society, represented by the UN, for gross offenses against populations. However, the practice has been patchy.

Economic and Social Questions

As we have discussed, conditions within states, including human rights, justice, development, and equality, have a bearing on global peace. The more integrated global context has meant that economic and social problems in one part of the world might affect other areas. Furthermore, promoting social and economic development is an important UN goal in itself. The preamble of the UN Charter talks of promoting "social progress and better standards of life in larger freedom" and the need to "employ international machinery for the promotion of the economic and social advancement of all peoples."

The number of institutions within the UN system that address economic and social issues has increased significantly since the founding of the UN. Nonetheless, the main contributor states have been giving less and less to economic and social institutions. In 2000, the UN convened a Millennium Summit, where heads of state committed themselves to a series of measurable goals and targets, known as the Millennium Development Goals (MDGs). These goals, to be achieved by 2015, include reducing by half the number of people living on less than a dollar a day, achieving universal primary education, and reversing the spread of HIV/AIDS and malaria (A/55/L.2). Since 2000, the UN has been integrating the MDGs into all aspects of its work at the country level, but progress on reaching the MDGs has been very uneven.

The UN Foundation was established with a gift of $1 billion from the founder of CNN, Ted Turner. He is a champion of public and private partnerships. Here he is giving Indian Congress party president Sonia Gandhi an award. The United Nations Foundation links the UN's work with others around the world; what does this mean in practice?

The Reform Process of the United Nations

In his important book *The Parliament of Man* (2006), Paul Kennedy suggests that any reform of the UN will need to be partial, gradual, and carefully executed. He argues that the need to make the UN more effective, representative, and accountable to its members is greater today than it was in the past because of a number of global developments, including the following:

1. The emergence of new great powers like India and Brazil and older powers like Japan and Germany who have been left out of the Security Council. Are the current members of the Security Council willing to add new members or even change the decision-making structure?

2. The presence of truly global issues that threaten the world as we know it. These include environmental degradation, terrorism, the proliferation of weapons of all kinds, and the persistence of global poverty. Is the UN interested in or capable of responding to these issues?

In the mid to late 1990s, alongside growing UN involvement in development issues, the UN economic and social arrangements underwent reform at two levels: first, reforms concerned with operations at the country (field) level; and second, reforms at the general, or headquarters, level.

Country Level

The continuing complaints of NGOs about poor UN performance in the field served as a powerful stimulus for reform. A key feature of the reforms at the country (field) level was the adoption of Country Strategy Notes. These were statements about the overall development process tailored to the specific needs of individual countries. They were written on the basis of discussions among the Specialized Agencies, Programmes and Funds, donors, and the host country. The merit of the Country Strategy Notes is that they clearly set out targets, roles, and priorities.

Other reforms at the country level included the strengthening of the resident coordinator's role and enhanced authority for field-level officers. There was also an effort to introduce improved communication facilities and information sharing. The activities of the various UN organizations were brought together in single locations, or "UN houses," which facilitated inter-agency communication and collegiality. The adoption of the MDG framework has also helped country field staff achieve a more coherent approach to development.

Headquarters Level

If the UN role in economic and social affairs at the country level was to be effective, reform was also required at the headquarters level. Because the Security Council is the main executive body within the UN, it is not surprising that many discussions of UN reform have focused on it.

The founders of the UN deliberately established a universal General Assembly and a restricted Security Council that required unanimity among the great powers. Granting permanent seats and the right to a veto to the great powers of the time—the United States, the Soviet Union (now Russia), France, the UK, and China—was an essential feature of the deal.

The composition and decision-making procedures of the Security Council were increasingly challenged as membership of the UN grew, particularly after decolonization. Yet the only significant reform of the Security Council occurred in 1965, when the Council was enlarged from eleven to fifteen members and the required majority from seven to nine votes. Nonetheless, the veto power of the permanent five (P-5) members was left intact.

The Security Council does not reflect today's distribution of military or economic power, and it does not reflect a geographic balance. Germany and Japan have made strong cases for permanent membership. Developing countries have demanded more representation on the Security Council, particularly South Africa, India, Egypt, Brazil, and Nigeria. However, it has proved impossible to reach agreement on new permanent members. Should the EU be represented instead of Great Britain, France, and Germany individually? How would Pakistan feel about India's candidacy? How would South Africa feel about a Nigerian seat? What about representation by an Islamic country? These issues are not easy to resolve. Likewise, it is very unlikely that the P-5 states will relinquish their veto. Nonetheless, although large-scale reform has proved impossible, changes in Security Council working procedures have made it more transparent and accountable to the member states.

Reform efforts in the 1990s focused on the reorganization and rationalization of the ECOSOC, the UN family of economic and social organizations. These efforts allowed ECOSOC to become more assertive and to take a leading role in the coordination of the UN system. They also aimed to eliminate duplication and overlap in the work of the functional commissions.

Overall, economic and social reorganization meant that the two poles of the system were better coordinated: the pole where intentions are defined through global conferences and agendas and the pole where programs are implemented. Programs at the field level were better integrated, and field officers were given enhanced discretion. The reform of ECOSOC sharpened its capacity to shape broad agreements into cross-sectoral programs with well-defined objectives. At the same time, ECOSOC acquired greater capacity to act as a conduit through which the results of field-level monitoring could be conveyed upward to the functional commissions. These new processes had the effect of strengthening the norms, values, and goals of a multilateral system.

The European Union and Other Regional Organizations

Regionalism can be seen as one of the few instruments available to states to try to manage the effects of globalization. We define it as the use of regional rather than central systems of administration or economic, cultural, or political affiliation. If individual states no longer have the effective capacity to regulate, regionalism might be a means to regain some control over global market forces—and to counter the more negative social consequences of globalization.

The Process of European Integration

In Europe, regionalism after 1945 has taken the form of a gradual process of integration leading to the emergence of the **European Union (EU)**. It was initially a purely West European creation among the "original six" member states, born out of the desire for reconciliation between France and Germany in a context of ambitious federalist plans for a united Europe. Yet the process has taken the form of a progressive construction of an institutional architecture, a legal framework, and a wide range of policies, which in 2007 encompassed twenty-seven European states.

The European Coal and Steel Community was created in 1951 (in force in 1952), followed

The EU's foreign policy chief meets with a Chinese official during a China–EU dialogue in Hungary in 2011. China's economic power makes it an attractive partner for the EU and its members. Does China's economic power give it political influence as well?

by the European Economic Community and the European Atomic Energy Community in 1957 (in force in 1958). These treaties involved a conferral of Community competence, or standards, in various areas—the supranational management of coal and steel, the creation and regulation of an internal market, and common policies in trade, competition, agriculture, and transport. Since then, powers have been extended to include new legislative competences in some fields such as the environment. Since the 1992 Treaty on European Union (the Maastricht Treaty, in force in 1993) the integration process has also involved the adoption of stronger forms of unification, notably monetary union, as well as cooperation in economic and employment policy, and more intergovernmental cooperation in foreign and security policy.

From very limited beginnings, in terms of both membership and scope, the EU has therefore gradually developed to become an important political and economic actor whose presence has a significant impact internationally and domestically. This gradual process of European integration has taken place at various levels. The first is the signature and reform of the basic treaties. These are the result of intergovernmental conferences, where representatives of national governments negotiate the legal framework within which the EU institutions operate. Such treaty changes require ratification in each country.

Within this framework, the institutions have considerable powers to adopt decisions and manage policies (Table 5.1), although the dynamics of decision making differ significantly across arenas. There are important differences between the more integrated areas of economic regulation and the more intergovernmental pillars of foreign policy and police or judicial cooperation in criminal matters. In some areas, a country might have to accept decisions imposed on it by the (qualified) majority of member states. In other areas, it might be able to block decisions.

To understand the integration process, one needs to take account of the role played by both member states *and* supranational institutions. Member states are not just represented by national governments, as a host of state, nonstate, and transnational actors participate in the processes of domestic preference formation and direct representation of interests in the key EU institutions. The relative openness of the European policy process means that political groups and economic interests will try to influence EU decision making if they feel that their position is not sufficiently represented by national governments. That is one reason the EU is increasingly seen as a system of multilevel governance, involving a plurality of actors on different territorial levels: supranational, national, and local.

The complexity of the EU institutional machinery, together with continuous change over time, has spawned a lively debate among integration theorists (Rosamond 2000; Wiener and Diez 2004). Some approaches are applications of more general theories of international relations. For example, the literature on both realism and liberalism has contributed to theorizing integration. Other scholars have regarded the EU as sui generis—in a category of its own—and therefore in need of the development of dedicated theories of integration.

Table 5.1 Institutions of the EU

EU Institution	Responsibilities	Location
European Commission	Initiating, administering, and overseeing the implementation of EU policies and legislation	Brussels and Luxembourg
European Parliament	Acting as directly elected representatives of EU citizens, scrutinizing the operation of the other institutions, and, in certain areas, sharing the power to legislate	Strasbourg, Brussels, and Luxembourg
Council of Ministers	Representing the views of national governments and determining, in many areas jointly with the EP, the ultimate shape of EU legislation	Brussels (some meetings in Luxembourg)
European Council	Holding regular summits of the heads of state or government and the president of the commission, setting the EU's broad agenda, and acting as a forum of last resort to find agreement on divisive issues (Note: different from the Council of Europe)	Brussels
European Court of Justice	Acting as the EU's highest court (supported by a Court of First Instance)	Luxembourg
European Central Bank	Setting interest rates and controlling the money supply of the single European currency, the euro	Frankfurt
Court of Auditors	Auditing the revenues and the expenditure under the EU budget	Luxembourg

The most prominent among these has been neofunctionalism, which sought to explain the evolution of integration in terms of "spillover" from one policy sector to another as resources and loyalties of elites were transferred to the European level. As aspects of EU politics have come to resemble the domestic politics of states, scholars have turned to approaches drawn from comparative politics or the study of governance in different states.

However, the exchange between "supranational" and "intergovernmental" approaches has had the greatest impact on the study of European integration. Supranational approaches regard the emergence of supranational institutions in Europe as a distinct feature and turn these into the main object of analysis. Here, the politics above the level of states is regarded as the most significant, and consequently the political actors and institutions at the European level receive the most attention.

Intergovernmental approaches, on the other hand, continue to regard states as the most important aspect of the integration process. Consequently, they concentrate on the study of politics *between* and *within* states. But most scholars would agree that no analysis of the EU is complete without studying both the operation and evolution of the central institutions and the input from political actors in the member states.

The prospect of an ever *wider* EU has raised serious questions about the nature and direction of the integration process. The 2004 enlargement has generally been seen as a qualitative leap for the EU. Concerns that the enlarged Union, if not reformed substantially, would find it difficult to make decisions and maintain a reliable legal framework led to several attempts to reform the treaties. The most wide-ranging proposals, and the most significant change in the language of integration, came with the treaty establishing a constitution for Europe that EU governments signed in 2004. The very fact that the EU should discuss something referred to in the media as a European Constitution is a sign of how far it has developed from its modest beginnings. However, the time might still not be right for such a project. The Constitutional Treaty was rejected in referendums in France and the Netherlands, raising serious doubts not only about this attempt at institutional reform but also about ambitions for a formal constitutional process more generally. In 2007, with intergovernmental negotiations about a revised "reform treaty," the EU seemed likely to continue along the established path of a succession of gradual developments rather than the big leaps.

President of European Central Bank Mario Draghi, right, and vice president Vitor Constancio chat during a European Finance ministers meeting at Zappeion Hall in Athens, on Wednesday, April 2, 2014. Draghi will need to deal with on-going Greek economic crisis. (AP Photo/Petros Giannakouris)

After eight years of debate and several disappointing negative national votes, the EU's reform treaty came into force on December 1, 2009. EU leaders believe the now-ratified Lisbon Treaty will rejuvenate the decision-making apparatus of all of the EU institutions, making the functioning of the twenty-seven-member Union more efficient and democratic.

In the recent global economic crisis, Germany has emerged as the clear leader of the eurozone and the EU. Some in Germany are talking about a remaking of the EU that would include more financial union, including some control over the members' budgets and spending; creating a eurobonds program; renegotiating many of the treaties that bind the EU members together; and even going so far as to create a federal Europe. Once again, a major crisis might serve as a catalyst for greater European integration

Other Regional Actors: The African Union and the Organization of American States

The **African Union (AU)** is the most important intergovernmental organization in Africa. It replaced the **Organization of African Unity (OAU)** in July 2002. At the time of this succession, fifty-three of the fifty-four African states were members (all but Morocco, which remains a nonmember at the time of this writing). The OAU was established in 1963 to provide a collective voice for Africa and to work to end all forms of colonization. It also sought to promote economic development and human rights and to improve the quality of life for all Africans. But the OAU's record here is not good, especially considering that eighteen of the twenty-one poorest countries in the world are in Africa. Some eight major conflicts are creating almost insurmountable human security problems across the continent. Many critics argue that the OAU was primarily a "talk shop" and was ineffective in many key areas. However, the OAU did succeed in encouraging its members to cooperate as a voting bloc in international organizations like the UN.

The AU still must deal with many of the same challenges as it attempts to fulfill its vision of creating "an integrated, prosperous and peaceful Africa, driven by its own citizens and representing a dynamic force in the global arena." The AU has a long way to go to be considered a successful regional organization. Achieving this success might be even more difficult as major powers like China, India, the United States, and European states all compete for access to African resources and turn a blind eye to abuses of governance in many states.

Turning to the Americas, the **Organization of American States (OAS)** is the world's oldest regional organization, founded in 1890. It was known at the time as the International Union of American Republics and changed its name to Organization of American States in 1948. Its charter states that the goals of the organization are to create "an order of peace and justice, to promote their solidarity, to strengthen their collaboration, and to defend their sovereignty, their territorial integrity, and their independence." The organization, which has thirty-five member states, might be more effective in the post–Cold War period. During the Cold War, the US obsession with communism drove the OAS to intervene in the affairs of states and at times use extralegal activities to make certain that friendly governments stayed in power. Although the United States remains the dominant power, the OAS could become a very effective regional organization and an effective part of global governance. The main pillars of the OAS are democracy, human rights, regional security, and economic development. With rising powers like Brazil, Chile, and Argentina and the intransigent Venezuela, the OAS could become a major player in global politics.

Global and regional state organizations are but one piece of the emerging pattern of global governance. We turn now to nongovernmental actors and examine their role in international life.

Nongovernmental Actors

In addition to states and international or regional government organizations, a range of nongovernmental actors play a role in global politics. Globalization has enhanced the ability of such actors to be significant players in all areas of global politics. As we will see, these powerful actors have many different agendas. In the next sections we explore who these actors are and what kinds of influences they have on the world stage.

The Growth of Global Civil Society

Leaders of global activist efforts include a variety of nongovernmental actors, such as **international nongovernmental organizations** (**INGOs**, or NGOs with members from at least three countries), philanthropic foundations that

Modern-day Robin Hoods? Rolling Jubilee, part of the Occupy movement that protested around the world in 2011 and 2012, spent $400,000 to buy $15 million of personal debts from banks and then set free those in debt. Most of the debt that was purchased was medical debt owed by 2,693 people across 45 states. The original Jubilee Movement aimed at forgiving third world debt.

give money to global social movements, and powerful, wealthy, or famous individuals (e.g., Bill Gates, Bono, and the Dalai Lama) who influence the formulation and implementation of public policy. All of these actors together make up what is known as a global or transnational **civil society**. We define civil society as citizens and groups that are neither in the public (governmental or state) sector nor the private (for-profit or corporate) sector and that engage in dialogue, debate, conflict, and negotiation.

Religious organizations, schools and other educational institutions, trade unions, and service organizations like Rotary International make up a traditional list of civil-society actors. Global civil society is not constrained by national boundaries, however. Scholars in this area (e.g., Keck and Sikkink 1998) have added to this list of actors INGOs, research groups or epistemic communities, foundations, and media organizations. Global civil society also includes social movements and advocacy networks. A **social movement** is a mode of collective action that challenges ways of life, thinking, dominant norms, and moral codes; seeks answers to global problems; and promotes reform or transformation in political and economic institutions. Transnational social movements (TSMOs), often made up of NGOs and like-minded governments and international organizations, have led many successful global campaigns to address issues such as famine in Africa, landmines, and corporate social responsibility in developing countries (Table 5.2).

Transnational advocacy networks (TANs) are "networks of activists, distinguishable largely by the centrality of principled ideas or values in motivating their formation" (Keck and Sikkink 1998, 1). Both INGOs and governments can play a central role in these networks. TANs and TSMOs have taken advantage of the forces of globalization to increase the political effectiveness of their various campaigns, and the ease of communicating online has contributed to their rise.

Table 5.2 Political Impacts of Transnational Social NGOs on States

NGO Impact	NGO Actions	Possible Effects of NGO Actions	Examples of NGOs on UN Registry
Partnership politics	Working with states to resolve a problem	More efficient use of scarce funding and workers	Ford Foundation, Save the Children
Information politics	Disseminating information to call attention to a problem or cause	Highlights the problem; this information is often not available anywhere else and can be used to influence policy-makers and to inform other activists.	General Confederation of Trade Unions, Water Environment Federation
Symbolic politics	Calling attention to a problem or event; both traditional and social media sources can be used to turn the facts about natural disasters and the aftermath of war and violence into human stories	Embarrasses state to take action; public pressure builds and governments are forced to stop ignoring and act	*Médecins Sans Frontières* (Doctors Without Borders), International Action Network on Small Arms
Leverage politics	Using material resources to achieve a goal; INGOs with a significant number of members and material resources can influence votes and help to shape the domestic and foreign policy process	Encourages greater state involvement	International Committee of the Red Cross
Accountability politics	Forcing states to meet public promises	Moral suasion to alter state behavior	Greenpeace, Gray Panthers Action Fund

These movements and networks, which target governments at all levels, in some cases provide critical resources for political change and innovation. Making connections with other actors across the world is much easier with social media, global media outlets, greater financial resources, and INGO links to governments, academic institutions, and even global corporations.

Nongovernmental Organizations

Nongovernmental organizations (NGOs) are autonomous organizations that are not instruments of any government, are not for profit, and are formal legal entities. These exist within societies as domestic NGOs, like the Sierra Club in the United States, or as INGOs. They campaign for certain causes (e.g., Amnesty International for human rights), represent the interests of specific professionals such as international trade unions, and include charitable organizations such as CARE and Oxfam.

As long as nation-states have fought wars or famine has plagued societies, civil-society organizations have played a role in trying to find solutions to these problems. In 1874, there were 32 registered INGOs, and in 1914 there were more

CASE STUDY | A Global Campaign:
The Baby Milk Advocacy Network

Background

The prototype for global campaigning by NGOs has been the International Baby Food Action Network (IBFAN), which challenges the marketing of dried milk powder by the major food and pharmaceutical transnational corporations (TNCs). In the early 1970s, medical staff in developing countries gradually became aware that the death rate for babies was rising because of decreased breast feeding. If the family was poor and used insufficient milk powder, the baby was undernourished. If the water or the bottle was not sterile, the baby developed gastric diseases. Bottle feeding today causes around 1.5 million deaths a year.

The Case

The question was first taken up by the *New Internationalist* magazine and War on Want (WoW) in Britain in 1973–1974. A Swiss NGO, the Third World Action Group (AgDW), then published a revised translation of WoW's report, under the title "Nestlé Kills Babies." When Nestlé sued for libel, AgDW mobilized groups from around the world to supply evidence for their defense. The Swiss Court found AgDW guilty in December 1976 on one of Nestlé's four original counts, on the technical basis that Nestlé was only indirectly responsible for the deaths.

The question moved to the United States when religious groups involved in Latin America fought another court case against Bristol-Myers. Increased awareness led to organization by a new group, the Infant Formula Action Coalition, of a boycott of Nestlé's products that spread to many countries. In the hope of diffusing the increasing pressure, the International Council of Infant Food Industries accepted a proposal by Senator Edward Kennedy for the WHO and UNICEF to hold a meeting on infant feeding in October 1979. Rather than seeing the issue depoliticized, the companies found they were facing demands to limit their marketing. The meeting also taught a group of NGOs how much they could benefit from working together with a common political strategy. They decided to continue to cooperate by forming IBFAN, as a global advocacy network.

The new network was able to mobilize a diverse coalition of medical professionals, religious groups, development activists, women's groups, community organizations, consumer lobbies, and the boycott campaigners. Against intense opposition from the TNCs and the US administration, IBFAN succeeded in achieving the adoption of an International Code of Marketing of Breast-Milk Substitutes, by WHO's assembly, in May 1981. The key provisions of the code were that "there should be no advertising or other form of promotion to the general public" nor any provision of free samples to mothers.

Outcome

As of 2006, thirty-two countries had implemented the code by means of a comprehensive law, another forty-four countries had implemented many, but not all, provisions as law, and a further sixty-four countries had weak legal provisions or voluntary policies. IBFAN's work continues along two tracks: It monitors and reports violations of the code by companies, including in countries where marketing is now illegal; and it also seeks to upgrade the law in countries that are only partially implementing the code.

Source: This account is based on A. Chetley (1986), The Politics of Baby Foods (London: Pinter) and information at www.ibfan.org, the IBFAN website.

than 1,000. The International Red Cross was founded by Jean Henri Dunant in 1859 after the Battle of Solferino and was awarded the Nobel Peace Prize in 1917, 1944, and 1963. The Red Cross directed the implementation of the first Geneva Convention on the humane treatment of wounded soldiers and prisoners of war. Another INGO, Save the Children, was formed after World War I, and Medecins Sans Frontieres (Doctors Without Borders) was started after the Biafran Civil War in Nigeria in the late 1960s. INGOs have been willing to work in crisis situations when governments are reluctant to get involved. The real growth in the number of INGOs took place in the 1990s. Simultaneously, INGOs began to work more closely with each other and with governments and intergovernmental organizations like the World Bank and the UN.

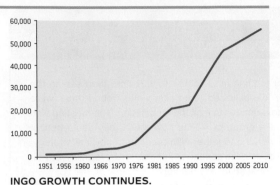

INGO GROWTH CONTINUES.
What impact does the growth of INGOs have on states?

NGOs often act collectively in pursuit of their interests or values, and some scholars believe that they are shifting political power away from the state. NGOs work with states and regional and international organizations, but most global politics scholars believe that the state no longer monopolizes the political world. Most of the NGOs working in what some have called the most idealist and "imagined" global communities are progressive organizations working to reform or transform the current global system. They aim to do so by making decision-making arenas more democratic, transparent, equitable, and environmentally friendly. As Rischard (2002) argues in his book on global problems, NGOs tend to work in three broad areas:

- *Sharing our planet*—issues such as global warming, ocean pollution, and biodiversity.
- *Sharing our humanity*—issues that focus on global health, education, human rights, war, violence, and repression.
- Governance, or *sharing our rule book*—issues that involve international laws and institutions.

Thus, concerns over trade and investment rules promoted by neoliberal institutions like the WTO and the World Bank have become the target of concern for many global activists.

Greenpeace activists boarded the Brent Spar oil platform in the North Sea in 1995. Recently, thirty Greenpeace activists were arrested for trespassing on a Russian Gazprom platform. Greenpeace uses these symbolic actions and its information resources to try to gain support for its positions on environmental issues.

Not all INGOs support progressive changes, however. Some represent the status quo, and some support authoritarian or racist preferred futures. Transnational or multinational corporations sponsor NGOs and advocacy networks that are also a part of this global civil society.

Celebrity Diplomacy

Celebrities, like any of us, use texts and blogs to communicate around the world, but they can also use their celebrity status to promote ideas, values, and positions. Traditional diplomats are critical of these celebrity actions, suggesting that they lack the expertise and dedication to the real goals of traditional diplomacy. Critics say it is okay for celebrities to raise funds for humanitarian issues but that because they are not representatives of states, they must take care not to interfere with any official diplomatic agenda.

In his book *Celebrity Diplomacy* (2007), Andrew Cooper suggests that these celebrities are part of an open and robust process of diplomacy that is the opposite of the insulated and secretive world of traditional diplomacy. Cooper suggests this new form of diplomacy could be eroding the authority and legitimacy of more traditional forms of diplomatic activity. He points out that the Latin root of the word ambassador is *ambactiare*, which means to go on a mission, and many celebrities have embraced that theme and have used their status and resources to achieve goals that reflect their own values. The International Campaign to Ban Landmines became headline news when Princess Diana became its international spokesperson, and Angelina Jolie and Brad Pitt have become spokespersons for a variety of causes related to children and refugees. Jolie and Pitt have created a new charitable foundation to aid humanitarian causes around the world. The newly formed Jolie/Pitt Foundation is giving away $2 million—$1 million to Global Action for Children and $1 million to Doctors Without Borders—to help families affected by HIV/AIDS and extreme poverty.

As governments cut social programs at home and development assistance programs and failed or fragile states are unable or unwilling to provide basic services for their citizens, foundations and individual philanthropists are willing to step up and fund water wells, schools, and hospitals. Some wealthy

Celebrity diplomacy is a common practice and brings attention to global problems. In 2012, actor George Clooney and a member of the U.S. House of Representatives were arrested outside the Sudanese Embassy in Washington, DC. The two were part of a group seeking to raise awareness of the human rights crisis in the Darfur region of Sudan.

individuals also support innovative programs that encourage local business development and local efforts to solve persistent societal challenges.

Foundations and Think Tanks

A foundation is a nonstate actor that is established as a charitable trust or a nonprofit INGO with the purpose of making grants to other institutions or to individuals for a variety of purposes. Many world leaders establish foundations when they leave office to continue to make a difference in global affairs. For example, the Nelson Mandela Foundation was established in 1999 to continue the work of this great leader, especially in the areas of reconciliation in divided societies and social justice. Another example is the William J. Clinton Foundation, which sponsors global initiatives that allow governments to respond to major global challenges such as the need for education, safe drinking water, and clean air. Tony Blair, the former prime minister of the UK, established the Tony Blair Faith Foundation in 2008 to promote "respect and understanding about the world's major religions."

As they have in the past, foundations are likely to continue to have an important role in global politics. They do not simply step in and provide funding where the state has left a vacuum. Rather, foundations want to be change agents and encourage reform and innovation in societies across the globe. Some of the more successful and enduring foundations are in the United States, but many wealthy individuals in Europe and Asia have established foundations to help their countries and their neighbors. For example, the Bharti Foundation, founded by telecom billionaire Sunil Mittal, has opened more than 200 schools to address the problem of illiteracy and has funded teacher training programs and libraries. Foundations play a major role in funding research institutes and communities of scholars and experts who are essential sources of information for those who formulate, implement, and eventually evaluate policy decisions and processes.

Other notable philanthropic foundations that have had a major impact on global politics include the Bill and Melinda Gates Foundation, the Rockefeller Foundation, the Open Society Foundations, the MacArthur Foundation, the Ford Foundation, and the Aga Kahn Foundation. Many of these foundations fund research institutes, universities, and think tanks.

Think tanks (also known as research institutes) vary in size, resource base, policy orientation, and political influence in either national or global politics. Some are scholarly and focus on nonpartisan research, whereas others represent a particular political position or ideology. Many focus on ideas like free market capitalism, socialism, or civic engagement.

Think tanks have increased in number and influence as critical players in global politics, and their increasing importance is the result of a variety of factors. One obvious reason has to do with the complexity of issues now facing policy makers. Most of the officials we elect or appoint to handle these issues are not experts. They depend on the communities of experts often found within think tanks and research institutes. Another reason for

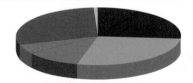

- Africa (554, 8.4%)
- Asia (1194, 18%)
- Europe (1836, 27.8%)
- Latin America and the Caribbean (721, 11%)
- Middle East and North Africa (329, 5.1%)
- North America (1919, 29.1%)
- Oceania (40, 0.6%)

NUMBER OF THINK TANKS IN THE WORLD, 2012.

Who shapes the policy agenda when European and North American research institutes dominate policy research? *Source: http://gotothinktank.com/ dev1/wp-content/uploads/2013/ 07/2012_Global_Go_To_Think_ Tank_Report_-_FINAL-1.28.13.pdf.*

Julian Assange, founder of the WikiLeaks website, noted for revealing confidential diplomatic cables in 2010. In what ways do nonstate actors influence foreign policy?

the growth of these actors is that although we are flooded with information, it is very hard to decide what information is reliable. Think tanks and research institutes with a long history of producing reliable information based on sound research offer public officials information they can use with confidence. These think tanks play a critical role by providing the following services:

- Disseminating research reports and other briefing documents.
- Promoting specific policy strategies and ideas.
- Providing essential information to political parties, public officials, policy bureaucracies, the media, and the general public.
- Evaluating policy programs and decision-making processes.

Multinational Corporations

Multinational corporations (MNCs) are firms with subsidiaries that extend the production and marketing of the firm beyond the boundaries of any one country. The foreign subsidiaries of an MNC are directly owned by the parent corporation. MNCs are not included under the umbrella of civil society because they are for-profit. They control scarce and critically important economic resources, move resources around the world, and have marketing influence and consumer loyalty. The number of MNCs increased exponentially after World War II.

MNCs often get a bad review as guilty of exploiting labor, crowding out local businesses, supporting oppressive governments, and contributing to pollution, poverty, and corruption. This view might be both outdated in some cases and limited, however, and views of MNCs vary according to one's theoretical perspective:

- Liberals see MNCs as a positive force, spreading technology, efficiency, and wealth.

The 1984 gas leak in Bhopal, India, was a terrible tragedy that continues to impact the quality of life for the people in the region. In 2012, these children live in a region with polluted water because of the former Union Carbide industrial complex. Transnational or global social movements often form around the injustices revealed by industrial disasters such as Bhopal.

- Economic nationalists, or neomercantalists, argue that MNCs threaten national sovereignty and dilute national wealth.
- Marxists see MNCs as representatives of the core capitalist states, creating dependencies in countries where they invest, and helping create and maintain a core–periphery global economic structure. According to this view, MNCs participate in predatory globalization, or the search for investment opportunities in countries where labor is cheap and where laws aimed at protecting the welfare of workers and the environment are either not enforced or nonexistent. Essentially, Marxists argue that MNCs put profits above all else. But many NGOs work with MNCs to create opportunities for work in developing countries and to respond to human needs.

The view of MNCs is changing because those who own and manage these corporations realize that they must provide a positive image to attract customers. Their ability to do so and to make profits depends in part on providing resources, expertise, and training to local populations. In many situations, MNCs have become partners in development by providing valuable resources for governments and their citizens. Not only do they provide jobs and help build infrastructure, but also MNCs are often engines of change and reform in corrupt and mismanaged governments.

Criminal and Terrorist Networks as Global Actors

Globalization has provided a number of opportunities for the spread of positive ideas and opportunities as well as trade, travel, and communications. There is, of course, a dark side to globalization, and that is the opportunities it provides for criminal networks to expand their activities, increase their profits, and increase their number of victims. A variety of informal organizations and criminal gangs engage in violent or criminal behavior across the globe. We can make a distinction between activity that is considered criminal around the world—such as theft, fraud, personal violence, piracy, or drug trafficking—and activity that is claimed by those undertaking it to have legitimate political motives. In reality, the distinction becomes blurred when criminals claim political motives or political groups are responsible for acts such as terrorism, torture, or involving children

WHAT'S YOUR WORLDVIEW

Is the idea of national sovereignty now obsolete? With globalization becoming a more important factor in shaping our quality of life, should we be more open to collective multilateralism, global governance, and even intervention from external actors?

in violence. For all governments, neither criminal activity nor political violence can be legitimate within their own jurisdiction and generally not in other countries.

Politically, the most important criminal industries are illicit trading in arms, drugs, and people. In a 2003 article in *Foreign Policy*, Moises Naim argues that the war on terrorism has obscured the importance of five other global wars that we are losing, on:

- drug interdiction,
- the illegal arms trade,
- the protection of intellectual property and the prevention of piracy and counterfeiting of products,
- human trafficking, and
- money laundering and the smuggling of money, gold coins, and other valuables.

Even when governments are strong and reasonably effective, a range of factors can hinder their ability to respond to the threats presented by global criminal networks. These include inadequate laws, bureaucratic jurisdictional disputes, and enforcement strategies that work well at home but not in a more complex global environment.

Is it possible to win any of these wars against powerful criminal networks? The answer is yes, but governments will not win without some serious thinking about how we organize states and how we think about the international system. World leaders must begin to share or even trade sovereignty. They must open their systems to global institutions sponsoring multilateral enforcement activities. States must find ways to regulate transboundary activities and to

The war on drugs has been going on for a long time. This national police special forces team from Colombia was trained by US forces back in 1989.

reach some agreement on a set of regulations that will be enforced in every market across the globe. Successful efforts to end these wars might also depend on a change in our attitudes about community and the individual. If we continue to promote the goal of individual advancement over peace and stability in our communities, these wars could continue for a long time.

We discuss terrorism and terrorist networks in depth in Chapter 6, so for now we merely want to emphasize that terrorist organizations are nonstate actors that have an impact on all actors in the international system. Terrorism is very difficult to eliminate because groups using terrorism are usually parts of larger, global networks that are decentralized and hydra-headed. President George W. Bush described the battle against it as "fourth-generation warfare," which involves nation-states in wars with nonstate global networks.

Terrorist networks are global networks composed of many different groups who might or might not share a common ideological position. These groups are usually united only in their desire to overthrow a government or a regional or global system of governance or replace a way of life or a hegemonic ideology. The major groups fighting the United States and much of the Western world today are fighting the dominant political, economic, and cultural actors and their belief systems. This *new terrorism* is characterized by its global reach, decentralized structure, a seemingly wide-open targeting strategy with no regard for civilians, and more obscure and extreme goals and objectives. Radical groups who are likely to use terrorism to overthrow governments and kill innocent civilians in the process are often linked to NGOs and foundations that are supported by sympathetic states or by states seeking to keep extremists out of their lands.

We should not forget that some states also support terrorist activities, and in some cases their military or police forces are the terrorists. In the pursuit of national interests, states might not always follow the rules.

Conclusion

International law, international and regional organizations, and INGOs collectively play an important role in the governance of our global society. These institutions provide the infrastructure of a truly global system in which it is possible to think about a global common good and a world where human interests trump national interests. There are three pillars of global governance (Muldoon 2004):

1. A political pillar that includes diplomacy, international law, and global and regional organizations like the UN, the WTO, and the EU.
2. An economic pillar that includes MNCs, international banking and industry associations, global labor movements, and global economic movements.
3. A social pillar that includes actors within the global civil society, such as INGOs, and global social movements.

Clearly, international and regional organizations play a critical role in governing the policy areas that transcend the nation-state. The effectiveness and perhaps the fairness of global policy will often depend on the efficacy of international law. Thus, all these institutions play a role in the governance of this global society.

The capacity of the UN in its economic and social work, its development work, and its management of peacekeeping and postconflict reconstruction has expanded since the 1990s. Nonetheless, further changes and adaptations within the UN system are necessary.

With regard to regional organizations, the EU is the best example of how far the integration process can go and how much sovereignty states are willing to share or surrender. The prospect of an ever-wider EU has raised serious questions about the nature and direction of the integration process. The most wide-ranging proposals, and the most significant change in the language of integration, came with the treaty establishing a constitution for Europe that EU heads of state or government signed in 2004. The very fact that the EU should discuss something referred to in the media as a European Constitution is a sign of how far it has developed from its modest beginnings. However, the time might still not be right for such a project.

Nongovernmental actors can also play an important role in making international society work. NGOs can hold governments accountable for their international commitments in a number of ways. Using modern communications methods, transnational social movements can call attention to a problem, recruit members to help, and bring needed relief, often faster than states are able to mobilize. However, nongovernmental actors do not have the stability that most states do, and their effectiveness can vary dramatically from year to year, from region to region, because their support and structure are entirely member dependent.

For all of these reasons we have outlined in this chapter, international law, international organizations, and INGOs remain works in progress.

The Organisation of Economic Co-operation and Development

Engaging With the
WORLD

The OECD, which was founded in 1961 and currently has thirty-four member countries, promotes policies to improve the economic and social well-being of people around the world. Through the OECD's Student Ambassador Program, an on-campus, year-long ambassadorship, you can engage with the OECD and plan activities to raise awareness. The OECD works with governments to understand what drives economic, social, and environmental change; measures productivity and global flows of trade and investment; and analyzes and compares data to predict future trends. To learn more about getting involved, check out www.oecd.org.

KEY TERMS

African Union (AU), p. 173
Civil society, p. 175
Collective security, p. 155
Economic sanctions, p. 158
European Union (EU), p. 170
Global governance, p. 147
Human security, p. 163
International Court of Justice (ICJ), p. 160
International institution, p. 150
International law, p. 148
International nongovernmental organization (INGO), p. 174
International organization, p. 150
Intervention, p. 164
League of Nations, p. 156
Multilateral diplomacy, p. 151

Multilateralism, p. 147
Multinational corporation (MNC), p. 181
Nongovernmental organization (NGO), p. 176
Nonstate actor, p. 147
Organization of African Unity (OAU), p. 173
Organization of American States (OAS), p. 174
Peace enforcement, p. 162
Peacekeeping, p. 162
Peacemaking, p. 162
Postconflict peace building, p. 162
Preventive diplomacy, p. 162
Regime, p. 148

Responsibility to Protect Resolution (R2P), p. 155
Social movement, p. 175
State sovereignty, p. 154
Supranational global organization, p. 154
UN Economic and Social Council (ECOSOC), p. 159
UN General Assembly, p. 158
UN Secretariat, p. 158
UN Security Council, p. 156
UN Trusteeship Council, p. 159
United Nations, p. 154
United Nations Charter, p. 155
Veto power, p. 156

REVIEW QUESTIONS

1. Can you think of other factors, in addition to the ones listed in the chapter, that contributed to the rise of modern international law in the past two centuries?

2. Do you find the argument that states create institutions to sustain international order persuasive?

3. What do you think are the strengths and weaknesses of the international legal system?

4. What have been the driving forces behind processes of regional integration and cooperation?

5. What impact have processes of regional integration had on the state?

6. Compare and contrast European integration with regional cooperation in other areas of the world.

7. How does the UN try to maintain world order?

8. How has UN peacekeeping evolved?

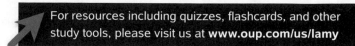

For resources including quizzes, flashcards, and other study tools, please visit us at **www.oup.com/us/lamy**

THINKING ABOUT GLOBAL POLITICS

Who Could Help Tomorrow? Twenty Global Problems and Global Issues Networks

This is a *problem-based* exercise that simply asks you to consider which public, private, and civil-society actors should pool their resources and effectively respond to global problems. The idea for this comes from a book by J. F. Rischard, *High Noon: Twenty Global Problems, Twenty Years to Solve Them* (2002). He is a vice president of the World Bank, and his book has been at the center of discussion at several major global conferences. Now, it is your turn to think about these issues and possible solutions. Rischard believes that two major stresses present unprecedented problems and opportunities. These two are demographic changes, including population growth and income distribution, and the new global economy that includes a technological revolution and the globalization of production, trade, and investment. These stress factors contribute to a number of global issues or challenges that require the attention of all citizens of the world. Here are the three issue areas and some specific challenges in each category:

- Sharing our planet: Issues involving the global commons, **global warming, biodiversity and ecosystem losses, fisheries depletion, deforestation, water deficits, and maritime safety and pollution.**

- Sharing our humanity: Issues requiring a global commitment, **poverty, peacekeeping, conflict prevention, counterterrorism, education for all, global infectious diseases, the digital divide, and natural-disaster prevention and mitigation.**

- Sharing our rule book: Issues needing a global regulatory approach; **reinventing taxation for the twenty-first century; biotechnology rules; global financial architecture; illegal drugs; trade, investment, and competition rules; intellectual property rights; e-commerce rules; and international labor laws and migration rules.**

Who can help to solve or manage these problems? How about a coalition of public, private, and civil-society actors? According to Rischard, partnerships like these are the only way forward. Global coalitions or global information networks (GINs) are similar in purpose to TANs and TSMOs. Each GIN enlists members from governments, international civil society organizations, and businesses to address the issues that challenge global stability and often create real human-security problems.

In small groups of three or four, identify one of the problems or challenges in the three preceding categories. In your group, discuss the nature of the problem and identify actors who you think could help respond to it. You need at least two actors in each of the three categories (six total actors): two governments, two NGOs, and two businesses. This is your problem-solving coalition, or GIN. Why did you select these actors? What resources or expertise do they bring to the problem-solving activities? How will each actor participate in the situation? How will each solve or manage the problem?

For example, if water pollution is the issue, maybe you should involve Canada and Saudi Arabia. Canada has large supplies of clean water, and Saudi Arabia has money to pay for the program and a need for water. NGOs might include the Global Water Campaign and Oxfam; businesses that sell water, like Nestlé and Coca-Cola, might also have skills, interests, and resources.

Your assignment is to put together the most effective coalition to respond to the potential crisis and tell us how it will work!

CONTRIBUTORS TO CHAPTER 5: *Devon Curtis, Christian Reus-Smit, Paul Taylor, Steven L. Lamy, and John Masker.*

6 Global Security, Military Power, and Terrorism

Only the dead have seen the end of war.

—Plato

With respect to terrorism, the locus of global concern is mainly restricted to Islamic countries with no willingness to address the terrorism of "covert operations" in the North, or to address the social causes of terrorism to the extent that recourse to such forms of political violence rests on injustices.

—Richard Falk

Wars in the twenty-first century have been and continue to be conflicts within failed or fragile states. About 39 percent of these conflicts are in Africa, another 39 percent are in Asia, and most of the rest are in the Middle East. The world must deal with wars that seem to have no meaning.

Consider the war in the Democratic Republic of Congo, which is the world's most lethal conflict since World War II. It has lasted more than fifteen years—although several rebel groups agreed to a cease-fire in late 2013—and taken the lives of over 5.4 million people, including an estimated 2.7 million children. Some twenty rebel groups and armies from nine nation-states are fighting in a territory as large as all of Western Europe, often committing acts of sexual violence in their assaults. Ethnic or tribal disputes, poverty, and the lust for power and treasure all contribute to this war. Fundamentally, there is no government to respond, and even 20,000 UN peacekeepers have been unable to contain the conflict. In December 2013, the eighth UN peacekeeping mission in Africa began operations in the Central African Republic. The primary goal of the mission was to stop the sectarian violence where Muslim and Christian groups preyed on each other, creating what UN officials called "pregenocidal" conditions. Civil wars and sectarian conflicts like the conflicts in the Democratic Republic of Congo and the Central African Republic present the biggest security challenges to those who seek global order.

The ongoing conflict in the Democratic Republic of the Congo has killed millions and forced millions more to become refugees. How might this conflict influence your life?

We have entered a period where the shape of war is changing. Nation-states are now unlikely to engage in wars of choice. The era of deploying large armies to fight large land wars might be over, replaced by precision strikes and drone raids. The new type of warfare lasts for years, is financially draining, costs thousands or even millions of lives, and poses extraordinary defensive challenges.

Although we seem to have become complacent over nuclear proliferation and the chances of a nuclear confrontation, the chances of a nuclear confrontation are still very real. Authoritarian states like North Korea and Iran are seeking to defend their interests in what they perceive as hostile environments, and nuclear powers like India and Pakistan are at each other's throats because of longstanding disputes over Kashmir. We must not forget that there are radicals always on the market for weapons of mass destruction.

Our material interests and lifestyle choices, if not our moral responsibilities, draw us all into these conflicts. For whatever reason, war has been a feature of life for most of recorded history. In this chapter we examine national security, international or global security, terrorism, and conflict from a number of academic perspectives. We will try to determine whether the arena of human conflict has changed in an age of globalization.

Introduction

Is global security possible to achieve? For much of the intellectual history of the world, a debate has raged about the causes of war. For some writers, especially historians, the causes of war are unique to each case. Other writers believe that it is possible to provide a wider, more generalized explanation. Some analysts, for example, see the causes lying in human nature, others in the outcome of the internal organization of states, and yet others in international anarchy.

The end of the Cold War reshaped the debate. Some liberal and many alternative theorists, like constructivists and radical liberals (discussed in Chapter 3), claimed to see the dawn of a new world order. For other analysts, however, realism or neorealism remained the best approach to thinking about international security. In their view, very little of substance had changed as a result of the events of 1989. The end of the Cold War initially brought into existence a new, more cooperative era between the superpowers. But this more harmonious phase was only temporary, because countries still interacted in an anarchic international system. For the thousands of people who have died, events seemed to support the realist and neorealist worldviews. With the first Gulf War (1990–1991), the ongoing civil wars in Africa and Asia, and then the 9/11 attacks, it became increasingly clear that states and nonstate actors (including international terrorist groups) continued to view force as an effective way to achieve their objectives.

We begin with a look at the basic definitions and disagreements central to the field, including what is meant by *security*, and we explore the relationship between national and international security. Then we examine the traditional ways of thinking about national security, and the influence these ideas about national security have had on contemporary thinking. We follow this examination with a survey of alternative ideas and approaches that have emerged in the literature in recent years. Next we turn to the pressing question of nuclear weapons proliferation, including a brief overview of these weapons and a discussion of attempts to prevent their spread in the years after the Cold War. Finally, we discuss a transnational trend—terrorism—that has changed the nature of global conflict and security.

Many small and middle powers recognize the importance of collective action and rely on regional and international organizations to provide security and stability. Here Austrian troops are part of a NATO-led peacekeeping force in Kosovo. They were there to prevent ethnic violence before a 2012 election in Serbia.

What Is "Security"?

Most writers agree that **security** is a contested concept. There is a consensus that it implies freedom from threats to core values (for both individuals and groups), but there is a major disagreement about whether the main focus of inquiry should be on *individual*, *national*, or *international* security. During the Cold War period, most writing on the subject was dominated by the idea of **national security** and the realist model that asserts states should develop military capabilities to deal with the threats they confront. More recently, however, a number of contemporary writers have argued for an expanded conception of security outward from the limits of parochial national security to include a range of other considerations and avoid ethnocentrism. It is known as the **widening school of international security** because of proponents' desire to widen the definition to include economic, political, social, and even environmental issues as part of a global security agenda.

Disagreements about definitions matter, because these academic arguments often influence the policy decisions that political leaders make. If the political leaders believe their primary responsibility is national security, then building a safe international system for all countries is of secondary importance. Barry Buzan (1991) concisely describes the security challenge:

> In the case of security, the discussion is about the pursuit of freedom from threat. When this discussion is in the context of the international system, security is about the ability of states and societies to maintain their independent identity and their functional integrity.

Do regions of the world have their own unique set of security challenges, or are the structural realists correct when they argue that all states respond to anarchy and the security dilemma in the same fashion?

Since the end of the Cold War, NATO members have taken on new security tasks. Here Turkish commandos captured five pirates operating in the Gulf of Aden near Somalia.

Today, many security specialists suggest that the most important contemporary trend is the broad process of **globalization** that is taking place. Globalization challenges what we expect a nation-state to provide its citizens. It might hinder the ability of leaders to protect its boundaries, provide order at home, and maintain and promote a productive economic system. We learned in Chapter 1 that a state's legitimacy, efficiency, and identity are challenged by the process of globalization. This process brings new risks and dangers. These include the increase in radical groups who are willing to use **terrorism** across the world, global climate change, a breakdown of the global monetary system, and the proliferation of weapons of mass destruction. These threats to security, on a planetary level, are viewed as being largely outside the control of a single state or groups of nation-states. Only the development of a global security **community**, theorists believe, can deal with this adequately.

In the aftermath of 9/11, and the new era of violence that followed it, Jonathan Friedman argued that we are living in a world "where polarization, both vertical and horizontal, both class and ethnic, has become rampant, and where violence has become more globalized and fragmented at the same time, and is no longer a question of wars between states but of substate conflicts, globally networked and financed, in which states have become one actor, increasingly privatized, amongst others" (J. Friedman 2003, ix). For many who feel like this, the post–9/11 era is a new and extremely dangerous period in world history. But whether the world is so different today from in the past is a matter of much contemporary discussion. To consider this issue we need to begin by looking at the way security has been traditionally conceived.

A striking feature of war in some parts of the contemporary world is its absence. The North Atlantic region has been described as a **security community**, a group of states for whom war has disappeared as a means of resolving disputes with each other, although they may continue to use war against opponents outside the security community. One common characteristic of these states is that they are all democracies, and it has been suggested that although democracies will go to war, they are not prepared to fight against a fellow democracy. The assumption of this **democratic peace** argument is that where groups of democracies inhabit a region, war will become extinct in that region, and that as democracy spreads throughout the world, war will decline. Neoconservative advisors in the Bush administration pushed the country into war, believing that democratic Iraq would become the seed from which democracy would grow in the Middle East. However, there is a danger that some wars will occur as democracies attempt to overthrow nondemocratic regimes to spread the "democratic zone of peace," so that wars will be fought in the name of peace. This was clearly the result of the 2003 invasion of Iraq.

The Changing Character of War

In the contemporary world, powerful pressures are significantly changing national economies and societies. Some of these pressures reflect the impact of globalization; others are the result of the broader effects of **postmodernity**, an international system where domestic and international affairs are intertwined. The cumulative effect has been to change perceptions of external threats. These changed perceptions have in turn influenced beliefs regarding (1) the utility of force as an instrument of policy and (2) the forms and functions of war. In the past two centuries, the modern era of history, some states have used war as a brutal form of politics (typified by the two world wars). In the post–Cold War period, however, the kinds of threats that have driven the accumulation of military power in the developed world have not taken the form of traditional state-to-state military rivalry. Instead, they have been more amorphous and less predictable threats such as terrorism, insurgencies, and internal crises in other countries.

In an era of unprecedented communications technologies, new fields of warfare have emerged. The tangible capacity for war making has also been developing. Military technology with enormous destructive capacity is becoming available to more and more states. This is important, not just because the technology to produce and deliver **weapons of mass destruction (WMD)** is spreading, but because highly advanced conventional military technology is

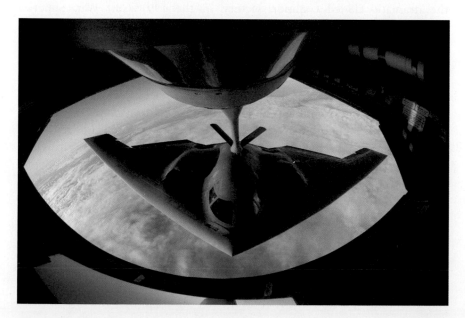

The US Air Force B-2 strategic bomber is designed to make it difficult for radar to see the aircraft.

Rocket scientists in Iran have developed guided missiles that can reach Saudi Arabia, Central Asia, and Israel. How do these ballistic missiles influence global politics?

becoming more widely available. One of the effects of the end of the Cold War was that there was a massive process of disarmament by the former Cold War enemies. This surplus weaponry flooded the global arms market, much of it highly advanced equipment being sold off comparatively cheaply.

The Nature of War

Wars are fought for reasons. The Western understanding of war, following the ideas of the Prussian military thinker and soldier, Carl Von Clausewitz, is that it is instrumental, a means to an end. Wars in this perspective are not random violence; they reflect a conscious decision to engage in them for a rational political purpose. Writing in the early 1800s, Clausewitz defined war as an act of violence intended to compel one's opponent to fulfill one's will. Often, people who initiate wars rationalize them by appealing to common belief and value systems. There are a wide variety of factors that can contribute to the outbreak of war, such as nationalism, class conflict, human nature, and so on. These are the main drivers of change rather than war itself. War is not something imposed by an outside force. The willingness to go to war comes from within states and societies.

Evolutions in Warfare

The concept of the **revolution in military affairs (RMA)** became popular after the dramatic US-led coalition victory in the 1991 Gulf War. Superior technology and doctrine appeared to give the United States and its allies an almost effortless victory. This outcome suggested that future conflicts would be decided by the possession of technological advantages such as advanced guided weapons and space satellites. Although by definition any RMA must involve a radical change or discontinuity in the history of warfare, there is disagreement as to when these changes take place or what causes them.

Most of the literature and debate on the RMA has been American and tends to take for granted the dominance conferred by technological superiority. There is little discussion of what might happen if the United States were to fight a country that has a similar capability or is able to deploy countermeasures. **Asymmetric conflicts** since 1990 have been fought by US-led "coalitions of the willing" against Iraq (in 1991 and again in 2003), the former Yugoslavia (mid-1990s), and, more recently, in Afghanistan (invaded in 2001). Because of the superiority in combat power of the coalition, the battle phases of these asymmetric conflicts have been fairly brief and have produced relatively few combat deaths compared with the Cold War period. Asymmetry works both ways, however. In the postconventional insurgency phases in Iraq and Afghanistan,

End the war in Afghanistan and stop the use of drones. The Peace and Civil Rights Movement Berlin prepare for President Obama's visit in June 2013 and promote an alternative to current NATO and US security strategies and actions.

the asymmetry produced guerrilla-style operations against the technological superiority of the coalition forces. Most battle deaths since 1945 have been caused by bullets and knives, not high-tech military equipment.

One feature of this evolution in warfare is the greatly increased role of the media. Portable satellite dishes enabling live broadcasts make media far more important in terms of shaping or even constructing understandings of particular wars. Media warfare has made war more transparent. Each side now goes to great lengths to manipulate media images of the conflict, and journalists have effectively been transformed from observers into active participants, facing most of the same dangers as the soldiers and helping to shape the course of the war through their reporting. This reflects a broader change. Just as modernity and its wars were based on the mode of production, so postmodernity and its wars reflect the mode of information.

Another postmodern development has been the increasing "outsourcing" of war to modern-day mercenaries and private contractors. Paramilitaries can be disciplined forces under some form of government control, or they can be private armies hired by wealthy private-sector leaders or even political leaders in unstable or failed states. Recently, paramilitary forces started fighting against the government in the Democratic Republic of the Congo. This paramilitary fought on behalf of the candidate who lost the election.

Paramilitary forces are inexpensive to arm, and they do not require the support and training that a regular army requires. These groups are usually not directly connected to governmental authorities, which allows governments to deny any connections with their activities. Although paramilitaries are used to secure political regimes and to protect the interests of their leaders, some have been caught participating in illegal activities. Paramilitary groups in Colombia, Indonesia, Rwanda, and the Balkans have participated in mass killings and even genocide.

CASE STUDY : US Drone Warfare: A Robotic Revolution in Modern Combat   **6.1**

Background

In the early years of its wars in Afghanistan and Iraq, the United States sparsely used its newly emerging unmanned aerial vehicle (UAV) drone technology. In 2001, the US Predator UAV fleet numbered only ten and only did reconnaissance. By 2012, however, the United States was using drones not just for reconnaissance, but also for precision attacks on critical enemy targets. In both Iraq and Afghanistan, the US military has used drones as an extension of conventional warfare. The use of drones has been successful in two major ways: first, by identifying and killing enemy combatants, and second, by avoiding deployment of traditional human forces. Drones perform the "Three Ds": dull jobs, dirty jobs, and dangerous jobs. Patrick Lin (2011) cites the emergence of a "fourth D": the capacity to perform with dispassion. Peter Singer (2012), a specialist on twenty-first-century warfare, suggests that the use of drones is "worryingly seductive" because it creates a policy view that war can be less costly in terms of blood and treasure.

The Case

Targeted killing of enemy fighters and their leaders appears to be an official policy of the US government. On September 2, 2012, a US-directed drone strike in Yemen killed thirteen civilians, including three women and three security officials. The strike occurred in a city known as Rada in the Al-Baitha province of Yemen. An estimated 200 suspected Al Qaeda members resided there at the time of the attack. This was the fourth reported US strike that week, among the hundreds that have taken place in

countries including Yemen, Pakistan, and Afghanistan. In the past eight years, CIA-directed drone strikes in the northwest territories of Pakistan have killed more than 2,400 people, including 479 civilians, according to the Bureau of Investigative Journalism in London ("March of the Robots" 2012). In 2005, the CIA is said to have used drone strikes in Pakistan three times; in 2011, there were 76 reported strikes. President Bush's administration authorized some 52 strikes between 2000 and 2008, and the Obama administration authorized nearly 300 strikes between 2008 and 2012. The United States and the United Kingdom are currently using these weapons, and more than fifty nations are expected to have or to soon develop similar military technology, including China and Iran, as well as nonstate actors including Hezbollah.

Outcome

Drones are a particularly potent instrument of combat, presenting a new and geographically unbound use of force. Predator drones have a better track record for accuracy than fighter jets. Leaders might believe that drones are morally preferable to other weapons of war because they enable capable, accurate, surgical strikes that limit civilian casualties, and their operators are not put at any risk. In 2009, then US Secretary of Defense Leon Panetta stated that the use of drones was "the only game in town in terms of confronting or trying to disrupt the Al Qaeda leadership." A major concern is that countries that develop these UAVs might be more inclined to launch attacks. Yet proponents of drone and other robot technology state that the technology protects soldiers and augments their ability to succeed while keeping them safe from the battlefield.

The United States uses drone warfare more extensively than any other country. The United States has drone bases in Afghanistan and in several African countries. This is a photo of the first drone landing on a nuclear aircraft carrier. This makes it possible for the United States to use drones anywhere in the world.

For Discussion

1. Any new weapon technology raises moral questions in light of the rules of war. Any lethal operations inside sovereign countries that are not at war with those using drones raise several legal and moral questions. Consider the following: The US government has implied that all military-age males in a drone strike area are legitimate targets. Do you agree with that position? Why or why not?

2. Do drones threaten to lower the threshold for lethal violence? Explain your position.

3. Is the decision to use drones ethically permissible? Is it ethically obligatory? Why or why not?

New Wars

Mary Kaldor (1999) has suggested that a category of **new wars** has emerged since the mid-1980s. Just as earlier wars were linked to the emergence and creation of states, the new wars are related to the disintegration and collapse of states, and much of the pressure on such states has come from the effects of globalization. In the past decade, 95 percent of armed conflicts have taken place within states rather than between them. The new wars occur in situations where the economy of the state is performing extremely poorly, or even collapsing, so that the tax revenues and power of the state decline dramatically, producing an increase in corruption and criminality. As the state loses control, access to weapons and the ability to resort to violence are increasingly privatized. Paramilitary groups proliferate, organized crime grows, and political legitimacy collapses. One of the effects of these developments is that the traditional distinction between the soldier and the civilian becomes blurred or disappears altogether.

Many of the features of the new wars are not new, in that they have been common in earlier periods of history—ethnic and religious wars, for example, or conflicts conducted with great brutality. However, it can be argued that the initiators of the new wars have been empowered by the new conditions produced by globalization, which have weakened states and created parallel economies and privatized protection. These new wars are made possible by the inability of certain governments to successfully exercise many of the functions associated with the traditional Westphalian state. Such conflicts will typically occur in **failed states**, countries like Somalia where the government has lost control of significant parts of the national territory and lacks the resources to reimpose control. Steven Metz (2004) has termed the countries falling into this category the **third-tier states** of the global political system.

> ### WHAT'S YOUR WORLDVIEW
>
> *So-called new wars tend to be internal wars between cultural or ethnic groups. Adversaries in these wars seek to eliminate those from different cultural communities. Ethnic cleansing and genocide are the results. Does the international community have a responsibility to prevent these types of war?*

For some observers, the economic rationale, rather than politics, is what drives the new wars, so that war has become a continuation of economics by other means. It is the pursuit of personal wealth, rather than political power, that is the motivation of the combatants. In some conflicts, therefore, war has become the end rather than the means.

Nuclear Proliferation and Nonproliferation

Although all wars since 1945 have been fought without the actual use of nuclear weapons, the issue of nuclear proliferation represents one of the more marked illustrations of globalization. Although only five states (China, France, Russia [Soviet Union], the United Kingdom, and the United States) are acknowledged by the Treaty on the Nonproliferation of Nuclear Weapons (NPT) as possessing nuclear weapons, others have the capability to construct nuclear devices. This was emphasized in May 1998 when India and Pakistan, previously regarded as "threshold" or near-nuclear states, demonstrated their

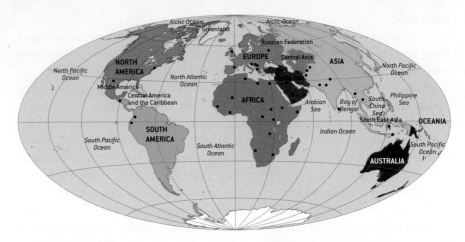

North America
Mexico War on Drugs (2006–present)
US Cyber Warfare (2009–present)

South America
Guatemala War on Drugs (current)
Columbian insurgency (2002–2010)
El Salvador gang/drug conflicts (2010–present)

Europe
Basque country ERA (1959–2011)
Northern Ireland Real IRA (1997–present)
National Liberation Army–Macedonia (2001)
Russia v. Chechnya (1994–2009)
Kosovo (1998–1999)
Croatian conflict (1991–1995)

Middle East
Israel v. Palestinian conflict (1948–present)
Turkish–Kurdish conflict (1978–present)
Iraq Sunni–Shi´a conflict (ongoing)
Arab Spring (2010–present)
Yemen (2010–present)
Syrian conflict (2011–present)

Oceania
East Timor (2006)
Indonesian conflicts (2002–present)

Africa
Lord's Resistance Army conflict (1989–present)
Sierra Leone (1991–2002)
Mozambique (1977–2002)
Angola (1975–2002)
Darfur and South Sudan (ongoing)
Somalia piracy (2005–present)
Democratic Rep. of Congo (1996–present)
Eritrea–Ethiopia (1998–2000)
Rwanda genocide (1994)
Ivory Coast (2002–present)
Mali conflict (2012–present)

Asia
Cambodia Khmer Rouge (1975–1979)
India–Kashmir (1947–present)
US–Taliban (2001–present)
Afghanistan–Taliban (2001–present)
Tibet–China (1962–present)
Sri Lanka civil war (1983–2009)
Nepalese civil war (1996–2006)
Tajikistan civil war (1992–1997)
Myanmar (1948–present)

Map 6.1 State-to-Nonstate Conflict.

respective capabilities by conducting a series of nuclear tests followed by ballistic missile launches.

These events highlighted another aspect of nuclear globalization: the potential emergence of a regionally differentiated world. Whereas in some regions nuclear weapons have assumed a lower significance in strategic thinking than they once held, other regions might be moving in the opposite direction. In Latin America, the South Pacific, Southeast Asia, Africa, and Central Asia the trend has been toward developing the region as a Nuclear Weapon Free Zone. In other regions, such as South Asia, the trend appears to be toward a higher profile for nuclear capabilities. What is unclear is the impact nuclearization (meaning nuclear weapons acquisition) will have in regions where states are moving toward denuclearization (meaning a process of removing nuclear weapons).

Developments stemming from the dissolution of the Soviet Union have also raised novel problems. This is the only case where a previously acknowledged **nuclear weapon state (NWS)** has been subjected to political disintegration. At the time, there was little understanding of what the nuclear consequences would be from such a tumultuous state implosion, and only in hindsight can we judge its full significance. It was unquestionably a period of unprecedented nuclear transformation requiring long-term cooperation between previously hostile states. Less obvious is that this period of transition was facilitated by the foresight of policy makers from both sides of the former Cold War divide who had created a framework of arms-control and disarmament agreements. Ensuring nuclear stability during this period might have been more difficult had it not been for policies such as the Cooperative Threat Reduction Program and agreements like the multilateral NPT and bilateral Strategic Arms Reduction Treaties, signed initially between the United States and the Soviet Union (and later between the United States and Russia).

Proliferation Optimism and Pessimism

One thesis that has sparked diverging responses asserts that the gradual spread of nuclear weapons to additional states should be welcomed rather than

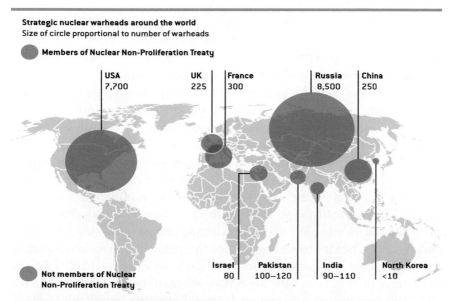

Strategic nuclear warheads around the world
Size of circle proportional to number of warheads

⬤ **Members of Nuclear Non-Proliferation Treaty**

USA	UK	France	Russia	China
7,700	225	300	8,500	250

Israel	Pakistan	India	North Korea
80	100–120	90–110	<10

⬤ **Not members of Nuclear Non-Proliferation Treaty**

GLOBAL MAP OF NUCLEAR ARSENALS.
All numbers are estimates because exact numbers are top secret.

feared. The thesis is based on the proposition that, just as nuclear **deterrence** maintained stability during the Cold War, so can it induce stabilizing effects in other conflict situations. This argument is challenged by those who hold that more will be worse, not better, and that measures to stem nuclear proliferation represent the best way forward (Sagan and Waltz 1995, 2003). In a series of articles, two leading thinkers on nuclear matters, Kenneth Waltz and Scott Sagan, present the arguments. Waltz writes that a controlled spread of nuclear weapons in countries like Pakistan and India is better than a rapid arms race. He contends that leaders of the new nuclear weapons countries would show the same restraint that the United States and the former Soviet Union demonstrated when they developed their nuclear arsenals.

Sagan disagrees strongly with Waltz's argument. His argument is based on the internal political dynamics of the second generation of nuclear weapons countries. According to Sagan, developing countries lack the stable political institutions that the United States and the Soviet Union had during the late 1940s and early 1950s. Instead, they have military-run or weak civilian governments, without the positive constraining mechanisms of civilian control, and military biases could serve to encourage nuclear weapons use—especially during a crisis.

The responses to nuclear proliferation encompass unilateral, bilateral, regional, and global measures that collectively have been termed the nuclear nonproliferation regime. Advocates of this regime argue it is these measures (including treaties like the NPT, export controls, international safeguards, nuclear-supplier agreements, and other standard-setting arrangements) that have constrained nuclear acquisition. Conversely, there have been several criticisms of this regime, and even some long-term supporters acknowledge it is in "need of intensive care" (Ogilvie-White and Simpson 2003). Among the criticisms are that it is a product of a bygone first nuclear age (1945–1990) and is not suited to the demands of the potentially more dangerous second nuclear age (1990–present); it is unable to alleviate the security dilemma that many states confront and, hence, does not address the security motivation driving nuclear weapons acquisition; and it is a discriminatory arrangement because the NPT only requires that the five NWSs pursue nuclear disarmament in good faith (under its Article VI), whereas all other parties—designated as **non-nuclear weapon states (NNWS)**—must forgo the acquisition of nuclear weapons.

Thus, there has always been a tension between two notions of the NPT: as primarily a nonproliferation measure or as a means for achieving nuclear disarmament. This tension was evident during discussion at the NPT Conference in 1995, when the treaty was extended indefinitely after an initial twenty-five years in operation (under Article X). It was also evident at the NPT Review Conference in 2000, when the five NWSs reiterated their commitment to the goal of nuclear weapons elimination. India was a leading critic of this position, asserting that states have an inherent right to provide for their defense. During these dialogues, emphasis was placed on the need for all parties to improve

Leaders from two intransigent states meet. Iran's new president, Hasan Rouhani, meets with a top North Korean official, Kim Yong Nam, at the time of Rouhani's swearing-in ceremony in Tehran. Both states have defied the international nuclear nonproliferation regime. Talks in 2013 with Iran may contain their efforts to create nuclear weapons, but North Korea has them as well as a very unpredictable leader.

transparency in their nuclear operations and for additional measures to enhance verification and compliance.

Nuclear Weapons Effects

The effects of nuclear weapons are considerable. Because of this, the UN Commission for Conventional Armaments in 1948 introduced a new category, WMD, to distinguish nuclear weapons from conventional forms. More recently, another concept, known as CBRN (referring to chemical, biological, radiological, and nuclear capabilities), has appeared in academic and policy papers. Some analysts have also argued that the term WMD should be unraveled because each of the weapons types has different effects, with nuclear weapons being the true WMD (Panofsky 1998).

Nuclear weapons are always dangerous because they can destroy the world as we know it. When used in conflict, nuclear weapons have indiscriminate effects—civilian deaths and injuries are impossible to avoid. Awareness of the effects stems from the two weapons dropped on Hiroshima and Nagasaki at the end of World War II, the only time nuclear weapons have been used. The weapons that destroyed these Japanese cities were relatively small in comparison to the destructive forces generated by later testing of thermonuclear weapons. The largest weapon of this kind known to have been tested was estimated to be a fifty-megaton device (i.e., the equivalent of 50 million tons of TNT) produced by the Soviet Union in 1961.

In recent years there has been a trend away from nuclear weapons with large explosive potential. Most security experts and world leaders agree that the spread of WMDs and the means to deliver them is the chief threat to global security. Yet, even among these leaders and experts, there is little agreement on how to control this proliferation. The risk is greater because the desire to possess nuclear weapons is spreading among states and also among nonstate actors like terrorist groups. The United States and other members of the UN Security Council have finally come together to pressure both Iran and North Korea to cease their nuclear weapons programs.

But the world is not united on these condemnations, and the sanctions continue to be ineffective. Russia and China refuse to impose strict sanctions on Iran because of their own political and economic concerns. North Korea presents a very special case that puzzles the entire world. Whereas the majority of world leaders are condemning the actions of the government of Syria in their destructive civil war, Kim Jong-un, the new leader of North Korea, sent a message in November 2012 in support of Syria's autocratic leader, Bashar Assad.

The Global Zero Movement

Launched in 2008 and led by 200 global leaders and thousands of citizens, the Global Zero movement is working toward the elimination of all nuclear weapons. The leadership of Global Zero has announced a two-phase plan aimed at stopping the spread of nuclear weapons, securing all existing weapons, and finally the elimination of all nuclear weapons. In the first phase of the project, the group has asked the United States and Russia to cut their weapons stock to 1,000 warheads and other nuclear states to freeze their arsenals.

Nuclear Deterrence

One issue of enduring resonance concerns the question of what can explain nuclear "nonuse" since 1945. This debate started early in the nuclear calendar as authors like Bernard Brodie argued that nuclear weapons were useful only in their nonuse (Brodie 1946; Gray 1996). Over the years, the main explanation of nonuse has centered on the notion of **nuclear deterrence**: States have been deterred from using nuclear weapons because of concerns of retaliation in kind by adversaries. On the US side, this became known as mutually assured destruction. Defense intellectuals in the United States believed that if both the United States and the former Soviet Union were able to absorb a surprise nuclear attack and still retaliate with what the analysts called "unacceptable damage," then neither side would risk a preemptive strike.

WHAT'S YOUR WORLDVIEW

What, in your opinion, is the cause of nuclear proliferation? What theory best describes the causes for nuclear proliferation? What theory poses the best solution(s)?

Nuclear Motivations

Given the economic cost of creating a nuclear weapons program, an obvious question is this: Why? Why would a state in the developing world choose to divert scarce resources to a program of questionable value? It is necessary to consider a range of factors that might influence nuclear weapons acquisition. These could include militarism and traditional technological factors that influence the availability of nuclear technology, as well as having a cadre of trained nuclear scientists. Another factor is domestic politics, including imperatives within a political party, or a domestic political situation that might propel a state toward nuclear weapons. Matters of diplomacy also influence the acquisition of nuclear weapons. Through diplomatic bargaining, the acquisition of a nuclear capability can be used to influence or bargain with both perceived allies and enemies. Ultimately, acquiring a nuclear capability deters other states from intervening in one's affairs.

Sagan (2004, 45–46) argues that beyond the *realist/neorealist* argument for building nuclear weapons—states develop these weapons when they face a significant threat—one must consider the influence of domestic interest groups and bureaucratic agencies that benefit from the production of nuclear weapons, missile systems, and other related technologies. In addition, one must consider the value of these weapons in domestic political debates about security and their normative value as symbols of power and modernity. What does it mean to be a major power? Nuclear weapons serve an important symbolic function and help to shape a state's identity (Sagan 2004, 64). In our current international system, the possession of nuclear weapons identifies a country as a major player, and thus some countries want to be seen as a member of this exclusive club. Yet we could just as easily have an international system that is defined by **norms** and values that emphasize disarmament and the elimination of nuclear weapons. This is a position that liberal institutionalists and transformers are working to achieve.

Studies conducted during the 1970s and 1980s on **nuclear terrorism** indicated that there were risks associated with particular groups acquiring a nuclear device or threatening to attack nuclear installations. One study by the International Task Force on Prevention of Nuclear Terrorism concluded that it was possible for a terrorist group to build a crude nuclear device provided it had sufficient quantities of chemical high explosives and weapons-usable fissile materials. More significantly, it was felt that such a group would be more interested in generating social disruption by making a credible nuclear threat rather than actually detonating a nuclear device and causing mass killing and destruction (Leventhal and Alexander 1987). More recent occurrences have served to alter this latter judgment.

Events in the mid-1990s, such as the first bombing of the World Trade Center in New York in 1993 and the attack against the US government building in Oklahoma in April 1995, revealed the extent of damage and loss of life that could be caused. Although both instances involved traditional methods of inflicting damage, the use of nerve agents (chemical weapons) in an underground train network in central Tokyo in March 1995 to cause both death and widespread panic has been viewed as representing a quantum change in methods. These concerns have intensified since the tragic events of September 11, 2001, when the World Trade Center was destroyed by a coordinated attack using civilian aircraft loaded with aviation fuel as the method of

After months of hints and warnings, in February 2013 North Korea announced a third successful test of a nuclear weapon. Given that government's aggressive actions and dismissal of UN Security Council sanctions, what should the UN do about this test?

destruction. The attack not only produced mass casualties, but also changed the assumption about terrorist use of CBRN capabilities (Wilkinson 2003).

Nuclear Capabilities and Intentions

The nuclear programs in Iraq, Iran, Pakistan, and North Korea have raised important issues concerning capabilities and intentions. These instances reveal the difficulties in obtaining consensus in international forums on how to respond to **noncompliance** and the problems associated with verifying treaty compliance in situations where special inspection or nuclear development arrangements are agreed. In the case of Iraq, a special inspection arrangement known as a United Nations Special Committee was established following the 1991 Gulf War to oversee the dismantlement of the WMD program that had come to light as a result of the conflict. By the late 1990s, problems were encountered over access to particular sites, and UN Special Committee inspectors were withdrawn. Disagreements also surfaced among the five permanent members of the UN Security Council concerning how to implement the UN resolutions that had been passed in connection with Iraq since 1991. These had not been resolved at the time of the 2003 intervention in Iraq, and subsequent inspections in that country were unable to find evidence of significant undeclared WMD.

The complexity associated with compliance is evident in the ongoing case of Iran. The country became the subject of attention from the International Atomic Energy Agency (IAEA) over delays in signing a protocol, added to Iran's safeguards agreement, requiring increased transparency by NNWS. Although Iran later did sign the protocol, the discovery by the IAEA of undeclared facilities capable of enriching uranium fueled speculation. In an effort to find a solution, a dialogue between Iran and the so-called EU-3 (France, Germany, and the United Kingdom) began in October 2003. Although an agreement was reached in Paris in November 2004, the situation was not resolved, and by 2006 the UN Security Council passed resolutions, under Chapter VII of the UN Charter, requiring Iran to comply with its international obligations. The Iranian case is a destabilizing factor in regional—and global— politics. As recently as the opening session of the 2012–2013 UN General Assembly, the Ahmadinejad government has denounced Israel, with the Iranian president himself calling for the destruction of the country. Thus, the difficulty of getting Iran to agree to verification mechanisms has complicated an already dangerous Middle East security picture.

Decisions regarding war and purchasing weapons needed to fight a war are state actions. However, increasingly since the end of the Cold War, states are facing security threats from nonstate actors. For the Cold War, the bipolar regime dominated a range of issues, reducing ethnonationalism or religious fundamentalism to secondary status. An aspect of globalization is the declining centrality of the state; this trend has created space for groups with subnational or pannational agendas to act. The subject of the next section—terrorism—is the preferred method of many of these groups.

Defining Terrorism

Terrorism and globalization share at least one quality—both are complex phenomena open to subjective interpretation. Definitions of terrorism vary widely, but all depart from a common point. Terrorism is characterized, first and foremost, by the use of violence. This tactic of violence takes many forms and often indiscriminately targets noncombatants. The purpose for which violence is used, and its root causes, is where most of the disagreements about terrorism begin.

Historically, the term *terrorism* described state violence against citizens, for example during the French Revolution or the Stalinist era of the Soviet Union. Over the past half-century, however, the definition of terrorism has evolved to mean the use of violence by nonstate groups or networks to achieve political change. Terrorism differs from criminal violence in its degree of political legitimacy. Those sympathetic to terrorist causes suggest that violence, including the death of innocent people, is the only remaining option that can draw attention to the plight of the aggrieved. Such causes have included ideological, ethnic, and religious exclusion or persecution.

Defining terrorism can be difficult because groups often advocate multiple grievances and compete with one another for resources and support. In addition, the relative importance of these grievances within groups can change over time. Those targeted by terrorists are less inclined to see any justification, much less legitimacy, behind attacks that are designed to spread fear by killing and maiming civilians. As

WHAT'S YOUR WORLDVIEW

Most people think that all groups that use terrorism are nonstate actors, but states can also use terrorist tactics. Do you think that is a legitimate use of force if used by a state?

a result, the term *terrorist* has a pejorative value that is useful in delegitimizing those who commit such acts.

Audrey Kurth Cronin, an academic authority on terrorism, has outlined different types of terrorist groups and their historical importance in the following way:

> There are *four types* of terrorist organizations currently operating around the world, categorized mainly by their source of motivation: left-wing terrorists, right-wing terrorists, ethnonationalist/separatist terrorists, and religious or "sacred" terrorists. All four types have enjoyed periods of relative prominence in the modern era, with left-wing terrorism intertwined with the Communist movement and currently practiced by Maoists in Peru and Nepal, right-wing terrorism employed by Neo-Nazi skinheads in several European countries drawing its inspiration from Fascism, and the bulk of ethnonationalist/separatist terrorism accompanying the wave of decolonization especially in the immediate post–World War II years and in places like Northern Ireland and Spain. Currently, "sacred" terrorism is becoming more significant. Of course, these categories are not perfect, as many groups have a mix of motivating ideologies—some ethnonationalist groups, for example, have religious characteristics or agendas—but usually one ideology or motivation dominates. (Cronin 2002/3, 39)

Even with the use of violence by states, there is disagreement on what constitutes the legitimate application of armed force. For example, during the 1980s Libya sponsored terrorist acts as an indirect method of attacking the United States, France, and the United Kingdom. Those states, in turn, condemned Libyan sponsorship as contravening international norms and responded with

A Boston Marathon bombing survivor rolls her wheelchair near a memorial for the victims of the blast. No place in the world is immune from violence and terrorism and no one seems to have an answer. What would you do prevent the alienation and estrangement that motivates individuals and groups to use terrorist tactics?

the customary methods of global politics: sanctions, international court cases, and occasional uses of force. Disagreement associated with the invasion of Iraq in 2003, led by the United States, relates to interpretations over whether the conditions for "just war" were met prior to commencement of military operations. Some suggest that the conditions were not met and that actions by the coalition should be considered an "act of terrorism" conducted by states. Leaders in the United States and the United Kingdom dismiss the charge on the basis that a greater evil was removed. Violating international norms in the pursuit of terrorists runs the risk of playing into perceptions that the state itself is a terrorist threat. Critics suggest that US policy toward terrorist detainees and "extraordinary renditions" damages US credibility as a global champion for individual rights and freedoms.

As with other forms of irregular, or asymmetric, warfare, terrorism is designed to achieve political change for the purpose of obtaining power to right a perceived wrong. However, according to some analysts, terrorism is the weakest form of irregular warfare with which to alter the political landscape. The reason for this weakness is that terrorist groups rarely possess the broader support of the population that characterizes insurgency and revolution, and the methods of terrorists often alienate potential supporters of the cause. Terrorist groups often lack support for their objectives because the changes they seek are based on radical ideas that do not have widespread appeal. To effect change, terrorists must provoke drastic responses that act as a catalyst for change or weaken their opponent's moral resolve. In a few cases, terrorist acts have achieved relatively rapid change.

As with definitions of terrorism, there is general agreement on at least one aspect of globalization. Technologies allow the transfer of goods, services, and information almost anywhere quickly and efficiently. In the case of information, the transfer can be secure and is nearly instantaneous. The extent of social, cultural, and political change brought on by globalization, including increasing interconnectedness and homogeneity in the international system, remains the subject of much disagreement and debate, as other chapters in this volume have outlined. These disagreements, in turn, influence discussion of the extent to which globalization has contributed to the rise of modern terrorism. There is little doubt that the technologies associated with globalization have been used to improve the effectiveness and reach of terrorist groups. The relationship between globalization and terrorism is best understood as the next step in the evolution of political violence since terrorism became a transnational phenomenon in the 1960s. To understand the changes perceived in terrorism globally, it is useful to understand the evolution of terrorism from a primarily domestic political event to a global phenomenon.

WHAT'S YOUR WORLDVIEW

Why would any individual resort to using terrorist tactics? Why would people decide to join extremist groups and use terrorism to achieve their goals?

Terrorism: From Domestic to Global Phenomena

Historically, nonstate terrorist groups have used readily available means to permit small numbers of individuals to spread fear as widely as possible. In the late nineteenth and early twentieth centuries, anarchists relied on railroads for travel and killed with revolvers and dynamite. Yet terrorists and acts of terrorism rarely had an impact beyond national borders, in part because the activists often sought political change within a specific country. Three factors led to the birth of transnational terrorism in 1968: (1) the expansion of commercial air travel, (2) the availability of televised news coverage, and (3) broad political and ideological interests among extremists that converged on a common cause. As a result, terrorism grew from a local to a transnational threat. Air travel gave terrorists unprecedented mobility.

For example, the Japanese Red Army trained in one country and attacked in another, as with the 1972 Lod Airport massacre in Israel. In the United States, some radicals forced airplanes to go to Cuba. Air travel appealed to terrorists for other reasons. Airport security measures, including passport control, were less stringent when terrorists began hijacking airlines. These **skyjackings** suited terrorist purposes well. Hijacked airliners offered a degree of mobility, and therefore security, for the terrorists involved. States also acquiesced to terrorist demands, frequently for money, which encouraged further incidents. The success of this tactic spurred other terrorist groups, as well as criminals and political refugees, to follow suit. As a result, incidents of hijacking increased dramatically from five in 1966 to ninety-four in 1969. Shared political ideologies stimulated cooperation and some exchanges between groups as diverse as the Irish Republican Army (IRA) and the Basque separatist organization Euzkadi Ta Askatasuna (ETA). Besides sharing techniques and technical experience, groups demanded the release of imprisoned "fellow revolutionaries" in different countries, giving the impression of a coordinated global terrorist network. The reality was that groups formed short-term relationships of convenience, based around weapons, capabilities, and money, to advance local political objectives. For example, members of the IRA did not launch attacks in Spain to help the ETA, but they did share resources.

Televised news coverage and the Internet also played a role in expanding the audience, who could witness the theater of

Terrorist attacks are nothing new in global politics. In 1972, Palestinian terrorist group Black September captured and killed eleven members of the Israeli Olympic team. Two West German policemen move into position to attempt to free the hostages.

CASE STUDY : Cyberterrorism   **6.2**

Background

In January 2010, Google announced that a computer attack originating from China had penetrated its corporate infrastructure and stolen information from its computers, most likely source code. The hackers had also accessed the Gmail accounts of some human rights activists and infiltrated the networks of thirty-three companies. Although it is difficult to pinpoint the origin of cyberattacks, the US National Security Agency traced the attacks first to servers in Taiwan and then to the Shanghai Jiaotong University and the Lanxiang Vocational School in China. The attacks on Google and other commercial and military targets indicate that China, like other countries including the United States, see the Internet and cyberespionage as a key part of the security arena. The Google hacking incident is only one of many similar cyberattacks originating from China.

The Case

Industries and other economic actors have become dependent on reliable, high-speed communications technology that allows for the instantaneous movement of capital, information, and ideas across the globe with the stroke of a key. The smooth functioning of all manner of government and critical infrastructure is now also contingent on the availability and dependability of communications technology. Unfortunately, in connecting people, the Internet also exposes them to vulnerabilities. As technology becomes more sophisticated and networks and information systems become more interdependent, there is increased risk of exploitation and disruption.

Most experts believe that terrorist groups and aggressive states are close to reaching the capability to launch major cyberattacks. More than twenty states have developed a significant cyberwarfare capability, but China provides a useful case study because it has been more brazen in its actions than Russia, France, or the United States, for example. According to the US Department of Defense, cyberwarfare is now an integrated part of China's

military strategy, and People's Liberation Army officers are undergoing training in it at Chinese military academies.

Outcome

The revolution in military affairs, which was so lauded in the 1990s and the early years of the twenty-first century, could prove to be the greatest vulnerability for the United States and other countries. Although the United States has focused on developing the world's greatest offensive capability in cyberspace, it has not developed an equally robust defensive capability. The development of and dependence on networked military systems—let alone critical national infrastructure—present significant weaknesses in modern military capability and strategic posture. Of particular concern is that potential adversaries' cyberwarriors might have already infiltrated these systems, leaving behind devices such as trapdoors (which allow hackers to return unnoticed and with greater ease at a later date) and logic bombs (which are programs hidden in software code and designed to eventually disrupt or destroy the software).

China is by no means alone in its motivation to build a cybercapability that can be used in conjunction with more conventional means of attack. Similarly, the United States is not the only country concerned about this new threat. All countries must guard against the need to engage in increased spending on the development of new and costly weapons systems.

For Discussion

1. Is it possible to defend against cyberattacks? Will this require a multinational response? Are states willing to share their defensive technologies with other states?
2. Do societies put themselves at a greater risk if they become more dependent on technology? Are we more vulnerable in a world that is so technologically connected?
3. Do cyber capabilities increase the power of smaller states and even groups within states and thus increase the vulnerabilities of even the great powers?

terrorism in their own homes. People who had never heard of what was called "the plight of the Palestinians" became more aware of the issue after live coverage of incidents such as the hostage taking conducted by Black September during the 1972 Munich Olympics. Although some considered media coverage "the oxygen that sustains terrorism," terrorists discovered that reporters and audiences lost interest in repeat performances over time. To sustain viewer interest and compete for coverage, terrorist groups undertook increasingly spectacular attacks, such as the seizure of Organization of Petroleum Exporting Countries delegates by "Carlos the Jackal," whose real name was Ilich Ramírez Sánchez, in Austria in December 1975. Terrorism experts speculated that terrorist leaders understood that horrific, mass-casualty attacks might cross a threshold of violence. This might explain why few terrorist groups attempted to acquire or use WMD, including nuclear, chemical, and biological weapons.

The Impact of Globalization on Terrorism

Al Qaeda, "The Base" or "The Foundation," received global recognition as a result of its attacks conducted in New York and Washington, DC, on September 11, 2001. Since the 2001 attacks, and even after the death of Osama bin Laden in 2011, experts have continuously debated what Al Qaeda is, what it represents, and the actual threat that it poses. In early 2006, the Office of the Chairman of the Joint Chiefs of Staff in the Pentagon released the *National Military Strategic Plan for the War on Terrorism*, which sought to characterize the fluid nature of the militant Islamic terrorism:

> There is no monolithic enemy network with a single set of goals and objectives. The nature of the threat is more complicated. In the GWOT [global war on terror], the primary enemy is a transnational movement of extremist organizations, networks, and individuals—and their state and nonstate supporters—which have in common that they exploit Islam and use terrorism for ideological ends. The Al Qaeda Associated Movement (AQAM), comprised of Al Qaeda and affiliated radical groups, is the most dangerous present manifestation of such extremism. The [Al Qaeda network's] adaptation or evolution resulted in the creation of an extremist "movement," referred to by intelligence analysts as AQAM, extending extremism and terrorist tactics well beyond the original organization. This adaptation has resulted in decentralizing control in the network and franchising its extremist efforts within the movement. (National Military Strategic Plan for the War on Terrorism [Unclassified], 13)

Efforts to explain the vitality of global terrorism in general—and Al Qaeda in particular—focus on three areas linked to aspects of globalization: culture, economics, and religion.

Cultural Explanations

Culture is one way to explain why militant Islam's call for armed struggle has been successful in underdeveloped countries. Culture also explains many of the ethnic conflicts, violence between religious and language groups, across the world. The 1990s were a period of unprecedented ethnic violence and terrorism that included the genocide in Rwanda and the ethnic cleansing in the former Yugoslavia. Many fundamentalist groups believe that violence is the only method to preserve traditions and values against a cultural tsunami of Western products and **materialism**. Once sought after as an entry method to economic prosperity, Western secular, materialist values are increasingly rejected by those seeking to regain or preserve their own unique cultural identity. The phenomenon of rejecting the West is not new; one could argue that it began almost 200 years ago as the strength of the Ottoman Empire waned. Since then, the social changes associated with globalization and the spread of free market capitalism appear to be overwhelming the identity or values of groups who perceive themselves as the losers in the new international system. In an attempt to preserve their threatened identity and values, groups actively distinguish

Former UN Secretary General Kofi Annan speaks at an event at the UN European headquarters honoring the late South African President Nelson Mandela. Both men dealt with ethnic conflict and the aftermath of such conflicts. Annan was a UN official involved in the UN interventions in the former Yugoslavia and the failure to intervene in Rwanda. Mandela helped end the heinous system of apartheid that separated the races and brutalized the Black population of South Africa.

themselves from despised "others." At the local level, this cultural friction could translate into conflicts divided along religious or ethnic lines to safeguard **identity**.

Economic Explanations

Not everyone agrees that defense of cultural identity is the primary motivation for globalized terrorist violence. Others see economic aspects as the crucial motivating factor in the use of violence to effect political change. Although globalization provides access to a world market for goods and services, the net result has also been perceived as a form of Western economic **imperialism**. The United States and the postindustrial states of Western Europe form the global North or economic core that dominates international economic institutions such as the **World Bank**, sets exchange rates, and determines fiscal policies. The actions and policies can be unfavorable to the underdeveloped countries, or global South, that make up the periphery or gap. Political decisions by the leaders of underdeveloped countries to deregulate or privatize industries to be competitive globally could lead to significant social and economic upheaval. The citizenry might shift loyalties to illegal activities such as terrorism if the state breaks its social contract (Junaid 2005, 143–144).

Wealth is also linked to personal security and violence. With little opportunity to obtain wealth locally, individuals will leave to pursue opportunities in other countries. The result is emigration and the rapid growth of

WHAT'S YOUR WORLDVIEW

Poverty might not be a direct cause of terrorist activities, but do you think it contributes to attitudes that make people susceptible to recruitment by radical groups?

burgeoning urban centers that act as regional hubs for the flow of global resources. Movement, however, is no guarantee that individual aspirations will be realized. In cases where they are not, individuals might turn to violence for reasons that are criminal (i.e., personal gain) or political (i.e., to change the existing political system through insurgency or terrorism). Paradoxically, rising standards of living and greater access to educational opportunities associated with globalization could lead to increased expectations. If those expectations are unmet, individuals can turn to extreme political views and action against "the system" that denies them the opportunity to realize their ambitions. A prominent study suggests that a sense of alienation and lack of opportunity among some Muslim males is a contributing factor for their decision to turn to violence globally (Sageman 2004, 95–96).

The explanation that recent terrorist violence is a reaction to economic globalization could be flawed for a number of reasons. These reasons include the personal wealth and social upbringing of a number of members of global terrorist groups, as well as trends in regional patterns of terrorist recruitment. Many former leaders and members of transnational terrorist groups, including the German Red Army Faction and the Italian Red Brigades, came from respectable middle- and upper-class families. The same holds true for a number of modern-day antiglobalization anarchists. Within militant Islamic groups, most of their leaders and senior operatives attended graduate schools around the globe in fields as diverse as engineering and theology and were neither poor nor downtrodden (Sageman 2004, 73–74). And, like the Bolshevik leaders, bin Laden and others have been able to convince less fortunate people to die for the cause.

The terrorist group Aum Shinrikyo (currently known as Aleph) released the nerve gas sarin in the Tokyo subway system in 1995, killing thirteen people and injuring thousands. How can any country anticipate and prevent these forms of terrorism?

Religion and "New" Terrorism

In the decade prior to 9/11, a number of scholars and experts perceived that fundamental changes were taking place in the character of terrorism. The use of violence for political purposes, to change state ideology or the representation of ethnic minority groups, had failed in its purpose and a new trend was emerging. **Postmodern** or **"new" terrorism** was conducted for different reasons altogether and seemed to be driven by the power of ideas of the kind that constructivist international relations theory describes (see Chapter 3). Motivated by promises of rewards in the afterlife, some terrorists are driven by religious reasons to kill as many of the nonbelievers and unfaithful as possible (Laqueur 1996, 32–33). Although suicide tactics had been observed in Lebanon as early as 1983, militant Islam had previously been viewed as a state-sponsored, regional phenomenon (Wright 1986, 19–21).

New terrorism, which some authors use to explain the global jihad, is seen as a reaction to the perceived oppression of Muslims worldwide and the spiritual bankruptcy of the West. As globalization spreads and societies become increasingly interconnected, Muslims have a choice: Accept Western beliefs to better integrate or preserve their spiritual purity by rebelling. Believers in the global **jihad** view the rulers of countries such as Pakistan, Saudi Arabia, or Iraq as apostates who have compromised their values in the pursuit and maintenance of secular, state-based power. The only possible response is to fight against such influences through jihad. Jihad is understood by most Islamic scholars and imams to mean the internal struggle for purity spiritually, although it has also been interpreted historically as a method to establish the basis for just war. Extremists who espouse militant Islam, including the now-deceased Osama bin Laden and his intellectual associate, Ayman al-Zawahiri, understand jihad in a different way. For the jihadi terrorist, there can be no compromise with either infidels or apostates.

The difference in value structures between secular and religious terrorists makes the responses to the latter difficult. Religious terrorists will kill themselves and others because they believe that they will receive rewards in the afterlife. Differences in value structures make the deterrence of religious terrorism difficult, if not impossible, as secular states cannot credibly threaten materially the ideas that terrorists value spiritually. Secular terrorism has had as its goal the pursuit of power to correct flaws within society but retain the overarching system. Religious terrorism, by contrast, does not seek to modify but rather to replace the normative structure of society (Cronin 2002/3, 41).

The use of religion, as a reaction to and an explanation for the phenomenon of global terrorism, contains some of the same incongruities as those focused on cultural and economic aspects. For Western observers, religious reasons appear to explain how individual terrorists are convinced to take their own lives and kill others. Personal motivations can include promises of financial rewards for family members, gaining fame within a community, taking revenge for some grievance, or simply achieving a form of self-actualization. Yet few religious terrorist leaders, planners, and coordinators martyr themselves. Religion provides terrorist groups with a crucial advantage: the mandate and sanction of the divine to commit otherwise illegal or immoral acts. There is a substantial difference between religious motivation as the single driving factor for individuals to commit acts of terrorism and the ultimate purpose for which violence is being used.

Globalization, Technology, and Terrorism

Few challenge the point that terrorism has become much more pervasive worldwide as a result of the processes and technologies of globalization. The technological advances associated with globalization have improved the capabilities of terrorist groups to plan and conduct operations with far more devastation

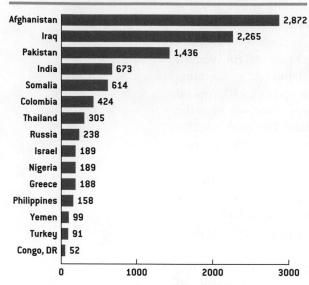

Country	Attacks
Afghanistan	2,872
Iraq	2,265
Pakistan	1,436
India	673
Somalia	614
Colombia	424
Thailand	305
Russia	238
Israel	189
Nigeria	189
Greece	188
Philippines	158
Yemen	99
Turkey	91
Congo, DR	52

TERRORIST ATTACKS, TOP 15 COUNTRIES, 2011.
Terrorist attacks are often aimed at governments or at different ethnic or ideological groups that are perceived as enemies. What do these numbers tell us about the states where they occur? Would you say all of these states are fragile or weak? What about Israel?

and coordination than their predecessors could have imagined. In particular, technologies have improved the capability of groups and cells to carry out attacks on a wider and more lethal scale.

Proselytizing

States traditionally have had an advantage in their ability to control information flows and use their resources to win the battle of hearts and minds against terrorist groups. Terrorist leaders understand how the Internet has changed this dynamic: "We [know that we] are in a battle, and that more than half of this battle is taking place in the battlefield of the media. And that we are in a media battle in a race for the hearts and minds of our Umma" (Office of the Director of National Intelligence 2005, 10).

The continued expansion of the number of Internet service providers, especially in states with relaxed or ambivalent content policies or laws, combined with capable and cheap computers, software, peripherals, and wireless technologies, has empowered individuals and groups to post tracts on or send messages throughout the World Wide Web. One form of empowerment is the virtual presence that individuals have. Although prominent jihadi terrorists' physical presence can be removed through imprisonment or death, their virtual presence and influence are immortalized on the World Wide Web.

Another form of empowerment for terrorist groups, brought on by globalization, is the volume, range, and sophistication of propaganda materials. Terrorist groups were once limited to mimeographed manifestos and typed communiqués. Terrorist supporters and sympathizers now build their own websites. An early example was a website sympathetic to the Peruvian Tupac Amaru Revolutionary Movement. This website posted the group's communiqués and videos during the seizure of the Japanese embassy in Lima in 1996. Webmasters sympathetic to terrorist groups also control the content and connotation of the material posted on their websites. The website of the Sri Lankan group Liberation Tigers of Tamil Eelam, for example, posts items that cast the group as an internationally accepted organization committed to conflict resolution. Messages, files, and polemics can be dispatched to almost anywhere on the globe via the Internet or text messaging, almost instantaneously.

Terrorist groups in Chechnya and the Middle East have also made increasing use of video cameras to record the preparations for attacks, and their results, including successful roadside bombings and the downing of helicopters. With the right software and a little knowledge, individuals or small groups can download or obtain digital footage and music and produce videos that appeal to specific groups. Video footage is useful in inspiring potential recruits and seeking donations from support elements within the organization. For example, terrorist recruiters distributed videos of sniper and other attacks against coalition forces in Iraq, produced by the Al Qaeda media-production group As-Sahab. The competition among global news outlets like CNN, MSNBC, and Al Jazeera ensures that the images of successful or dramatic attacks reach the widest audience possible.

Security of Terrorist Organizations

Terrorist cells without adequate security precautions are vulnerable to discovery and detection. Translations of captured Al Qaeda manuals, for example, demonstrate the high value their writers place on security, including surveillance and countersurveillance techniques. The technological enablers of globalization assist terrorist cells and leaders in preserving security in a number of ways, including distributing elements in a coordinated network, remaining mobile, and utilizing clandestine or encrypted communications.

The security of terrorist organizations has historically been preserved by limiting communication and information exchanges between cells. This ensures that if one cell is compromised, its members only know each other's identities and not those of other cells. Thus the damage done to the organization is

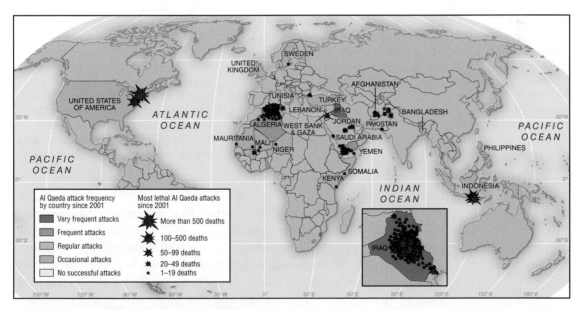

Map 6.2 The Global Reach of Al Qaeda.
Can a nation-state respond to networks like this without global cooperation?

THEORY IN PRACTICE

The Realist-Theory Perspective and the War on Terror

The Challenge

Debates about political theories have had an important role in government debates about how secular Western democracies can best fight terrorism. The realist tradition asserts that countries are the most important, sometimes the only, actors that matter in international politics. Many political scientists in the realist tradition also maintain that questions of morality should not restrain the actions of a country that is under threat of an attack.

Options

These components of realism can explain why the Bush administration was seemingly surprised by the September 11, 2001, attacks and why the government reacted the way it did to those events. For example, on August 6, 2001, National Security Advisor Condoleezza Rice gave President Bush a briefing that included a memo titled "Bin Laden Determined to Strike in US," which documented plans of the Al Qaeda organization (*The 9/11 Commission Report*, New York: Norton; p. 261). This was the most recent of a series of warnings about possible terrorist attacks on the United States or on American interests around the world.

Realist theory helps us to understand why the Bush administration did not act aggressively on these reports: The theory asserts that *states* are the primary threat to other *states*. Despite the previous successful Al Qaeda attacks on the US embassies in Kenya and Tanzania, and the near sinking of the destroyer USS *Cole*, members of the Bush administration might have believed that a small nonstate group was not able to launch another attack. In addition, the Bush administration was preoccupied with North Korea's nuclear weapons program and an incident in which a Chinese fighter aircraft had damaged a US Navy maritime surveillance aircraft, forcing it to land in China. Logically for President Bush and his advisors, North Korea and China presented a more pressing threat to the United States.

Realist international relations theory also provides an explanation for the Bush administration's actions after September 11, 2001. If, as the memo said, bin Laden was determined to attack the United States, President Bush was equally determined that it would not happen again. Therefore, the United States soon attacked Afghanistan, seeking to

depose the Taliban government that had offered sanctuary to bin Laden and other members of the Al Qaeda leadership. More telling, however, was the Bush administration's decision to label as "unlawful combatants" anyone that US military personnel captured and detain them at the US Navy base at Guantánamo, Cuba or in secret prisons around the world. The increasingly unpopular practice of "extraordinary rendition" was another component of the policy. Extraordinary rendition was the capture and transfer of suspected terrorists to unspecified foreign sites for purposes of detention and often torture. Some nongovernmental human rights organizations called the actions violations of international law, but the Bush administration, echoing a key aspect of the realist perspective, called the decisions morally necessary to protect the United States.

For Discussion

The terrorist challenge facing nation-states raises the enduring question of international relations: When is it appropriate for national leaders to violate international law and moral codes of conduct to protect their citizens? Is torture acceptable if it protects a nation-state?

minimized. Security is even more important to **clandestine** or **"sleeper" cells** operating on their own without central direction. The use of specific codes and ciphers, known only to a few individuals, is one way of preserving the security of an organization. Although code and ciphers inevitably have been broken and information has been obtained through interrogation, such activities take time. During that time, terrorist groups adjust their location and operating methods in an attempt to stay ahead of counterterrorist forces. Technological advancements, including faster processing speeds and software developments, now mean that those sympathetic to terrorist causes can contribute virtually through servers located hundreds or thousands of miles away.

Mobility

The reduced size and increased capabilities of personal electronics also give terrorists mobility advantages. Mobility has always been a crucial consideration for terrorists and insurgents alike, given the superior resources that states have been able to bring to bear against them. In open societies that have well-developed infrastructures, terrorists have been able to move rapidly within and between borders, and this complicates efforts to track them because they exploit the very societal values they seek to destroy.

The globalization of commerce has also improved terrorist mobility. The volume of air travel and goods that pass through ports has increased exponentially through globalization. Between states, measures have been taken to ease the flow of goods, services, and ideas, to improve efficiency, and to reduce costs. One example is the European Schengen Agreement, in which border security measures between EU member states have been relaxed to speed deliveries. Market demands for efficiencies of supply, manufacture, delivery, and cost have complicated states' efforts to prevent members of terrorist groups from exploiting gaps in security measures. Additional mobility also allows terrorist groups to transfer expertise, as demonstrated by the arrest of three members of the IRA suspected of training counterparts in the Fuerzas Armadas Revolucionarias de Colombia in Bogota in August 2001.

The use of air travel by terrorists prior to 9/11 has been well documented. Mohamed Atta, for example, traveled extensively between Egypt, Germany, and the Middle East before the attacks. In this respect, the latest generation of terrorists resembles their transnational predecessors in exploiting travel methods for attacks. Terrorist use of transportation is not necessarily overt, as the volume of goods transported in support of a globalized economy is staggering and difficult to monitor effectively. For example, customs officials cannot inspect all of the vehicles or containers passing through border points or ports. To illustrate the scale of the problem, the United States receives 10 million containers per year, and one port, Los Angeles, processes the equivalent of 12,000 twenty-foot containers daily. Western government officials fear that terrorist groups will use containers as a convenient and cheap means to ship WMD. Incidents in Italy in 2001 and Israel in 2004 confirm that terrorist groups are aware of the convenience and cheapness of globalized shipping to improve their mobility.

> ### WHAT'S YOUR WORLDVIEW
>
> *With the aspects of globalization—affordable travel, technology, and the free flow of capital— do you think it is possible to provide complete security and safety for all citizens in a society?*

Combating Terrorism

States plagued by transnational terrorism responded individually and collectively to combat the phenomenon during the Cold War. These responses ranged in scope and effectiveness and included passing antiterrorism laws,

Another TSA airport check and the most visible illustration of the impact of terrorism on the lives of all citizens who travel. Is it likely that these types of interventions will increase? Are citizens likely to face more oversight?

taking preventative security measures at airports, and creating special-operations counterterrorism forces such as the West German Grenzschutzgruppe-9 (GSG-9). Successful rescues in Entebbe (1976), Mogadishu (1977), and Prince's Gate, London (1980), demonstrated that national counterterrorism forces could respond effectively both domestically and abroad. A normative approach to tackling the problem, founded on the principles of international law and collective action, was less successful. Attempts by the UN to define and proscribe transnational terrorism bogged down in the General Assembly over semantics (i.e., deciding on the definition of a terrorist), but other cooperative initiatives were successfully implemented. These included the conventions adopted through the International Civil Aviation Organization to improve information sharing and legal cooperation, such as The Hague Convention for the Suppression of Unlawful Seizure of Aircraft (1970). Another collective response to improve information sharing and collaborative action was the creation of the Public Safety and Terrorism Sub-Directorate within Interpol in 1985. However, most initiatives and responses throughout this decade were unilateral, regional, or ad hoc in nature.

Counterterrorism Activities

Paul Pillar (2001, 29–39), a former high-level CIA official, suggests that counterterrorist policies must address at least four important issue areas. These include the following:

- Develop a thorough *understanding* of the variety of economic, political, and sociocultural issues and conditions that contribute to decisions by individuals or groups to use terrorist tactics. Know that some people who become terrorists will not give up that role no matter what is done to correct unacceptable conditions.
- Completely assess the *capabilities* of terrorist groups and design programs that reduce their ability to attack.
- Review and understand the *intentions* of terrorists and make certain not to reward any of their activities with concessions.
- Create a *defense* based on counterterrorist measures that would convince terrorists that it is not worth an attack (deterrence).

Both Purdy (2004–2005) and Pillar (2001) discuss in detail the policy instruments available to those trying to prevent further terrorist attacks. The first counterterrorist instrument that states might use is *diplomacy*. Leaders might use persuasion and various incentives to encourage foreign governments to suppress certain group activities and to abide by rules and procedures that might prevent terrorist activities. Global policies are welcome, but usually bilateral diplomatic agreements are more effective. It is easier to reward or punish a single state for its compliance or noncompliance with a bilateral or regional agreement than to try to monitor the activities of some 200 nation-states.

A second counterterrorism strategy is the *mobilization of NGOs* to promote international law and to educate the world about the causes of terrorism, the importance of the rule of law, and the human costs of violence and terrorism.

A third counterterrorist activity is *law enforcement*. Terrorist activities are illegal—violating both national and international law. New laws, special courts, prisons, and new penalties are all part of the war on terrorism. Police forces across the world are now cooperating to identify, arrest, and punish terrorist groups.

Stricter law enforcement and increased surveillance have caused some concerns related to the loss of certain civil liberties. The most controversial aspects of the global war on terrorism have been the long-term imprisonment of terrorists, the use of torture and other punitive forms of interrogation, and the illegal transferring of prisoners to nondemocratic states where torture is regularly used.

A fourth counterterrorism strategy involves the use of *financial controls* that track, freeze, and seize financial resources that support terrorist activities. There is an international convention, or treaty, that criminalizes the collection of funds for any terrorist activity. Unfortunately, because of numerous offshore accounts, Internet banking, and a global banking and financial system that makes it easy to hide and transfer funds, controlling this financial process is extremely difficult and will require both private- and public-sector collaboration.

A fifth counterterrorist strategy is the *use of military force*. The use of military force against states that support terrorism is a just cause and is supported by international law. Problems arise when the enemy is a nonstate actor, a network of terrorist organizations operating in a variety of states. How do you justify retaliating strikes against sovereign states that might not support terrorists within their boundaries?

The strategic use of force might be the only way to respond to groups willing to use force to achieve their goals. If supported by the international community and international law, force can be an effective tool. The multilateral effort to end Taliban rule in Afghanistan, and the continuing **NATO** operation, provides an example of a just multilateral effort to close terrorist training camps, arrest leaders of Al Qaeda, and build an effective state that is capable of providing for its citizens.

The final counterterrorist tool is *intelligence and covert action*. This involves both the use of technical intelligence, such as the

Another outcome of the war on terrorism is the expanding role of the National Security Agency as it monitors phone traffic around the world. South Korean protestors denounce the US National Security Agency's alleged spying and demand that the South Korean government protest this activity by its ally. Do you think the United States has gone too far? Does this hurt the image of the United States among its friends?

WHAT'S YOUR WORLDVIEW ?

Providing security is the primary task of all nation-states. Do you think states will willingly share resources and intelligence with other states or international organizations to defeat terrorist networks? What factors work against multilateralism in this area?

monitoring of phone calls and e-mails, and human intelligence, and information collected by spies. The collection of information is not easy, because extremists and others willing to use terrorism are difficult to find. Pillar (2001, 110) also points out that analysis is as difficult as collecting information. He suggests that there might just be too much information, and it is difficult to decide what is relevant and what is simply useless chatter.

To deal with transnational terrorism, the global community must address its most problematic modern aspect: the appeal of messages that inspire terrorists to commit horrific acts of violence. Killing or capturing individuals does little to halt the spread of extremist viewpoints that occur under the guise of discussion and education. In the case of Islam, for example, radical mullahs and imams twist the tenets of the religion into a doctrine of action and hatred, where spiritual achievement occurs through destruction rather than personal enlightenment. In other words, suicide attacks offer the promise of private goods (spiritual reward) rather than public goods (positive contributions to the community over a lifetime). Precisely how the processes and technologies of globalization can assist in delegitimizing the pedagogy that incites terrorists will remain one of the most vexing challenges for the global community for years to come.

Conclusion

Questions of war and peace are central to the existence of every country. In this chapter we have examined the many ways academics analyze security affairs and how these ideas influence the decisions political leaders make on war and weapons procurement, especially nuclear weapons and nuclear proliferation. Terrorism, another salient issue in global security, remains a complex phenomenon in which violence is used to obtain political power to redress grievances that might have become more acute through the process of globalization. The challenge for the global community will be in utilizing its advantages to win the war of ideas that motivates and sustains those responsible for the current wave of terrorist violence.

Engaging with the

Global Security Institute

The GSI offers a series of programs on disarmament as well as an internship program. It is dedicated to strengthening international cooperation and security based on the rule of law, with a particular focus on nuclear arms control, nonproliferation, and disarmament. Visit www.gsinstitute.org.

KEY TERMS

Al Qaeda, p. 210
Asymmetric conflicts, p. 194
Clandestine or "sleeper" cells, p. 216
Community, p. 192
Democratic peace, p. 192
Deterrence, p. 200
Failed states, p. 197
Globalization, p. 192
Identity, p. 211
Imperialism, p. 211
Jihad, p. 213
Materialism, p. 211
National security, p. 191

NATO, p. 219
New wars, p. 197
Noncompliance, p. 204
Non-nuclear weapon state
    (NNWS), p. 200
Norms, p. 203
Nuclear deterrence, p. 202
Nuclear terrorism, p. 203
Nuclear weapon state (NWS),
    p. 199
Postmodern or "new" terrorism,
    p. 212
Postmodernity, p. 193

Revolution in military affairs
    (RMA), p. 194
Security, p. 191
Security community, p. 192
Skyjackings, p. 208
Terrorism, p. 192
Third-tier states, p. 197
Weapons of mass destruction
    (WMD), p. 193
Widening school of international
    security, p. 191
World Bank, p. 211

REVIEW QUESTIONS

1. Why is security a "contested concept"? How do academic disagreements about the term reflect the theory perspectives we studied in Chapter 3?
2. According to realists, why do states find it difficult to cooperate? How do constructivists explain cooperation?
3. Is the tension between national and global security resolvable?
4. Has international security changed since the United States began its global war on terrorism? How?
5. What are the main arguments for and against the proliferation of nuclear weapons? To what extent might these arguments be the result of a person's theory-based worldview?
6. How might nonstate actors represent a new nuclear-proliferation challenge?
7. Why do some authors believe that war between the current great powers is highly unlikely?
8. What is "asymmetric warfare"?
9. When and how did terrorism become a truly global phenomenon?
10. Of all the factors that motivate terrorists, is any one more important than others, and if so, why?
11. What is the role that technology plays in terrorism, and will it change how terrorists operate in the future? If so, how?
12. What is the primary challenge that individual states and the global community as a whole face in confronting terrorism?
13. How can globalization be useful in diminishing the underlying causes of terrorism?

For resources including quizzes, flashcards, and other study tools, please visit us at **www.oup.com/us/lamy**

THINKING ABOUT GLOBAL POLITICS

Perspectives on the Arms Race

OBJECTIVE

The goal of this exercise is difficult to reach: consensus on a national security policy or national strategy for the United States with regard to nuclear weapons. After doing some research online and in your library, you will explore with your classmates the importance of world-views in determining national interests. Your professor might put you into groups.

PROCEDURE

This is not a debate but a discussion. You should try to consider the assumptions of national security from three significant groups participating in arms debates within the United States. These are the major groups:

- Arms advocates (Realists)
- Arms control advocates (Liberals)
- Disarmament advocates (Select an Alternative Theory; see Chapter 3)

1. Review with your classmates the basic worldview positions and corresponding policy priorities of each group (reread Chapters 2 and 3).

2. Divide your class into three groups representing these views.
3. Explore these general questions in your discussion:
   - What does the United States want its nuclear weapons to do?
   - What should our nuclear strategy be?
   - How can the United States use nuclear weapons to achieve its foreign policy and national security goals?

FOLLOW-UP

Take the evening to review your readings from the semester so far (both in this textbook and in whatever supplemental readings your professor has assigned). Make a list of statements made in these materials that support your position, which you will use in your next class. During class, your professor might choose to have you (or a group leader) write these statements on the board and ask others in the class to respond to your selections.

CONTRIBUTORS TO CHAPTER 6: *John Baylis, Darryl Howlett, James D. Kiras, Steven L. Lamy, and John Masker.*

Human Rights and Human Security

7

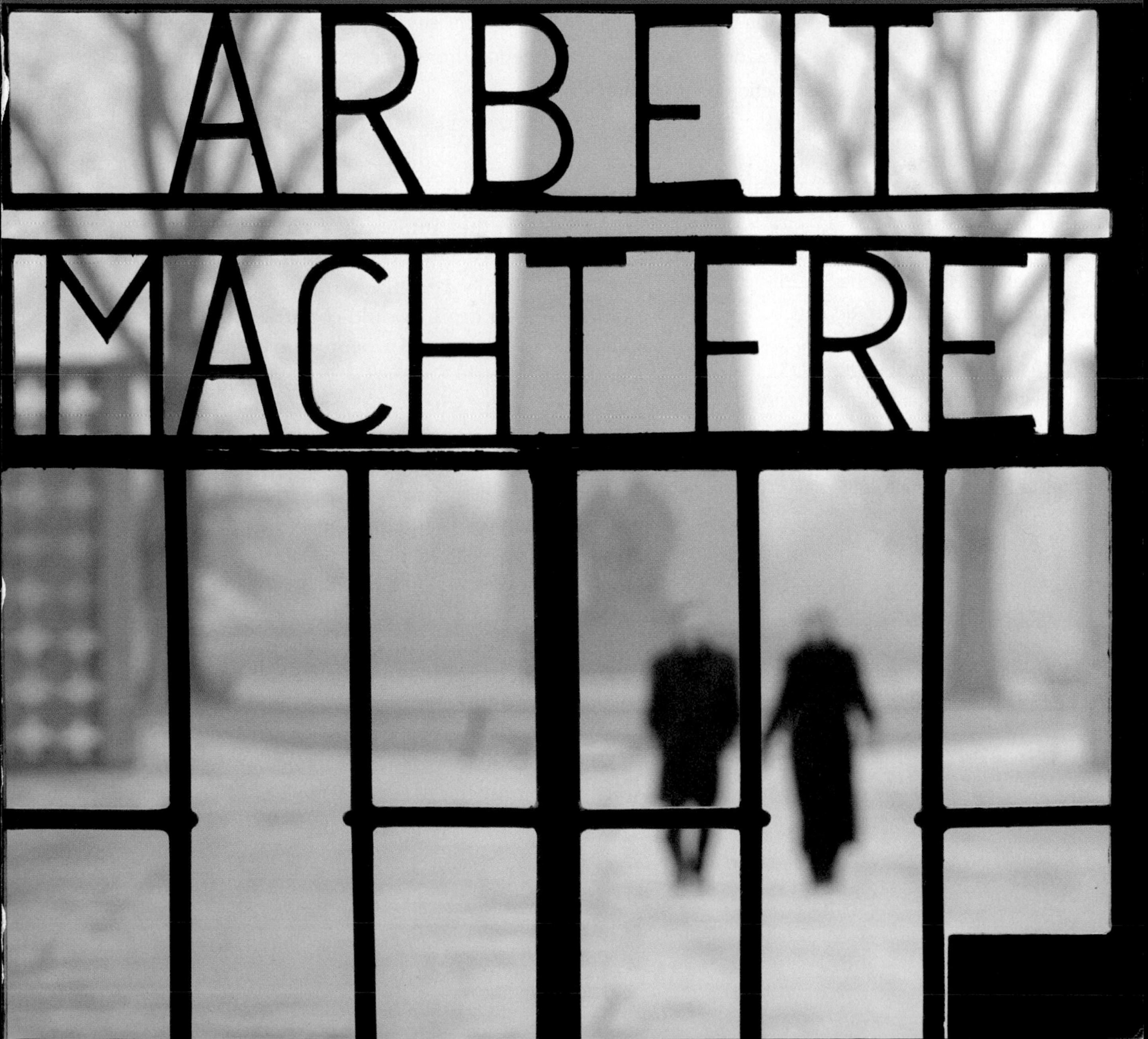

The crime of genocide should be recognized therein as a conspiracy to exterminate national, racial, or religious groups. . . . The formulation of the crime may be as follows: Whoever, while participating in a conspiracy to destroy religious, national, or racial groups, undertakes an attack against life, liberty, or property of members of such groups is guilty of the crime of genocide.

—*Raphael Lemkin*

Human security naturally connects several kinds of freedom—such as freedom from want and freedom from fear, as well as freedom to take action on one's behalf.

—*Commission on Human Security*

The term *genocide* was created after World War II, as leaders of the antifascist coalition struggled to understand the magnitude of human tragedy before them. Immediately after the war, the victorious powers promised "never again" would countries stand by as tyrants massacred their own people or launched wars of aggression.

And yet sadly, since 1945, genocidal violence has occurred in the Congo, Cambodia, East Timor, Rwanda, Bosnia, Kosovo, Chechnya, Somalia, Darfur, and many other places. In this chapter we examine the linked concepts of human rights and human security, both of which emerged from the effects of World War II. We will see that there are many reasons for hope that the world community will be able one day to stop human rights abuses and to provide security to all people. But because the successful promotion of both human rights and human security depends on the international community, there might be just as many reasons to be pessimistic about the prospects for a better world. After all, protecting the rights of individuals can infringe on the prerogatives of governments and thus on the notion of sovereign equality of countries.

"Arbeit macht frei" literally means "work makes you free." This is a modern-day picture of the front gates leading into Auschwitz. In 1945, states pledged that genocide would never occur again. Have the states kept their promise?

As we have seen elsewhere in this book, however, globalization is changing many traditions in world affairs.

This tension between the rights of the *individual* and the rights of *society* is a significant barrier to the creation of human security. As we will see in the first section of this chapter, there were intellectual disagreements in the nineteenth and early twentieth centuries about answers to basic questions: What is a human right? What rights should be protected and by whom? Must these rights be universal? We are still looking for answers to these questions. How can we discuss such a broad issue as global security on a smaller, human scale—what should it look like, and why is it important? What opportunities still exist for political and military leaders to circumvent, undermine, and exploit international laws?

Introduction

As in other areas of the study of global politics, there are disagreements about human rights and human security. And, like the debates in other areas, the splits tend to be down the same lines as the international relations theories we discussed in Chapter 3. However, the fundamental question is a simple one: Do countries have an obligation to improve the living conditions and protect the rights of people who live in other countries?

Furthermore, if there is such an obligation, what are its legal foundations? And who would define the terms of human rights? Clearly such rights would rest within a legal system—but whose? And what kind? Some of the contemporary disagreement about the obligation to promote human rights and human security stems from a history of colonialism. For example, the modern concept of individual human rights developed originally in Europe. Yet, as many European countries colonized other regions of the world (and other parts of Europe, even), these rights were often not extended to other peoples who were seen as not "human." Today, for many people who live in Africa and Asia these human rights might appear to derive from their problematic colonial heritage. Why should it necessarily mean something different to be human in Africa than in Europe?

What Are Human Rights?

The modern concept of human rights has developed over many years. This the idea that all human beings share fundamental natural rights that are an essential part of their humanity. These universal rights are not granted by governments and cannot be taken away by sovereign powers.

Origin of the Concept

The theory of human rights developed in Europe during the Middle Ages, and it rested on the idea of **natural law**—that humans have an essential nature. Natural law theorists differed on many issues, but they agreed on the

LEARNING OBJECTIVES

After reading and discussing this chapter, you should be able to:

Define human rights, natural law, and charter rights.

Explore what responsibility states have to intervene in other states where rights are being abused or suspended.

Explain the concept of human security and how it relates to human rights.

Give an account of the history of humanitarian challenges and the variety of international responses to these challenges.

Describe the roles that various actors play in promoting and protecting human rights and human security.

following: (1) there are universal moral standards that support individual rights; (2) there is a general duty to adhere to these standards; and (3) the application of these standards is not limited to any particular legal system, community, state, race, religion, or civilization (Finnis 1980). These central propositions are the origin of modern rhetoric on *universal* human rights.

Natural law provided the theory, but in the rougher world of medieval political practice, rights had different connotations. There, rights were concessions extracted from a superior, probably by force. The Magna Carta (1215) is a case in point. In it the barons of England obliged King John to grant to them and their heirs in perpetuity a series of liberties that are, for the most part, very specific and related to particular grievances. The Magna Carta is based on the important principle that the subjects of the king owe him duty only if he meets their claims. This is clearly a political bargain or contract.

Although rights as part of natural law and those established by political contract are not inherently incompatible, these two kinds of rights are actually based on *opposed* principles. Whereas rights based on natural law are derived from the notion of human flourishing and are universal, **charter rights** are the result of a political contract and, by definition, are limited to the parties to the contract and thus restricted in time and space.

The Liberal Account of Rights

The complex language of medieval thinking on rights carried over into the modern period. Political philosophers such as Hugo Grotius, Thomas Hobbes, and John Locke continued to use notions of natural law, albeit in radically different ways from their predecessors. Gradually, a synthesis of the concepts of natural rights and charter rights emerged. Known as the **Liberal Account of Rights**, this position is made up of two basic components:

1. Human beings possess rights to life, liberty, the secure possession of property, the exercise of freedom of speech, and so on, which are inalienable—cannot be traded away—and unconditional. The only acceptable reason for constraining any one individual is to protect the rights of another.

2. The primary function of government is to protect these rights. Political institutions are to be judged on their performance of this function, and political obligation rests on their success in this. In short, political life is based on a kind of implicit or explicit contract between people and government.

From a philosophical and conceptual point of view, this position is easy to denigrate as a mishmash of half-digested medieval ideas. As G. W. F. Hegel and many subsequent communitarian thinkers have pointed out, it assumes that individuals and their rights predate society—and yet how could they exist without being part of a society? For philosopher Jeremy Bentham, the function of government was to promote the general good (which he called utility), and the idea that individuals might have the right to undermine this seemed to him madness, especially because no one could tell him where these rights came from; the whole idea was "nonsense upon stilts." Karl Marx, on the other hand, and many subsequent radicals, pointed out that the liberal position stresses property rights, to the advantage of the rich and powerful. All these points raise compelling questions, but they underestimate the powerful rhetorical appeal of the liberal position. Most people are less likely to be worried about the philosophical inadequacies associated with the liberal position on human rights than they are to be attracted by the obvious benefits of living in a political system based on or influenced by it.

People around the world live with poverty and insecurity. The drug trade in developing countries provides jobs and income but also causes deadly violence. Drug gangs have taken control of vast regions of Mexico. Here, more than 200 weapons were seized in a 2011 arrest in Mexico City.

One of the uncertain features of the liberal position is the extent to which the rights it describes are universal. For example, the French Revolutionary Declaration of the Rights of Man and of the Citizen clearly, by its very title, is intended to be of universal scope, but even here the universalism of Article 1, "Men are born and remain free and equal in respect of rights," is soon followed by Article 3, "The nation is essentially the source of all sovereignty." When Revolutionary and Napoleonic France moved to bring the Rights of Man to the rest of Europe, the end result looked to most contemporaries remarkably like a French empire. The liberal position, although universal in principle, is particular in application, and it more or less takes state boundaries for granted.

The humanitarianism and international standard-setting of the nineteenth and twentieth centuries brought these issues to the foreground. The Congress of Vienna of 1815 saw the great powers accept an obligation to end the slave trade, which was finally abolished by the Brussels Convention of 1890, and slavery itself was formally outlawed by the Slavery Convention of 1926. The Hague Conventions of 1907 and the Geneva Conventions of 1926 were designed to introduce humanitarian considerations into the conduct of war. The International Labor Office, formed in 1901, and its successor the International Labor Organization, attempted to set standards in the workplace via measures such as the Convention Concerning Forced or Compulsory Labor of 1930.

In short, for Western European proponents of the Liberal Account of Rights, human rights were intended to be protections for individuals against oppressive rulers, whether unelected monarchs or the choice of democratic majorities. The English and French colonizers of Asia and Africa took that notion of individual rights with them, and many believed that it could take root in other cultures. As we will see, our modern notion of human rights is tied to the colonial

WHAT'S YOUR WORLDVIEW

Not all ideas regarding human rights come from Europe. What ideas about human rights came from non-Western societies and religious traditions?

experience, and over the centuries this notion has evolved and been the subject of many disagreements.

Human Rights and State Sovereignty

Humanitarian measures taken together may provide a framework for some kind of global governance, but in many states it is difficult to override a policy of **nonintervention**—not intervening in the affairs of other states—which is related to the notion of sovereignty. For example, abolishing the slave trade, which involved international transactions, was much easier than abolishing slavery, which concerns what states do to their own people; indeed, pockets of slavery survive to this day in parts of Africa, Asia, and the Middle East.

Although sovereignty remains a norm of the system, humanitarian impulses have often been reduced to no more than laudable speech. One problem in realizing them is that a basic principle of international society is the sovereignty of states, which requires respect toward, and noninterference with, the institutions of member states. In nineteenth-century England, Manchester School radical liberals such as John Bright and Richard Cobden were bitterly critical of traditional diplomacy but supported the norm of nonintervention. They argued that their opponents, who claimed moral reasons in support of interventions, were in fact motivated by power politics. This is, of course, a familiar line of argument—one most likely, in the twenty-first century, to be directed at the American heirs of Britain's position in the world.

Cobden was a consistent anti-interventionist and anti-imperialist; other liberals were more selective. Gladstone's 1870s campaign to throw the Ottoman Empire out of Europe was based on the more common view that different standards applied between "civilized" and "uncivilized" peoples. In Gladstone's view, the Ottoman Empire—although since 1856 a full member of international society—could not claim the rights of a sovereign state because its institutions did not come up to the requisite standards. Indeed, this latter position was briefly established in international law in the notion of **standards of civilization**, a nineteenth-century, European discourse about what made a country "civilized" or "uncivilized." Now, in the twenty-first century, this notion might disturb and unsettle us, yet current conventional thinking on human rights is based on very similar ideas.

The willingness of liberals to extend their thinking on human rights toward direct intervention was characteristic of the second half of the twentieth century. The horrors of World War I stimulated attempts to create a peace system based on a form of international government, and although the League of Nations of 1919 had no explicit human rights provision, the underlying assumption was that its members would be states governed by the rule of law and respecting individual rights. The UN Charter of 1945, in the wake of World War II, does have some explicit reference to human rights—a tribute to the impact, on the general thought climate, of the horrors of that war and, in particular, of the murder of millions of Jews, Gypsies, and Slavs in the extermination camps of National Socialist Germany. In this context, the need to assert a universal position was deeply felt, and the scene was set for the burst of international human rights legislation of the postwar era.

International Human Rights Legislation

The post–World War II humanitarian impulse led to a burst of lawmaking and standard-setting, which gave rise to what are known as *generations* of rights. First-generation rights focus on individual rights such as free speech, freedom of religion, and voting rights—rights that protect the individual from the potential abuses of the state. Second-generation rights include social, economic, and cultural rights. This group of rights includes the right to employment, housing, health care, and education. First- and second-generation rights are covered by the Universal Declaration of Human Rights and the EU's Charter of Fundamental Rights. Third-generation rights are more focused on collective or group rights and have not been adopted by most states. These include the right to natural resources, the right to self-determination, and the right to clean air.

The Universal Declaration of Human Rights

In 1948, the UN General Assembly established a baseline of human rights for its member states to follow. The **Universal Declaration of Human Rights** set out thirty basic political, civil, economic, and social rights that sought to define which specific rights all people share as humans. In the words of the Preamble to the Declaration, "the peoples of the United Nations reaffirmed their faith in fundamental human rights, in the dignity and worth of the human person and of the equal rights of men and women." The enumerated entitlements included freedom from torture, freedom of opinion, equal treatment before the law, freedom of movement within a country, the right to own property, the right to education, and the right to work.

There were two shortcomings in the Universal Declaration. First, it was nonbinding on the member states of the UN. Countries' leaders could pledge to support the goals of the document but then point to a range of political or economic problems that stopped them from full implementation. Article 29 bolstered their rationale for nonintervention: "Everyone has duties to the community in which alone the free and full development of

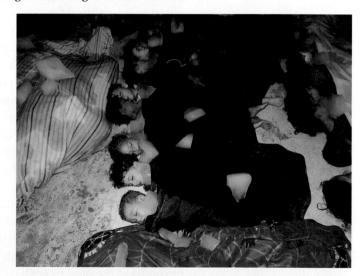

Under the 1993 Chemical Weapons Convention there is a worldwide ban on the production, stockpiling, and use of chemical weapons. A country using chemical weapons is breaking international law. Further, any country using chemical weapons is guilty of violating human rights. What if a leader uses these heinous weapons against his own citizens? Syria has allegedly killed hundreds using chemical weapons. Why has the world done nothing?

WHAT'S YOUR WORLDVIEW

Do you think US constitutional rights should be extended to noncitizen residents? Why or why not?

his personality is possible." A second difficulty was the European origins of these rights. As the wave of decolonization swept Asia and Africa, newly independent countries eagerly embraced the tenets of human rights law. Unfortunately, as civil strife threatened to split some of these countries, some leaders blamed it on the pattern of oppression that the colonizers had created, and they used the provisions of Article 29 as the political justification for postcolonial repression.

Despite its shortcomings, the Universal Declaration of Human Rights is, symbolically, a central piece of legislation. This was the first time in history that the international community had attempted to define a comprehensive code for the internal government of its members. During the late 1940s, the UN was dominated by the West, and the contents of the Declaration represented this fact, with its emphasis on political freedom. The voting was forty-eight for and none against. Eight states abstained, for interestingly different reasons.

South Africa abstained. The white-dominated regime in South Africa denied political rights to the majority of its people and clearly could not accept that "all are born free and equal in dignity and rights" (Article 1), claiming it violated the protection of the domestic jurisdiction of states guaranteed by Article 2(7) of the UN Charter. This is a clear and uncomplicated case of a first-generation (political) rights issue.

The Soviet Union and five Soviet-bloc countries abstained. Although Stalin's USSR was clearly a tyranny, the Soviet government did not officially object to the political freedoms set forth in the Declaration. Instead, the Soviet objection was to the absence of sufficient attention to social and economic rights by comparison to the detailed elaboration of "bourgeois" freedoms and property rights. The Soviets saw the Declaration as a Cold War document, designed to stigmatize socialist regimes—a not wholly inaccurate description of the motives of its promulgators.

Saudi Arabia also abstained, although for different reasons. The Saudi state was one of the few non-Western members of the UN in 1948 and just about the only one whose system of government was not, in principle, based on some Western model. Saudi Arabia objected to the Declaration on religious grounds, specifically objecting to Article 18, which specifies the freedom to change and practice the religion of one's choice. These provisions did not merely contravene specific Saudi laws, which, for example, forbade (and still forbid) the practice of the Christian religion in Saudi Arabia, but they contravened the tenets of Islam, which does not recognize a right of apostasy. Here, to complete the picture, we have an assertion of third-generation rights and a denial of the universalism of the Declaration. Thus, the opening moment of the universal human rights regime sees the emergence of the themes that will make up the politics of human rights over the next sixty years.

Table 7.1 UN Conventions Following the 1948 Universal Declaration of Human Rights

Convention	Year
International Convention on the Elimination of All Forms of Racial Discrimination (ICERD)	1965
International Covenant on Civil and Political Rights (ICCPR)	1966
International Covenant on Economic, Social, and Cultural Rights (ICESCR)	1966
Optional Protocol to the International Covenant on Civil and Political Rights (ICCPR-OP1)	1966
Convention on the Elimination of All Forms of Discrimination Against Women (CEDAW)	1979
Convention Against Torture and Other Cruel, Inhuman, or Degrading Treatment or Punishment (CAT)	1984
Convention on the Rights of the Child (CRC)	1989
Second Optional Protocol to the International Covenant on Civil and Political Rights, aiming to abolish the death penalty (ICCPR-OP2)	1989
International Convention on the Protection of the Rights of All Migrant Workers and Members of Their Families (ICRMW)	1990
Optional Protocol to the Convention on the Elimination of Discrimination Against Women (OP-CEDAW)	1999
Optional Protocol to the Convention on the Rights of the Child on the Involvement of Children in Armed Conflict (OP-CRC-AC)	2000
Optional Protocol to the Convention on the Rights of the Child on the Sale of Children, Child Prostitution, and Child Pornography (OP-CRC-SC)	2000
Optional Protocol to the Convention Against Torture and Other Cruel, Inhuman, or Degrading Treatment or Punishment (OP-CAT)	2002
Optional Protocol to the Convention on the Rights of Persons With Disabilities (OP-CRPD)	2006
International Convention for the Protection of All Persons From Enforced Disappearance (CPED)	2006
Convention on the Rights of Persons With Disabilities (CRPD)	2006
Optional Protocol of the Covenant on Economic, Social and Cultural Rights (ICESCR-OP)	2008

Subsequent UN Legislation

Building on the promise of the Universal Declaration, the UN took the lead in creating major legally binding international conventions that define rights of specific groups, including women, children, and migrant workers, and that aim to eliminate torture and racial discrimination (see Table 7.1).

These conventions provide the intellectual and legal basis for the concept of human security, which we examine in later in the chapter.

What Is Human Security?

Like the doctrines of human rights, the concept of **human security** represents a powerful but controversial attempt (as we discuss later) by sections of the academic and policy community to redefine and broaden the meaning of security. Traditionally, security meant protection of the sovereignty and territorial integrity of states from external military threats. This was the essence of the concept of national security, which dominated security analysis and policy making during the Cold War period. In the 1970s and 1980s, academic literature on security, responding to the Middle East oil crisis and the growing awareness of worldwide environmental degradation, began to describe security in broader, nonmilitary terms. Yet the state remained the object of security, or the entity to be protected.

The concept of human security challenges the state-centric notion of security by focusing on the individual. Human security is about security for the people, rather than for states or governments. As such, it has generated much debate. Critics wonder whether such an approach would widen the boundaries of security studies too much and whether "securitizing" the individual is the best way to address the challenges facing the international community from the forces of globalization. On the other side, advocates of human security find the concept effectively highlights the dangers to human safety and survival posed by poverty, disease, environmental stress, and human rights abuses, as well as armed conflict. These disagreements notwithstanding, the concept of human security captures a growing realization that, in an era of rapid globalization, security must encompass a broader range of concerns and challenges than simply defending the state from external military attack.

Origin of the Concept

The origin of the concept of human security can be traced to the publication of the *Human Development Report* of 1994, issued by the UN Development Programme (UNDP 1994). The report defined the scope of human security to include seven areas:

- **Economic security**—ensuring basic income for all people, usually from productive and remunerative work or, as the last resort, from some publicly financed safety net.
- **Food security**—ensuring that all people at all times have both physical and economic access to basic food.
- **Health security**—guaranteeing a minimum protection from diseases and unhealthy lifestyles.
- **Environmental security**—protecting people from the short- and long-term ravages of nature, man-made threats in nature, and deterioration of the natural environment.
- **Personal security**—protecting people from physical violence, whether from the state or external states, from violent individuals and substate factors, from domestic abuse, or from predatory adults.
- **Community security**—protecting people from the loss of traditional relationships and values and from sectarian and ethnic violence.

CASE STUDY   Human Insecurity in Southeast Asia

Background

Whether going by the narrow (freedom from fear) or broad (freedom from want) conception, Southeast Asia faces some of the most critical challenges to human security in the world. The region, including Vietnam, Laos, Cambodia, Burma (Myanmar), Indonesia, Malaysia, Thailand, Philippines, Brunei, and Singapore, has witnessed some of the worst violence of the twentieth century.

The Case

The Khmer Rouge regime in Cambodia killed about 1.7 million (a quarter of the Cambodian population) during its brutal rule between 1975 and 1979 (Yale University Cambodian Genocide Program). In Indonesia, anti-communist riots in the mid-1960s, which accompanied he transition from President Sukarno to President Suharto, claimed about 400,000 lives (Schwarz 1999, 20). The US war in Vietnam produced 250,000 South Vietnamese, 1.1 million North Vietnamese, and 60,000 American casualties (Olson 1988). Ethnic and separatist movements in East Timor and Aceh have claimed 200,000 and more than 2,000 lives, respectively (Wessel and Wimhofer 2001). And although there are no proper collated figures for ethnic separatism in Myanmar—usually low-scale, random casualties and conflicts—600,000 internally displaced persons from these conflicts have been recorded (US Department of State 2003).

The region has been free of major conflict since the fighting in Cambodia (1979–1991) ended. But internal conflicts in southern Thailand, southern Philippines, and Myanmar pose a serious challenge to human security. Military rule, which accounted for some of the worst human rights violations in the region, continues in Myanmar, has returned in Thailand, and remains a possibility in the Philippines.

Outcome

Southeast Asia also faces other threats to human security. Absolute poverty levels have declined, but the prevalence of underweight children under five years of age in Southeast Asia is third highest in the world (28 percent), after sub-Saharan Africa (30 percent) and South Asia (47 percent). In Asia, national HIV-infection levels are highest in Southeast Asia. The outbreaks of highly pathogenic H5N1 avian influenza, which began in Southeast Asia in mid-2003 and have now spread to parts of Europe, are the largest and most severe on record.

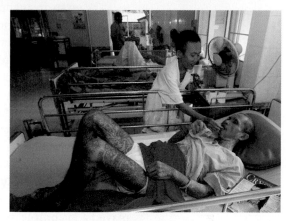

An AIDS hospice in Thailand was the site of a test of anti-HIV drugs in 2009. Should states make such medicines available at reduced costs to all citizens in the world?

Southeast Asia has also experienced a range of transnational threats in recent years. These include the Asian economic crisis of 1997, described by the World Bank as "the biggest setback for poverty reduction in East Asia for several decades" (Ching 1999). Other challenges include the recurring haze problem (1997, 2006) from forest fires in Indonesia, the severe acute respiratory syndrome outbreak in 2003, and the Indian Ocean tsunami that devastated coastal areas in Indonesia, Thailand, and other Southeast Asian nations in December 2004 and killed at least 200,000 people in Asia, with Indonesia suffering 128,000 dead and 37,000 missing.

Conceptually, Southeast Asia shows a link between underdevelopment and conflict. Its poorest areas—Indonesia, Cambodia, Myanmar, and the southern regions of Thailand and the Philippines—have been especially prone to conflict. Economic development has led to relative stability in Singapore and Malaysia.

For Discussion

1. Should the countries of Asia be left to work out their own problems, without intervention from European or North American states?
2. How does the constructivist perspective help us to understand the crisis of insecurity in Asia?
3. To what extent has globalization increased or decreased threats to human security in Asia?

Source: Acharya 2007.

- **Political security**—ensuring that people live in a society that honors their basic human rights and ensuring the freedom of individuals and groups from government attempts to exercise control over ideas and information.

The seven areas appear to describe the basic purpose of every country; and yet, as with other UN programs, the *Human Development Report* has had numerous critics. The primary complaint has been that the UNDP has issued an unfunded mandate: The report could be used to admonish countries that did not reach the standards, yet the UNDP provided little or no funding to reach them. As you will see in the next section, this tension between standard-setting in human rights and human security and assessing country performance has been a consistent strain since 1945. The leaders of many governments resent what they perceive as interference in the sovereign affairs of their countries.

Human Security and Development

Unlike many other efforts to redefine security, where political scientists played a major role, human security was the handiwork of a group of development economists, such as the late Pakistani economist Mahbub ul Haq, who conceptualized the UNDP's *Human Development Report*. They were increasingly dissatisfied with the orthodox notion of development, which viewed it as a function of economic growth (as we discuss in depth in Chapter 8). Instead, they proposed a concept of **human development** that focuses on building human capabilities to confront and overcome poverty, illiteracy, diseases, discrimination, restrictions on political freedom, and the threat of violent conflict: "Individual freedoms and rights matter a great deal, but people are restricted in what they can do with that freedom if they are poor, ill, illiterate, discriminated against, threatened by violent conflict or denied a political voice" (UNDP 2011, 18–19).

Closely related to the attempt to create a broader paradigm for development was the growing concern about the negative impact of defense spending on development, or the "guns versus butter" dilemma. As a global study headed by Inga Thorsson of Sweden concluded, "the arms race and development are in a competitive relationship" (Roche 1986, 8). Drawing on this study, a UN-sponsored International Conference on the Relationship Between Disarmament and Development, in 1986 in Paris, sought "to enlarge world understanding that human security demands more resources for development and fewer for arms."

Human security includes freedom from fear, freedom from want and the rule of law. But it also includes education. A Syrian child answers a teacher's question at a UN refugee camp in Amman, Jordan. With the civil war continuing in Syria and conflicts in Africa, refugee numbers are increasing worldwide.

Common Security

The move toward human security was also advanced by the work of several international commissions. They offered a broader view of security that looked beyond the Cold War emphasis on East–West military competition. Foremost among them was the Palme Commission of 1982, which proposed the doctrine of **common security**, emphasizing noncompetitive, cooperative approaches to achieving human security for all. Its report stressed that "in the Third World countries, as in all our countries, security requires economic progress as well as freedom from military fear" (Palme Commission 1982, xii). In 1987, the report of the World Commission on Environment and Development (also known as the Brundtland Commission) highlighted the linkage between environmental degradation and conflict: "The real sources of insecurity encompass unsustainable development, and its effects can become intertwined with traditional forms of conflict in a manner that can extend and deepen the latter" (Brundtland et al. 1987, 230).

Along with attempts to broaden the notion of security to include nonmilitary threats, there was also a growing emphasis on the individual as the central object of security. The Palme Commission's notion of common security became the conceptual basis of the Conference on Security and Cooperation in Europe (CSCE). The CSCE made East–West security cooperation conditional on the improvement of the human rights situation in the former Soviet bloc. The North–South Roundtable on the "Economics of Peace," held in Costa Rica in 1990, called for a shift from "an almost exclusive concern with military security … to a broader concern for overall security of individuals from social violence, economic distress and environmental degradation" (Jolly and Ray 2006, 3).

> **WHAT'S YOUR WORLDVIEW**
>
> *Are the elements of human security rights or privileges? On what evidence and theoretical perspective do you base your argument?*

History of Humanitarian Activism and Intervention

As the concepts of human rights and human security have developed, many opinion leaders and politicians in democratic societies have become increasingly aware that the state must take action in the face of challenges to human lives and dignity. In effect, many politicians have come to believe that the state should do more than defend borders and that cooperative and purposeful international action might be necessary to safeguard people.

One reason human security has become a more salient issue in recent decades is that civil wars and intrastate conflicts have become more frequent. These have entailed huge losses of life, ethnic cleansing, displacement of people within and across borders, and disease outbreaks. Traditional national-security approaches have not been sufficiently sensitive toward conflicts that arise over cultural, ethnic, and religious differences, as happened in Eastern Europe, Africa, and Central Asia in the post–Cold War era (Tow and Trood 2000).

The world's newest state, South Sudan, is in an internal conflict as rival tribal leaders fight for control of the government. The US UN Ambassador, Samantha Power, considered by many a "humanitarian hawk," listens to the UN Security Council debate that resulted in an increase of peacekeeping troops in South Sudan from 7000 to 12,500. Power is a strong advocate for humanitarian intervention.

Another reason for increasing humanitarian awareness is the spread of democratization (see Map 7.1), which has been accompanied by increased emphasis on human rights and **humanitarian intervention**. Proponents of interventions take the position that the international community is justified in intervening in the internal affairs of states accused of gross violation of human rights. This has led to the realization that although the concept of national security has not been rendered irrelevant, it no longer sufficiently accounts for the kinds of danger that threaten societies, states, and the international community.

The notion of human security has also been brought front and center by crises induced by accelerating globalization. For example, the widespread poverty, unemployment, and social dislocation caused by the Asian financial crisis in 1997 underscored the vulnerability of people to the effects of economic globalization (Acharya 2004).

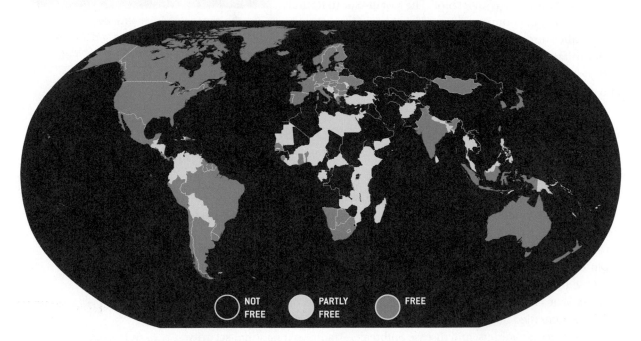

NOT FREE   PARTLY FREE   FREE

Map 7.1 Democracy in the World.

This 2012 map from Freedom House represents a specifically American view of democracy. In many countries, democracy is only tenuously established, and human rights abuses continue. *Source: Freedom in the World 2013: Democratic Breakthroughs in the Balance; Freedom House Report (pp. 14–18). http://www.freedomhouse.org/sites/default/files/FIW%202013%20Booklet.pdf.*

During the current global economic recession, international aid agencies saw a sharp decline in donations for countries and individuals, thus undermining their ability to provide basic needs.

Intervention and Nonintervention in the 1990s

It has become common to describe the immediate post–Cold War period as something of a golden era for humanitarian activism and intervention. Thomas Weiss (2004, 136) argues that "the notion that human beings matter more than sovereignty radiated brightly, albeit briefly, across the international political horizon of the 1990s." There is no doubt that, during the 1990s, states began to contemplate intervention to protect imperiled strangers in distant lands. This was symbolized for many by NATO's intervention to halt Serb atrocities in Kosovo in March 1999 and the Australian-led intervention to end mass atrocities in East Timor. But the 1990s also saw the world stand aside during the genocides in Rwanda and Srebrenica. To make sense of these developments, let's focus on international interventions in northern Iraq, Somalia, Rwanda, and Kosovo and divide our discussion into three parts: the place of humanitarian impulses in decisions to intervene, the legality and legitimacy of the interventions, and the effectiveness of these military interventions.

In the cases of northern Iraq in April 1991 and also Somalia in December 1992, domestic public opinion played an important role in pressuring policy makers into using force for humanitarian purposes. In the face of a massive refugee crisis caused by Saddam Hussein's oppression of the Kurds in the aftermath of the 1991 Gulf War, US, British, French, and Dutch military forces intervened to create protected "safe havens" for the Kurdish people. Similarly, the US military intervention in Somalia in December 1992 was a response to sentiments of compassion on the part of US citizens. This sense of solidarity disappeared, however, once the United States began sustaining casualties.

> **WHAT'S YOUR WORLDVIEW**
>
> *Why is the idea of humanitarian intervention so controversial? Why are states so unwilling to intervene to save people in danger?*

The fact that the White House pulled the plug on its Somali intervention after the loss of eighteen US Rangers in a firefight in October 1993 indicates how capricious public opinion is. Television pictures of starving and dying Somalis had persuaded the outgoing Bush administration to launch a humanitarian rescue mission, but once the US public saw dead Americans dragged through the streets of Mogadishu, the Clinton administration announced a timetable for withdrawal. What the Somalia case demonstrates is that the "CNN effect" is a double-edged sword: It can pressure governments into humanitarian intervention yet with equal speed produce public disillusionment and calls for withdrawal. These cases also suggest that even if there are no vital national interests at stake, liberal states might launch humanitarian rescue missions if sufficient public pressure is mobilized. Certainly, there is no evidence in either of these cases to support the realist claim that states cloak power-political motives behind the guise of humanitarianism.

By contrast, the French intervention in Rwanda in July 1994 seems to be an example of abuse. The French government emphasized the strictly humanitarian character of the operation, but this interpretation lacks credibility given the evidence that it was covertly pursuing national self-interest. France had propped up the one-party Hutu state for twenty years, even providing troops when the Rwandan Patriotic Front (RPF), consisting largely of members of the rival Tutsi population and operating out of neighboring Uganda, threatened to overrun the country in 1990 and 1993. The French president, François Mitterrand, was reportedly anxious to restore waning French influence in Africa and was fearful that an RPF victory in French-speaking Rwanda would bring the country under the influence of Anglophones. France therefore did not intervene until the latter stages of the genocide against the Tutsis, which was ended primarily by the RPF's military victory. It seems, therefore, that French behavior accords with the realist premise that states will risk their soldiers only in defense of the national interest. French leaders might have been partly motivated by humanitarian sentiments, but this seems to be a case of a state abusing the concept of humanitarian intervention, because the primary purpose of the intervention was to protect French national interests.

The moral question raised by French intervention is why international society failed to intervene when the genocide began in early April 1994. French intervention might have saved some lives, but it came far too late to halt the genocide. Some 800,000 people were killed in a mere 100 days. The failure of international society to stop the genocide indicates that state leaders remain gripped by the mind-set of national interests trumping human interests. There was no intervention for the simple reason that those with the military capability to stop the genocide were unwilling to sacrifice troops and treasure to protect Rwandans. International solidarity in the face of genocide was limited to moral outrage and the provision of humanitarian aid.

If the French intervention in Rwanda can be criticized for being too little, too late, NATO's intervention in Kosovo in 1999 was criticized for being too much, too soon. At the beginning of the war, NATO said it was intervening to prevent a humanitarian catastrophe. To do this, NATO aircraft were given two objectives: reduce Serbia's military capacity and coerce Serbian president Slobodan Milosevic into accepting the Rambouillet settlement, with the emphasis initially placed on the former. Three arguments were adduced to support NATO's claim that the resort to force was justifiable. First, it was argued that Serbian actions in Kosovo had created a humanitarian emergency and breached a whole range of international legal commitments. Second, NATO governments argued that the Serbs were committing crimes against humanity, possibly including genocide. Third, it was contended that the Milosevic regime's use of force against the Kosovar Albanians challenged global norms of common humanity.

> **WHAT'S YOUR WORLDVIEW** **?**
>
> *Economic, social, and cultural rights were very controversial during the Cold War and remain so today. Why do you think these proposed rights remain so controversial? Do they challenge the power and influence of certain economic and political interests?*

Closer analysis of the justifications articulated by Western leaders suggests that although humanitarianism might have provided the primary impulse for action, it was by no means the exclusive impulse, and the complexity of the motives of the interveners colored the character of the intervention. Indeed, NATO was propelled into action by a mixture of humanitarian concern and self-interest gathered around three sets of issues. The first might be called the "Srebrenica syndrome"—a fear that, left unchecked, Milosevic's henchmen would replicate the carnage of Bosnia. The second is related directly to self-interest and was a concern that protracted conflict in the southern Balkans would create a massive refugee crisis in Europe. Finally, NATO governments were worried that if they failed to contain the crisis, it would spread and engulf several neighboring states, especially Macedonia, Albania, and Bulgaria (Bellamy 2002, 3). This suggests that humanitarian intervention might be prompted by mixed motives. This only becomes a problem if the nonhumanitarian motives undermine the chances of achieving the humanitarian purposes.

The Cambodian genocide lasted from 1975 to 1979 and during this period 1.7 million people (21 percent of Cambodia's population) lost their lives. The Khmer Rouge regime led by Pol Pot operated one of the most repressive regimes in the history of humankind. In this photo, Cambodian villagers line up for the trial of two Khmer Rouge leaders at the October 2013 combined UN/Cambodian tribunal in Phnom Penh.

Universalism Challenged

Paradoxically, the success of the global human rights regime caused a growing backlash to the development of international norms of behavior. If taken seriously and at face value, human rights laws after 1945 would create a situation where all states would be obliged to conform to a quite rigid template that dictated most aspects of their political, social, and economic structures and policies. And so, from 1945 opponents of both the human rights and the human security regimes objected that (1) the norms were an unwarranted intrusion in the affairs of sovereign states and (2) these norms also sought to overturn existing assumptions about the role of the state and its jurisdiction.

Conventional defenders of human rights and human security argue that universalism would be a good thing—the spread of best practice in these matters is in the interest of all people. Others disagree. Does post-1945 law actually constitute best practice? The feminist critique of universal human rights is particularly appropriate here. The universal documents all, in varying degrees, privilege a patriarchal view of the family as the basic unit of society. Even such documents as the Convention on the Elimination of All Forms of Discrimination Against Women of 1979 do no more than extend to women the standard liberal package of rights, and modern feminists debate whether this constitutes a genuine advance (Peters and Wolper 1995).

More fundamentally, is the very idea of "best practice" sound? We have already met one objection to the idea in the Saudi abstention of 1948. The argument is simple: Universalism is destructive not only to undesirable differences between societies, but also to desirable and desired differences. The human rights movement stresses the *common* humanity of the peoples of the world, but for many, the things that distinguish us from one another are as important as the things that unify us. For example, the Declaration of Principles of Indigenous Rights adopted in Panama in 1984 by a nongovernmental group, the World Council of Indigenous Peoples, lays out positions that are designed to preserve the traditions, customs, institutions, and practices of indigenous peoples (many of which, it need hardly be said, contradict contemporary liberal norms). As with feminist critiques, the argument here is that the present international human rights regime rests too heavily on the experiences of one part of humanity, in this case Western Europe, Canada, and the United States—of course, in practice, the cultural critique and the feminist critique might lead in different directions.

This philosophical point took on a political form in the 1990s. In the immediate post–Cold War world, and especially after the election of US president Bill Clinton in 1992, there was some talk of the United States adopting active policies of democracy promotion, and a number of East Asian governments and intellectuals asserted in response the notion that there were specifically "Asian values" that required defending from this development. The argument was that human rights boil down to no more than a set of particular social choices that need not be considered binding by those whose values (and hence social choices) are differently formed—for example, by Islam or Confucianism rather than by an increasingly secularized Christianity. The wording of the Vienna Declaration on Human Rights of 1993, which refers to the need to bear in mind "the significance of national and regional particularities and various historical, cultural and religious backgrounds" when considering human rights, partially reflects this viewpoint—and has been criticized for this by some human rights activists.

Returning to the history of rights, it is here that the distinction between rights grounded in natural law and rights grounded in a contract becomes crucial. As noted earlier, it is only if rights are grounded in some account of human progress and reason that they may be regarded as genuinely universal in scope. But is this position, as its adherents insist, free of cultural bias, a set of ideas that all rational beings must accept? It seems not, at least insofar as

Human rights activist Ka Hsaw Wa (left), an ethnic Karen from Burma, has led the struggle for minority national rights and environmentalism within that country.

many apparently rational Muslims, Hindus, Buddhists, atheists, utilitarians, and so on clearly do not accept its doctrines. It seems that either the standards derived from natural law (or a similar doctrine) are cast in such general terms that virtually any continuing social system will exemplify them or, if the standards are cast more specifically, they are not in fact universally desired.

Of course, we are under no obligation to accept all critiques of universalism at face value. Human rights might have first emerged in the West, but this does not in itself make rights thinking Western. It could be that an apparently principled rejection of universalism is, in fact, no more than a rationalization of tyranny. How do we know that the inhabitants of Saudi Arabia, say, actually prefer not to live in a democratic system with Western liberal rights, as their government asserts? There is an obvious dilemma here: If we insist that we will only accept democratically validated regimes, we will be imposing an alien test of legitimacy on these societies—yet what other form of validation is available?

In any event, the body of legal acts for the protection of universal human rights applies, does it not, even if rights are essentially convenient fictions? Again, defenders of difference will argue that international law is itself a Western, universalist notion, and, in any event, they rightly note that the Western record of adherence to universal norms does not justify any claim to moral superiority. They point to the many crimes of the age of imperialism as well as to contemporary issues such as the treatment of asylum seekers and refugees, and, of course, the by-products of the global war on terror such as torture and imprisonment without trial.

There is no neutral language for discussing human rights. Whatever way the question is posed reflects a particular viewpoint, and this is no accident. It is built into the nature of the discourse. Is there any way in which the notion of universal rights can be saved from its critics? Two modern approaches seem fruitful. Even if we find it difficult to specify human *rights*, it might still be possible to talk of human *wrongs*—similarly, some have argued that it is easier to specify what is *unjust* than what is *just* (see Booth 1999). To use Michael Walzer's terminology (1994), there might be no thick moral code that is universally acceptable, to which all local codes conform, but there might be a thin code that at least can be used to delegitimize some actions. Thus, for example, the Genocide Convention of 1948 seems a plausible example of a piece of international legislation that outlaws an obvious wrong, and, similarly, although some local variations in the rights associated with gender might be unavoidable, it is still possible to say that practices that severely restrict human capabilities, such as female genital mutilation, are simply wrong. Any code that did not condemn such suffering would be unworthy of respect.

This might not take us as far as some would wish—essential to this approach is the notion that there are going to be some practices that many would condemn but that will have to be tolerated—but it might be the most appropriate response to contemporary pluralism. An alternative approach involves recognizing that human rights are based on a particular culture—Richard Rorty (1993) calls this the "human rights culture"—and defending them in these terms rather than by reference to some cross-cultural code. This approach would involve abandoning the idea that human rights exist. Instead, it involves proselytizing on behalf of the sort of culture in which rights are deemed to exist. The essential point is that human life is safer, pleasanter, and more dignified when rights are acknowledged than when they are not.

Humanitarian Dimensions

Both human rights and human security have become part of an international discourse about proper norms of behavior and the best methods to promote these norms. The disagreements that exist today tend to be questions about the responsibilities of governments to live up to these standards. In this section we discuss some dimensions of this discourse, with particular emphasis on political and economic rights and security, human rights and human security during times of conflict, rights to and security of natural resources, and women's rights.

Political and Economic Rights and Security

"No one shall be subjected to torture or to cruel, inhuman or degrading treatment or punishment" (UN Declaration Article 5, Covenant on Civil and Political Rights Article 7, Convention on Torture, etc.). This is an immunity that is now well established, but what in practice does this mean for someone faced with the prospect of such treatment? If the person is fortunate enough to live in a country governed by the rule of law, domestic courts may well uphold his or her immunity, and the international side of things will come into play only on the margins. Thus, a European who is dissatisfied with treatment at home might be able to take a legal dispute over a particular practice beyond his or her national courts to the European Commission on Human Rights and the European Court of Human Rights. In non-European countries governed by the rule of law, no such direct remedy is available, but the notion of universal rights at least reinforces the rhetorical case for rights that are established elsewhere.

The more interesting case emerges if potential victims do not live in such a law-governed society—if, that is, "their" government and courts are the problem and not the source of a possible solution. What assistance should they expect from the international community? What consequences will flow from their government's failure to live up to its obligations? The problem is that even in cases where violations are quite blatant, it can be difficult to see what other states are able to actually do, even supposing they are willing to act—which cannot be taken for granted, because states rarely if ever act simply in terms of human rights considerations.

Thus, during the Cold War, the West regularly issued verbal condemnations of human rights violations by the Soviet Union and its associates but rarely acted on these condemnations—the power of the Soviet Union made direct intervention imprudent, and even relatively minor sanctions would be adopted only if the general state of East–West relations suggested this would be appropriate. Similar considerations apply today to relations between Western countries and China. Conversely, violations by countries associated with the West were routinely overlooked or, in some cases, even justified—the global war on terror provides contemporary examples. With the ending of the Cold War it seemed possible that a more evenhanded approach to human rights violations might emerge, and, indeed, more active policies have been pursued in some cases, but expectations of major changes in attitude have not been met. In 1997, for example, the incoming Labour government in Britain declared its determination to place human rights at the heart of its foreign policy. Perhaps predictably, the actual policy of the government was frequently seen to be as determined by political and commercial considerations as in the past, and this was true even before the impact of 9/11 and the war on terror is taken into consideration (Smith and Light 2001).

The Chinese government is not afraid to censor the media and arrest citizens who defy them. Press freedom does not exist in China. Here a policeman arrests a supporter of the *Southern Weekly* newspaper in Guangzhou, China. China also limits access to the Internet and other social media.

All told, it seems unlikely that individuals ill-treated by nonconstitutional regimes will find any real support from the international community unless their persecutors are weak, of no strategic significance, and commercially unimportant—and even then it is unlikely that effective action will be taken unless one further factor is present, namely, the force of public opinion. This is the one positive factor that could goad states into action: The growth of humanitarian NGOs has produced a context in which sometimes the force of public opinion can make itself felt, not necessarily in the oppressing regime, but in the policy-formation processes of the potential providers of aid.

The situation with respect to second-generation rights is more complicated. Consider, for example, "the right of everyone to an adequate standard of living for himself and his family, including adequate food, clothing and housing, and to the continuous improvement of living conditions" (Covenant on Economic, Social and Cultural Rights, Article 11.1), or the "right of everyone to be free from hunger" (Article 11.2). It has been argued by numerous cosmopolitan writers that such rights are, or should be, central. For example, Henry Shue (1996) argues that only if such basic rights are met can any other rights be claimed, and Thomas Pogge (2002) sees the relief of world poverty as a central task for the human rights regime.

The Covenant makes the realization of these rights an obligation on its signatories, but this is arguably a different kind of obligation from the obligation to refrain from, for example, "cruel or degrading" punishments. In the latter case, as with other basically political rights, the remedy is clearly in the hands of national governments. The way to end torture is, simply, for states to stop torturing. The right not to be tortured is associated with a duty not to torture. The right to be free from hunger, on the other hand, is not simply a matter of a duty on the part of one's own and other states not to pursue policies that lead to starvation. It also involves a duty to act to "ensure an equitable distribution of world food supplies in relation to need" (Covenant on Economic, Social and Cultural Rights, Article 11.2[b]). The distinction here is sometimes seen as that between "negative" and "positive" rights, although this is not entirely satisfactory, because negative (political) rights often require positive action if they are to be protected effectively. In any event, there are problems with the notion of economic rights.

First, it is by no means clear that, even assuming goodwill, these social and economic goals could always be met, and to think in terms of having a right to something that could not be achieved is to misuse language. In such circumstances, a right simply means "a generally desirable state of affairs," and this weakening of the concept could have the effect of undermining more precise claims to rights that actually can be achieved (such as the right not to be tortured).

Second, some states might seek to use economic and social rights more directly to undermine political rights. Thus, dictatorial regimes in poor countries quite frequently justify the curtailment of political rights in the name of promoting economic growth or economic equality. In fact, there is no reason to accept the general validity of this argument—Amartya Sen argues cogently that development and freedom go together (Sen 1999)—but it will still be made, and not always in bad faith.

Finally, if it is accepted that all states have a positive duty to promote economic well-being and freedom from hunger everywhere, then the consequences go beyond the requirement of the rich to share with the poor, revolutionary though such a requirement would be. Virtually all national social and economic policies become a matter for international regulation. Clearly, rich states would have a duty to make economic and social policy with a view to its consequences on the poor, but so would poor states. The poor's right to assistance creates a duty on the rich to assist, but this in turn creates a right of the rich to insist that the poor have a duty not to worsen their plight—for example, by failing to restrict population growth or by inappropriate economic policies. Aid programs promoted by the Commonwealth and World Bank, and the structural-adjustment programs of the International Monetary Fund, regularly include conditions of this kind. They are, however, widely resented because they contradict another widely supported economic and social right: "All peoples have the right of self-determination. By virtue of that right they freely determine their political status and freely pursue their economic, social and cultural development" (Covenant on Economic, Social and Cultural Rights, Article 1.1). Even when applied in a well-meaning and consistent way, external pressures to change policy are rarely popular, even with those they are intended to benefit.

On the other hand, it is certainly true that people suffering from brutal poverty and severe malnourishment are unlikely to be able to exercise any rights at all unless their condition is attended to, and it might be true, as Pogge argues, that the transfers actually required to raise living standards to an acceptable level across the world are sufficiently modest that they would not actually raise the problems just outlined. Still, most economic and social "rights" are best seen as collectively agreed-on aspirations rather than as rights as the term has conventionally been used.

Human Rights and Human Security During Conflict

Why the continued importance of national security over human rights and human security? For developing countries, state sovereignty and territorial integrity take precedence over security of the individual. Many countries in the developing world are artificial nation-states, whose boundaries were drawn arbitrarily by the colonial powers in the nineteenth century without regard for the actual ethnic composition or historical linkages among peoples. State responses to ethnic separatist movements (now conflated with terrorism), which are partly rooted in people's rejection of colonial-imposed boundaries, have been accompanied by the most egregious violations of human security by governments. Moreover, many third-world states, as well as China, remain under authoritarian rule. Human security is stymied by the lack of political space for alternatives to state ideologies and by restrictions on civil liberties imposed by authoritarian regimes to ensure their own survival.

In the developed as well as the developing world, one of the most powerful challenges to human rights and human security has come from the war on terror led by the United States in response to the 9/11 attacks. These attacks revived the traditional emphasis of states on national security (Suhrke 2004, 365). Although terrorists target innocent civilians and thus threaten human security, governments have used the war on terror to restrict and violate civil liberties. The United States' decision to put Saddam Hussein on trial in an Iraqi court rather than the ICC illustrated the continued US defiance of a key policy instrument of human security, even though it focused on the more Western-oriented conception of "freedom from fear." The US questioning of the applicability of the Geneva Conventions, and the abandoning of its commitments on the issue of torture in the context of war in Iraq, further undermined the agenda of human security. So did Russia's flouting of a wide range of its international commitments—including the laws of war, CSCE and Organization for Security and Co-operation in Europe commitments, and international and regional conventions on torture—in the context of its war in Chechnya.

A pioneering report released by the Human Security Center at the University of British Columbia (2005) points to several significant trends in armed conflicts around the world. What explains the overall downward trend in armed conflicts? The report lists several factors: growing democratization (the underlying assumption here being that democracies tend to be better at peaceful resolution of conflicts); rising economic interdependence (which increases the costs of conflict); the declining economic utility of war, owing to the fact that resources can be more easily bought in the international marketplace than acquired through force; the growth in the number of international institutions that can mediate in conflicts; the impact of international norms against violence such as human sacrifice, witch burning, slavery, dueling, war crimes, and genocide; the end of colonialism; and the end of the Cold War. A specific reason identified by the report is the dramatic increase in the UN's role: its work in areas such as preventative diplomacy and peacemaking activities, its postconflict peacebuilding, the willingness of the UN Security Council to use military action to enforce peace agreements, the deterrent effects of war crime trials by the ICC and other tribunals, and the greater resort to reconciliation and addressing the root causes of conflict. The 80 percent decline in the most deadly civil conflicts since the early 1990s, argued the report, is caused by the dramatic growth of international efforts at preventive diplomacy, peacemaking, and peacebuilding (University of British Columbia, Human Security Center 2005, Part V).

Yet, the optimism created by the report did not last long. The more recent 2009–10 Human Security Report found a 25% increase in armed conflicts between 2003 to 2008. (See Figure 10.1) A large percentage of these conflicts—a quarter of those that started between 2004 and 2008—were related to "Islamist political violence." These increases were partly due to "minor conflicts" with few casualties. While the "war on terror" played an important part in the increasing number and the deadliness of conflicts, viewed from a longer-term perspective, the level of conflict in the Islamic world is lower than two decades earlier. And in terms of casualty levels, the average annual battle-death toll per conflict was less than 1000 in the new millennium compared to the 1950s. Yet there remains the possibility of violence associated with the "Arab Spring" and its aftermath, which, although low for now, could escalate due to the ongoing strife in Syria and instability in transitional societies.

And there are some horrific costs associated with these conflicts. For example, deaths directly or indirectly attributed to the conflict in the Democratic Republic of the Congo since 1998 have surpassed casualties sustained by Britain in World War I and World War II combined. The conflict in Sudan's Darfur region displaced nearly 2 million people (UNDP 2005, 12). In Iraq, a team of American and Iraqi epidemiologists estimated that Iraq's mortality rate more than doubled following the US invasion: from 5.5 deaths per 1,000 people in the year before the invasion to 13.3 deaths per 1,000 people per year in the postinvasion period. In all, some 655,000 more people died in Iraq since the invasion in March 2003 than would have died if the invasion had not occurred (D. Brown 2006, A12).

WHAT'S YOUR WORLDVIEW

Genocide continues and states have often not responded, despite the fact that many states have signed international agreements requiring it. Why do you think states have failed to act effectively?

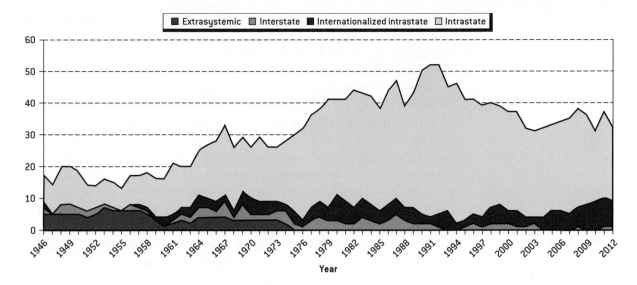

Figure 7.1 Armed Conflicts, 1946–2012.
Source: Journal for Peace Research, http://jpr.sagepub.com/content/early/2013/06/28/0022343313494396.full.

The share of civilian casualties in armed conflict has increased since World War II. Civilians accounted for 10 percent of the victims during World War I and 50 percent of the victims during World War II. They constitute between 80 and 85 percent of the victims of more recent wars. Many of these victims are children, women, the sick, and the elderly (*Gendering Human Security* 2001, 18). Although death tolls from organized campaigns against civilians have declined in recent years, the number of such campaigns increased by 55 percent between 1989 and 2005 (University of British Columbia, Human Security Center 2006, 3).

International terrorist incidents and related fatalities increased worldwide between 2002 and 2005. Most of the increases were associated with the war in Iraq, where the number of fatalities grew from about 1,700 in 2004 to approximately 3,400 in 2005 (National Counterterrorism Center 2005). Excluding Iraq, however, terrorist action killed fewer people worldwide in 2005—1,500 as opposed to 3,000 in 2004 (National Counterterrorism Center 2005).

Furthermore, some of the most serious issues of human security in armed conflicts still need to be overcome, such as child soldiers and landmines. According to one study, 75 percent of the armed conflicts today involve child soldiers (University of British Columbia, *Human Security Center* 2005, 35). Landmines and unexploded ordnance cause between 15,000 and 20,000 new casualties each year (US Campaign to Ban Landmines, accessed April 4, 2013). Despite the justified optimism generated by the Ottawa Treaty (to be discussed later), there remain 80 million live mines undetected—someone steps on a landmine every twenty-eight minutes—and 80 percent of those killed or injured by landmines are civilians (Koehler 2007).

Finally, the decline in armed conflicts around the world is not necessarily irreversible. Some of the factors contributing to the decline of conflicts, such as democratization and the peace-operations role of the UN, can suffer setbacks because of a lack of support from major powers and the international community. And there remain serious possible threats to international peace and security that can cause widespread casualties, such as a conflict in the Korean Peninsula and war between China and Taiwan.

Battle deaths are not themselves an adequate indicator of threats to human security posed by armed conflict. Many armed conflicts have indirect consequences on human life and well-being. Wars are a major source of economic disruption, disease, and ecological destruction, which in turn undermine human development and thus create a vicious cycle of conflict and underdevelopment. As the *Human Development Report* (UNDP 2005, 12) puts it: "Conflict undermines nutrition and public health, destroys education systems, devastates livelihoods and retards prospects for economic growth." It found that of the fifty-two countries that are reversing or stagnating in their attempts to reduce child mortality, thirty have experienced conflict since 1990. A British government white paper on international development notes:

> Violent conflict reverses economic growth, causes hunger, destroys roads, schools and clinics, and forces people to flee across borders. Women and girls are particularly vulnerable because they suffer sexual violence and exploitation. And violent conflict and insecurity can spill over into neighboring countries and provide cover for terrorists or organized criminal groups. (Department for International Development 2006, 45)

Wars also damage the environment, as happened with the US use of Agent Orange defoliant during the Vietnam War and Saddam Hussein's burning of Kuwaiti oil wells in the 1990–1991 Gulf War, leading to massive air and land pollution. Similar links can be made between conflict and the outbreak of disease: "[W]ar-exacerbated disease and malnutrition kill far more people than missiles, bombs and bullets" (University of British Columbia, Human Security Center 2005, 7). Disease accounts for a significant percentage of the 5.4 million people who have died in the conflict in the Democratic Republic of the Congo (UNDP 2005, 45).

Just as wars and violent conflict have indirect consequences such as economic disruption, ecological damage, and disease, levels of poverty and environmental degradation contribute to conflict and hence must be taken into consideration in human security research (as we discuss in Chapters 9 and 10). One study shows that a country at $250 GDP per capita has an average 15 percent risk of experiencing a civil war in the next five years, whereas at a GDP per capita of $5,000, the risk of civil war is less than 1 percent (Humphreys and Varshney 2004, 9; Department for International Development 2005, 8). Although no direct link can be established between poverty and terrorism, terrorists often "exploit poverty and exclusion in order to tap into popular discontent—taking advantage of fragile states such as Somalia, or undemocratic regimes such as in Afghanistan in the 1990s, to plan violence" (UNDP 2005, 47).

Women, Conflict, and Human Security

The relationship between gender and human security has multiple dimensions. The UN Inter-Agency Committee on Women and Gender Equality notes five aspects: (1) violence against women and girls, (2) gender inequalities in control over resources, (3) gender inequalities in power and decision making, (4) women's human rights, and (5) women (and men) as actors, not victims (UN Inter-Agency Committee on Women and Gender Equality 1999, 1). Recent conflicts have shown women as victims of rape, torture, and sexual slavery. For example, between 250,000 and 500,000 women were raped during the 1994 genocide in Rwanda. Such atrocities against women are now recognized as a crime against humanity (Rehn and Sirleaf 2002, 9).

War-affected areas often see a sharp increase in domestic violence directed at women and a growth in the number of women trafficked to become forced laborers or sex workers. Women and children comprise 73 percent of an average population but account for 80 percent of the refugees in the world today and perhaps a larger percentage as internally displaced persons. Another important aspect of the gender dimension of human security is the role of women as actors in conflicts. This involves considering the participation of women in combat. In the Eritrean war of independence, women made up 25 to 30 percent of combatants. A similar proportion of women were fighting with the Tamil Tigers. Women play an even larger role in support functions, such as logistics, staff, and intelligence services, in a conflict. It has been noted that women become targets of rape and sexual violence because they serve as a social and cultural symbol. Hence violence against them might be undertaken as a deliberate strategy to undermine the social fabric of an opponent. Similarly, securing women's participation in combat might be motivated by a desire, among the parties to a conflict, to increase the legitimacy of their cause. It signifies "a broad social consensus and solidarity, both to their own population and to the outside world" (*Gendering Human Security* 2001, 18).

In recent years, there has been a growing awareness of the need to secure the greater participation of women in international peace operations. The UN Department of Peacekeeping Operations noted in a 2000 report:

> Women's presence [in peacekeeping missions] improves access and support for local women; it makes male peacekeepers more reflective and responsible; and it broadens the repertoire of skills and styles available within the mission, often with the effect of reducing conflict and confrontation. Gender mainstreaming is not just fair, it is beneficial. (cited in Rehn and Sirleaf 2002, 63)

In 2000, the UN Security Council passed a resolution (Security Council Resolution 1325) mandating a review of the impact of armed conflict on women

Gendered Perspective on Human Rights

The Challenge

Until recently, it has been conventional for human rights treaties to be cast in language that assumes that the rights bearer is a man and the head of a household. Many feminists argue that this convention reflects more than an old-fashioned turn of phrase. The classic political and civil rights (freedom of speech, association, from arbitrary arrest, etc.) assume that the rights bearer will be living, or would wish to live, a life of active citizenship, but, until very recently, such a life was denied to nearly all women in nearly all cultures. Instead of this public life, women were limited to the private sphere and subjected to the arbitrary and capricious power of the male head of the household. It is only very recently in the Western liberal democracies that women have been able to vote, to stand for office, or to own property in their own name, and issues such as the criminalization of rape in marriage and the effective prevention of domestic violence against women are still controversial. The situation is even worse in some non-Western polities. It could be that a genuinely gender-neutral account of human rights is possible, but some radical feminists argue that an altogether different kind of thinking is required (see Mackinnon 1993).

Options

Both cultural critics and feminists argue, convincingly, that the model of a rights bearer inherent in the contemporary international human rights regime is based on the experiences of Western men. Agreement collapses, however, when the implications of this common position are explored. Liberal feminists wish to see the rights of men extended to women, whereas radical feminists wish to promote a new model of what it is to be human that privileges neither men nor women. Most cultural critics, on the other hand, wish to preserve inherited status and power differences based on gender.

Application

The contradictions here are sharpest when it comes to relations between the world of Islam and the human rights regime, largely because relations between Islam and the West are so fraught on other grounds that all differences are magnified. Radical or traditional Islamists argue for conventional gender roles, support quite severe restrictions on the freedom of women, and promote the compulsory wearing of restrictive clothing such as the niqab or the burqa. Many of these petty restrictions have no basis in the Koran or the sayings of the Prophet and can simply be understood as methods of preserving male dominance—although it should be said that they are often accepted by Muslim women as ways of asserting their identity. More serious for the human rights regime are those verses of the Koran that unambiguously deny gender equality. It is often, and truly, said that the Koran's attitude toward the status of women was in advance of much contemporary seventh-century thought—including Christian and Jewish thought of the age—but it remains the case that, for example, in a sharia court the evidence of a woman is worth less than that of a man, and sexual intercourse outside marriage is punishable for a woman even in the case of rape. The other Abrahamic religions continue to preserve misogynist vestiges, but mainstream Christian and Jewish theologians have reinterpreted those aspects of their traditions that radically disadvantage women. Given the importance attached to the literal text

A global press and the Internet have made local and national decisions in one country the concern of communities across the globe. In this picture, for example, Indonesian Muslim students protest the French decision to ban Muslim headscarves and other religious clothing in public schools.

of the Koran, this reinterpretation will prove more difficult for Muslims, although many Islamic thinkers discuss women's rights. The role of women under Islam will be a continuing problem for the international human rights regime as it attempts to divest itself of its Western Judeo-Christian heritage and adopt a more inclusive framework. It will, of course, be an even bigger problem for those women who live in oppressive Muslim regimes.

For Discussion

1. Should local cultural standards outweigh externally derived norms?
2. The rights of women all over the world, including in many OECD countries, are at risk. To what extent is the focus on women in Islamic societies justified?
3. Are certain human rights not "universal"?

and the role of women in peace operations and conflict resolution. The review was released in 2002 and entitled *Women, Peace and Security* (UN 2002). In his introduction to the report, UN Secretary-General Kofi Annan noted that that "women still form a minority of those who participate in peace and security negotiations, and receive less attention than men in post-conflict agreements, disarmament and reconstruction" (UN 2002, ix). There is still a long way to go before the international community can fully realize the benefits of greater participation by women in UN peace operations and conflict-resolution activities.

Globalization has made it more difficult for leaders of countries to assert that national cultural norms are more important than global standards of behavior. Transnational corporations, the globalized entertainment industry, and the UN itself all penetrate national borders and erode traditional values. As we will see in the next section, the international community of countries is actively involved in this process.

The Role of the International Community

Because of the broad and contested nature of the idea of human security, it is difficult to evaluate policies undertaken by the international community that can be specifically regarded as human security measures. But the most important multilateral actions include the ICC, the Antipersonnel Landmines Treaty, and the 2005 R2P document adopted by the UN, which (as discussed earlier in this book) asserted the moral obligations for states to intervene against human rights violations in other states.

The ICC was established on July 1, 2002, with its headquarters in The Hague, Netherlands, although its proceedings may take place anywhere. It is a permanent institution with "the power to exercise its jurisdiction over persons for the most serious crimes of international concern" (Rome Statute, Article 1). These crimes include genocide, crimes against humanity, war crimes, and the crime of aggression, although the court would not exercise its jurisdiction over the crime of aggression until such time as the state parties agree on a definition of the crime and set out the conditions under which it may be prosecuted. The ICC is a "court of last resort." It is "complementary to national criminal jurisdictions," meaning that it can only exercise its jurisdiction when national courts are unwilling or unable to investigate or prosecute such crimes (Rome Statute, Article 1). The court can only prosecute crimes that were committed on or after July 1, 2002, the date its founding treaty entered into force. Since its establishment, the ICC has been involved in the prosecution of some high-profile war criminals in the former Yugoslavia, Liberia, and Congo, including the former president of Yugoslavia, Slobodan Milosevic (whose trial ended without a verdict after he was found dead in his cell in March 2006), and former Liberian president Charles Taylor.

The Convention on the Prohibition of the Use, Stockpiling, Production, and Transfer of Anti-Personnel Mines and on Their Destruction, signed in Ottawa on December 3–4, 1997, bans the development, production, acquisition, stockpiling, transfer, and use of antipersonnel mines (Ottawa Treaty, Article 1, General Obligations, 1997). It also obliges signatories to destroy existing stockpiles. Among the countries that have yet to sign the treaty are the People's Republic of China, the Russian Federation, and the United States.

The surge in UN peacekeeping and peacebuilding operations has contributed to the decline in conflict and enhanced prospects for human security. The number of UN peacekeeping operations increased threefold between the first forty years of the UN's founding and the twenty years since—from thirteen to forty-seven missions (UN Peacekeeping website, n.d.). More recently, a UN Peacebuilding Commission was inaugurated in 2006. Its goal is to assist in post-conflict recovery and reconstruction, including institution building and sustainable development, in countries emerging from conflict. The UN has also been center stage in promoting the idea of humanitarian intervention, a central policy element of human security. The concept of humanitarian intervention was endorsed by the report of the UN Secretary-General's High-Level Panel on Threats, Challenges and Change, *A More Secure World* (UN 2004, 66, 106), the subsequent report by the secretary-general, entitled *In Larger Freedom* (UN 2005), and finally by the UN Summit in September 2005.

UN specialized agencies play a crucial role in promoting human security. For example, the UNDP and the World Health Organization have been at the forefront of fighting poverty and disease, respectively. Other UN agencies, such as the UN High Commissioner for Refugees, UNICEF, and UN Development Fund for Women (UNIFEM), have played a central role in getting particular issues, such as refugees and the rights of children and women, onto the agenda for discussion and in providing a platform for advocacy and action (MacFarlane and Khong 2006).

NGOs contribute to human security in a number of ways: giving information and early warning about conflicts, providing a channel for relief operations (often being the first to do so in areas of conflict or natural disaster), and supporting government- or UN-sponsored peacebuilding and rehabilitation missions. NGOs also play a central role in promoting sustainable development. A leading NGO with a human security mission is the International Committee of the Red Cross. Established in Geneva, it has a unique authority based on the international humanitarian law of the Geneva Conventions to protect the lives and dignity of victims of war and internal violence, including

The UN High Commissioner for Refugees special envoy, Angelina Jolie, speaks to refugees from the Syrian civil war at a military camp in Jordan. Reports in 2013 from this UN agency state that most of the refugees in the world have fled from five war-affected countries: Afghanistan, Somalia, Iraq, Syria, and Sudan.

the war wounded, prisoners, refugees, civilians, and other noncombatants, and to provide them with assistance. Other NGOs include Médecins Sans Frontières (Doctors Without Borders; emergency medical assistance), Save the Children (protection of children), and Amnesty International (human rights).

At times these agencies overlap in the services they provide or the issue for which they advocate. As you will see, this tends to be the case in international relations. However, given the complex nature of international human rights law and the demands of providing for human security, each organization can play a part in helping to advance the international agenda.

Conclusion

For more than sixty years, leaders and citizens of countries have worked to develop the paired concepts of human rights and human security. Although governments around the world—including some in Europe and North America, the intellectual homelands of the concepts—from time to time violate the very freedoms they once endorsed when they ratified the various human rights treaties, it is understood that these are transgressions of long-standing norms of behavior. Certainly, more can be done to promote freedom from fear and freedom from want. The *Human Development Report* of 2005 estimates that the rich nations of the world provide ten dollars to the military budget for every one dollar they spend on aid. For example, the current global spending on HIV/AIDS, "a disease that claims 3 million lives a year, represents three days' worth of military spending" (UNDP 2011, 8).

Perhaps the greatest challenge today in the issue area of human rights and human security is the need to change the ways in which government officials and citizens see the role of the state. Does it exist solely to defend the country, along the lines suggested in the Westphalian model of an independent and sovereign state? Or do we have an obligation as humans to help other humans in need? Until this is resolved, debates about human rights and human security will continue.

Human Rights Watch Film Festival

This is a program of the well-respected organization Human Rights Watch, which is dedicated to defending and protecting human rights. The festival chooses films that expose human rights abuses through storytelling in a way that challenges viewers to empathize with and demand justice for all people. It is held annually in several cities across the United States and abroad. Visit http://ff.hrw.org/.

Reliefweb

This is a database of jobs, workshops, conferences, and courses in development, international policy, and assistance. It is a particularly useful resource if you want to do humanitarian work abroad. The majority of listings are conferences outside the United States, but there are more than 400 listings most days. Visit reliefweb.int.

KEY TERMS

Charter rights, p. 226
Common security, p. 235
Genocide, p. 224
Human development, p. 234

Humanitarian intervention, p. 236
Human security, p. 231
Liberal Account of Rights, p. 226
Natural law, p. 225

Nonintervention, p. 228
Standards of civilization, p. 228
Universal Declaration of Human
　Rights, p. 229

REVIEW QUESTIONS

1. What is the relationship between rights and duties?

2. Why is the promotion of human rights so rarely seen as an appropriate foreign policy goal of states? If you were a policymaker, what kinds of arguments would you construct in favor of human rights as a policy goal?

3. What are the problems involved in assigning rights to peoples as opposed to individuals?

4. In what ways can gender bias be identified in the modern human rights regime?

5. What is the relationship between democracy and human rights? Is it always the case that democracies are more likely to respect human rights than authoritarian regimes?

6. Can the compromising of human rights in the face of the threat of terrorism ever be justified as the lesser of two evils?

7. What is human security? How is it different from the concept of national security?

8. Describe the main difference between the two conceptions of human security: "freedom from fear" and "freedom from want." Are the two understandings irreconcilable?

9. How do you link poverty and health with human security?

10. What are the main areas of progress in the promotion of human security by the international community?

11. What are the obstacles to human security promotion by the international community?

12. Why do we need to give special consideration to the suffering of women in conflict zones?

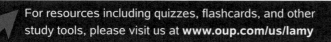

THINKING ABOUT GLOBAL POLITICS

What Should Be Done? National Interests Versus Human Interests

BACKGROUND

Takastand is a new nation-state that once was part of a large authoritarian empire. It is resource rich and is located in a strategic region that is important to many of the major powers, including China, India, Russia, and the United States. It is a multiethnic state with five major ethnocultural communities. Although it professes to be a democratic state, one political party controls the government. This political party also represents the dominant ethnic community, and it openly discriminates against the other ethnic communities. The police and the military have led secret raids against ethnic minorities, and international human rights organizations have found mass graves. The Takastand government denies any connections to the human rights abuses and blames international criminal networks or fundamentalist religious groups that are attempting to overthrow the government. The government also believes that stability is more important than rights at this stage of the country's development. Also, the government's claim that it is being attacked by fundamentalist Islamic forces backed by Al Qaeda has led to significant security assistance from the US government and its NATO partners.

Most of the opposition groups claim that they stand for individual rights and freedoms and democracy, and they all claim that they will implement a true democracy that protects the rights and freedoms of all citizens. They also claim that they will end the country's dependence on the West and that they will challenge the hegemony of the United States and its allies.

Although this is a very poor country, it has significant energy reserves, but most of the profits end up in the hands of the political and military elites. Close to 85 percent of the wealth is controlled by 13 percent of the population. A number of European governments and NGOs have established effective development programs focusing on the UN's MDGs. More women and children in rural areas are now receiving health care, food, and education. The government representatives in these regions control the programs and usually demand payments to allow them to continue. Recently, they have arrested NGO workers and local activists who challenged their authority. Four NGO project leaders were arrested, prosecuted before a military court, and sentenced to death.

ASSIGNMENT

This action has prompted an international conference to address the human security problems and the repression in Takastand. The conference is modeled after similar conferences held to decide how to help Rwanda, Iraq, and Afghanistan. Your assignment is to describe how the world should respond. Take a look at other international assistance conferences and use those as models for your work. Is this a military, political, economic, or human rights issue? Then follow these three steps in planning your conference. This can be a group activity.

> Step One: What issues should the conference address? Consider economic, political, military, and human rights and security issues.
>
> Step Two: Consider who should be involved. Should this be an action of the UN, or should the great powers take care of this crisis? What role should NGOs play in this human security crisis?
>
> Step Three: Answer these questions:
>
> Is stability in this region more important than human rights? Why or why not?
>
> Is it more important to provide access to economic opportunities or to provide cultural and political freedoms? Why?
>
> Should citizens of some countries be forced to give up rights and freedoms so that others may have access to material goods and resources that help them enjoy the good life? Why?

CONTRIBUTORS TO CHAPTER 7: *Amitav Acharya, Alex J. Bellamy, Chris Brown, Nicholas J. Wheeler, Steven L. Lamy, and John Masker.*

8 | Global Economics and Trade

The ideas of economists and political philosophers, both when they are right and when they are wrong, are more powerful than is commonly understood. Indeed, the world is ruled by little else.

—*John Maynard Keynes*

Trade is the oldest and most important economic nexus among nations. Indeed, trade along with war has been central to the evolution of international relations.

—*Robert Gilpin*

There can be different brands of free-market vanilla and you can adjust your society to it by going faster or slower. But, in the end, if you want higher standards of living in a world without walls, the free market is the only ideological alternative left. One road. Different speeds. But one road.

—*Thomas L. Friedman*

How did it happen? One day the global economy was cruising along in the economic fast lane. Stock prices seemed to have no ceiling, with each day bringing a new all-time high. The annual bonuses that CEOs of multinational corporations and bond traders of Wall Street gave themselves were more than the gross domestic products of most developing countries. Then, although the danger was there to see for some time, subprime mortgages in the United States sparked a worldwide economic collapse in 2008. Bad mortgages had become part of the new pattern of global investments that were, for the most part, unfettered by government regulation. The Nobel Prize–winning economist Joseph Stiglitz stated in 2010 that one of the legacies of this crisis will be a new debate on which kind of economic system "is most likely to deliver the greatest benefit." Communism is out of the debate, but what about Asian capitalism, which emphasizes an economy that enriches the state, or the Nordic social democratic

More than 20,000 Ukrainian activists are protesting in Independence Square in Kiev, Ukraine, in December 2013. They opposed the government's decision to reject a deal to associate with the EU in favor of a closer cooperation with Russia. After the Russian annexation of Crimea the future integrity and sovereignty of Ukraine is at stake.

model, which is creating economic stability and growth in Sweden and Norway? Time will tell whether the future of capitalism will include more or less government intervention in the market and whether states will continue to provide their citizens with a wide variety of social services.

But the economic recession that began in 2008 was more than bad personal finances and massive government bailouts for banks and corporations. It also constituted a serious global security challenge, as Dennis Blair warned in early 2009. Blair, who was at the time the Director of National Intelligence for the United States, stated that 25 percent of the world's countries have experienced low-level instability attributed to unemployment and poor economic conditions. Effective global trade and financial systems are critical elements of global security.

The notion of a free market unfettered by any sort of government intervention is a chimera. Governments often determine the direction the economy may take. The government of Ukraine abandoned over five years of negotiations with the EU and decided to move closer to Russia. This was more than an economic choice. It was an existential choice between a post-Soviet system that is corrupt and dysfunctional and an EU that is built on the rule of law and a respect for both markets and individuals. Note how the leaders of the liberal global economy responded to the recent economic crisis. As the global economic crisis that had begun in 2008 simply continued, France and Germany took the lead in discussing ways of protecting the eurozone against economic collapse.

By the end of 2012, Georgia, Ukraine, Hungary, the Seychelles, Pakistan, Latvia, and Belarus had all taken loans from the IMF. The financial crisis was the result of serious shortcomings in domestic financial regulation and the failure of global cooperation, especially with regard to global financial institutions. Many politicians and academic specialists argued that it was time for world leaders to reform the international economic institutions that were created after World War II. As you will see in this chapter, much has changed since 1945: There are now more state actors, more global financial actors, and more transnational corporations. The worldwide economic recession of 2008–2013 revealed that globalization has made all of this more difficult to manage, if not control. Open economies grew much faster than closed economies, but they also opened themselves to the spread of financial difficulties.

Introduction

International political economy (IPE) is about the interplay of economics and politics in world affairs. The core question of IPE is this: What drives and explains events in the world economy? For some people, this comes down to a battle of "states versus markets." But this description is misleading. The "markets" of the world economy are not like local street bazaars, in which all items can be openly and competitively traded and exchanged. Further, politicians cannot rule the global economy, much as they might like to. World markets—and countries, local firms, and multinational corporations that trade and invest within them—are all shaped by layers of rules, norms, laws, organizations, and even habits. Political scientists call all these features of the system *institutions*. IPE tries to explain what creates and perpetuates institutions and what impact they have on the world economy.

Since the 1970s, IPE has continued to advance as a core subject of international relations, in part because of the effects of globalization. Furthermore, the end of the Cold War introduced several economic challenges, such as integrating the former Eastern bloc countries into the world system. At the same time, an explosion of tribal, religious, and ethnic conflicts around the world forced analysts to more closely examine the links among poverty, economic stagnation, and the indebtedness of countries on the one hand and intrastate conflict on the other. Finally, the end of the Cold War thrust international institutions into the limelight. The United Nations, the IMF, the **World Bank Group**, and the newly created **World Trade Organization (WTO)** all became an important focus of study and attention.

The globalization of world politics involves, among other things, a globalization of economics. As we discussed in previous chapters, politics and economics are inseparable within most societies. Economics does not explain everything, but no account of world politics (and hence no analysis of globalization as a key issue of contemporary world history) is adequate if it does not explore the economic dimension.

Like the Bretton Woods system, which was developed after World War II and which we discuss later, the global trade and finance systems developed in reaction to the events that followed World War I. The freewheeling capitalism of the Roaring Twenties, many people believed, helped cause the **Great Depression**. In the United States, for example, overproduction and underconsumption, buying stocks on margin, the corrupt investment strategies known as Ponzi schemes (made famous again by the recent actions of Bernie Madoff), and land speculation were all parts of the problems inherent when governments did not regulate business activity. Once the Great Depression struck in 1929, international trade measures such as increased tariffs exacerbated the preexisting domestic market distortions.

International trade, however, did not lend itself to solutions like the IMF and World Bank of the Bretton Woods system. John Maynard Keynes, Harry Dexter White, and the other economists and political leaders who met at Bretton Woods, New Hampshire, in July 1944 planned a third part of the system, the International Trade Organization. Unfortunately, largely because of opposition in the US Senate, the Havana Charter of the International Trade Organization never entered into force. In its place, the General Agreement on Tariffs and Trade (GATT) secretariat—which was intended to oversee trade on a temporary basis—took on the task of organizing global trade negotiations.

We begin this chapter with a brief review of important postwar events that laid much of the groundwork for the economic realities we live with today; we then focus on some of the key institutions and ideas that have helped create our globalized world of commerce. As the chapter unfolds, we also consider how this of all fits together—practically and intellectually—and we conclude the chapter by examining the debate surrounding globalization: Where do we go from here? Of course, to understand where we are today and how we got here, we must first dial back the clock—to the 1940s, after World War II.

The Postwar World Economy

The institutions and framework of the world economy have their roots in the planning for a new economic order that took place during the last phase of World War II. In 1944, policy makers gathered in New Hampshire at the Bretton Woods resort to consider how to resolve two very serious problems. First, they needed to ensure that the Great Depression of the 1930s would not

How did the Bretton Woods conference of July 1944 set up a political and economic system that clearly benefitted the United States and its allies?

happen again. In other words, they had to find ways to ensure a stable global monetary system and an open world-trading system. Second, they needed to rebuild the war-torn economies of Europe.

At the meeting in Bretton Woods, policy makers planned three institutions to promote a new world economic order:

- They created the IMF to ensure a stable exchange rate regime and the provision of emergency economic assistance.
- They created the International Bank for Reconstruction and Development (later called the World Bank) to facilitate private investment and reconstruction in Europe. The bank was also charged with assisting **development** in other countries, a mandate that later became the main reason for its existence.
- Finally, they planned the GATT, which was later signed (in 1947) and became a forum for negotiations on **trade liberalization**, the removal or reduction of barriers to free trade.

The 1944 plans for the world economy, however, were soon postponed when in 1945 the United States made its first priority the containment of the Soviet Union. Fearing the rise of communism in war-ravaged Europe, the United States took a far more direct role than planned in reconstructing Europe and managing the world economy. The United States announced the **Marshall Plan** in 1947, which directed massive financial aid to Europe and permitted the United States to set conditions on it. Proposed by Secretary of State George Marshall, and officially known as the European Recovery Program, it was offered to all European states, including the Soviet Union. These funds played a critical role in European recovery. That same year, the planned gold standard was replaced by the **dollar standard**, which the United States managed directly, backing the dollar with gold. Unsurprisingly, by the time the IMF, the World Bank, and the GATT began to function in the 1950s, they were distinctly Western-bloc organizations that depended heavily on the United States.

US support for what became known as the **Bretton Woods system** began to change when weaknesses emerged in the US economy. After 1965, the United States widened its costly military involvement in Vietnam and also started to spend more money on public education and urban redevelopment programs at home (President Johnson's Great Society programs), and all without raising taxes. The damage was dramatic. As prices rose within the US economy, the competitiveness of US goods and services in the world economy dropped. Likewise, confidence in the US dollar plummeted. Firms and countries turned away from the dollar, and the US capacity to back its currency with gold was brought into question.

Meanwhile, other countries in the world economy were enhancing their position. European allies were benefiting from the growing and deepening economic integration in Europe. By the late 1960s, the development of the

European Economic Community provided a springboard for European policy makers to diverge from US positions on such subjects as NATO, military exercises, and support for the gold standard. In Asia, the phenomenal success of **export-led growth** in Japan and in newly industrializing countries such as South Korea and Taiwan created a new challenge to US trade competitiveness and a new agenda for trade negotiations. These countries took advantage of cheap labor to gain control of industries like electronics and textiles, thereby controlling most of the exports to the world.

Facing these pressures, the United States changed the rules of the international monetary system in 1971. The government announced that it would no longer convert dollars to gold at $35 per ounce and that it was imposing a 10 percent surcharge on import duties (to improve its trade balance by curtailing imports, which were flooding into the United States, and to try to stem the outflow of dollars to the rest of the world). These actions broke the Bretton Woods system. This was not the only change in the world economy in the 1970s.

In the 1970s, the period of high growth that followed World War II came to an abrupt end, leaving very high inflation. Further compounding the problem, the first oil crisis in 1973 plunged the world economy into stagflation (a combination of economic stagnation, or low growth, and high inflation). In the monetary system, the role of the IMF collapsed when the Bretton Woods system broke down in 1971 and the major industrialized countries failed to find a way to coordinate their exchange rate policies within the IMF framework. Instead, the major currencies floated, and industrialized countries began to discuss monetary issues among themselves in groups such as the Group of Seven (the United States, Japan, Germany, the United Kingdom, France, Italy, and Canada), which first met in 1975.

In the trading system, cooperation had steadily grown in negotiations under the auspices of the GATT. However, in the 1970s, the gains that had been made in reducing tariff barriers, especially among industrialized countries, were reversed by an emerging **protectionism**—actions to protect domestic industries from more efficient foreign producers. As each country grappled with stagflation, many introduced new forms of barriers (or "nontariff barriers"), in particular to keep out the new competitive imports from successful developing countries like those experiencing export-driven growth. An egregious example of the new protectionism was the Multifiber Arrangement of 1973, which placed restrictions on all textile and apparel imports from developing countries, blatantly violating the GATT principle of nondiscrimination.

The GATT was an interim agreement signed in 1947 in the expectation that it would be superseded by an international trade organization. A permanent trade organization was not created until 1994, however. In essence, the GATT created a forum for trade negotiations. Numerous rounds of talks culminated in the very successful Kennedy Round of 1962–1967, where breakthroughs were made in the reduction of trade barriers among industrialized countries. However, when protectionism flourished in the 1970s, the GATT proved unable to restrain powerful members such as the United States and European countries from imposing trade barriers (e.g., the Multi-fiber Arrangement of 1973, restricting textile imports) and abusing the many exceptions and safeguards written into the agreement. The GATT also functioned as a forum for dispute settlement (i.e., upholding trade rules). However, it was both slow and impotent in this regard, constrained by the need for consensus on any decision regarding disputes. The GATT was replaced by the WTO as a result of agreements forged in the last round of GATT talks, the Uruguay Round (1986–1994). Established on January 1, 1995, the WTO has the following functions: administering WTO trade agreements, providing a forum for trade negotia-

The WTO and the UN work together to address issues that divide the rich and poor states. Here Pascal Lamy, the former director general of the WTO, and UN Secretary-General Ban Ki-moon meet in 2011 to discuss aid and trade issues.

tions, handling trade disputes, monitoring national trade policies, supplying technical assistance and training for developing countries, and cooperating with other international organizations. It is located in Geneva with a secretariat staff of 500.

The new protectionism in industrialized countries further fueled the anger of people in developing countries, who, in the 1970s, launched a concerted campaign in the UN General Assembly for a New International Economic Order (NIEO). Organized as the Group of 77 (G-77), the developing countries were determined to alter the rules of the game, and their strategy for change was bolstered by the success of Organization of the Petroleum-Exporting Countries oil-producing developing countries in raising oil prices in 1973. The agenda of the NIEO covered trade, aid, investment, the international monetary and financial system (including debt forgiveness), and institutional reform. Developing countries sought better representation in international economic institutions, a fairer trading system, more aid, the regulation of foreign investment, the protection of economic sovereignty, and reforms to ensure a more stable and equitable financial and monetary system.

A kind of **summit diplomacy** also took place in the 1970s between North (the industrialized countries) and South (developing countries). These direct, leader-to-leader negotiations were underpinned by a different kind of thinking and scholarship about IPE. The developing countries' push for reform of the international economic system reflected **dependency theory** and Marxist theories of international economic relations that highlighted negative aspects of **interdependence**, a condition where states (or peoples) are affected by others' decisions. Interdependence can be symmetric, in that both actors are affected equally, or it can be asymmetric, where the impact varies between actors. If political or economic costs of interdependence are high, a state is in a vulnerable position. If costs are low, it is a situation of sensitivity interdependence, as we discussed in Chapter 3 in our discussion of neoliberal theories. In a global economy, leaders must manage their trade and financial relations to reduce their vulnerability in this complex system. This is not an easy task, as the United States and many European states have discovered.

As you will remember from Chapter 3, dependency and Marxist theorists sought to identify aspects of the international economy and institutions that impeded the possibilities of development in the South. Their central concern was to answer why so many countries within the world economy remained underdeveloped, despite their promises of modernization and global growth. The most sympathetic official "Northern" answer to these concerns was voiced in the Brandt Report in 1980, the findings of a group of high-level policy makers from rich and poor states that had been asked to examine how and why the international community should respond to the challenges of interdependence and development. The Brandt Report urged the wealthy states in the North to increase development assistance and to reduce trade and investment restrictions for poor countries in the South. Closing the gap between rich and poor states was presented as the biggest security challenge facing world leaders.

The NIEO campaign was unsuccessful for several reasons. The UN General Assembly was an obvious institution for developing countries to choose in making their case, because, unlike the IMF or World Bank, it offers every country one vote. However, the UN General Assembly had no power to implement the agenda of the developing countries. Furthermore, although many industrialized countries were sympathetic to the developing countries' case in the 1970s, these governments did not act, and by the 1980s a new set of governments with a distinctly less sympathetic **free market** ideology had come to power in the United States, the United Kingdom, and West Germany. According to this ideology, markets should be ruled only by the forces of supply and demand, and buying and selling should not be constrained by government regulations or interventions.

The 1980s opened with a shift in US economic policy. In 1979, the US Federal Reserve dramatically raised interest rates in an effort to stem inflation by contracting economic activity in the United States. However, the reverberations in the rest of the world economy were immediate and extensive. During the 1960s and 1970s, US and European policies had facilitated the rapid growth of **global capital markets** (institutions that transfer funds to industries globally) and financial flows. In the 1970s these flows were further buoyed by the investments of oil producers who needed to find outlets for the vast profits made from the oil-price rise of 1973.

WHAT'S YOUR WORLDVIEW

In a global economy run by transnational corporations seeking cheap labor, cheap resources, and minimal rules concerning safety, health, and the environment to maximize their profits, should governments seek to protect their citizens and protect their jobs?

The money found its way to governments in developing countries, which were offered loans at very low prices. The rise in interest rates in 1979 was an abrupt wake-up call to both borrowers and creditors (many of whom were US-based banks), who suddenly realized that many of the loans could not be repaid. The IMF was immediately called in to prevent any developing country from defaulting on these loans, as it was feared that such a default would cause a global financial crisis.

The debt crisis meant that the IMF's role in the world economy became largely one of ensuring that indebted countries undertook "structural adjustment" in their economies. Structural adjustment meant immediate measures to reduce inflation, government expenditure, and the role of the government in the economy, including trade liberalization, privatization, and **deregulation**. These "neoliberal" policies were in marked contrast to the Keynesian analysis that had prevailed until the 1980s, during the decades of growth in the world economy. Keynesians (named after economist John Maynard Keynes) believe that governments should play an active and interventionist role in the economy to ensure both growth and equity. By contrast, neoliberalism sought to roll back the state and the role of government, leaving decisions about allocation, production, and distribution in the economy to the market. By the late 1980s, the term **Washington Consensus** was being used, sometimes pejoratively, to imply that these policies were mainly a reflection of US interests.

The 1990s brought the challenge of how to integrate Central and Eastern European countries and the former Soviet Union into the global economy. The IMF and World Bank became deeply involved, but the Washington Consensus was not broad enough for the purpose. Both institutions began to embrace a broader and deeper view of **conditionality** aimed at promoting "good governance" in member countries. This conditionality meant that regional and international lending agencies required recipient national governments to accept certain policy conditions to receive loans and economic assistance. But many thought conditionality had gone too far when, in the wake of the East Asian financial crisis in 1997, the IMF imposed far-reaching and overly draconian conditions on countries such as Korea. The impact would be felt in subsequent years as the IMF's lending role waned in most emerging-market economies. Over this period, the World Bank sought to broaden its appeal through enhanced relations with governments as well as with NGOs. At the same time, the newly established WTO began operations in 1995, opening up a new forum for negotiating a broad range of international issues, including not just traditional trade but also such issues as **intellectual property rights** (which protect content owners), trade-related investment measures, and food-safety standards.

In the first decade of the twenty-first century, a shift in global economic power was occurring. In September 2003, during global trade negotiations in Mexico, a group of twenty countries, including Brazil, South Africa, India,

A construction worker stands on a scaffold at a new building in the northern Greek port city of Thessaloniki. In a November 2013 an OECD report predicted that the Greek economy will shrink further next year and the EU may need to step in once again.

and China, resisted the powerful United States and EU and refused to engage unless some of their terms were heeded. In the IMF in 2006 a shift in voting power was conceded in favor of China, Mexico, Turkey, and Korea, and further shifts were conceded in the wake of the financial crisis. Yet few believed this would be enough to fully engage these countries in the institutions. Several emerging countries—with China in the lead—became more powerful donors in their own right. As world energy consumption grew, so too did the power of countries supplying energy resources. In Venezuela, President Hugo Chavez painted the world in the style made popular in the 1970s, blaming the United States and other countries of the global North for the economic conditions in the global South.

The **G-20** is a new global economic actor that may play a major role in future talks about trade, development, and economic stability. It is made up of the finance ministers and central bank governors of the EU and nineteen non-EU countries, both developed and developing: Argentina, Australia, Brazil, Canada, China, France, Germany, India, Indonesia, Italy, Japan, Mexico, Russia, Saudi Arabia, South Africa, the Republic of Korea, Turkey, the United Kingdom, and the United States. The managing director of the IMF, the president of the World Bank, and chairs of some of the critical committees of the IMF and World Bank also participate in G-20 meetings. The G-20 was established in 1999 after the 1997 Asian financial crisis in an effort to stabilize the global financial market. Finance ministers and the members' central bank administrators meet regularly to discuss strategies to promote global financial stability and sustainable growth and development. The member states of the G-20 represent nearly 90 percent of global gross national product, 80 percent of global trade, and 67 percent of the world's population. The G-20 has successfully created a stronger regulation and policy coordination system and has improved macroeconomic cooperation among G-20 members, but it has yet to prove that it is able to coordinate the economic policies of the major global economies. In a 2011 summit, the members failed to agree on a financial assistance program for European states like Greece and Italy.

WHAT'S YOUR WORLDVIEW ?

How is the G-20 different from the established Bretton Woods institutions? Do you think the member states of the G-20 can find a way out of our current economic crises? Why or why not?

Approaches to IPE

We have learned that in international relations contending theories or traditions offer competing descriptions and explanations of conditions and events. Next we outline both traditional and new approaches to IPE.

Traditional Approaches: Liberal, Mercantilist, and Marxist

As we try to understand the complexities of the global economy—past, present, and future—we should consider three competing traditions, or economic belief systems:

- The *liberal tradition* (free market belief system) dominated most discussion of the international economic system that was created after World War II. This tradition assumes that free trade and the free movement of capital will ensure that investment flows to where it will be most profitable (e.g., into less developed areas where maximal gains might be made). Free trade permits countries to benefit from their comparative advantages so that goods and services are efficiently and equitably distributed in the world economy.

- The *mercantilist tradition* focuses on competition among states, emphasizing that states must protect their own interests and power to protect their citizens in the competitive international economy. This stands in stark contrast to the liberal tradition. Simply put, for mercantilists, the international system is like a jungle in which each state has to do what it can to survive. The aim of every state must be to maximize its wealth and independence.

- The *Marxist or socialist tradition* also sees the global economy as an area of competition, but not among states. It favors a more equitable political economy, one that ends the exploitation of workers around the world and closes the gap between rich and poor states. For Marxists, world economic relations are best conceived as a class struggle between the oppressors (capitalists, who own the means of production) and the oppressed (the working class).

These three traditions have a particular moral and analytical slant on global economic relations.

Comparing these different traditions also highlights aspects of IPE at three levels of analysis:

- *National*: The nature of a particular government or competition within its institutions and the role of interest groups and societal forces within a country.

- *Systemic*: The structure of the international system.
- *Global*: The role of global actors including INGOs and transnational corporations.

At each of these levels of analysis, what drives the actors concerned? How might we therefore explain their preferences, actions, and outcomes? (See the levels-of-analysis discussions in Chapters 1 and 4.) In answering these questions we enter into more methodological preoccupations that divide the study of IPE today.

New Approaches

The traditions already outlined highlight normative concerns and analytical questions that divide the study of IPE. The discipline is now subject to a lively methodological debate about how scholars might best explain policies and outcomes. In essence, this debate is about whether you can assume what states' (and other actors') preferences and interests are. If you can, then rational-choice (or "neo-utilitarian") approaches to IPE make sense. However, if you open up the questions of why and how states and other actors come to have particular preferences, then you are pushed toward approaches now often labeled constructivism.

Rational choice:

- The *political-economy approach* applies rational choice to groups within the state. (*Rational* in this sense implies that an actor selects the optimal choice when making a decision, given the specific incentives, institutional constraints, and opportunities.) This approach assumes that governments and their policies are important but that the policies and preferences of governments reflect the actions of specific interest groups within the economy.
- The *institutionalist approach* applies the assumptions of rational choice to states in their interaction with other states. The core assumption is that states create international institutions and delegate power to them to maximize utility within the constraints of world markets and world politics. Frequently, this comes down to the need to resolve collective-action problems. For example, states realize that they cannot achieve their goals in areas such as trade or environment unless all other states also embark on a particular course of action.

In contrast to rational choice analysis, *constructivist approaches* to IPE assume that historical and sociological factors affect policies within the world economy. This approach pays much more attention to the ways in which actors formulate preferences and make decisions. In other words, rather than assuming that a

CASE STUDY : NAFTA and Mexico

Background

Most people in the United States had not heard of the North American Free Trade Agreement (NAFTA) prior to the 1992 presidential election campaign. In the first televised presidential debate, independent candidate H. Ross Perot skewered then-president George H. W. Bush, asserting that the NAFTA—the terms of which were largely unknown in the United States—would result in what Perot called "a giant sucking sound" as American jobs went south to Mexico. As expected, the three candidates said little about what the deal would mean for Mexico. With the agreement more than twenty years old, what has the NAFTA done for Mexico?

The Case

According to statistics found on the website of the Office of the US Trade Representative (USTR), by 2003 all sectors of the Mexican economy had benefited from the country's NAFTA membership. For example, exports of Mexican-grown agricultural products to the United States increased 103 percent from 1993 to 2000. Overall farm production increased by over 50 percent during the same period, with changes of 25 percent in pork production, 27 percent in fruit production, and a stunning 80 percent increase in poultry production.

In higher wage industrial manufacturing jobs, similar changes swept most sectors by 2003. In export-oriented industries, according to the USTR, the NAFTA is responsible for more 3.5 million new jobs, and these jobs on average pay 37 percent more than non-export-linked manufacturing employment.

Statistics, as Mark Twain famously said, can lie. Put somewhat more diplomatically, statistics are but one perspective on a complex economic situation. Government-compiled economic figures tell only part of the story. Ignored in government data are those sectors of an economy in which payment for a job completed might be in the form of a basket of fruit or a chicken. Or, if people are paid in cash and do not report this payment on their income tax forms, the transaction escapes the notice of the government. This is often the case in developing countries with what is disparagingly called "women's work."

There are several signs that the NAFTA is not working for most Mexicans, if people in the United States are willing to look beyond official data. When US college students on spring break trips descend on Cancun and Puerto Vallarta, they could, if they stopped to think, recognize the limited extent of the NAFTA's success. Jobs in support of the tourist industry are low paid, low status, and high stress. Cleaning up after

NAFTA's terms have helped some economic sectors and harmed others.

Continued

CASE STUDY NAFTA and Mexico *continued*

tourists from *El Norte*, as the United States is called, is unrewarding at best.

Another sign of the very focused character of NAFTA's success for Mexico can be seen in the thousands of young Mexicans, primarily males, who risk arrest and death by trekking across the Sonoran desert to gain illegal entry into the United States. Once here, these "illegal immigrants," as US opponents of the current immigration policies call them, compete for low-wage jobs. They can be seen in neighborhoods throughout the southwestern states, waiting to be hired as day laborers. Immigration also became a part of the November 2012 presidential elections in the United States and in the 2010 California election, the Republican candidate for governor in California had to explain why she had hired an "undocumented" and therefore "illegal" immigrant as a domestic helper.

Outcome

The irony of the economic recession of 2008–2012 is seen in a surprising statistic: The US Border Patrol is intercepting fewer people trying to gain illegal entry into the country. With few jobs in *El Norte*, why risk death in the desert, abuse at the hands of human traffickers, or arrest in the United States? Better, perhaps, to stay in Mexico and hope that NAFTA will bring you a job.

For Discussion

1. What are the ways in which the NAFTA case is about "free trade" but not "fair trade"?
2. Should the United States reform its immigration laws to permit workers to seek employment regardless of their citizenship?
3. Does the United States have a responsibility to improve working conditions in Mexico? Why? Why not?

Applying Levels of Analysis

Why would US leaders sign the NAFTA treaty, connecting the United States economically with both Canada and Mexico?	
Level	**Explanation**
Individual	The leaders of each country saw this as a way of increasing their power and prestige. The US president saw this as an application of his liberal capitalist ideas.
Domestic/national	Economic interest groups seeking access to new markets put pressure on political leaders to sign the treaty.
International system	The end of the Cold War created a more multipolar system, and every country is seeking new alliances and new markets.
Global	Transnational corporations seeking access to markets, investment opportunities, cheap labor, and resources are pushing states to open their markets and create a truly global market.

state or decision maker's preferences reflect rational choices within given constraints and opportunities, analysts in a broader tradition of IPE examine the beliefs, roles, traditions, ideologies, and patterns of influence that shape preferences, behavior, and outcomes.

These academic debates highlight the essential question of whether to treat states' interests and preferences as given or fixed. We return to this question in the final section of this chapter. There we examine why states form institutions and what role such institutions might play in managing globalization. First, however, we need to establish what globalization in the world economy is and what its implications are.

International Institutions in the Globalizing World Economy

We have seen that globalization is increasing interdependence among states. It is also increasing global interconnectedness and the capacity of some states to influence others. The Asian financial crisis exhibited all three of these changes. The countries of Asia had "liberalized" into global capital markets (with much encouragement from the United States and other industrialized countries) and soon became recipients of large inflows of short-term capital. As soon as confidence in Thailand faltered, reactions were instantaneously transmitted to investors (through the new communications networks). The subsequent debacle of 1997 demonstrated how quickly, easily, and devastatingly a financial crisis in one country can spill over into others.

The management of the Asian financial crisis led some policy makers to call for stronger, more effective international institutions, including a capacity to ensure better information and monitoring, deeper cooperation, and regulation in the world economy. At the same time, however, others argued that the crisis revealed the problems and flaws of existing international institutions and the bias or interests they reflect. These positions echo a larger debate in IPE about the nature and impact of institutions in the world economy. This debate is important in helping us to determine what role international institutions might play in managing the new problems and challenges arising from globalization (see Table 8.1).

Competing accounts of institutions echo the differences in approaches to IPE already discussed. Institutionalists (Chapter 3) tell us that states will create institutions to better achieve gains through policy **coordination** and cooperation. However, several preconditions are necessary for this to occur. Under certain conditions, institutionalists argue, states will agree to be bound by certain rules, norms, or decisions of **international organizations**. This does not mean that the most powerful states in the system will always obey the rules. Rather, institutions affect international politics because they open up new reasons to cooperate, they permit states to define their interests in a more cooperative way, and they foster negotiations among states as well as compliance with mutually agreed rules and standards.

Table 8.1 Debates About Institutions

	Institutionalist (or Neoliberal Institutionalist)	Realist (or Neorealist)	Constructivist
Under what conditions will states create international institutions?	For mutual gains (rationally calculated by states).	Only where relative position vis-à-vis other states is not adversely affected.	Institutions arise as a reflection of the identities and interests of states and groups, which are themselves forged through interaction.
What impact do institutions have on international relations?	Expand the possible gains to be made from cooperation.	Facilitate the coordination of policies and actions but only insofar as this does not alter the balance of power among states.	Reinforce particular patterns of interaction and reflect new ones.
What are the implications for globalization?	Institutions can manage globalization to ensure a transition to a more "liberal" economy.	Institutions will "manage" globalization in the interests of dominant and powerful states.	Changing patterns of interaction and discourse will be reflected in institutional responses to globalization.

The institutionalist account offers reasons for a certain kind of optimism about the role international institutions will play in managing globalization. Institutions will smooth over many gaps and failures in the operation of markets and serve to ensure that states make genuinely rational and optimizing decisions to cooperate. Globalization will be managed by existing institutions and organizations, and, indeed, new institutions will probably also emerge. Globalization managed in this way will ensure that the world economy moves more toward the liberal model and that both strong and weak states benefit. Although there have been many protests about international organizations, these are the result of people misunderstanding the advantages of free trade and free movements of capital in the world economy.

Let us consider what this means in practice. Take a state deciding whether to sign up to a new trade agreement or support the decision of an international organization. The institutionalists argue that policy makers will consider the absolute gains to be made from the agreement, including the potential longer term gains, such as advancing a more stable and credible system of rules. The structural realists, by contrast, argue that policy makers will primarily be concerned with relative gains. In other words, rather than asking, "Do we gain from this?," they will ask, "Do we gain more from this than other states?" If other states stand to gain more, then the advantages of signing up are outweighed by the fact that the power of the state will be diminished in relation to other states.

For realists, cooperation and institutions are heavily constrained by underlying calculations about power. Having signed an agreement or created an international organization, a powerful state will not necessarily be bound by it.

Indeed, if it gets in the way of the state's interests (defined in realist terms), a powerful state will simply sweep the institution aside. The implications for globalization and its impact on weak states are rather grim. International institutions, including the IMF, the World Bank, the WTO, the G-20, and the EU, will manage globalization, but in the interests of their most powerful members. Institutions will only accommodate the needs and interests of weaker states where in so doing they do not diminish the dominant position of powerful states. From a realist perspective, it follows that antiglobalization protesters are right to argue that the international institutions do not work for the interests of poor and developing countries. However, the realists are equally certain that such protests will have little impact.

Constructivists reject the idea that institutions reflect the "rational" calculations of states, either within interstate competition (realists) or as part of a calculation of longer term economic advantage and benefits from cooperation (institutionalists). In fact, what constructivists reject is the idea that states' interests are objectively definable and fixed. Instead, they argue that any one state's interests are affected by its identity as a state and that both its interests and identity are influenced by a social structure of interactions, normative ideas, and beliefs. If we cannot assume that states have a particular identity or interest prior to their interactions, then the institutionalists are wrong to assume that institutions emerge as rational responses to the needs of markets, trade, finance, and the like. Equally, the realists are wrong to assume that institutions can only be reflections of power politics. To quote constructivist Alexander Wendt (1992),

Stock markets across the world are interconnected. On this day in January 2014, Japanese stock markets sank after a sell-off of stocks in the United States. The interdependence of global economies means that one state's economic security may be dependent on economic security and stability around the world.

"Anarchy is what states make of it." In other words, identities and interests are more fluid and changing than realists permit. Through their interactions and discourse, states change, and these changes can reflect in institutions.

The constructivist approach examines actors and processes involved in globalization that are neglected in realist and institutionalist accounts and have important ramifications for institutions. For example, the protesters against the WTO, the IMF, and the World Bank can be construed as part of an ongoing dialogue that affects states in several ways. The international attention to these issues places them on the agenda of international meetings and organizations. It also puts pressure on political leaders and encourages interest groups to form within the state. As a result, the beliefs, ideas, and conceptions of interest in international relations change, and this can shift the attention, nature, and functions of international institutions. On this view, globalization is not just a process affecting and managed by states. Several other actors are involved, both within and across societies, including international institutions, which play a dynamic role. The governance or management of globalization is shaped by a mixture of interests, beliefs, and values about how the world works and how it ought to be. The existing institutions doubtless reflect the interests of powerful states. However, these interests are the products of the way states interact and are subject to reinterpretation and change.

WHAT'S YOUR WORLDVIEW ?

Why do these disputes about the character of globalization matter? In your own life, is globalization a positive or negative process?

Global Trade

The distinctiveness of **transborder**, **supraterritorial** economic relations becomes clearer with illustrations. Examples concerning global trade are given in this section. Others regarding global finance are discussed in the next section. In each case, their significance relates mainly to contemporary history (although the phenomena in question made some earlier appearances).

The rules of the global trading system are to a great extent only those the countries themselves put on the firms that operate within their borders. Most of the world's trade takes place within the framework of the WTO; however, as the organization's press office indicates, it is a multilateral discussion forum, not a global trade system. Member states of the WTO agree, among other things, to lower tariffs and to eliminate nontariff barriers to trade, but it is left to the member states to enforce the agreements. Following the concept of international regime that you read about in Chapter 3, the principle that guides the WTO is that multilateral free trade pacts are better than bilateral deals. Another key principle is **most favored nation status**, whereby member states pledge not to discriminate against their trading partners.

Of course, disputes occur in the world's trading system, often to serve a domestic political purpose. For example, the United States and the EU from time to time have disagreements about bovine growth hormone in beef products grown in the United States, and the United States has had a long-running dispute with China over trade in intellectual property rights. To address such

When the euro became the new currency, old bills were shredded. How will the euro stay strong with economic crises and the addition of more countries from the former Soviet bloc?

disagreements, the WTO has a dispute-resolution panel that keeps the process at the multilateral level, so that members will not take unilateral action that could undermine the WTO's goals. Frequently, however, once a country begins the Dispute Settlement Body process, both parties settle the dispute before it reaches the full panel. From the creation of the WTO in 1995 to September 17, 2012, members filed 450 unfair-trade complaints, but less than a third reached the Dispute Settlement Body panel stage. Because of the risk of retaliation, members prefer to utilize the good offices, reconciliation, and mediation services of the secretary-general, as provided for in Article 5 of the WTO covenant.

Transborder Production

Transborder production arises when a single process is spread across widely dispersed locations both within and between countries. Global coordination links research centers, design units, procurement offices, material-processing installations, fabrication plants, finishing points, assembly lines, quality control operations, advertising and marketing divisions, data processing offices, after-sales services, and so on.

Transborder production can be contrasted with territorially centered production. In the latter instance, all stages of a given production process—from initial research to after-sales service—occur within the same local or national unit. In global production, however, the stages are dispersed across different and often widely scattered countries. Each of the various links in the transborder chain specializes in one or several functions, thereby creating economies of scale or exploiting cost differentials between locations. Through **global sourcing**, the company draws materials, components, machinery, finance,

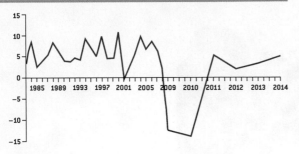

VOLUME OF WORLD MERCHANDISE EXPORTS.
This graph represents the annual percentage change
in the volume of world merchandise exports. What do these
data tell you about world trade over the past three decades?
What patterns do you notice here? What patterns might have
influenced each of the significant fluctuations?

*Source: p. 14 of World Trade 2012 Report by Belgian Foreign
Trade Agency, http://www.abh-ace.be/en/binaries/World%20
Trade%202012_BD_tcm450-228713.pdf.*

and services from anywhere in the world. Territorial
distance and borders figure only secondarily, if at all, in
determining the sites. Indeed, a firm might relocate certain stages of production several times in short succession in search of profit maximization.

What have been described as global factories were
unknown before the 1940s. They did not gain major
prominence until the 1960s and have mainly spread
since the 1970s. Transborder production has developed
mainly in the manufacture of textiles, garments, motor
vehicles, leather goods, sports articles, toys, optical products, consumer electronics, semiconductors, airplanes,
and construction equipment. As you can see, there is
little that is not produced transnationally. In this world
of more open borders, various globalists have described
MNCs as "footloose" and "stateless." This is a process
that Cynthia Enloe calls "the globetrotting sneaker."

With the growth of global production, a large proportion of purportedly international transfers of goods
and services have entailed **intrafirm trade** within transborder companies.
When the intermediate inputs and finished goods pass from one country to
another they are officially counted as "international" commerce, yet they primarily involve movements within a global company rather than between national economies. Conventional statistics do not measure intrafirm transfers,
but estimates of the share of such exchanges in total cross-border trade have
ranged from 25 to over 40 percent.

Much (although far from all) transborder production has taken advantage
of what are variously called special economic zones, export processing zones,
or free production zones. Within these enclaves, the ruling national or provin-
cial government exempts assembly plants, and other facilities for transborder
production, from the usual import and export duties. The authorities might
also grant other tax reductions, subsidies, and waivers of certain labor and environmental regulations. The first such zone
was established in 1954 in Ireland, but most were created
after 1970, mainly in Asia, the Caribbean, and the maquila-
dora areas along the Mexican frontier with the United States.
Several thousand export processing zones are now in place
across more than 100 countries. One distinguishing trait of
these manufacturing centers is their frequent heavy reliance
on female labor.

WHAT'S YOUR WORLDVIEW

*It might be comforting to travel around the
world and find Nike shops, Xerox machines,
and Starbucks—but what are the costs to local
businesses? What is lost economically and
culturally? Do you think this form of global
homogenization is a good or bad thing?*

Transborder Products

Much of the output of both transborder and country-based production has acquired a planet-spanning market in the contemporary globalizing economy.
Hence a considerable proportion of "international" trade now involves the

distribution and sale of **global goods**, often under a transworld brand name. Consumers dispersed across many corners of the planet purchase the same articles at the same time. The country location of a potential customer for, say, a Xerox photocopier, a Britney Spears CD, or Kellogg's Corn Flakes is of secondary importance. Design, packaging, and advertising determine the market far more than territorial distances and borders.

Like other aspects of globalization, supraterritorial markets have a longer history than many contemporary observers appreciate. For example, Campbell's Soup and Heinz began to become household names at widely dispersed locations across the world in the mid-1880s, following the introduction of automatic canning. From the outset, Henry Ford regarded his first automobile, the Model T, as a world car. Coca-Cola was bottled in twenty-seven countries and sold in seventy-eight by 1929 (Pendergrast 1993, 174). On the whole, however, the numbers of goods, customers, and countries involved in these earlier global markets were relatively small.

In contrast, global goods pervade the contemporary world economy. They encompass a host of packaged foods, bottled beverages, tobacco products, designer clothes, household articles, music recordings, audio-visual productions, printed publications, interactive communications, office and hospital equipment, armaments, transport vehicles, and travel services. In all of these sectors and more, global products inject a touch of the familiar almost wherever on earth a person might visit. The countless examples include Nescafé (sold in 200 varieties worldwide), Heineken beer (quaffed in more than 170 countries), Kiwi shoe polish (applied in almost 200 countries), Nokia mobile phones (used in more than 130 countries), Thomas Cook tourist offices (available in 140 countries), American International Group insurance policies (offered in more than 130 countries), television programs by Globo of Brazil (distributed in 128 countries), and the *Financial Times* newspaper (printed in 19 cities across the globe). Covering smokers in 170 lands, "Marlboro Country" is a distinctly global place.

Today many shops are mainly stocked with transborder articles. Moreover, since the 1970s a number of retail chains have gone global. Examples include Italy-based Benetton, Japan-based 7-Eleven, Sweden-based IKEA, UK-based Body Shop, and US-based Toys "R" Us. Owing largely to the various megabrands and transborder stores, shopping centers of the twenty-first century are in good part global emporia. Unfortunately for many of these

Where are your sneakers manufactured?

globalized corner stores, the economic recession of 2008–2012 caused a global fire sale of products.

Other supraterritorial markets have developed since the 1990s through **electronic commerce**. Today's global consumer can—equipped with a credit card and telephone, television, or Internet link—shop across the planet from home. Mail-order outlets and telesales units have undergone exponential growth, and e-commerce on the World Wide Web has expanded hugely.

Through transborder production and transworld products, global trade has become an integral part of everyday life for a notable proportion of the world's firms and consumers. Indeed, these developments could help to explain why the recessions of contemporary history have not, despite frequently expressed fears of "trade wars," provoked a wave of protectionism. In previous prolonged periods of commercial instability and economic hardship (e.g., during the 1870s–1890s and 1920s–1930s), most states responded by imposing major protectionist restrictions on cross-border trade. Reactions to the 2008–2012 recession have been more complicated (see Milner 1988). Although many territorial interests have pressed for protectionism, global commercial interests have generally resisted it. Thus, many transborder companies actively promoted the Uruguay Round and have, on the whole, vigorously supported the WTO.

The Globalization Debate in Political Economy

The nature and impact of globalization is the subject of profound debate within IPE (as within other areas of international relations discussed in this book). The term *globalization* is used to refer to at least four different sets of forces or processes in the world economy. As summarized in Table 8.2, this is a multifaceted process.

In IPE, several competing claims are made about globalization. For example, whereas some scholars argue that globalization is nothing new, others posit that globalization is dramatically diminishing the role of the state (see Chapter 1). Still others claim that globalization is exacerbating inequalities and giving rise to a more unjust world. To make sense of these different arguments, and the evidence adduced to support them, it is worth thinking about the approaches to IPE covered in previous sections because they help to identify key differences in emphasis that give rise to conflicting interpretations of globalization. For example, skeptics who deny that globalization is transforming world politics tend to focus on the "internationalization" element of globalization (see Table 8.2). They can then draw on evidence that throws into doubt whether the number of transactions taking place among states has indeed risen (UNDP 1997) and make the argument that there is "nothing new" in the growing interdependence of states. By

Table 8.2 Four Aspects of Globalization

1. Internationalization	Describes the increase in transactions among states, reflected in flows of trade, investment, and capital (see the argument that these flows have not increased as much as is claimed; UNDP 1997). The processes of internationalization have been facilitated and are shaped by international agreements on trade, investment, and capital, as well as by domestic policies permitting the private sector to transact abroad.
2. The technological revolution	Refers to the way modern communications (Internet, satellite communications, high-tech computers), made possible by technological advances, have made distance and location less important factors not just for government (including at local and regional levels), but equally in the calculations of other actors, such as firms' investment decisions or in the activities of social movements.
3. Deterritorialization	Accelerated by the technological revolution and refers to the declining influence of territorial places, distances, and boundaries over the way people collectively identify themselves or seek political recognition. This permits an expansion of global civil society but equally an expansion of global criminal or terrorist networks.
4. Liberalization	Describes government policies that reduce the role of the state in the economy, such as through the dismantling of trade tariffs and barriers, the deregulation and opening of the financial sector to foreign investors, and the privatization of state enterprises.

contrast, liberal enthusiasts of globalization focus on technological innovation and the nonpolitical "objective" forces that are shrinking the world economy. They argue that this is creating a less political, more efficient, more unified world order. Those who focus on deterritorialization highlight that there is also a negative side to globalization. Just as technological innovation permits a more active global civil society, so too it permits the growth of an uncivil one.

Conclusion

In this chapter, we have seen the basics of the major post–World War II international financial institutions and how they work. The global economic events of 2008–2012 put a major strain on the ability of these institutions to cope with the collapse. Some analysts of international political economy believe that the very institutions that were intended to bring stability to the system helped to cause the recent global recession. Institutions like the IMF and World Bank looked to adapt to a more pluralistic economic system in which economic power is diffused among a number of states and nonstate actors. The present economic system is no longer controlled by the United States. The Washington Consensus, with its emphasis on limited government and free markets, is now being challenged by the Bejing Consensus, where government controls the market to strengthen the state. The 2008–2012 crisis has forced rich and poor states to come together, reform the present global economic institutions, and create new ones—like the G-20 group of leaders, which first met in November 2008 in Washington, DC, bringing together the Group of Seven and major emerging economies. When the subprime mortgage crisis struck the US markets in the summer of 2008, the effects were felt worldwide. World leaders must react and

THEORY IN PRACTICE

What Course to Follow Out of the Global Recession?

The Challenge

The debates about international relations theories that you studied in Chapter 3 might have struck you as somewhat sterile. But if you were a political leader seeking a way to bring your country out of the economic recession that began in 2008, you would probably have a clear idea of what the theories mean for the policies you were considering. Although as of this writing in 2014 there was one socialist in the Senate (Bernie Sanders of Vermont), in the United States political leaders tend to follow one of two dominant models: realism or liberalism.

Options

The realist perspective on international relations stresses the need to defend the state and its interests. In the past, the recommendations of realism tended to sound like mercantilism, popular in the seventeenth and

eighteenth centuries. Countries should seek to be self-sufficient, a condition called **autarchy**, and keep as much gold and silver within national control as possible. In modern times, realists might not call it mercantilism, but their protectionist recommendations can sound like that doctrine; for example, increase tariff barriers to protect domestic industries, buy products made domestically, and stop outsourcing jobs to other countries.

Liberal international relations theories make a very different set of recommendations, many of which are embodied in the WTO. For adherents of this perspective, the way out of an economic recession is by increasing foreign trade, by making trade as free as possible. This means reducing or eliminating tariffs and nontariff barriers and encouraging the process of global sourcing of goods and services. The result of

such outward-looking policies would hopefully be what economists call *comparative advantage*. This is a complex idea that in simplest terms asserts that if a country produces and sells what it can make most efficiently, it will be able to buy the other products that it needs with the profits from its own production.

Application

For our hypothetical political leader, the choice is not as simple as it seems. In democratic political systems, politicians must stand for reelection, and they must account for their decisions. In some ways, the realist perspective is the easiest to defend. The politician has promised to defend American jobs and pursued policies that could do that. If the recession is made worse by these protectionist ideas, at least the politician can claim to have tried.

India's Tata Group acquired Jaguar Land Rover in 2008. The global economic meltdown hurt the auto industry around the world.

Working against the protectionist counsels of realism is the more than sixty years of effective trade practices, first in GATT and then after 1995 in the WTO. Therefore, a politician seeking reelection has the historical record to fall back on when debating with a realism-inspired opponent. Beginning in 1947 with twenty-three countries, the eight rounds of trade talks worked to reduce global restrictions on trade in goods and services.

Of course, no politician would want to tell a worker that it is a good thing that the factory closed its doors and the jobs went to another country where production costs are lower. In good economic times, this is perhaps not necessary; during an economic recession, there is often no choice.

For Discussion

1. How would economic policy recommendations from a feminist perspective differ from those of a realist perspective?
2. When a crisis such as the global recession hits, it is easy to blame politicians. Is that fair? To what extent are citizens responsible for the 2008 economic meltdown?
3. Is autarchy possible in a globalized economy? What about mercantilism?

reform the present system or risk further turbulence as new crises emerge. We are facing several potential problems. First, we will need to address the growing inequality within and between states; second, we will need to address new vulnerabilities and risks unleashed by globalized financial markets; and third, the world must deal with the growing scarcity of critical resources like oil and water. Otherwise, we face a future of resource wars and collapsing economies.

We began this chapter by asking, "How did it happen?" Prior to the summer of 2008, the world's economy seemed to be gaining wealth. Aside from the historic high price for petroleum products, most economic sectors showed no sign of distress. Yet the seeds of the economic recession that began in 2008 were already planted. As you learned in this chapter, the complex relationship of trade in goods and financial instruments was seemingly doomed to fail. Too much of the money was invested in arcane instruments like derivatives and mortgages served up as secure investments. The globalized trade and finance sectors were largely unregulated by host countries. Governments tried financial methods that worked in past recessions and economic crises. Slowly, many of these reforms and interventions—both new and old—have worked to arrest the economic crisis and to help many counties stabilize their banking industries and their financial markets. The US economy is slowly recovering but partisan political disputes and the rising cost of health care and social security without increasing taxes and other revenues may trigger another economic crisis in the United States that will create economic instability around the world. Europe's debt crisis is far from over and may result in slow growth in the rest of the world. In addition, several of the emerging economic leaders such as India, China, and Brazil are not growing as fast as they were before the crisis. The worst of the financial crisis might be past, but the pain of loss is still being felt in rich and poor states across the world.

Engaging with the

G-8 and G-20 Youth Summits

The G-8 and G-20 Youth Summits are premier international youth conferences that bring together young leaders representing the Group of Eight (G-8) and Group of Twenty (G-20) nations to facilitate discussions of international affairs, promote cross-cultural understanding, and build global friendships. The most recent summits were held in Washington, DC, in June 2012. You can find further information on the summits at www.g8-g20-youth-summits.org.

WTO Secretariat

The WTO Secretariat maintains a limited internship program for postgraduate university students wishing to gain practical experience and deeper knowledge of the multilateral trading system. Only a limited number of such internship posts are available. Intake to the program is on a continuing basis, with no specific recruitment period. Assignments are intended to enhance interns' knowledge and understanding of the WTO and of trade policy more generally. Visit http://www.wto.org.

KEY TERMS

Autarchy, p. 280
Bretton Woods system, p. 261
Conditionality, p. 265
Coordination, p. 271
Dependency theory, p. 263
Deregulation, p. 265
Development, p. 261
Dollar standard, p. 261
Electronic commerce, p. 278
Export-led growth, p. 262
Free market, p. 264

G-20, p. 266
Global capital markets, p. 264
Global goods, p. 277
Global sourcing, p. 275
Great Depression, p. 259
Intellectual property rights, p. 265
Interdependence, p. 263
International organization, p. 271
Intrafirm trade, p. 276
Marshall Plan, p. 261
Most favored nation status, p. 274

Political-economy approach, p. 268
Protectionism, p. 262
Summit diplomacy, p. 263
Supraterratoriality, p. 274
Trade liberalization, p. 261
Transborder, p. 274
Washington Consensus, p. 265
World Bank Group, p. 259
World Trade Organization (WTO),
    p. 259

REVIEW QUESTIONS

1. In what ways did the Bretton Woods framework for the postwar economy try to avoid the economic problems of the interwar years?

2. Did a loss of US hegemony cause the breakdown of the Bretton Woods system?

3. What is different about the Marxist and mercantilist depictions of power in the international economy?

4. Does rational-choice theory explain more about outcomes than actors' preferences?

5. In what way do constructivists invoke structure in their explanation of IPE?

6. Why do skeptics doubt that globalization is transforming IPE?

7. How can we explain the different impact globalization has on different states?

8. How does transborder production differ from territorial production?

9. To what extent has contemporary economic globalization marked "the end of geography"?

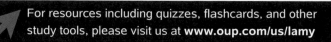

THINKING ABOUT GLOBAL POLITICS

The Possibilities of Cooperation: The Global Commons Challenge

INTRODUCTION

In a world of finite resources, restraint and cooperation on the part of individuals and nation-states might be the only means of maintaining and promoting the delicate balance and unity of the world's ecosystem. This activity will enable you to judge the value of cooperation in serving human needs and the validity of unrestrained self-interest in an interdependent world.

SCENARIO I: THE PROBLEM OF THE COMMONS I

Once there was a small pasture held in common by a village of cattle herdsmen. Being rational beings, free, and shrewd, they each sought to maximize their gains from pasturing their animals on the commons. Currently, each herdsman has two animals grazing on the commons.

One day, herdsman Smith began to think about increasing the number of animals he had grazing on the commons from two to three. Should he?

Discussion Questions I

1. What does the problem of the commons have to do with you?
2. Are you ever confronted with problems similar to the ones faced by Smith? If so, what considerations do you make?
3. Is your community, nation-state, or world faced with problems similar to the one faced by the village?
4. What is the difference between self or national interest and human interest? Give examples.
5. What is the purpose of understanding "The Problem of the Commons"?

SCENARIO II: THE PROBLEM OF THE COMMONS II

Once there was a small planet, the fate of which was held in common by a number of large and small nation-states. Being rational, free, and shrewd, the peoples of these nation-states sought to maximize their gains by utilizing the resources of the small planet to further each of their own particular ends. The people of one particular nation-state, consisting of 5 percent of the planet's population, use 27 percent of the natural resources of the small planet. Should they continue this level of use? (Note that the original "Global Commons" story is attributed to G. Hardin. This one is adapted.)

Discussion Questions II

1. What are some possible arguments for and against the country presented in this scenario using a disproportionately high percentage of resources?
2. As a citizen of the country presented in this scenario, how would you respond to the demands to reduce, share, or conserve resources?
3. If you lived in one of the other countries, what type of world redistribution strategy would you support?
4. Is it possible to create a more equitable international system? Why or why not?

MULTILATERALISM, COOPERATION, AND BURDEN SHARING

This part of the activity might require some library research. In small groups, assign each member a research task. One student should find an international issue where nation-states still act unilaterally with minimal

Continued

THINKING ABOUT GLOBAL POLITICS *continued*

cooperation. A second student should find information about a policy area where states engage in limited cooperation but do not give up significant sovereignty. A third student should find evidence where nation-states collaborate by sharing resources, expertise, and some decision making. A fourth research task should be allocated to one who will find examples where nation-states share decision-making authority and actually transfer authority to a regional or international institution.

As you conduct your research, look for answers to the following questions:

1. What are the benefits of cooperation in these areas?
2. Why do you think that states are more willing to cooperate in some policy areas and not in others?

3. In the policy areas your group identified, is cooperation beneficial?
4. Do you think cooperation changes citizens' images of the international system?
5. Do you think continued cooperation will change the attitudes of leaders in the system?

In the next class session, review your notes with your colleagues in your work group. Your instructor will ask each group to share its findings and its responses to the assigned questions. The end result should be an interesting and useful record of cooperative multilateralism and unilateralism in international relations.

CONTRIBUTORS TO CHAPTER 8: *Ngaire Woods, Steven L. Lamy, and John Masker.*

Poverty, Development, and Hunger

Wherever there is great property there is great inequality. For one very rich man there must be at least 500 poor, and the affluence of the few supposes the indigence of the many.

—*Adam Smith*

All societies used to be poor. Most are now lifting out of it; why are others stuck? The answer is traps. Poverty is not intrinsically a trap, otherwise we would all still be poor. Think, for a moment, of development as chutes and ladders. In the modern world of globalization there are some fabulous ladders; most societies are using them. But there are also some chutes, and some societies hit them. The countries at the bottom are an unlucky minority, but they are stuck.

—*Paul Collier*

As we saw in Chapter 5 and explore in this chapter, advocacy campaigns linked to celebrities like Kanye West, Radiohead, U2, Angelina Jolie, America Ferrera, Madonna, and George Clooney have come to play an important part in shaping the range of choices that politicians make about eliminating poverty, building economic development, and ending hunger worldwide.

Since 1945 we have witnessed not only increasing individual advocacy but also unprecedented official development policies and impressive global economic growth. Yet global polarization is increasing, with a growing economic gap between rich and poor states and people. As we have seen in other issue areas in this book, people who work in the academic discipline of international relations have had different ways of thinking about this gap:

- Traditionally, realists have concentrated on issues relating to war and have seen security and development economics as separate issue areas.

The thirty-ninth G-8 summit was held in Northern Ireland in June 2013. A variety of charities in the United Kingdom launched the Big IF campaign to pressure the G-8 countries to increase funding for development and hunger projects. These paper flowers represent the millions of children who die each year from malnutrition. Are you part of an organization that seeks to make such a difference in the world?

- Mainstream realist and liberal scholars have largely neglected the challenges that global underdevelopment presents to human well-being.
- Dependency theorists have been interested in persistent and deepening inequality and relations between North and South, but for decades they received little attention in the discipline.
- During the 1990s, debate flourished, and several subfields developed that touched on matters of poverty, development, and hunger, albeit tangentially (e.g., global environmental politics, gender, international political economy).
- The contributions of a range of theorists and scholars in the 1990s significantly raised the concerns of the majority of humanity and states: postcolonial theorists, Marxist theorists (Hardt and Negri), scholars adopting a **human security** approach (Nef, Thomas), and the few concerned directly with development (Saurin, Weber).

Now, in the twenty-first century, the discipline is better placed to engage with the interrelated issues of poverty, development, and hunger by influencing the diplomatic world, where interest in these issues is increasing, spurred on by fears of terrorist threats and recognition of the uneven impact of globalization (C. Thomas and Wilkin 2004).

Introduction

Despite the trend toward increased activism, poverty, hunger, and disease remain widespread, and women and girls continue to comprise the majority of the world's poorest people. Since the 1980s and 1990s, the worldwide promotion of neoliberal economic policies (the so-called **Washington Consensus**) by **global governance** institutions has been accompanied by increasing inequalities within and among states. During this period, the second-world countries of the former Eastern bloc have been incorporated into the third world grouping of states, and millions of people previously cushioned by their governments have been thrown into poverty. As a result, the developing world is characterized by rising social inequalities and, within the third-world countries, the adverse impact of globalization has been felt acutely. Countries have been forced to adopt free market policies as a condition of debt rescheduling and in the hope of attracting new investment to spur development. The global picture is very mixed, with other factors such as gender, class, race, and ethnicity contributing to local outcomes (Buvinic 1997, 39).

More recently, the enormity of the current challenges was recognized by the UN in 2000 with the acceptance of the MDGs (www.undp.org). These set time-limited, quantifiable targets across eight areas, including poverty, health, gender, education, environment, and development. The first goal was the eradication of extreme poverty and hunger, with the target of halving the proportion of people living on less than a dollar a day by 2015.

LEARNING OBJECTIVES

After reading and discussing this chapter, you should be able to:

Define the terms poverty, development, and hunger as they related to global politics.

Explain international economic liberalism as a development model.

Explain why the orthodox development model did not provide for economic development in former European colonies.

Analyze development using the theories of realism, liberalism, Marxism, constructivism, and feminism.

Describe the Washington Consensus, and identify three of its effects on developing countries.

Explain why poverty, development, and hunger affect women and children more than men in developing societies.

The global poor are short of food for all or part of the year. Some eat only one meal a day. Demonstrators at the UN headquarters in New York urge world governments in 2007 to meet the MDG to reduce hunger by 50 percent by 2015.

The attempts of the majority of governments, INGOs, and NGOs since 1945 to address global hunger and poverty can be categorized into two very broad types, depending on the explanations they provide for the existence of these problems and the respective solutions they prescribe. These can be identified as the dominant mainstream, or orthodox, approach, which provides and values a particular body of developmental knowledge, and a critical alternative approach, which incorporates other, more marginalized understandings of the development challenge and process (see Table 9.1). Most of this chapter is devoted to an examination of the differences between the mainstream or orthodox approach and the critical alternative approach in view of the three related topics of poverty, development, and hunger, with particular emphasis placed on the topic of development. The chapter concludes with an assessment of whether the desperate conditions in which so many of the world's citizens find themselves today are likely to improve.

Poverty

Different conceptions of poverty underpin the mainstream and alternative views of development. There is basic agreement on the material aspects of poverty, such as lack of food, clean water, and sanitation, but disagreement on the importance of nonmaterial aspects. Also, key differences emerge in regard to how material needs should be met, and hence about the goal of development.

Most governments, international organizations (like the IMF and World Bank), and citizens in the West, and many elsewhere, adhere to the orthodox conception of **poverty**, which refers to a situation where people do not have the money to buy adequate food or satisfy other basic needs and are often classified as un- or underemployed.

Since 1945, this mainstream understanding of poverty based on money has arisen as a result of the globalization of Western culture and the attendant

Table 9.1 Mainstream and Alternative Conceptions of Poverty, Development, and Hunger

	Poverty	Development	Hunger
Mainstream approach	Unfulfilled material needs	Linear path—traditional to modern	Not enough food to go around
Critical alternative approach	Unfulfilled material and nonmaterial needs	Diverse paths, locally driven	There is enough food; the problem is distribution and entitlement

Goals and Targets	Africa		Asia				Oceania	Latin America & the Caribbean	Caucasus & Central Asia
	Northern	Sub-Saharan	Eastern	South-Eastern	Southern	Western			

GOAL 1 | Eradicate extreme poverty and hunger

Goals and Targets	Northern	Sub-Saharan	Eastern	South-Eastern	Southern	Western	Oceania	Latin America & the Caribbean	Caucasus & Central Asia
Reduce extreme poverty by half	low poverty	very high poverty	moderate poverty*	moderate poverty	very high poverty	low poverty	very high poverty	low poverty	low poverty
Productive and decent employment	large deficit in decent work	very large deficit in decent work	large deficit in decent work	large deficit in decent work	very large deficit in decent work	large deficit in decent work	very large deficit in decent work	moderate deficit in decent work	moderate deficit in decent work
Reduce hunger by half	low hunger	very high hunger	moderate hunger	moderate hunger	high hunger	moderate hunger	moderate hunger	moderate hunger	moderate hunger

GOAL 2 | Achieve universal primary education

Goals and Targets	Northern	Sub-Saharan	Eastern	South-Eastern	Southern	Western	Oceania	Latin America & the Caribbean	Caucasus & Central Asia
Universal primary schooling	high enrolment	moderate enrolment	high enrolment	high enrolment	high enrolment	high enrolment	—	high enrolment	high enrolment

GOAL 3 | Promote gender equality and empower women

Goals and Targets	Northern	Sub-Saharan	Eastern	South-Eastern	Southern	Western	Oceania	Latin America & the Caribbean	Caucasus & Central Asia
Equal girls' enrolment in primary school	close to parity	close to parity	close to parity	parity	parity	close to parity	close to parity	parity	parity
Women's share of paid employment	low share	medium share	high share	medium share	low share	low share	medium share	high share	high share
Women's equal representation in national parliaments	low representation	moderate representation	moderate representation	low representation	low representation	low representation	very low representation	moderate representation	low representation

GOAL 4 | Reduce child mortality

Goals and Targets	Northern	Sub-Saharan	Eastern	South-Eastern	Southern	Western	Oceania	Latin America & the Caribbean	Caucasus & Central Asia
Reduce mortality of under-five-year-olds by two thirds	low mortality	high mortality	low mortality	low mortality	moderate mortality	low mortality	moderate mortality	low mortality	moderate mortality

GOAL 5 | Improve maternal health

Goals and Targets	Northern	Sub-Saharan	Eastern	South-Eastern	Southern	Western	Oceania	Latin America & the Caribbean	Caucasus & Central Asia
Reduce maternal mortality by three quarters	low mortality	very high mortality	low mortality	moderate mortality	high mortality	low mortality	high mortality	low mortality	low mortality
Access to reproductive health	moderate access	low access	high access	moderate access	moderate access	moderate access	low access	high access	moderate access

GOAL 6 | Combat HIV/AIDS, malaria and other diseases

Goals and Targets	Northern	Sub-Saharan	Eastern	South-Eastern	Southern	Western	Oceania	Latin America & the Caribbean	Caucasus & Central Asia
Halt and begin to reverse the spread of HIV/AIDS	low incidence	high incidence	low incidence	low incidence	low incidence	low incidence	low incidence	low incidence	intermediate incidence
Halt and reverse the spread of tuberculosis	low mortality	moderate mortality	low mortality	moderate mortality	moderate mortality	low mortality	high mortality	low mortality	moderate mortality

GOAL 7 | Ensure environmental sustainability

Goals and Targets	Northern	Sub-Saharan	Eastern	South-Eastern	Southern	Western	Oceania	Latin America & the Caribbean	Caucasus & Central Asia
Halve proportion of population without improved drinking water	high coverage	low coverage	high coverage	moderate coverage	high coverage	high coverage	low coverage	high coverage	moderate coverage
Halve proportion of population without sanitation	high coverage	very low coverage	low coverage	low coverage	very low coverage	moderate coverage	very low coverage	moderate coverage	high coverage
Improve the lives of slum-dwellers	moderate proportion of slum-dwellers	very high proportion of slum-dwellers	moderate proportion of slum-dwellers	high proportion of slum-dwellers	high proportion of slum-dwellers	moderate proportion of slum-dwellers	moderate proportion of slum-dwellers	moderate proportion of slum-dwellers	—

GOAL 8 | Develop a global partnership for development

Goals and Targets	Northern	Sub-Saharan	Eastern	South-Eastern	Southern	Western	Oceania	Latin America & the Caribbean	Caucasus & Central Asia
Internet users	high usage	moderate usage	high usage	high usage	moderate usage	high usage	low usage	high usage	high usage

---

The progress chart operates on two levels. The words in each box indicate the present degree of compliance with the target. The colours show progress towards the target according to the legend below:

▪ Target already met or expected to be met by 2015.

▪ Progress insufficient to reach the target if prevailing trends persist.

▪ No progress or deterioration.

▪ Missing or insufficient data.

* Poverty progress for Eastern Asia is assessed based on China's data only.

For the regional groupings and country data, see *mdgs.un.org*. Country experiences in each region may differ significantly from the regional average. Due to new data and revised methodologies, this Progress Chart is not comparable with previous versions.

Sources: United Nations, based on data and estimates provided by: Food and Agriculture Organization of the United Nations; Inter-Parliamentary Union; International Labour Organization; International Telecommunication Union; UNAIDS; UNESCO; UN-Habitat; UNICEF; UN Population Division; World Bank; World Health Organization – based on statistics available as of June 2013.

Compiled by Statistics Division, Department of Economic and Social Affairs, United Nations.

Figure 9.1 2013 Progress Chart for UN Millennium Development Goals.

expansion of the market. Thus a community that provides for itself outside monetized cash transactions and wage labor, such as a hunter-gatherer group, is regarded as poor. This meaning of poverty has been almost universalized. Poverty is seen as an economic condition dependent on cash transactions in the marketplace for its eradication. These transactions in turn are dependent on development defined as economic growth. The same economic yardstick is used to measure all societies and to judge whether they merit development assistance.

Poverty has widely been regarded as characterizing the third world, and it has a gendered face that realist and liberal perspectives often ignore. By the mid-1990s an approach had developed whereby it was seen as incumbent on the developed countries to help the third world eradicate poverty. Because studies show that women and children are most severely impacted by the consequences of poverty, development economists are increasingly addressing female poverty and women's roles in economic development. The solution advocated to overcome global poverty is the further integration of the global economy (C. Thomas 2000) and of women into this process (Pearson 2000; H. Weber 2002). Increasingly, however, as globalization has intensified, poverty defined in such economic terms has come to characterize significant sectors of the population in advanced developed countries such as the United States (see Bello 1994).

But for some, poverty cannot be measured merely in terms of cash. Critical, alternative views of poverty place the emphasis not simply on money but also on spiritual values, community ties, and availability of common resources. In traditional subsistence methods, a common strategy for **survival** is provision for oneself and one's family via **community**-regulated access to common water, land, and fodder. The work of the UNDP since the early 1990s is significant here for distinguishing between income poverty (a material condition) and human poverty (encompassing human dignity, opportunity, and choices).

The issue of poverty and the challenge of poverty alleviation moved up the global political agenda at the close of the twentieth century, as evidenced in the UN's first MDGs, cited earlier in this chapter. Although World Bank figures for the 1990s showed a global improvement in reducing the number of people living on less than a dollar a day (its orthodox measurement of extreme poverty), the picture was uneven: In sub-Saharan Africa the situation deteriorated, and elsewhere, such as the Russian Federation, the Commonwealth of Independent States, Latin America and the Caribbean, and some non-oil-producing Middle Eastern states, the picture remains bleak. In 2005, the World Bank stated that almost half the world—more than 3 billion people—lived below the

WHAT'S YOUR WORLDVIEW

The poorest 1.4 billion are living below the $1.25 global poverty line and more than 1 billion are going hungry. Why is it so hard to get the world to care? Could you make choices that might help the bottom billion?

new poverty line, $2.50 a day, and at least 80 percent of the world's population lived on less than $10 a day. Most of the global improvement resulted from trends in China and India, and even there, extensive pockets of poverty remain.

Development

Having considered the orthodox and critical alternative views of poverty, we now turn to an examination of the important topic of development. This examination is conducted in three main parts. The first part starts by examining the orthodox view of development and then proceeds to an assessment of its effect on postwar development in the third world. The second part examines the critical alternative view of development and its application to subjects such as empowerment and democracy. In the third part, we consider the ways the orthodox approach to development has responded to some of the criticisms made of it by the critical alternative approach.

When we consider the topic of **development**, it is important to realize that all conceptions of development necessarily reflect a particular set of social and political values. Since World War II, the dominant understanding—favored by the majority of governments and multilateral lending agencies—has been **modernization theory**, a theory that considers development synonymous with economic growth, within the context of a free market international economy. Economic growth is identified as necessary for combating poverty, defined as the inability of people to meet their basic material needs through cash transactions. This is seen in the influential reports of the World Bank, where countries are categorized according to their income. Those countries that have lower national incomes per capita are regarded as being less developed than those with higher incomes, and they are perceived as being in need of increased integration into the global marketplace.

As the wave of decolonization swept the world in the 1960s and early 1970s, an alternative view of development has emerged from a few governments, UN agencies, grass-roots movements, NGOs, and some academics. Their concerns have centered broadly on entitlement and distribution. Poverty is identified as the inability to provide for the material needs of oneself and one's family by subsistence or cash transactions and by the absence of an environment conducive to human well-being broadly conceived in spiritual and community terms. These voices of opposition are growing significantly louder, as ideas polarize following the apparent universal triumph of economic liberalism at the end of the Cold War. The language of opposition is changing to incorporate matters of democracy such as political empowerment, participation, meaningful self-determination for the majority, protection of the commons, and an emphasis on growth that benefits the poor. The fundamental

Table 9.2 **Development: A Contested Concept**

The Orthodox View	The Alternative View
Poverty: A situation suffered by people who do not have the *money to buy food* and satisfy other *basic material needs*.	**Poverty:** A situation suffered by people who are not able to meet their *material and nonmaterial needs* through their own effort.
Purpose: Transformation of traditional subsistence economies defined as "backward" into industrial, commodified economies defined as "modern." Production of surplus. Individuals sell their labor for money, rather than producing to meet their family's needs.	**Purpose:** Creation of human well-being through sustainable societies in social, cultural, political, and economic terms.
Core ideas and assumptions: The possibility of unlimited economic growth in a free market system. Economies would reach a "takeoff" point, and thereafter, wealth would trickle down to those at the bottom. Superiority of the Western model and knowledge. Belief that the process would ultimately benefit everyone. Domination, exploitation of nature.	**Core ideas and assumptions:** Sufficiency. The inherent value of nature, cultural diversity, and the community-controlled commons (water, land, air, forest). Human activity in balance with nature. Self-reliance. Democratic inclusion, participation: for example, a voice for marginalized groups such as women and indigenous groups. Local control.
Measurement: Economic growth; gross domestic product (GDP) per capita; industrialization, including of agriculture.	**Measurement:** Fulfillment of basic material and nonmaterial human needs of everyone; condition of the natural environment. Political empowerment of marginalized.
Process: Top-down; reliance on "expert knowledge," usually Western and definitely external; large capital investments in large projects; advanced technology; expansion of the private sphere.	**Process:** Bottom-up; participatory; reliance on appropriate (often local) knowledge and technology; small investments in small-scale projects; protection of the commons.

differences between the orthodox and the alternative views of development can be seen in Table 9.2, supplemented by Case Study 9.1, which illustrates the impact of ideas about development from the contemporary coffee-producing sector. In the following two sections, we examine how the orthodox view of development has been applied at a global level and assess what measure of success it has achieved.

Post-1945 International Economic Liberalism and the Orthodox Development Model

During World War II, there was a strong belief among the Allied powers that the protectionist trade policies of the 1930s had contributed significantly to the outbreak of the war. As we learned in Chapter 8, even before World War II had ended, the United States and the United Kingdom drew the plans for the creation of a stable postwar international order, with the UN, its affiliates the IMF and the World Bank Group, plus the GATT providing the institutional bases. The latter three provided the foundations of a liberal international economic order, based on the pursuit of free trade but allowing an appropriate role for state intervention in the market in support of national security and

Contemporary debate on the coffee sector provides a graphic example of competing ideas and values concerning development and has relevance far beyond coffee. The impact of commodity price volatility and a long-term decline in terms of trade of primary products has profound effects on livelihoods of millions of rural householders in the poorest countries. In the case of coffee, about 25 million small farmers in more than fifty countries depend directly on coffee production. During the 1980s, export production increased in poor countries, fueled significantly by policy advice from the World Bank and IMF that hard-currency earnings had to be boosted through increased commodity exports to pay off spiraling third-world debt. Oversupply since the early 1980s has resulted in a decline of about 70 percent in nominal coffee prices, with prices reaching a thirty-year low in 2001. The impact on livelihoods of smallholder peasant farmers and plantation workers has been devastating. At the eleventh World Coffee Conference in Salvador da Bahia in September 2005, twelve groups representing peasant farmers and workers launched an alternative approach to coffee production, in the Salvador Declaration:

> For a truly sustainable coffee sector, all who take part in coffee production must share its wealth: small-scale producers, permanent and seasonal rural workers, industry and retail workers. Many say

Fair trade NGOs seek to get a fair price for producers of tea, coffee, cocoa, and other food products grown in the developing world.

that the solutions to the crisis are only associated with methods of production, including increased investment in substitutes for local coffee varieties, use of toxic fertilisers and pesticides, and mechanization—all aimed at greater productivity. This vision . . . allows for the consolidation of production and marketing by a small group of companies that do not practise social responsibility but make decisions that impact millions of people while they reap the lion's share of the benefits of the trade. This vision is not sustainable. . . . Real sustainability of the coffee sector should not be viewed through an economic lens alone but must include ethical and political perspectives.

From an ethical perspective, the citizenship rights of people who participate in wealth generation must be guaranteed. Those rights are: stability of prices; recognition of efforts to protect the rural landscape and biological diversity by improving cultivation, harvest, and post harvesting practices; and recognition of the basic rights of rural workers, including the fundamental rights of association and collective bargaining, particularly for seasonal rural workers. . . .

From a political perspective, . . . governments (must) agree to and implement public policies that guarantee the rights of coffee producers and rural workers. It should be possible to develop a sustainable model based on food security and sovereignty.

In conclusion, we expect the World Coffee Conference to acknowledge . . . the issue of sustainability from the perspective of all actors involved in the coffee chain and sanction space for direct representation by small-scale farmers and rural workers organisations . . . (and) seek to establish the basis for fair trade between nations.

For Discussion

1. Do ethics matter in most economic development stories? Why or why not?
2. Are you willing to pay more for your cup of coffee if you know that the coffee farmers were paid a fair wage? Why or why not?
3. How do we all benefit if those producing valuable commodities are paid well and live in stable and free countries?
4. Sustainable development means considering the needs of future generations when we make choices today. Why is it so hard to develop this foresight?

national and global stability (Rapley 1996). This has been called **embedded liberalism**. Because the decision-making procedures of these international economic institutions favored a small group of developed Western states, their relationship with the UN, which in the General Assembly has more democratic procedures, has not always been an easy one.

In the early postwar years, reconstruction of previously developed states took priority over assisting developing states. This reconstruction process really took off in the context of the Cold War, with the transfer of huge sums of money from the United States to Europe in the form of bilateral aid from the Marshall Plan of 1947. In the 1950s and 1960s, as decolonization progressed and developing countries gained power in the UN General Assembly, the focus of the World Bank and the UN system generally shifted to the perceived needs of developing countries. The United States was heavily involved as the most important funder of the World Bank and the UN and also in a bilateral capacity.

There was a widespread belief in the developed Western countries, among the managers of the major multilateral institutions, and throughout the UN system that third-world states were economically backward and needed to be "developed." Western-educated elites in those countries believed this process would require intervention in their economies. In the context of independence movements, the development imperative came to be shared by many citizens in the third world. The underlying assumption was that the Western lifestyle and mode of economic organization were superior and should be universally aspired to.

The Cold War provided a context in which there was a competition between the West and the Eastern bloc to win markets in the third world. The United States believed that the path of liberal economic growth would result in development and that development would result in a global capitalist system, which favors the United States. The USSR, by contrast, attempted to sell its centralized economic system as the most rapid means for the newly independent states to achieve industrialization and development. Unfortunately for the Soviet government, because of its own food-supply and consumer-goods production problems, the country's material foreign assistance was usually limited to military equipment.

The majority of third-world states were born into and accepted a place within the Western, capitalist orbit, primarily because of preexisting economic ties with their former colonial occupiers, whereas a few, either by choice or by lack of options, ended up in the socialist camp. Yet in the early postwar and postcolonial decades, all newly independent states favored an important role for the state in development.

With the ending of the Cold War and the collapse of the Eastern bloc after 1989, this neoliberal economic and political philosophy came to dominate development thinking across the globe. The championing of unadulterated liberal economic values played an important role in accelerating the globalization process, representing an important ideological shift. The "embedded liberalism" of the early postwar decades gave way to the neoclassical economic policies that favored a minimalist state and an enhanced role for the market: the Washington Consensus. The belief was that global welfare would be maximized by the **liberalization** of trade, finance, and investment and by the restructuring of national economies to provide an enabling environment for capital. Such policies would also hopefully ensure the repayment of debt. The former Eastern bloc countries were now seen to be in transition from centrally planned to market economies, and throughout the third world the role of government was reduced and the market was given the role of major engine of growth and associated development. This approach was presented as common sense, with the attendant idea that "There Is No Alternative" (C. Thomas 2000). It informed the strategies of the IMF and World Bank, and, importantly, through the Uruguay Round of trade discussions carried out under the auspices of GATT, it shaped the WTO.

By the end of the 1990s, the G-7 (later the G-8, when Russia joined in 1996) and associated international financial institutions were championing a slightly modified version of the neoliberal economic orthodoxy, labeled the **post-Washington Consensus**, which stressed growth benefiting the poor and poverty reduction based on institutional strength, continued domestic policy reform, and growth through trade liberalization. Henceforth, locally owned national poverty-reduction strategy (PRS) papers would be the focus for funding (Cammack 2002). These papers quickly became the litmus test for funding from an increasingly integrated lineup of global financial institutions and donors.

The Post-1945 International Economic Order: Results

There has been an explosive widening of the gap between the rich and the poor since 1945 compared with previous history. Nevertheless, there have been major gains for developing countries since 1945 as measured by the orthodox criteria of economic growth, GDP per capita, and industrialization. A striking feature of both is the marked **regional diversity**. The East Asian experience has been generally positive throughout this period, but the African experience not so. China has been strong since the early 1980s, and India has fared better since the late 1980s.

In the 1990s, the picture was far from positive. The UNDP reports "no fewer than 100 countries—all developing or in transition—have experienced serious economic decline over the past three decades. As a result, per capita income in these 100 countries is lower than it was 10, 20, even 30 years ago" (UNDP 1998, 37). Moreover, the 1990s saw 21 countries experience decade-long declines in social and economic indicators, compared with only 4 in the 1980s (UNDP 2003). Financial crises spread across the globe and indicated marked reversals in Mexico, the East Asian states, Brazil, and Russia.

The African continent looked increasingly excluded from any economic benefits of globalization, and 33 countries there ended the 1990s more heavily indebted than they had been two decades earlier (Easterly 2002). By the end of the century, not a single former second- or third-world country had joined the ranks of the first world in a solid sense. Significant growth occurred in a handful of countries, such as China, India, and Mexico—the "new globalizers"—but the benefits were not well distributed within those countries. Despite significant improvements in global social indicators like adult literacy, access to safe water, and infant mortality rates, global deprivation continues.

Having outlined the broad development achievements and failures of the postwar international economic order, we now evaluate these from two different development perspectives: a mainstream orthodox view and a critical alternative view.

Economic Development: Orthodox and Alternative Evaluations

The orthodox liberal assessment of the past sixty years of development suggests that states that have integrated most deeply into the global economy through trade liberalization have grown the fastest, and it praises these "new globalizers." It acknowledges that neoliberal economic policy has resulted in greater inequalities within and between states, but regards inequality positively as a spur to competition and the entrepreneurial spirit.

It was clear at least from the late 1970s that "trickle-down" (the idea that overall economic growth as measured by increases in the GDP would automatically bring benefits for the poorer classes) had not worked. Despite impressive rates of growth in GDP per capita enjoyed by some developing countries, this success was not reflected in their societies at large, and although a minority became substantially wealthier, the mass of the population saw no significant change. For some bankers in multilateral organizations and conservative politicians in rich countries, the even greater polarization in wealth evident in recent decades is not regarded as a problem, so long as the social and political discontent the inequality creates is not so extensive as to potentially derail implementation of the liberalization project itself. This discontent will be alleviated by the development of national PRSs, which it is claimed put countries and their peoples in the driver's seat of development policy, thus empowering the local community and ensuring a better distribution of benefits.

Advocates of a critical alternative approach emphasize the pattern of distribution of gains within global society and within individual states, rather than growth. They believe that the economic liberalism that underpins the process of globalization has resulted, and continues to result, in increasing economic differentiation between and within countries and that this is problematic. Moreover, they note that this trend has been evident over the very period when key global actors have been committed to promoting development worldwide and, indeed, when there were fairly continuous world economic growth rates and positive rates of GDP growth per capita (I. R. Brown and Kane 1995).

The increasing gap between rich and poor was regarded as inevitable, and undesirable, by dependency theorists such as Andre Gunder Frank (1967). Writing in the 1960s and 1970s, these theorists stressed how the periphery, or third world, was actively underdeveloped by activities that promoted the growth in wealth of the core Western countries and of elites in the periphery (see Case Study 9.2).

At the beginning of the twenty-first century, however, exponents of a critical alternative—in contrast to their orthodox colleagues—question the value of national PRSs, arguing that although a new focus on issues such as health and education is important, the more fundamental issue of possible links between Washington Consensus policies and poverty creation is ignored.

The orthodox and alternative evaluations are based on different values and they are measuring different things. Glyn Roberts' words are pertinent: "GNP growth statistics might mean a good deal to an economist or to a maharajah, but they do not tell us a thing about the quality of life in a Third World fishing village" (G. Roberts 1984, 6).

A Critical Alternative View of Development

Since the early 1970s, there have been numerous efforts to stimulate debate about development and to highlight its contested nature. Critical alternative ideas have been put forward that we can synthesize into an alternative approach. These have originated with various NGOs, grass-roots development organizations, individuals, UN organizations, and private foundations. The Nobel Prize committee recognized the alternative approach when in 2006 it gave the Nobel Peace Prize to Muhammad Yunus and the microcredit loan institution, Grameen Bank, that he founded. Disparate **social movements** not directly related to the development agenda have contributed to the flourishing of alternative viewpoints; for example, the women's movement, the peace movement, movements for democracy, and green movements (C. Thomas 2000). Noteworthy was the publication in 1975 by the Dag Hammarskjöld Foundation of *What Now? Another Development?* This alternative conception of development (see Ekins 1992, 99) argued that the process of development should be

- need-oriented (material and nonmaterial);
- endogenous (coming from within a society);
- self-reliant (in terms of human, natural, and cultural resources);
- ecologically sound; and
- based on structural transformations (of economy, society, gender, power relations).

Since then, various NGOs, such as the World Development Movement, have campaigned for a form of development that takes aspects of this

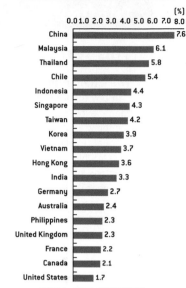

REAL GDP GROWTH.
This chart shows the per-capita GDP growth of selected countries (2010–2011). Does anything about these data surprise you? Based on what you have read in this book and studied in your course, how would you explain the data presented here?

Source: Bureau of Labor Statistics International Comparison of GDP per Capita pg. 9 http://www.bls.gov/fls/intl_gdp_capita_gdp_hour.pdf.

THEORY IN PRACTICE

The Terms of Development

The Challenge

Can any theory of international relations explain the problems of economic underdevelopment? International relations specialists even have trouble deciding what to call the countries of the world once held in European colonial bondage. "Third world" made sense at one time. The term originated with Alfred Sauvy, a French demographer, who in 1952 compared the economic and political conditions of European colonies with those endured by the Third Estate in France prior to the Revolution. The typology was a simple one: First-world countries had capitalist free market economies, second-world countries in the Soviet bloc and China had centrally planned economies, and third-world countries lacked industrial bases and provided raw materials for export. With the end of the Cold War, this tripartite typology made less sense.

Options

Until 1989, "third world" provided a less demeaning alternative to terms often found in the political science literature on Africa, Asia, Oceania, and Latin America: "underdeveloped," or "less developed country" (LDC), sometimes called "least developed country" (also LDC). A brief look at a map reveals another problem. The "global South" is another term often used to indicate the former European colonies in Africa, Asia, and Latin America; the other side of this dyad is the "global North," meant to describe the former colonial occupiers. But not all countries in the global South are "poor," and not all countries that were once colonial occupiers—Portugal and Spain, for

Residents play table tennis at the Santa Marta slum in Rio de Janeiro, Brazil. Police and government officials are rooting out gangs and bringing services to these favelas to make the city safer for the 2014 World Cup and the 2016 Olympics.

instance—are "rich." Instead, there are pockets of wealth and poverty in both the South and the North.

Application

Beyond debates about terminology, there is another problem for theorists. What do we mean by the term *development* itself? The term might mean industrial output and its related exchange of goods and services. If that is the case, then the term implies that industrialization itself is a proper goal. The problem of global climate change suggests that industrialization, as it has been practiced, is not a good thing (see Chapter 10). Moreover, the term, according to some gender theorists, only considers transactions that can be counted or that rely on an amount calculated in a currency. This method of accounting can overlook transactions that take place in a barter market or economic activities traditionally done by women: raising crops for household consumption,

cutting firewood, and caring for children, for example. In a capitalist economy, in Western Europe or the United States, such activities could have a dollar amount attached. For example, the US tax code gives a deduction for the cost of child care.

The realist perspective looks at the problems of economic and political underdevelopment, using the standard definitions found in scholarly books, with an almost Calvinist sensibility: Countries are poor because they are poor. Because international politics is a constant struggle for power in conditions of anarchy, then some countries must lose in that struggle. This perspective can help to explain the series of internal and transborder wars in central Africa since the late 1980s. Short on their own resources, the neighbors of the Congo tried to destabilize that country to gain access to mineral wealth.

Continued

THEORY IN PRACTICE   *continued*

Radical perspectives like Marxism once offered hope for a restructured global system. However, whatever comfort the doctrine once promised, the demise of the Soviet Union ended it. What was left was a theory that outlined the causes and results of political and economic exploitation but proposed an apparently bankrupt solution.

For analysts in the liberal tradition, the policy prescription does not offer much hope either. This tradition tends to recommend that the former colonies integrate themselves into the global economy, perhaps by planting a cash crop for export or by utilizing untapped resources. As we have seen in this chapter, however, countries that borrow money from international financial institutions can get caught in a debt trap if the price for the export commodity declines. This can leave the country economically worse off.

Unfortunately, no matter what they are called—the third world, the global South, the LDCs—for many countries, poverty and hunger prevail.

For Discussion

1. Instead of disagreeing about terminology, should leaders work on comprehensive plans to help the poor of the world?
2. Are there alternative views of development that might challenge the orthodox position?
3. What does a state-centric focus (on states as the primary actor in global politics) overlook?

alternative approach on board. Grass-roots movements have often grown up around specific issues, such as dams (Narmada in India) or access to common resources (the rubber tappers of the Brazilian Amazon; the Chipko movement, which began as a women's movement to secure trees in the Himalayas). Such campaigns received a great impetus in the 1980s with the growth of the green movement worldwide. The two-year preparatory process before the UN Conference on Environment and Development in Rio, in June 1992, gave indigenous groups, women, children, and other previously voiceless groups a chance to express their views. This momentum has continued, and it has become the norm to hold alternative NGO forums parallel to all major UN conferences. Also, the World Social Forum meets annually.

Democracy, Empowerment, and Development

Democracy is at the heart of the alternative conception of development. Grass-roots movements are playing an important role in challenging entrenched structures of power in formal democratic societies. In the face of increasing globalization, with the further erosion of local community control over daily life and the increased extension of the power of the market and **transnational corporations**, people are standing up for their rights as they define them. They are making a case for local control and local empowerment as the heart of development. They are protecting what they identify as the immediate source of their survival—water, forest, and land. They are rejecting the dominant agenda of private and public (government-controlled) spheres and setting an alternative one. Examples include the Chiapas uprising in Mexico and Indian peasant protests against foreign-owned seed factories. Protests at the annual meetings of the WTO, as well as protests of the IMF and World Bank, have become routine since the late 1990s and are indicative of an increasingly

CASE STUDY | Haiti: Poverty and Hunger 9.2

With its per-capita income of $556, Haiti is the poorest country in the Western hemisphere. Two-thirds of people live in rural areas; 80 percent are poor. Nearly half the population consumes less than 75 percent of the recommended intake of food energy. Rice is a major staple of the diet and mainly produced by small farmers. Twenty percent of people depend on rice cultivation for their livelihoods, and the sector has a major economic spin-off, with thousands of agricultural laborers, traders, and millers earning their living from it.

In recent years Haiti has undergone rapid trade liberalization, and it is now one of the most open economies in the world. Liberalization of the rice market started in the 1980s, but the final stroke came in 1994–1995, when, under pressure from the international community (notably the IMF and the United States), the tariff on rice was cut from 35 percent to 3 percent.

Rice producers reported that prices fell by 50 percent during 1986–1987, after the first wave of liberalization. In 1995, local production fell by 27 percent. Rice imports increased by thirty times between 1985 and 1999 as a result of the market slump. Food aid in rice surged from zero in 1994 to 16,000 metric tons in 1999. Most rice imports are of subsidized US rice.

These trends have severely undermined the livelihoods of more than 50,000 rice-farming families and led to a rural exodus. Although cheap imports initially benefited poor consumers, in recent years these benefits have vanished. The FAO says that overall malnutrition has increased since the start of the trade liberalization, affecting 48 percent of the population in 1979–1981 and 62 percent in 1996–1998. Even before the recent devastating earthquake, almost half of Haiti's food needs were met by imports (Oxfam 2003, 10).

For Discussion

1. Haiti is a fragile state and dependent on external assistance to survive. What should the OAS or the UN be doing to help it become more self-reliant?
2. Is liberalization for some states the wrong way to organize an economy? Explain your answer.
3. How could the United States help here, and does it have a responsibility to help?

widespread discontent with the process of globalization and the distribution of its benefits.

Such protests symbolize the struggle for substantive democracy that communities across the world are working for. In this context, development is about facilitating a community's participation and lead role in deciding what sort of development is appropriate for it; it is not about assuming the desirability of the Western model and its associated values. This alternative conception of development therefore values diversity above universality and is based on a different conception of rights.

For some commentators, national PRSs offer the opportunity—albeit as yet unrealized—for greater community participation in development policy making in the South. If all parties operate in the spirit that was intended, the PRS process could enhance representation and voice for states and peoples in the South, and it offers the best hope available for expanding national ownership of economic policy.

Now that we have looked at the critical alternative view of development, we look at the way the orthodox view has attempted to respond to the criticisms of the alternative view.

The Orthodoxy Incorporates Criticisms

In the mainstream debate, the focus has shifted from growth to sustainable development. The concept was championed in the late 1980s by the influential Brundtland Commission (officially entitled the World Commission on Environment and Development—see Brundtland et al. 1987) and supported in the 1990s by a series of UN global conferences. Central to the concept of **sustainable development** is the idea that the pursuit of development by the present generation should not be at the expense of future generations. Similarly, when faced with critical NGO voices, the World Bank eventually in 1994 came up with its "Operational Policy 4.20" on gender. The latter aimed to "reduce gender disparities and enhance women particularly in the economic development of their countries by integrating gender considerations in its country assistance programs" (www.worldbank.org).

Most recently, the language of poverty reduction being incorporated into World Bank and IMF policies includes words like "growth with equity" and "pro–poor growth," which some would argue are nothing more than buzzwords, because they underlie macroeconomic policy that remains unchanged. An examination of the contribution of the development orthodoxy to increasing global inequality is not on the agenda. The gendered outcomes of macroeconomic policies are largely ignored.

Despite promises of new funding at the UN Monterrey Conference on Financing for Development in 2002, new transfers of finance from developed to developing countries have been slow in coming; meanwhile, most expected

A new antiglobalization organization in Europe, the "Blockupy" movement, confronts a police barricade in front of the European Central Bank in Frankfurt, Germany, in May 2013. This new alliance of activists is critical of globalization and the neoliberal institutions that support and promote economic globalization.

In Zimbabwe, a corrupt and inept government tried to reduce prices on basic commodities and left markets with nothing.

new promises to be made by the G-8 during their summit in 2009. In addition to new finance, that summit saw commitments to write off $40 billion of debt owed by the heavily indebted poor countries. However, the commitment was not implemented with immediate effect and didn't cover all needy countries. The North–South agenda has changed little in the years since the Rio Summit, when sustainable development hit the headlines.

It is important to note that some parts of the UN family have been genuinely responsive to criticisms of mainstream development. The UNDP is noteworthy for its advocacy of the measurement of development based on life expectancy, adult literacy, and average local purchasing power—the Human Development Index (HDI). The HDI results in a very different assessment of countries' achievements than does the traditional measurement of development based on per-capita GDP (A. Thomas et al. 1994, 22). For example, China, Sri Lanka, Poland, and Cuba fare much better under HDI assessments than they do under more orthodox assessments, whereas Saudi Arabia and Kuwait fare much worse.

An Appraisal of the Responses of the Orthodox Approach to Its Critics

During 2000, a series of official "+ 5" miniconferences were held, such as Rio + 5, Copenhagen + 5, and Beijing + 5, to assess progress in specific areas since the major UN conferences five years earlier. The assessments suggested that the international community had fallen short in its efforts to operationalize conference action plans and to mainstream these concerns in global politics.

Voices of criticism are growing in number and range. Even among supporters of the mainstream approach, voices of disquiet are heard, as increasingly the maldistribution of the benefits of economic liberalism is seen to have been a threat to local, national, regional, and even global order. Moreover, the social protest that accompanies economic globalization is regarded by some as a potential obstacle to the neoliberal project. Thus supporters of globalization are keen to temper its most unpopular effects by modification of neoliberal policies. Small but nevertheless important changes are taking place. For example, the World Bank has guidelines on the treatment of indigenous peoples, resettlement, the environmental impact of its projects, gender, and disclosure of information. It is implementing social safety nets when pursuing structural-adjustment policies, and it is promoting microcredit as a way to empower women. With the IMF, it developed an initiative for heavily indebted poor countries to reduce the debt burden of the poorest states. What is important, however, is whether these guidelines and concerns really inform policy and whether these new policies and facilities result in practical outcomes that impact the fundamental causes of poverty.

The bank has admitted that such changes have been incorporated largely because of the efforts of NGOs, which have monitored its work closely and undertaken vigorous international campaigns to change its general operational processes and the way it funds projects. These campaigns continue. The Bretton Woods Campaign, Fifty Years Is Enough, Jubilee 2000, and, most recently, the Make Poverty History campaign have been particularly significant in calling for open, transparent, and accountable decision making by global economic institutions, for local involvement in project planning and implementation, and for debt write-off. As noted at the start of this chapter, for many years Bob Geldof and Bono have been very active in advocating change. In addition to the NGO pressure for change, pressure is building within the institutional champions of the neoliberal development orthodoxy.

There is a tremendously long way to go in terms of gaining credence for the core values of the alternative model of development in the corridors of power, nationally and internationally. Nevertheless, the alternative view, marginal though it is, has had some noteworthy successes in modifying orthodox development. These could be significant for those whose destinies have until now been largely determined by the attempted universal application of a selective set of local, essentially Western, values.

Hunger

In addressing the topic of global hunger, it is necessary to face the paradox that although "the production of food to meet the needs of a burgeoning population has been one of the outstanding global achievements of the post-war period" (International Commission on Peace and Food 1994, 104, 106), there were nevertheless in 2006 around 852 million malnourished people in about eighty countries, and at least 40,000 die every day from hunger-related causes. The current depth of hunger across different world regions is shown in Map 9.1. Famines might be exceptional phenomena, but hunger is ongoing. Why is this so?

The Orthodox, Nature-Focused Explanation of Hunger

The orthodox explanation of hunger, first mapped out in its essentials by Thomas Robert Malthus in his *Essay on the Principle of Population* in 1798, focuses on the relationship between human population growth and the food supply. It asserts that population growth naturally outstrips the growth in food production,

In parts of the developing world such as the Congo, more than 50 percent of the population is malnourished.

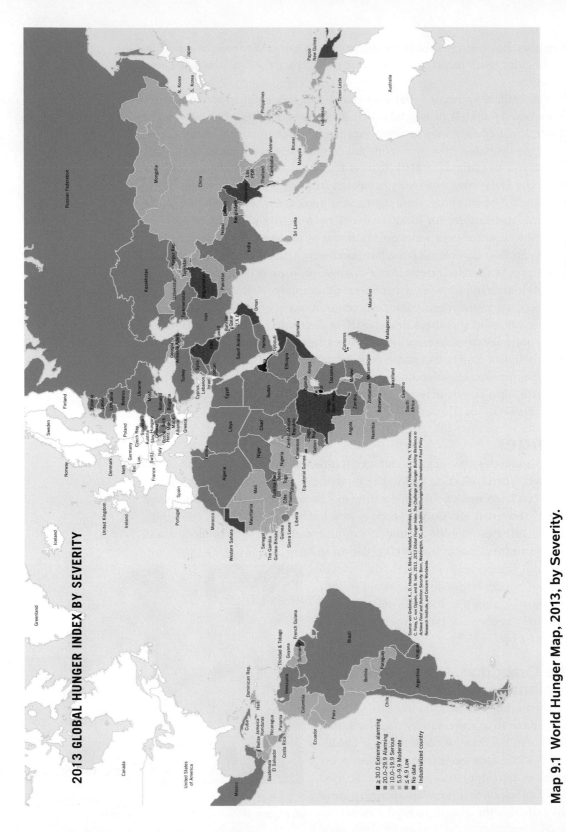

2013 GLOBAL HUNGER INDEX BY SEVERITY

■ ≥ 30.0 Extremely alarming
■ 20.0–29.9 Alarming
■ 10.0–19.9 Serious
■ 5.0–9.9 Moderate
■ ≤ 4.9 Low
□ No data
□ Industrialized country

Source: von Grebmer, K., D. Headey, C. Béné, L. Haddad, T. Olofinbiyi, D. Wiesmann, H. Fritschel, S. Yin, Y. Yohannes, C. Foley, C. von Oppeln, and B. Iseli. 2013. *2013 Global Hunger Index: The Challenge of Hunger: Building Resilience to Achieve Food and Nutrition Security.* Bonn, Washington, DC, and Dublin: Welthungerhilfe, International Food Policy Research Institute, and Concern Worldwide.

Map 9.1 World Hunger Map, 2013, by Severity.

What patterns of hunger do you see around the world? What responsibilities might industrial nation-states have toward helping less developed nation-states?

so that a decrease in the per-capita availability of food is inevitable, until eventually a point is reached at which starvation, or some other disaster, drastically reduces the human population to a level that can be sustained by the available food supply. This approach therefore places great stress on human overpopulation as being the cause of the problem and seeks ways to reduce the fertility of the human race, or, rather, that part of the human race that seems to reproduce faster than the rest—the poor of the third world. Recent supporters of this approach, such as Meadows, Meadows, and Randers (1972), argue that there are natural limits to population growth—principally that of the carrying capacity of the land—and that when these limits are exceeded, disaster is inevitable.

The available data on the growth of the global human population indicate that it has quintupled since the early 1800s and is expected to grow from 6 billion in 1999 to 10 billion in 2050. Over 50 percent of this increase is expected to occur in seven countries: Bangladesh, Brazil, China, India, Indonesia, Nigeria, and Pakistan. Figure 9.2 provides data on world population growth, focusing on the most populous countries—almost all of which are located in the third world. The combined populations of the top eleven countries account for over half of the world's population. Figures like these have convinced many adherents of the orthodox approach to hunger that it is essential for third-world countries to adhere to strict family-planning policies that one way or another limit their population growth rates. Indeed, in the case of the World Bank, most women-related efforts until very recently were in the area of family planning.

The Entitlement, Society-Focused Explanation of Hunger

Critics of the orthodox approach to hunger and its associated implications argue that it is too simplistic in its analysis and ignores the vital factor of food distribution. They point out that it fails to account for the paradox we observed at the beginning of this discussion on hunger: Despite the enormous

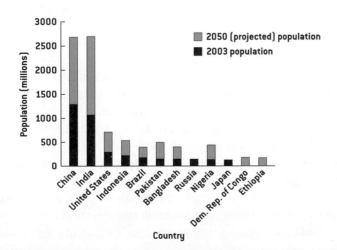

Figure 9.2 **World Population Growth: Comparison of 2003 (Actual) and 2050 (Projected).**

increase in food production per capita that has occurred over the postwar period (largely as a result of the development of high-yielding seeds and industrial agricultural techniques), little impact has been made on the huge numbers of people in the world who experience chronic hunger. For example, the UN Food and Agriculture Organization estimates that although there is enough grain alone to provide everyone in the world with 3,600 calories a day (i.e., 1,200 more than the UN's recommended minimum daily intake), there are still more than 800 million hungry people.

Furthermore, critics note that the third world, where the majority of malnourished people are found, produces much of the world's food, whereas those who consume most of it are located in the Western world. Meat consumption tends to rise with household wealth, and a third of the world's grain is used to fatten animals. A worrying recent trend is the use of corn grown in the United States to produce green fuel, thus reducing what is available to feed the hungry overseas. Such evidence leads opponents of the orthodox approach to argue that we need to look much more closely at the social, political, and economic factors that determine how food is distributed and why access to food is achieved by some and denied to others.

WHAT'S YOUR WORLDVIEW

The One Campaign and NGOs like Oxfam have worked hard to end global poverty and hunger, so why do poverty and hunger persist? What appear to be the root causes? Best solutions?

A convincing alternative to the orthodox explanation of hunger was set forward in Amartya Sen's pioneering book, *Poverty and Famines: An Essay on Entitlement and Deprivation*, which was first published in 1981. From the results of his empirical research work on the causes of famines, Sen concluded that hunger is the result of people not having enough to eat, rather than there not being enough to eat. He discovered that famines have frequently occurred when there has been no significant reduction in the level of per-capita food availability and that some famines have occurred during years of peak food availability. For example, the Bangladesh famine of 1974 occurred in a year of peak food availability, yet because floods wiped out the normal employment opportunities of rural laborers, the latter were left with no money to purchase the food that was readily available, and many of them starved.

Therefore, what determines whether people starve or eat is not so much the amount of food available to them but whether they can establish an entitlement to that food. For example, if there is plenty of food available in the stores, but a family does not have the money to purchase that food and does not have the means of growing their own food, then they are likely to starve. With the globalization of the market, and the associated curtailing of subsistence agriculture, the predominant method of establishing an entitlement to food has become that of the exercise of purchasing power, and consequently it is those without purchasing power who will go hungry amid a world of plenty (Sen 1981, 1983).

Sen's focus on entitlement enables him to identify two groups who are particularly at risk of losing their access to food: landless rural laborers, such as in South Asia and Latin America, and pastoralists, such as in sub-Saharan Africa.

The landless rural laborers are especially at risk because no arrangements are in place to protect their access to food. In the traditional peasant economy there is some **security** of land ownership, and therefore rural laborers have the possibility of growing their own food. However, this possibility is lost in the early stages of the transition to capitalist agriculture, when the laborers are obliged to sell their land and join the wage-based economy. Unlike in the developed countries of the West, no social security arrangements are in place to ensure that their access to food is maintained. In this context, it is important to note that the IMF and World Bank austerity policies of the 1980s ensured that any little welfare arrangements that were previously enjoyed by vulnerable groups in developing countries were

In parts of the developing world such as Kenya, enough food is available. However, the increased global demand for biofuels has started to push farmers to grow crops like corn that they can sell in that emerging market for a higher price.

largely removed, and therefore these policies directly contributed to a higher risk of hunger in the third world.

Building on the work of Sen, the researcher Susan George in *The Hunger Machine* (Bennett and George 1987, 1–10) details how different groups of people experience unequal levels of access to food. She identifies six factors that are important in determining who goes hungry:

1. The North–South divide between developed and developing countries.
2. National policies on how wealth is shared.
3. The rural–urban bias.
4. Social class.
5. Gender.
6. Age.

One could add to the list two other very important, and often neglected, factors determining hunger: race and disability. Consequently, a person is more likely to experience hunger if he or she is disabled rather than able-bodied, black rather than white, a child rather than an adult, poor rather than wealthy, a rural dweller rather than a town dweller, and an inhabitant of a developing country rather than an inhabitant of a developed country.

Globalization and Hunger

It is possible to explain the contemporary occurrence of hunger by reference to the process of globalization. Globalization means that events occurring in one part of the globe can affect, and be affected by, events occurring in other, distant parts of the globe. Often, as individuals, we remain unaware of our role in this process and its ramifications. When we drink a cup of tea or coffee, or eat imported fruit and vegetables, in the developed countries, we tend not to reflect on the changes experienced at the site of production of these cash crops in the developing world. However, it is possible to look at the effect of the establishment of a global system of food production, as opposed to a local, national, or regional one. This has been done by David Goodman and Michael Redclift (1991) in their book *Refashioning Nature: Food, Ecology and Culture,* and the closing part of this discussion on hunger is largely based on their findings.

Since 1945, a global food regime has been established, and as we enter the twenty-first century we are witnessing an increasingly global organization of food provision and of access to food, with transnational corporations playing the major role. In other words, local subsistence producers, who traditionally have produced to meet the needs of their family and community, might now be involved in cash-crop production for a distant market. Alternatively, they might have left the land and become involved in the process of industrialization. The most important actor in the development and expansion of this global food regime has been the United States, which, at the end of World War II, was producing large food surpluses. These surpluses became cheap food exports and initially were welcomed by the war-ravaged countries of Europe. They were also welcomed by many developing countries, for the model of development prevalent then depended on the creation of a pool of cheap wage labor to serve the industrialization process. Hence, to encourage people off the land and away from subsistence production, the incentive to produce for oneself and one's family had to be removed. Cheap imported food provided this incentive, and the resulting low prices paid for domestic subsistence crops made them unattractive to grow; indeed, for those who continued to produce for the local market, such as in Sudan, the consequence has been the production of food at a loss (Bennett and George 1987, 78). Not surprisingly, therefore, in the developing world, the production of subsistence crops for local consumption drastically declined in the postwar period.

The postwar, US-dominated, global food regime has therefore had a number of unforeseen consequences. First, the domestic production of food staples in developing countries was disrupted. Second, consumer preferences in the importing countries changed in line with the cheap imports, and export markets for US-produced food were created. Effectively, a dependence on food aid was created (Goodman and Redclift 1991, 123). Third, there has been a stress on cash-crop production. The result has been the drive toward export-oriented, large-scale, intensively mechanized agriculture in the South. Technical progress resulted in the "Green Revolution," with massively increased yields produced from high-yield seeds and industrialized agricultural practices. This has, in some respects, been an important achievement. However, the cost has been millions of peasants thrown off the land because their labor was no longer required; the greater concentration of land in a smaller number of hands; and environmental damage from pesticides, fertilizers, and inappropriate irrigation techniques.

Since the early 1980s, the reform of national economies via structural-adjustment policies has given a further boost to the undermining of the national organization of agriculture and an added boost to the activities of agribusiness. Also, the aggressive pursuit of unilateralist trade policies by the United States, such as the invocation of free trade to legitimize opening the Korean agricultural market, has added to this. Global trade liberalization since the early 1980s, and especially the Uruguay Round's Agreement on Agriculture (the original text of which was drafted by the multinational Cargill's vice president Dan Amstutz; Oxfam 2003, 23), are also eroding local food security and throwing peasant producers and their families off the land. The Haitian example portrayed in Case Study 9.2 is repeated across the developing world; for example, the crisis facing Niger in 2005–2006 has been called a "free market famine" (Mousseau and Mittal 2006, 1). This has fueled resentment in the South about the global rules governing agriculture. For example, in India, disputes over intellectual property rights in regard to high-yielding crop seeds have resulted in violent protest by peasant farmers at foreign-owned seed factories. In the North, NGOs have campaigned against the double standards operated by their governments in expecting Southern countries to liberalize their food markets as the Northern countries continue to heavily subsidize and protect their own.

In many parts of the world, farmers use hand tools, not tractors, to cultivate their crops.

Conclusion

In this chapter, we have seen the ways in which poverty, development, and hunger are more than merely domestic political issues. Academic theories of international relations tended to ignore these problems until the mid-1980s, when the third-world debt crisis threatened to undermine key parts of the global financial system. Political leaders in the rich countries of the North—and in many cases the South—acted the way realism predicted: to protect the interests of their own states.

Engaging with the WORLD

InterAction Internships

If you are looking for experience in NGO coordination, development, and humanitarianism, check out InterAction's openings for interns in the Office of the President, Humanitarian Affairs, IT, Annual Forum, and Policy and Communications at http://www.interaction.org/about/internship-program.

Blue Kitabu

Blue Kitabu sponsors summer fellows to work on a number of projects in areas such as sustainability and education, primarily in sub-Saharan Africa. This organization works with communities and community leaders to build educational infrastructure, needed business and markets, materials, and teacher training for the most vulnerable populations. Visit http://www.bluekitabu.org.

KEY TERMS

Community, p. 290
Development, p. 291
Embedded liberalism, p. 294
Global governance, p. 287
Human security, p. 287
Liberalization, p. 295

Modernization theory, p. 291
Post-Washington Consensus, p. 295
Poverty, p. 288
Regional diversity, p. 295
Security, p. 307
Social movement, p. 297

Survival, p. 290
Sustainable development, p. 301
Transnational corporations, p. 299
Washington Consensus, p. 287

REVIEW QUESTIONS

1. What does poverty mean?

2. Explain the orthodox approach to development and outline the criteria by which it measures development.

3. Assess the critical alternative model of development.

4. How effectively has the orthodox model of development neutralized the critical alternative view?

5. Compare and contrast the orthodox and alternative explanations of hunger.

6. What are the pros and cons of the global food regime established since World War II?

7. Account for the increasing gap between rich and poor states and people after fifty years of official development policies.

8. Use a gendered lens to explore the nature of poverty.

9. Is the recent World Bank focus on poverty reduction evidence of a change of direction by the bank?

10. Which development pathway—the reformist or the alternative—do you regard as the more likely to contribute to global peace in the twenty-first century?

11. Are national poverty-reduction strategies contributing to national ownership of development policies in the third world?

For resources including quizzes, flashcards, and other study tools, please visit us at **www.oup.com/us/lamy**

THINKING ABOUT GLOBAL POLITICS

Development Assistance as Foreign Policy Statecraft

EXPECTATIONS

You will be asked to evaluate contending arguments for aid (Official Development Assistance, or ODA) and then make a case supporting ODA and a case against supporting ODA to developing states.

PROCEDURE

Step One

Participants will be divided into three groups and asked to evaluate proposals requesting development assistance with a specific worldview in mind. The groups and their designated worldview:

1. Western Security Organization—Realists who have a competitive view of international relations.
2. European Social Democrats—Liberal internationalists favoring multilateral cooperation.
3. World Federalists—Modern-day utopians or radical liberals who seek to create a world government based on human-centric values and world law.

Step Two

Your task is to make recommendations on where aid or development assistance should be allocated. You might recommend the following:

A. Project Aid—Funds for specific activities such as the construction of roads, irrigation systems, etc.
B. Program Aid—Funds that are loaned to correct problems in a country's capital flow. The funds are used to correct balance of payment problems or simply to give the country funds to increase its supply of capital in the form either of savings or foreign currency.
C. Technical Assistance—This includes experts and advisors, training or educational programs, and the supply of equipment for projects.
D. Food Aid—Food, medicine, and equipment sent to countries to feed the starving or simply increase the available stocks of food.

E. Specific Aid—To deal with emergency situations (e.g., drought relief, natural disasters).
F. Military Assistance—To maintain order and to make certain the country is stable and the government is not at risk because of extreme poverty or radical movements.

Step Three

You must decide on ODA allocations for the following countries.

Country #1 has requested $100 million in aid from the developed donor countries. The country is governed by a weak democratic system. A Marxist party is strong but holds few government positions. The party currently in power was always pro–United States and now is an active participant in US-led multilateral activities. The economy depends heavily on the export of one crop and one mineral. There is little industry. The aid money will be used to improve and extend the road system, improve the dock and port facilities in the country's only port city, and fund agricultural extension projects.

Country #2 has requested $50 million in aid. The country is governed by a socialist party and has strong ties with Europe's more social democratic states. The president of the country often participates in meetings of heads of state of nonaligned nations, and the country's leaders are very active in multilateral organizations. This country has a diversified economy that exports agricultural products, some minerals, and light manufactured goods. The requested aid will be used to improve the national university, send students abroad for advanced college degrees in business management and science, import farm machinery, and purchase high-technology equipment to develop manufacturing in computers and technology related to the environment.

Country #3 has requested $150 million in aid. The country is totally dependent on outside support. The country has suffered from a severe drought, and three tribal groups continue to challenge the military

Continued

THINKING ABOUT GLOBAL POLITICS *continued*

government. The country's only resources are uranium and an abundance of cheap labor. Most aid has ended up in the hands of the elites and has not been used to improve the quality of life of most of the population. Recently, the leaders have begun to discuss a possible alliance with Syria and Iran. The aid will be used to develop a comprehensive education system, develop facilities in rural areas, and build a national highway and rail system. Based on the assumptions of your group's worldview:

1. Rank the three countries in terms of aid priority.
2. Select an appropriate program (e.g., military assistance and drought relief for Country *X*).
3. Be prepared to defend your choices. Each group will have an opportunity to decide on its priorities and then present them. Each group should also be prepared to critically review the allocations made by the other groups.

Step Four

As you debate your group's position on these requests, consider the following questions. You might want to ask the other groups to justify their positions by responding to these questions. As you finish the exercise, these three questions could provide useful debriefing or evaluation of your debate.

1. What is the strongest argument for giving or not giving some form of aid to each country?
2. What assumptions about each country and the international system defined your allocation priorities?
3. Discuss the relative strengths and weaknesses of bilateral and multilateral aid programs. Would you agree with the statement that suggests that the complexity of world development problems requires multilateral responses?

CONTRIBUTORS TO CHAPTER 9: *Caroline Thomas, Steven L. Lamy, and John Masker.*

Environmental Issues

10

Today, the pressure humanity puts on the planet, its Ecological Footprint, is 50 percent greater than the planet's ability to withstand this pressure. It now takes the Earth one year and six months to regenerate what we use in a single year. This global ecological overshoot is depleting the natural capital on which all of life depends.

—*Global Footprint Network*

The "control of nature" is a phrase conceived in arrogance, born of the Neanderthal age of biology and philosophy, when it was supposed that nature exists for the convenience of man.

—*Rachel Carson (1962)*

Is "weather panic" the new normal? As global temperatures rise, climate scientists predict side effects such as droughts, flooding, and ferocious storms. No one is certain of the direct link, but CO_2 emissions are rising by record amounts. Without a doubt, the world's environmental problems have only gotten worse since 1987, when the Brundtland Commission released its UN-sponsored report on the global environment, "Our Common Future."

Despite leadership from past politicians such as Nobel Prize winner Al Gore, and despite strong grassroots efforts by citizens in some industrial countries to "Reduce, Reuse, and Recycle"—to "Think Globally, Act Locally"—why are other international leaders and many other citizens unwilling to change their lifestyles to respond to urgent challenges like climate change, air and water pollution, and resource scarcity? Why is it so hard to reach agreement when scientific reports clearly confirm the severity of environmental degradation across the globe? Why are some leaders of political and economic organizations rejecting climate science? There are no easy answers to these global problems, but such questions can at least be understood more clearly

The Black Marble, or the earth, our very fragile home at night. This is an image of Asia and Australia with some of the brighter lights revealing the wildfires in Western Australia. Lights in uninhabited areas include images of fishing boats, gas flaring, lightning, oil drilling, and mining operations.

with a careful examination of the facts, along with some perspective afforded us by considering the history and theory of international co-operation involving environmental issues.

Introduction

Although humankind as a whole now appears to be living well above Earth's carrying capacity, the **ecological footprints** of individual states vary to an extraordinary extent. See, for example, Map 10.1, an unusual map where the size of countries is proportionate to their carbon emissions. Indeed, if everyone were to enjoy the current lifestyle of the developed countries, more than three additional planets would be required.

This situation is rendered all the more unsustainable by the process of globalization, even though the precise relationship between environmental degradation and the overuse of resources on the one hand and globalization on the other is complex and sometimes contradictory. Globalization has stimulated the relocation of industry to the global South, caused urbanization as people move away from rural areas, and contributed to ever-rising levels of consumption, along with associated emissions of effluents and waste gases. Although often generating greater income for poorer countries exporting basic goods to developed-country markets, ever-freer trade can also have adverse environmental consequences by disrupting local **ecologies** (communities of plants and animals), cultural habits, and livelihoods.

On the other hand, some analysts believe there is little evidence that globalization has stimulated a "race to the bottom" in environmental standards,

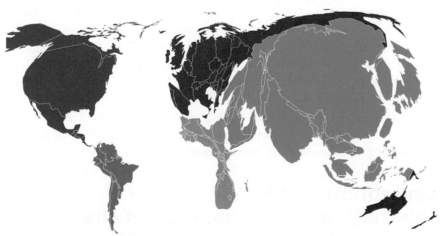

Map 10.1 World Carbon Emissions.

Countries are sized in proportion to their annual CO_2 emissions from fossil fuel use and cement production. What patterns of CO_2 emission do you see around the world? Does a nation's responsibility toward ending global climate change increase if its CO_2 emission is higher? Which laws govern the global emissions of CO_2? How can they be enforced?

One of the last frontiers is the Arctic and demonstrations against drilling are likely to increase. Here, in 2013, Greenpeace leads a campaign in London against the Shell Oil Company. Shell is one of the firms drilling in the Arctic.

and some even argue that increasing levels of affluence have brought about local environmental improvements, just as birth rates tend to fall as populations become wealthier. Economists claim that globalization's opening up of markets can increase efficiency and reduce pollution, provided that the environmental and social damage associated with production of a good is properly factored into its market price. Similarly, as we see in this chapter, globalization has promoted the sharing of knowledge and the influential presence of NGOs in global environmental politics. Whatever the ecological balance sheet of globalization, the resources on which human beings depend for survival, such as fresh water, a clean atmosphere, and a stable climate, are now under serious threat.

Global problems may need global solutions and pose a fundamental requirement for **global environmental governance**. Yet the history of environmental cooperation demonstrates that local or regional action remains a vital aspect of responses to many problems. One of the defining characteristics of environmental politics is the awareness of such interconnections and of the need to "think globally—act locally." NGOs have been very active in this respect, as we saw in Chapter 8.

Despite the global dimensions of environmental change, an effective response still has to depend on a fragmented international political system of more than 190 sovereign states. Global environmental governance consequently involves bringing to bear interstate relations, international law, and transnational organizations in addressing shared environmental problems. Using the term *governance*—as distinct from *government*—implies that regulation and control have to be exercised in the absence of a central government, delivering the kinds of service that a world government would provide if it were to exist. In this chapter we briefly explore essential concepts employed in regime analysis, which is commonly applied in the study of international governance.

Environmental Issues on the International Agenda: A Brief History

Before the era of globalization there were two traditional environmental concerns: conservation of natural resources and damage caused by pollution (see Table 10.1). Pollution, like wildlife, does not respect international boundaries, and action to mitigate or avert environmental harm sometimes had to involve more than one state. Early international agreements were designed to

Table 10.1 **Chronology of Environmental Issues and Actions**

1938	Trail Smelter case
1946	International Convention for the Regulation of Whaling
1955	UK Clean Air Act to combat "smog" in British cities
1958	International Convention for the Prevention of Pollution of the Sea by Oil
1959	Antarctic Treaty
1962	Rachel Carson publishes *Silent Spring*
1967	*Torrey Canyon* oil tanker disaster
1969	Greenpeace founded
1971	At the Founex meeting in Switzerland, Southern experts formulate a link between environment and development
1972	United Nations Conference on the Human Environment (UNCHE) in Stockholm United States creates Environmental Protection Agency First Earth Day Establishment of the United Nations Environment Programme (UNEP)
1973	MARPOL Convention on oil pollution from ships Convention on International Trade in Endangered Species (CITES)
1979	Convention on Long-Range Transboundary Air Pollution (LRTAP)
1980	Convention on the Conservation of Antarctic Marine Living Resources
1982	UN Law of the Sea Convention (enters into force in 1994)
1984	Bhopal chemical plant disaster
1985	Vienna Convention for the Protection of the Ozone Layer; Antarctic ozone hole confirmed
1986	Chernobyl nuclear disaster
1987	Brundtland Commission Report Montreal Protocol on Substances That Deplete the Ozone Layer
1988	Establishment of the Intergovernmental Panel on Climate Change (IPCC)
1989	Basel Convention on the Control of Transboundary Movements of Hazardous Wastes and Their Disposal
1991	Madrid Protocol (to the Antarctic Treaty) on Environmental Protection
1992	United Nations Conference on Environment and Development (UNCED) held at Rio de Janeiro; publication of the Rio Declaration and Agenda 21; United Nations Framework Convention on Climate Change (UNFCCC) and Convention on Biological Diversity (CBD) both signed; establishment of the Commission on Sustainable Development (CSD)

Continued

Table 10.1 *continued*

1995	World Trade Organization (WTO) founded
1997	Kyoto Protocol to the UNFCCC
1998	Rotterdam Convention on Hazardous Chemicals and Pesticides Aarhus Convention on Access to Information, Public Participation in Decision-Making, and Access to Justice in Environmental Matters
2000	Cartagena Protocol on Biosafety Millennium Development Goals set out
2001	US President Bush revokes signature of the Kyoto Protocol
2002	World Summit on Sustainable Development (WSSD), Johannesburg; Johannesburg Plan of Implementation
2005	Entry into force of the Kyoto Protocol and introduction of the first international emissions-trading system by the European Union
2006	International discussions commence on the climate change regime after 2012
2007	Fourth Assessment Report of the IPCC
2008	First Commitment Period of Kyoto begins
2009	Copenhagen Accord UNFCCC (Cop 15)
2010	Cancun Conference (COP 16) BP oil spill in the Gulf of Mexico
2011	The Fukushima Daiichi nuclear disaster, a failure at the Fukushima Nuclear Plant in Japan
2011	Durban Platform on climate change agreed on
2012	Rio +20 UN Environmental Conference
2015	Paris New climate change agreement scheduled for signing

conserve specific resources, such as fisheries (1867 convention between France and Great Britain) or fur seals (1891, 1892, and 1911 conventions between Great Britain, the United States, and Russia). In 1935, with the Trail Smelter case, leaders of countries recognized that reducing transboundary pollution required joint effort and could be accomplished peacefully. In this landmark case, pollutants from a mineral smelter in Canada drifted south to contaminate portions of the US state of Washington. The resulting treaty between the two countries asserted the legal principle that countries are liable for damage that their citizens cause in another country.

There were also numerous, mostly unsuccessful, attempts to regulate exploitation of maritime resources lying beyond national jurisdiction, including several multilateral fisheries commissions. The development of the 1946 International Convention for the Regulation of Whaling (and its International Whaling Commission) marked an interesting move away from the goal of the late nineteenth-century fur seal conventions, which entailed conserving an industry by regulating catches, toward the preservation of the great whales by declaring an international moratorium on whaling. This shift still generates bitter confrontation among NGOs, most members of the International Whaling Commission, and the small number of nations—Japan, Norway, and Iceland—that wish to resume commercial whaling and still kill what they call "research whales."

After World War II, global economic recovery brought with it evidence of damaging pollution of the atmosphere, of watercourses, and of the sea, notably the Mediterranean, leading to international agreements in the 1950s and 1960s covering such matters as discharges from oil tankers. This worthy activity was, however, not the stuff of great power politics. Such "apolitical" matters were the domain of new UN specialized agencies, like the Food and Agriculture Organization, but were hardly central to diplomacy at the UN General Assembly in New York.

However, the salience of environmental issues grew in the 1960s, and in 1968 the General Assembly accepted a Swedish proposal for what became the 1972 UN Conference on the Human Environment (UNCHE) "to focus governments' attention and public opinion on the importance and urgency of the question." The Stockholm Conference led to the creation of the United Nations Environment Programme (UNEP) and the establishment of environment departments by many governments. Yet it was already clear that for the countries of the South, constituting the majority in the UN General Assembly, environmental questions could not be separated from their demands for development, aid, and the restructuring of international economic relations. This was the political context surrounding the emergence of the concept of **sustainable development** (i.e., that meets the needs of the present without compromising future ability to meet needs). Before this concept was formulated by the Brundtland Commission in 1987, however, the environment had been pushed to the periphery of the international agenda by the global economic downturn of the 1970s and then the onset of the second Cold War.

Environmental degradation continued nonetheless. Awareness of new forms of transnational pollution, such as sulfur dioxide, or "acid," rain, joined existing concerns over point-source pollution (when the pollutant comes from a definite source), followed by a dawning scientific realization that some environmental problems—the thinning of the stratospheric ozone layer and the possibility of climate change—were truly global in scale. The attendant popular concern over such issues, and the relaxation of East–West tension, created the opportunity for a second great UN conference, for which the connection between environment and development had been explicitly drawn through the Brundtland Commission's notion of sustainable development. Although this conference was subject to many subsequent interpretations, its political essence is an accommodation of the environmental concerns of developed

WHAT'S YOUR WORLDVIEW

Do you think that citizens should pressure governments to take action to protect the environment? At what level of government do citizens have the greatest influence on environmental issues—local, state, or national? Why do you think this is so?

UN Secretary General Ban Ki-moon and Danish Prime Minister Helle Thorning-Schmidt meet in Copenhagen at a Global Green Growth Forum in 2011 to discuss ways to update and continue the expiring Kyoto Protocol.

states and the development demands of the South, without which there could have been no Earth Summit and no Rio process.

The 1992 UN Conference on Environment and Development (UNCED), or "Earth Summit," was the largest international conference so far held. It raised the profile of the environment as an international issue while concluding several significant documents and agreements, such as Agenda 21 and international conventions on climate change and the preservation of biodiversity. The event's underlying politics were captured in its title—it was a conference on "environment and development," where the most serious arguments concerned aid pledges to finance the environmental improvements under discussion.

A process was created at the UN to review the implementation of the Rio agreements, including meetings of the new Commission on Sustainable Development and a Special Session of the General Assembly in 1997.

On UNCED's tenth anniversary in 2002, the World Summit on Sustainable Development was held in Johannesburg. The change of wording indicated how conceptions of environment and development had shifted since the 1970s. Now discussion was embedded in recognition of the importance of globalization and of the dire state of the African continent. Poverty eradication was clearly emphasized, along with practical progress in providing clean water, sanitation, and agricultural improvements. One controversial element was the role to be played in such provision by private–public sector partnerships.

The UN conferences marked the stages by which the environment entered the international political mainstream, but they also reflected underlying changes in the scope and perception of environmental problems. As scientific understanding expanded, it was becoming a commonplace, by the 1980s, to speak in terms of global environmental change, as most graphically represented by the discovery of the ozone hole and the creeping realization that human activities might be dangerously altering the global climate itself.

Alongside environmental degradation and advances in scientific knowledge, the international politics of the environment has responded to the issue–attention cycle in developed countries, peaking at certain moments and then declining. The causes are complex, and during the 1960s they reflected the countercultural and radical movements of the time, along with wider public reactions to a series of trends and events. The most influential of these was Rachel Carson's (1962) book *Silent Spring*, which powerfully conjoined the conservationist and antipollution agendas by bringing to light the damage inflicted on bird life by industrial pesticides like DDT. Well-publicized environmental

Farmers in Madagascar, like many in the developing world, have used slash and burn techniques to clear forests. The 2012 Doha climate change meetings expanded a green fund to pay for the restoration of forests like this one.

disasters, such as the 1959 mercury poisoning at Minamata in Japan and the 1967 wreck of the *Torrey Canyon* oil tanker close to beaches in southwestern England, fed public concern. The failure of established political parties to effectively respond to these issues encouraged the birth of several new high-profile NGOs—Friends of the Earth, Greenpeace, and the World Wildlife Fund for Nature—alongside more established pressure groups such as the US Sierra Club and the British Royal Society for the Protection of Birds. The interest in international environmental action and, indeed, most of the NGOs exerting pressure to this end were an almost exclusively developed-world phenomenon.

Public attention then receded, until the end of the second Cold War coincided with a new concern over global environmental problems, providing the political impetus for the 1992 Earth Summit. Interest waned again during the ensuing decade, although by 2005–2006 public alarm over the impact of climate change again propelled environmental issues up the political agenda. The demand was, of course, for international action and governance, but what exactly did this mean?

The Environment and International Relations Theory

Academics who study the international relations of the environment try to understand the circumstances under which potentially effective international cooperation can occur. The later discussion of climate change shows that this question remains important (see "Climate Change" in this chapter). Most scholars have used the concept of regime. Note, for instance, how the defining characteristics of regimes—principles, norms, rules, and decision-making procedures—can be applied to the environmental cases mentioned in this chapter. Those who try to explain the record of environmental regimes tend to adopt a liberal-institutionalist stance, stressing as a key motivating factor the joint gains arising from cooperative solutions to the problem of providing public goods such as a clean atmosphere (see Chapters 3 and 4). One important addition to the regime literature, made by scholars of environmental politics, points out the importance of scientific knowledge and the roles of NGOs in this area. Whereas orthodox regime approaches assume that behavior is based on the pursuit of power or interest, analysts of international environmental cooperation have noted the independent role played by changes in knowledge (particularly scientific understanding). This cognitive approach appears in studies of the ways in which transnationally organized groups of scientists and policy makers—often referred to as epistemic communities—have influenced the development of environmental regimes.

Liberal-institutionalist analysis of regime creation might still be the predominant approach to global environmental change, but it is not the only one. It makes the important, but often unspoken, assumption that the problem to be solved is how to obtain global governance in a fragmented system of sovereign states. Marxist writers would reject this formulation (see Chapter 4). For them, the state system is part of the problem rather than the solution, and the proper object of study is the way global capitalism reproduces relationships that are profoundly damaging to the environment. The global spread of neoliberal policies accelerates those features of globalization—consumerism, the relocation of production to the South, and the thoughtless squandering of resources—driving the global ecological crisis. Proponents of this view also highlight the incapacity of the state to do anything other than assist such processes. It follows that the international cooperation efforts described here at worst legitimize this state of affairs and at best provide some marginal improvements to the devastation wrought by global capitalism. For example, they would point to how free market concepts are now routinely embedded in discussions of sustainable development and how the WTO rules tend to subordinate attempts to provide environmental regulation of genetically modified organisms (GMOs). This argument is part of a broader debate among political theorists concerning whether the state can ever be "greened." The opposing view would be that within any time frame that is relevant to coping with a threat as large and immediate as climate change, state and international cooperation remain the only plausible mechanisms for providing the necessary global governance, and we shall simply have to do the best we can with existing state and international organizational structures.

With the end of the Cold War, some realist international relations specialists began to apply their ideas about anarchy and war to the study of environmental politics. As a result, they contended that conflict, not cooperation, shaped the issue, and they went looking for proof of this hypothesis. Largely ignoring the many examples of cooperation, like the Antarctic treaty system, they argued that environmental change contributes to the incidence of both internal conflict and even interstate war, even though the causal connections are complex and involve many factors. It is already evident that **desertification** (the extreme deterioration of land due to loss of vegetation and soil moisture) and the degradation of other vital resources are intimately bound up with cycles of poverty, destitution, and war in Africa. But these factors can also be attributed to the effects of European colonization of the continent. However, if we consider such predicted consequences of climate change as mass migrations of populations across international boundaries and acute scarcity of water and other resources, the outlines of potential future conflicts come into sharper focus.

Thus, the more immediate and persistent consequence of warfare could very well be the destruction of **ecosystems** (systems of organisms sharing a habitat) that such conflict causes. For example, during World War I, artillery shelling devastated farmland along the trench lines in northern France and Belgium, creating eerie moonscapes for years after the war. Similarly, in Vietnam the detrimental environmental effects of US weapons, including the use of the herbicide Agent Orange (a form of the carcinogenic compound dioxin) and the carpet bombing of wide swaths of jungle and rice paddies, remain visible today. More recently, tank-training exercises in the Mojave Desert of California have increased erosion of the fragile landscape. During both Gulf Wars, fires set at oil wells sent carcinogenic materials aloft to be carried downwind, where people who breathed the air became sick. In addition, the depleted-uranium antitank bullets fired during those wars put radioactive material into the air and soil. Even the less obvious effects of warfare can have unforeseen, negative impacts: A recent lawsuit filed in US federal court has charged that US Navy sonar-training exercises can hurt the hearing of migrating whales, causing them to become disoriented.

Left out of most discussions about international relations theory and the environment is the **ecotopian** perspective. The **deep ecology** movement, or the **ecocentric** view, represents a radical or transformational perspective. Deep ecologists are purists rejecting the idea of inherent human superiority and giving equal moral weight to all elements of nature. Many of these utopians who seek system transformation have called for an alliance between red (socialist) and green (environmentalist) organizations to address the two overarching political issues of our time: human inequality and environmental destructions.

Deep ecologists lack faith in capitalist systems that are technologically dependent; prone to move toward large centralized corporate control; and protected by undemocratic, elitist political institutions. Strongly opposed to materialism and consumerism, they argue that our throw-away, shop-til-you-drop consumer culture should be replaced by an emphasis on meeting basic human needs. Otherwise, they fear, the environment will be devastated.

CASE STUDY | The "Doomsday" Seed Vault

Background

One day in February 2008, like a scene out of a post-apocalyptic science fiction movie, more than 200 invited guests hunkered inside puffy parkas at the official opening of the Svalbard Global Seed Vault. The luminaries included Wangari Maathai, Nobel Prize winner for her work in reforestation in Africa, the European Commission president, and several heads of government. Unfortunately dubbed in news media the "Doomsday Vault," the facility is located on an island over 600 miles north of Norway and not far from the North Pole. There, at the end of a 400-foot tunnel carved into a mountain and isolated from the outside by a series of air locks, governments will be able to store as many as 2 billion seeds, representing almost 4.5 million species of food plants. It is intended to be the storehouse of last resort for the world's plants.

The Case

The seed vault is the idea of an NGO based in Rome, Italy, called the Global Crop Diversity Trust. An affiliate of the Food and Agriculture Organization, the trust will administer the facility, which cost more than $9 million. The vault is one response to fears about the long-term effects global warming might have on biodiversity and crop output. It will be a repository for samples of food seeds in the event that a temperature increase causes plant extinctions. One sign that the host Norwegian government—which covered the entire cost of construction—and Crop Diversity Trust believe the threat of global warming is very real is the location of the tunnel. It is far above the current high tide mark and also well above where mean high tide will be if the Arctic, Antarctic, and Greenland ice sheets all melt.

Billing itself as "A Foundation for Food Security," the Global Crop Diversity Trust gives grants in support of food-plant research and to maintain gene banks in accordance with the goals of the 1983 International Treaty on Plant Genetic Resources for Food and Agriculture and the 1993 Biodiversity Convention. In addition, the trust seeks to maintain vital food products eaten in the developing world such as bananas, sorghum, barley, cassava, lentils, and several varieties of beans.

There seems to be little not to like about the Svalbard Global Seed Vault, aside from the eminent threat of highly negative effects of global warming. However, the Global Crop Diversity Trust website (www.croptrust.org) FAQ section provides some hints about one possible controversy. The site carefully asserts that it is national governments that will deposit seeds and that each government will retain ownership of its seeds. A look at the donors section of the website suggests an explanation for this statement of seed ownership. There, among a list of donors such as EU governments, USAID, the Rockefeller Foundation, and the Bill and Melinda Gates Foundation, are the names of two giants of the agribusiness chemical industry: DuPont and Syngenta AG. Many environmentalists remember what Syngenta AG posts on its corporate-history web page: Prior to changing its name to Syngenta AG in 2001, the chemical firm was known by several names, including Ciba. It was Ciba employees, says the corporate website, who invented both DDT and 2,4-D (http://www.syngenta.com). The former (DDT) was the villain in Rachel Carson's *Silent Spring;* the latter (2,4-D) is better known as a component of Agent Orange, an herbicide that US forces sprayed in uncounted millions of gallons on Vietnam during the 1960s and early 1970s.

The entry corridor to the Global Seed Vault on Svalbard Island, Norway.

Continued

CASE STUDY   The "Doomsday" Seed Vault   *continued*

Outcome

As we have seen so far in this book, perspective matters when seeking to understand international politics. Some environmental activists resent the fact that agribusiness seems to be trying to exploit global warming by supporting the Global Crop Diversity Trust, especially because the chemical industry bears some of the guilt for causing the greenhouse gas problem in the first place. However, as Syngenta AG's website indicates, the company is trying to do its best to save biodiversity. Which side is

correct? The answer might be buried under a mountain in the permafrost zone at the end of a tunnel 600 miles from the North Pole.

For Discussion

1. If the goal of the Global Seed Vault is good, does it matter who the donors are?
2. Should the concept of national sovereignty extend to control of the world's seeds?
3. Who is to blame for climate change?

Ecological and natural laws should help shape morality in human affairs, and the costs of environmental degradation must be considered as policy choices are made. Following their recommendations would certainly require a significant transformation in our political and economic thinking and in our policy priorities.

Clearly, the environmental degradation caused by wars, and the instruments of war, is impossible to dismiss yet even more difficult to address because by its very nature warfare is a breakdown of international cooperation. However, when states are not at war and cooperation *is* a viable option, what does it look like and how does it function? Now that we have explored some of the theories surrounding international environmental cooperation, in the next section we will talk more about global mechanisms—or how states and transnational actors attempt to solve environmental issues through formal agreements and cooperative actions.

WHAT'S YOUR WORLDVIEW

How do alternative theories like the constructivist, radical-liberal, ecotopian, and some feminist theories of international relations help us to understand environmental problems in ways that traditional theories like realism and liberalism do not?

The Functions of International Environmental Cooperation

Because environmental issues, such as pollution control, often involve more than one country—or region, or hemisphere—states must establish international governance regimes to regulate these transboundary environmental problems and sustain the global commons. Yet these regimes encompass more than formal agreements between states, although such agreements are very important. Moreover, there are other functions and consequences of international cooperation beyond regime formation, which we learn about in the following sections.

Transboundary Trade and Pollution Control

When pollution, water, fish, or animals crosses national frontiers, the need for international cooperation arises. The regulation of transboundary environmental problems is a long-established function of international cooperation, reflected in hundreds of multilateral, regional, and bilateral agreements providing for joint efforts to manage resources and control pollution.

An important example is provided by the 1979 Convention on Long-Range Transboundary Air Pollution and its various protocols. They responded to the growing problem of acidification and so-called acid rain by providing mechanisms to study atmospheric pollution problems in Europe and North America and securing commitments by the states involved to control and reduce their emissions. Another set of multilateral environmental agreements regulates the transboundary movement of hazardous wastes and chemicals, in the interest of protecting human health and the environment, and requires that when hazardous chemicals and pesticides are traded, the government from whose territory the exports originate shall obtain the "prior informed consent" of the importing country (see Table 10.2).

Controlling, taxing, and even promoting trade has always been one of the more important functions of the state, and trade restrictions can also be used as an instrument for nature conservation. The 1973 Convention on International Trade in Endangered Species (CITES) does this by attempting to monitor, control, or prohibit international trade in species (or products derived from them) whose continued survival might be put at risk by the effects of such trade. Species at risk are "listed" in three appendices to the convention; some 600 animal and 300 plant species currently enjoy the highest level of protection (a trade ban) through listing in Appendix I, although decisions on the "up-listing" and "down-listing" of species are sometimes controversial, as in the case of the African elephant or the northern spotted owl, bald eagle, and gray wolves in the United States.

The use of trade penalties and restrictions by multilateral environmental agreements has been a thorny issue whenever the objective of environmental protection has come into conflict with the rules of the GATT/WTO trade regime. Such a problem arose when the international community attempted to address the controversial question of the new biotechnology and GMOs. There was much resistance to the claims of (primarily American) biotechnology corporations that had made huge investments in developing GMO seed, pharmaceutical, and food products and argued that these innovations had positive environmental and development potential (through reducing pesticide use and increasing crop yields). European publics, supermarkets, and

Regime Theory and the Montreal Protocol

The Challenge

Academic advocates of international regime theory discussed in this chapter contend that four factors—context, knowledge, interest, and power—can explain why and when countries decide to create a formal commitment in a given issue area. The same four factors also help to explain what kinds of restraints countries permit on their behaviors. The evolution of international cooperation to protect the ozone layer provides an excellent case on which to test this hypothesis. In brief, if there are significant disagreements about the scientific evidence and one or more countries wants to limit cooperation, then it is unlikely that other countries will be able to establish an effective international regime.

Options

The consequences of the thinning of the stratospheric ozone layer include excessive exposure to UVB radiation, resulting in increased rates of skin cancer for human beings and damage to immune systems. Stratospheric ozone depletion arose from a previously unsuspected source—artificial chemicals containing fluorine, chlorine, and bromine that were involved in chemical reaction with ozone molecules at high altitudes. Most significant were the chlorofluorocarbons (CFCs), which had been developed in the 1920s as "safe" inert industrial gases and which had been blithely produced and used over the next fifty years for a whole variety of purposes from refrigeration to air conditioning and as propellants for hairspray. Despite growing scientific knowledge, there was no universal agreement on the dangers posed by these chemicals, and production and use continued—except, significantly, where the US Congress decided to ban some non-essential uses. This meant that the US chemical industry found itself under a costly obligation to find alternatives. Until a US-based chemical company developed an alternative to the harmful CFC compound, the US diplomats blocked serious discussions at the international level. As evidence on the problem began to mount, the UNEP acted to convene an international conference in Vienna. It produced a relatively weak "framework convention"—the 1985 Vienna Convention for the Protection of the Ozone Layer—agreeing that international action might be required and that the parties should continue to communicate and to develop and exchange scientific findings. These findings proved to be very persuasive, particularly with the added public impetus provided by the dramatic discovery of the Antarctic "ozone hole."

Application

Within two years, the Montreal Protocol was negotiated. Some analysts point to a change in US negotiating stance as the reason for the rapid passage of the protocol. Why did this change occur? An American chemical giant found a replacement compound for the ozone-depleting CFCs, seemingly confirming part of the regime-creation hypothesis. In the Montreal Protocol, parties agreed to a regime under which the production and trading of CFCs and other ozone-depleting substances would be progressively phased out. The developed countries achieved this for CFCs by 1996, and Meetings of the Parties have continued to work on the elimination of other substances since that time. There was some initial resistance from European chemical producers, but the US side had a real incentive to ensure international agreement because otherwise its chemical industry would remain at a commercial disadvantage. The other problem faced by the negotiators involved the developing countries, which themselves were manufacturing CFC products. As the Indian delegate put it, it was the developed countries' mess and their responsibility to clear it up! Why should developing countries be forced to change over to higher cost CFC alternatives? There were two responses to this. The first was an article in the protocol giving the developing countries a period of grace. The second was a fund, set up in 1990, to finance the provision of alternative non-CFC technologies for the developing world.

Illegal production and smuggling of CFCs was evident in the 1990s. This tested the monitoring and compliance systems of the protocol (which included a possible use of trade sanctions against offenders). Nonetheless, the regime has generally proved to be effective and has continually widened the scope of its activities to deal with further classes of ozone-depleting chemicals. The damage to the ozone layer will not be repaired until the latter part of the twenty-first century, given the long atmospheric lifetimes of the chemicals involved. However, human behavior has been significantly altered, to the extent that the scientific subsidiary body of the Montreal Protocol has been able to report a measurable reduction in the atmospheric concentration of CFCs. Therefore it seems that the context, knowledge, interest, and power hypothesis is correct.

For Discussion

1. How might the alternative theories we have studied explain the case of CFCs and regime creation?
2. Can you think of examples in which a leader in one environmental issue is a laggard on another?
3. Given the apparent pace of climate change in the polar regions, is the regime-creation process too slow to solve the Earth's problems?

Table 10.2 **Some Environmental Treaties with Weight in International Environmental Law**

Atmospheric Pollution	
1985	Convention on Long-Range Transboundary Air Pollution
1988	Protocol on the Reduction of Sulfur Emissions or Their Transboundary Fluxes
1988	Protocol Concerning the Control of Emissions of Nitrogen Oxides
Stratospheric Ozone Layer	
1985	Vienna Convention for the Protection of the Ozone Layer
1987	Montreal Protocol on Substances That Deplete the Ozone Layer
Hazardous Wastes	
1989	Basel Convention on the Control of Transboundary Movements of Hazardous Wastes and Their Disposal
1991	Bamako Convention on the Ban of the Import Into Africa and the Control of Transboundary Movement and Management Within Africa of Hazardous Wastes
Marine Pollution	
1969	International Convention on Civil Liability for Oil Pollution Damage
1971	Brussels Convention Relating to Civil Liability in the Field of Maritime Carriage of Nuclear Material
1973/1978	International Convention for the Prevention of Pollution from Ships (MARPOL)
1992	London Convention on the Prevention of Marine Pollution by Dumping Wastes and Other Matter
Wildlife	
1971	Ramsar Convention on Wetlands of International Importance Especially as Waterfowl Habitat
1973	International Convention for the Regulation of Whaling
1973	Convention on International Trade in Endangered Species (CITES)
1979	Bonn Convention on the Conservation of Migratory Species of Wild Animals

some developing countries were very wary of GMO technologies on safety and other grounds, which led to pressure for controls on their transboundary movement and to negotiation of the Biosafety Protocol to the Convention on Biological Diversity that had been agreed at Rio in 1992. The resulting Cartagena Protocol was signed in 2000 and establishes an advanced informed agreement procedure between governments, to be applied when GMOs are transferred across frontiers for ultimate release into the environment. The criteria to guide decisions on locking imports reflected a precautionary approach rather than insistence on conclusive scientific evidence of

The red panda (**Ailurus fulgens**) is listed on the CITES "endangered list" because of commercial logging in its habitat of Nepal and northern Burma.

harmfulness. Much of the argument in negotiating the Cartagena Protocol concerned the relationship of these new environmental rules to the requirements of the trade regime and arose from the concern of the United States and other potential GMO exporters that the protocol would permit a disguised form of trade protectionism. Whether the WTO trade rules should take precedence over the emerging biosafety rules was debated at length, until the parties agreed to avoid the issue by providing that the two sets of rules should be mutually supportive.

Norm Creation

The development of international environmental law and associated norms of acceptable behavior has been rapid and innovative over the past thirty years. Some of the norms mentioned earlier are in the form of quite technical policy concepts that have been widely disseminated and adopted as a result of international discussion. The precautionary principle has gained increasing but not uncritical currency. Originally coined by German policy makers, the precautionary principle states that where there is a likelihood of environmental damage, banning an activity should not require full and definitive scientific proof. As we saw in the earlier example of GMOs, the latter has tended to be the requirement in trade law. The norm of "prior informed consent" has also been promoted alongside that of "the polluter pays." In the longer term, one of the key effects of the climate-change regime (dealt with in detail later) might well be the dissemination of new approaches to pollution control, such as emissions trading and joint implementation.

The UN Earth Summits were important in establishing environmental norms. The 1972 Stockholm Conference produced its "Principle 21," which combines sovereignty over national resources with state responsibility for external pollution. This should not be confused with Agenda 21, issued by the 1992 Rio Earth Summit. Agenda 21 was a complex forty-chapter document of some 400 pages that took two years for members of the UN to negotiate in UNCED's Preparatory Committee. Agenda 21 was frequently derided, not least because of its nonbinding character, but this internationally agreed compendium of environmental "best practice" subsequently had a wide impact and remains a point of reference. For example, many local authorities have produced their own local "Agenda 21s." Under the Aarhus Convention (1998), North American and European governments agreed to guarantee to their publics a number of environmental rights, including the right to obtain environmental information held by governments, to participate in policy decisions, and to have access to judicial processes.

> ### WHAT'S YOUR WORLDVIEW ?
>
> *The international community seems to understand environmental challenges, but most states seem reluctant to give up sovereignty to solve any global-commons problem. Why?*

Aid and Capacity Building

Although not a specific norm of the type just dealt with, sustainable development provides a normative framework built on an underlying deal between developed and developing worlds. Frequent North–South arguments since Rio about the levels of aid and **technology transfer** that would allow developing countries to achieve sustainable development have ended in many disappointments and unfulfilled pledges. In 1991, the UNEP, UNDP, and the World Bank created the Global Environmental Facility as an international mechanism specifically for funding environmental projects in developing countries. Between 2003 and 2006 it attracted donations of around $3 billion. Most environmental conventions now aim at **capacity building** through arrangements for the transfer of funds, technology, and expertise, because most of their member states simply lack the resources to participate fully in international agreements. The stratospheric-ozone and climate-change regimes aim to build capacity and could not exist in their current form without providing for this function.

A river of trash: In many developing countries, finding enough water is not the problem; common practices like dumping garbage create major health hazards and make rivers impassable, as shown in this photo from Jakarta, Indonesia.

Scientific Understanding

International environmental cooperation relies on shared scientific understanding, as evidenced by the form of some important contemporary environmental regimes. An initial framework convention will signal concern and establish mechanisms for developing and sharing new scientific data, thereby providing the basis for taking action in a control protocol. Generating and sharing scientific information has long been a function of international cooperation in public bodies such as the World Meteorological Organization and myriad academic organizations such as the International Council for the Exploration of the Seas and the International Union for the Conservation of Nature. Disseminating scientific information on an international basis makes sense, but it needs funding from governments, because, except in areas like pharmaceutical research, the private sector has no incentive to do the work. International environmental regimes usually have standing scientific committees and subsidiary bodies to support their work. Perhaps the greatest international effort to generate new and authoritative scientific knowledge has been in the area of **climate change**, through the Intergovernmental Panel on Climate Change (IPCC).

Set up in 1988 under the auspices of the World Meteorological Organization and UNEP, the IPCC brings together the majority of the world's climate-change scientists in three working groups: on climate science, impacts, and economic and social dimensions. They have produced assessment reports in 1990, 1995, 2001, and 2007, which are regarded as the authoritative scientific statements on climate change. The reports are carefully and cautiously drafted with the involvement of government representatives and represent a consensus view.

The Fourth Assessment Report, published in February 2007, concluded that "warming of the climate system is unequivocal, as is now evident from observations of increases in global average air and ocean temperatures, widespread melting of snow and ice and rising global sea level" (IPCC 2007, 4). Most of the temperature increase "is *very likely* due to the observed increase in anthropogenic greenhouse gas concentrations" (8). The use of words is significant here, because the IPCC defines *"very likely"* as being more than 90 percent certain. This represents a change from the previous report, which had only estimated that human activity was *"likely,"* or more than 66 percent certain, to be responsible for temperature increases.

The IPCC agreed to prepare a Fifth Assessment Report in 2008. This report (AR5, scheduled for completion in 2014) is focused on assessing the socioeconomic aspects of climate change and the implications for sustainable development policies and risk management efforts across the world.

WHAT'S YOUR WORLDVIEW

Which is more important: economic development or environmental protection? Is it possible to achieve both goals? Can we achieve sustainable development?

Governing the Commons

The **global commons** are usually understood as areas and resources not under sovereign jurisdiction—in other words, not owned by anybody. The high seas

In South Sudan, a local official points to open pools of chemical liquids, by-products of oil production that pollute farms and waterways.

and the deep ocean floor come within this category (beyond the 200 nautical mile exclusive economic zone that states could claim under the 1992 UN Convention on the Law of the Sea), as does Antarctica (based on the 1959 Antarctic Treaty). Outer space is another highly important commons area, its use being vital to modern telecommunications, broadcasting, navigation, and surveillance. Finally, there is the global atmosphere.

The global commons have an environmental dimension, not only as resources but also as a kind of garbage dump for waste products from cities and industry. The fish and whale stocks of the high seas have been relentlessly overexploited, to the point where some species have been wiped out and long-term protein sources for human beings are imperiled. The ocean environment has been polluted by land-based effluent and oil and other discharges from ships. It has been a struggle to maintain the unique wilderness of the Antarctic in the face of increasing pressure from human beings, and even outer space now faces an environmental problem in the form of increasing orbital debris left by decades of satellite launches. Similarly, the global atmosphere has been degraded in a number of highly threatening ways, through damage to the stratospheric ozone layer and, most important, by the enhanced **greenhouse effect** now firmly associated with changes to the earth's climate. This is often characterized as a "tragedy of the commons." Where there is unrestricted access to a resource owned by no one, there will be an incentive for individuals to grab as much as they can and, if the resource is finite, there will come a time when it is ruined by overexploitation as the short-term interests of individual users overwhelm the longer run collective interest in sustaining the resource.

Environmental Regimes

Within the jurisdiction of governments it might be possible to solve the problem by turning the commons into private property or nationalizing them, but for the global commons such a solution is, by definition, unavailable. Therefore the function of international cooperation in this context is the very necessary one of providing a substitute for world government to ensure that global commons are not misused and subject to tragic collapse. Regimes have been created that have enjoyed varying degrees of effectiveness. Many of the functions already discussed can be found in these global-commons regimes, but their central contribution is a framework of rules to ensure mutual agreement among users about acceptable standards of behavior and levels of exploitation, consistent with sustaining commons ecology.

Enforcement poses difficult challenges because of the incentives for users to "free ride" by taking more than a fair share or refusing to be bound by the collective arrangements. Free riding can potentially destroy regimes because other parties will then see no reason to restrain themselves either. In local commons regimes, inquisitive neighbors might deter rule breaking, and a similar role at the international level can be performed by NGOs. However, it is very difficult to enforce compliance by sovereign states—this is a fundamental difficulty for international law and hardly unique to environmental regimes. Mechanisms have been developed to cope with the problem, but how effective they, and the environmental regimes to which they apply, can be is hard to judge because this involves determining the extent to which governments are in legal and technical compliance with their international obligations. Moreover, it also involves estimating the extent to which state behavior has actually been changed as a result of the international regime concerned. Naturally, the ultimate and most demanding test of the effectiveness of global-commons regimes is whether the resources or ecologies concerned are sustained or even improved.

Some of the first and least successful global-commons regimes were the various fisheries commissions for the Atlantic and elsewhere, which sought agreement on limiting catches to preserve stocks. Pollution from ships has been controlled by MARPOL (the 1973 international marine environmental convention—short for "marine pollution"), and there is a patchwork of other treaties to manage such issues as the dumping of radioactive waste at sea. For the Antarctic, a remarkably well-developed set of rules designed to preserve the ecological integrity of this last great wilderness has been devised within the framework of the 1959 treaty. The Antarctic regime is a rather exclusive club: The treaty's "Consultative Parties" include the states that had originally claimed sovereignty over parts of the area, and new members of the club have to demonstrate their involvement in scientific research on the frozen continent. There is a comprehensive agreement on conserving the marine ecosystem around the continent, and in the late 1980s preparations for regulated mineral mining were defeated and replaced by a new 1988 Protocol on Environmental Protection, which included a fifty-year mining ban. The success, with only a minimal level of formal organization, of a restricted group of countries in governing this crucial laboratory for understanding global environmental change demonstrates what can be achieved by international action.

Antarctic science was crucial to the discovery of a problem that resulted in what is perhaps the best example of effective international action to govern the commons. In 1985, a British Antarctic Survey balloon provided definitive evidence of serious thinning of the stratospheric ozone layer. A diminishing ozone layer is a global problem par excellence, because the ozone layer protects the earth and its inhabitants from the damaging effects of the sun's ultraviolet B radiation. A framework convention was signed in 1985, followed in 1987 by its Montreal Protocol imposing international controls over

WHAT'S YOUR WORLDVIEW ?

International relations describes a world of nation-states and sovereignty. How would you convince these states to give up or share sovereignty to address common problems like pollution or climate change?

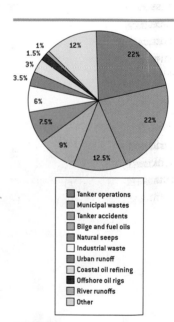

SOURCES OF MARINE POLLUTION.

What do you notice about the top five sources of pollution in this chart? Based on these data and what you have read in this chapter so far, what do you think world governments can do about transboundary pollution? (Note: These data do not include the BP oil spill in the Gulf of Mexico in 2010.)

ozone-depleting chemicals. The further evolution of the ozone-layer regime offers the paramount example of how international cooperation can achieve an effective solution to a global environmental problem. The problem's causes were isolated, international support was mobilized, compensatory action was taken to ensure that developing countries participated, and a set of rules and procedures were developed that proved to be effective, at least in reducing the concentration of the offending chemicals in the atmosphere, if not yet fully restoring the stratospheric ozone layer.

Climate Change

Unlike the ozone-layer problem, which was clearly the result of damage caused when people used CFCs in industry, air conditioning, and personal products like hairspray, climate change and the enhanced greenhouse effect had long been debated among scientists. Only in the late 1980s did sufficient international scientific and political consensus emerge to stimulate action—a clear case of the development and influence of an epistemic community. There were still serious disagreements, however, over the likelihood that human-induced changes in mean temperatures were altering the global climate system.

Naturally occurring greenhouse gases in the atmosphere insulate the earth's surface by trapping solar radiation. Before the Industrial Revolution, carbon dioxide concentrations in the atmosphere were around 280 parts per million. They have since grown exponentially. In 2007 they were measured at 379 ppm, by 2013 they had reached 400 ppm. This rising concentration was because of the burning of fossil fuels and reductions in some of the "sinks" for carbon dioxide—notably forests. Methane emissions have also risen with the growth of agriculture (IPCC 2007, 11).

The best predictions of the IPCC are that if nothing is done to curb intensive fossil fuel emissions, there will be a likely rise in mean temperatures on the order of 4.3 to 11.5 degrees Fahrenheit (or 2.4–6.4 degrees Celsius) by 2099. The exact consequences of this are difficult to predict on the basis of current climate modeling, but sea level rises and turbulent weather are generally expected. In 2010 it was internationally agreed that to avoid climate catastrophe, it would be necessary to hold temperature increases below 3.6 degrees Fahrenheit (or 2 degrees Celsius) by keeping atmospheric CO_2 concentrations below

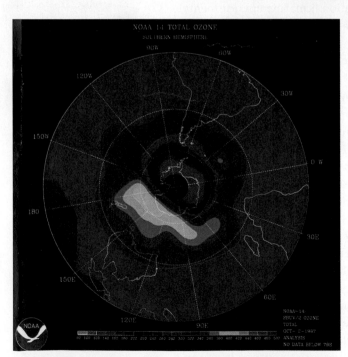

International agreements have reduced the amount of ozone-depleting gases that industries release, but the gases remain a cause of atmospheric damage, as this NASA satellite image shows.

550 ppm. In the first decade of the twenty-first century, unusual weather patterns, storm events, and the melting of polar ice sheets have added a dimension of public concern to the fears expressed by the scientific community.

As a common problem, climate change is on a quite different scale from anything that the international system has previously encountered. Climate change is really not a "normal" international environmental problem—it threatens huge changes in living conditions and challenges existing patterns of energy use and security. There is almost no dimension of international relations that it does not actually or potentially affect, and it has already become the subject of "high politics," discussed at G-8 summits and in high-level meetings between political leaders. Indeed, the UK foreign secretary stated in 2006 that climate change and climate security must now be a priority for foreign policy. Although recognizing the importance of this issue for the health of the planet and all living creatures, national leaders are still attempting to negotiate a comprehensive climate agreement.

One way of examining the dimensions of the problem and the steps taken at the international level to respond to the threat is to make a comparison to the stratospheric-ozone problem discussed in the previous section. There are, of course, some similarities. CFCs are in themselves greenhouse gases, and the international legal texts on climate change make it clear that controlling them is the responsibility of the Montreal Protocol. The experience with stratospheric ozone and other recent conventions has clearly influenced efforts to build a climate-change regime. At the very start of climate discussions, the same approach was adopted: a framework convention followed by protocols.

The UN Framework Convention on Climate Change (UNFCCC) was signed at the Rio Earth Summit in 1992. It envisaged the reduction of greenhouse gas emissions and their removal by carbon sequestration, a process through which carbon-based gases are injected into the ground or into peat bogs. The signatories hoped that including a commitment from the developed nations to cut their emissions back to 1990 levels by 2000 could make a start. In a US election year this proved to be impossible, and the parties had to be content with a nonbinding declaration that an attempt would be made. There was a binding commitment, however, for parties to draw up national inventories of sources and sinks. Because this included the developing nations, many of whom were ill equipped to fulfill this obligation, there was also funding for capacity building. Most important, the convention locked the signatories into holding a continuing series of annual Conferences of Parties to consider possible actions and review the adequacy of existing commitments, supported by regular meetings of the subsidiary scientific and implementation bodies. By the Conference of Parties in Kyoto in 1997, the parties agreed on a "control" measure—the Kyoto Protocol involving emissions reductions by developed countries facilitated by "flexibility mechanisms."

The problem faced by the framers of the Kyoto Protocol was vastly more complex and demanding than that which their counterparts at Montreal had

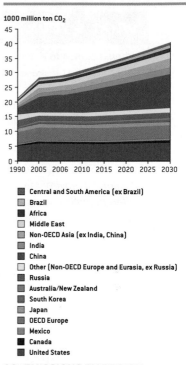

1000 million ton CO_2

- Central and South America (ex Brazil)
- Brazil
- Africa
- Middle East
- Non-OECD Asia (ex India, China)
- India
- China
- Other (Non-OECD Europe and Eurasia, ex Russia)
- Russia
- Australia/New Zealand
- South Korea
- Japan
- OECD Europe
- Mexico
- Canada
- United States

CO_2 EMISSIONS BY REGION.
Global CO_2 emissions increased from 15.3 billion tons in 1970 to 22.5 billion tons in 1990; by 2012 emissions had increased to 33 billion tons. What are governments doing to reverse this trend? What impediments do they face in implementing their plans?
Source: Netherlands Environmental Assessment Agency.

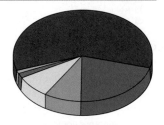

THE PROPORTIONS OF GREENHOUSE GASES.

This chart combines the potency and volume of major-heat absorbing gases in the atmosphere. Since the Industrial Revolution, carbon dioxide concentrations have grown exponentially, from 280 parts per million to 400 parts per million in 2011.
If nothing is done to curb intensive fossil fuel emissions, what will happen to the average global temperature? What effects might that have?

- Carbon Dioxide
- Ozone
- Methane
- Nitrous Oxide
- CFC 12
- CFC 11

confronted so successfully in 1987. Instead of controlling a single set of industrial gases for which substitutes were available, reducing greenhouse gas emissions would involve energy, transport, and agriculture—the fundamentals of life in modern societies. This challenges the whole idea of sustainable development. Whether this must involve real sacrifices in living standards and "impossible" political choices is a tough question for governments, although there are potential economic benefits from cutting emissions through the development of alternative energy technologies. Politicians in Europe have taken the lead in trying to reduce greenhouse gas emissions. Unfortunately, for most of the 1990s and the first decade of the new millennium, US politicians—representing one of the worst greenhouse-gas-offending countries by several indicators—were reluctant to make the necessary adjustments.

The Kyoto Protocol to the Climate Convention entered into force in 2005. It committed developed countries to make an average 5.2 percent cut in their greenhouse gas emissions from a 1990 baseline. Within this range, different national targets were negotiated: for example 8 percent for the EU, 6 percent for Japan, and 7 percent for the US. (The US eventually refused to participate on the grounds that its economic competitors, China and India, were not required to make similar cuts). These targets were to be achieved by the first commitment period—2008–2012. To provide flexible ways of achieving these targets, three mechanisms were also agreed on:

1. First there was **emissions trading,** where rights to emit carbon could be bought and sold. The EU established its own emissions trading system and carbon markets began to grow up elsewhere. Second and third were two offset mechanisms, **Joint Implementation** and the **Clean Development Mechanism** (CDM). They allow countries to meet their own national targets by investing in carbon reduction projects elsewhere in the world. The CDM has been very extensively used, especially in China. It was hoped that there would be a renewal of the Kyoto Protocol covering all the developed countries and lasting from 2013 to 2020, in the event only a limited second phase was achieved, covering only 15% of global emissions and without commitments from the US and Japan.

2. Joint implementation. Under this mechanism, a developed country can receive credits against its own emissions-reduction target by financing projects in another developed country. The argument is that a given amount of money is best spent where it can achieve the greatest reduction in world emissions of greenhouse gases. Countries with very efficient power plants will have an incentive to use this scheme.

3. The clean development mechanism. This mechanism applies the same principle to relations between developed and developing countries. This has stimulated a good deal of interest in China and elsewhere because it is a source of new funds and technology transfer.

Even with what appeared to be a flexible framework and some useful mechanisms built into the Kyoto Protocol, there was much disagreement and international posturing. Another reason for dissent was that, despite a quite unprecedented international scientific effort in support of the IPCC to establish the causes and consequences of warming, there was not the kind of scientific consensus that had promoted agreement on CFCs—at least not in 1997. At the time, there was disagreement over the significance of human activities and over projections of future change (which has since narrowed dramatically). And there were those who had an economic interest in denying or misrepresenting the science, including fossil fuel interests and producers such as Saudi Arabia. At the other end of the spectrum, the Alliance of Small Island States, some of whose members' territory would simply disappear under projected sea level rises, were desperately concerned that these projections be taken seriously.

At a landfill in California methane gas created by garbage is converted to liquid natural gas for use as fuel. Have you ever wondered where your trash goes?

There is a further problem in that, even though the effects of climate change are not fully understood, there is enough evidence for some nations to calculate that there might be benefits to them from climatic alterations. Regions of Russia, for example, might become more temperate with rises in mean temperature and more suitable for agricultural production (although one could equally well argue the extremely damaging effects of melting permafrost in Siberia). In North America, variations in rainfall patterns have already begun to disrupt agriculture that relies on irrigation.

What is happening to the bees? A bee works on collecting nectar from a fruit tree. Bee experts say conditions that create a honeybee die-off include mild winters and unseasonably warm early spring weather that creates conditions for an explosion in the mite populations that kill off many colonies.

Snowfall patterns in the major mountain ranges are changing, and some species of frogs and insects—especially honey bees necessary for crop pollination—are slowly disappearing. One generalization that can be made with certainty is that the developing nations, with limited infrastructure and major populations located at sea level, are most vulnerable. In recognition of this, and on the understanding that a certain level of warming is now inevitable, international attention has begun to shift toward the problem of adaptation to the effects of climate change as well as mitigation of its causes. Once again, the comparative simplicity of the stratospheric-ozone problem is evident—the effects of ozone

Global industrial growth has caused an increased demand for power generation, often through the burning of fossil fuels that produce greenhouse gases.

depletion were spread across the globe and affected North Europeans as well as those living in the Southern Hemisphere.

At the heart of the international politics of climate change as a global environmental problem is the structural divide between North and South. For the Montreal Protocol there was a solution available at an acceptable price, delivered through the Multilateral Ozone Fund. Once again, climate change is different. One of the most significant principles set out in the UNFCCC was that of common but differentiated responsibilities. That is to say that although climate change was the "common concern" of all, it had been produced as a consequence of the development of the old industrialized nations, and it was their responsibility to take the lead in cutting emissions.

The Kyoto Protocol, in its first phase, accomplished relatively little and much more greenhouse gas reduction occurred under the Montreal protocol in the same period, for chlorofluorocarbons are also powerful greenhouse gases. It became increasingly clear that, given the fact that by 2005 developing countries were responsible for the majority of current emissions and that in 2007 China overtook the US as the primary emitter, an effective climate agreement would have to include all the Parties to the Convention. This continues to be very difficult to achieve because of the legitimate claims to development and climate justice made by Southern countries and, of course, because many of the emissions from a country like China have been displaced by the globalization of production from Europe and America. It is also true that developed countries, suffering from the world economic crisis of 2008, were not prepared to take risks with their economies. In 2007 it was agreed to have two negotiation tracks, one on the future of Kyoto and the other on the future of the Convention. The US was prepared to participate in the latter because it avoided Kyoto 'targets and timetables'. It was hoped that a new comprehensive agreement could be reached at Copenhagen in 2009.

Copenhagen was a high profile event, attended by the new US President Obama and other world leaders. They failed to produce a new legally binding and comprehensive agreement. Instead, the US and the BASIC countries (a coalition of large emerging economies including Brazil, China, India and South Africa) struck a deal known as the Copenhagen Accord. This has tended to set the course of negotiations through to the agreement on the 'Durban Platform' in 2011. The key assumptions are that a new agreement, unlike Kyoto, will be 'bottom up'—that is

WHAT'S YOUR WORLDVIEW ?

The political culture of some countries emphasizes individual rights and responsibilities, yet protecting the environment asks us to live collectively and consider the other. Is it possible to change this perspective?

In 2007, the Nobel Prize Committee recognized the IPCC and former vice president Al Gore for their work on the causes and ramifications of global warming.

countries will offer their 'contributions' to emissions reductions that they regard as appropriate. All countries will participate, which breaks down the strict divide between developed and developing countries, but the CBDR principle will remain so that contributions can be 'differentiated'. How strictly contributions will be assessed and how far they will be legally binding, remains to be seen. These issues are scheduled to be resolved in Paris in 2015, for an agreement that will enter into force in 2020. It is clear that the contributions offered at the moment will not be sufficient to put the world on a pathway that avoids breaching the 2 degree Celsius threshold. There will have to be much greater ambition amongst the major emitters before 2015, if the task is not to become much more costly and difficult to achieve in future decades.

Conclusion

In this chapter, we have seen that cooperation to protect the global environment, although sometimes difficult to achieve, is possible. The determinants of successful cooperation can be found in international-regime theory, beginning with the acceptance of proper norms of behavior, because the costs of not cooperating are potentially too great. Indeed, the environmental issues we are faced with today—global climate change, desertification, and other environmental degradations—can become more severe and less manageable for future generations, as we have seen in our own brief history of the twentieth and early twenty-first century. Solving these issues now requires new perspectives and unprecedented cooperation on a global scale.

Engaging with the
WORLD

Worldwide Opportunities on Organic Farms (WWOOF)

WWOOF links people who want to volunteer on organic farms with farmers who are looking for volunteer help. Volunteers are paired with a farm anywhere within participating countries. In return for volunteer help, WWOOF hosts offer food, accommodations, and opportunities to learn about organic lifestyles. Visit www.wwoof.org.

Greenpeace Ship

Do you have sailing experience and care about the environment? The Greenpeace Ship takes on enthusiastic volunteers and professionals to work as crew members, sailing around the world on environmental campaigns to protect the global commons. Visit www.greenpeace.org.

KEY TERMS

Capacity building, p. 330
Climate change, p. 331
Deep ecology, p. 323
Desertification, p. 323
Ecocentric, p. 323

Ecological footprint, p. 315
Ecologies, p. 315
Ecosystem, p. 323
Ecotopian, p. 323
Global commons, p. 331

Global environmental
  governance, p. 316
Greenhouse effect, p. 332
Sustainable development, p. 319
Technology transfer, p. 330

REVIEW QUESTIONS

1. What are the possible connections, both negative and positive, between globalization and environmental change?

2. Why did environmental issues appear on the international agenda, and what were the key turning points?

3. Summarize the consequences of the 1972 UN Conference on the Human Environment and the 1992 UNCED.

4. How would you interpret the meaning of sustainable development?

5. How can regime concepts be applied to the study of international environmental cooperation?

6. Can international trade and environmental protection ever be compatible?

7. Why did the framework convention/control protocol prove useful in the cases of stratospheric ozone depletion and climate change?

8. How does the "tragedy of the commons" story help to illustrate the need for governance of the global commons?

9. Describe the free rider problem in relation to the climate-change regime.

10. Consider the possible security implications of the climate predictions made by the IPCC.

The Environment: Images and Options

INTRODUCTION

This exercise asks students to evaluate different and contending images of the future. These images of the future consider environmental, political, economic, and sociocultural factors.

Reluctantly, many citizens are now coming to the realization that there are real environmental costs associated with humankind's goal to achieve the "good life." Citizens and leaders alike are also now recognizing the potential challenges posed by continuing policies that abuse the delicate ecological balance. These challenges to economic and political security and the good life are explored in this exercise.

PROCEDURE

Before beginning to explore the four alternative futures, students should read and review journal articles or texts that explore environmental problems associated with the contending images. Here are some suggested readings:

> The World Commission on Environment and Development, *Our Common Future* (Oxford: 1987).

> Barry Hughes, *World Futures: A Critical Analysis of Alternatives* (Johns Hopkins: 1985).

> Robert Woyach, "Global Resources and Growth," in S. Lamy (editor), *Contemporary International Issues* (Reinner: 1988).

Second, review the different elements of the four possible futures. What are the fundamental similarities and differences between these images? Consider which future you feel would be most beneficial to you and your family. Would this future create a world society in which all people could benefit? Why or why not? Which future would result in the following conditions?

1. Full employment
2. Less air pollution
3. More time for recreational activities
4. Less government
5. Greater equality
6. More citizen participation
7. Exploration and use of alternative energy sources
8. A world economy that encourages equitable and balanced growth
9. A reduction of waste and overconsumption
10. Less spending on military
11. More economic opportunities
12. Increased conflict

Debriefing Questions

1. What image of the future is challenged by a more balanced ecological view?
2. Do these images of the future correspond in any way with the different theories in Chapter 3?
3. Why are environmental issues becoming so significant in international politics?
4. Is a sustainable development strategy a possibility for the future?

Note: Sustainable development is usually defined as a process of development that meets the needs of the present without compromising the ability of future generations to meet their own needs.

The Four Possible Futures			
Future One	**Future Two**	**Future Three**	**Future Four**
A society that provides the necessities for all while encouraging equal opportunities for self-development.	A free enterprise society in which major economic growth provides economic benefits for all.	A society in which people recognize the limits to uncontrolled growth: people limit personal wealth, build communities that are in harmony with nature, and encourage reduction of waste.	A society in which independent people are given opportunities to develop themselves without harming the environment.

Continued

THINKING ABOUT GLOBAL POLITICS *continued*

	Future One	Future Two	Future Three	Future Four
Society	As well as being individuals, most people live in social groups. People need support from one another to grow and be happy.	People benefit most when there is equal opportunity for all people to seek their own best interest. Government must not tell them what to do or what not to do.	People must cooperate, not compete. They must blend their own self-interest into that of the greater good.	A society where well-informed individuals can exercise freedom of choice to satisfy their own interest. This will contribute to creative problem solving and increased well-being for all.
Environment	The world around us is to be used. New inventions will make some resources (like the sun and wind) useful before or after others (coal and gas) are used up.	The land and sea around us are full of riches. They should be used to the fullest in making us happy and prosperous.	It is important to preserve the balance between ourselves and the land and sea around us. They belong both to us and to those who come after us.	By inventing new ways of using our resources, we can prosper without harming our natural riches.
Government	Central government should be strong and guarantee a job for all with equal pay for equal work. It must also allow people to develop private businesses, too.	Central government should play a very limited role in our lives. Its main jobs are to keep peace at home and protect us from attack.	Attention should be turned away from central government and toward local community government. Local government aids social and natural harmony.	Central government should give some support to its citizens. It should provide education and information and protect our natural resources.
Economics	Maximum effort will be made to cut our dependence on foreign resources. The government will pay for basic human services such as health care and education.	Large-scale industry can best use the natural resources of our land and oceans. They are most fit to lead development and make the most money in a world eager to buy our goods.	Local economies promote doing more with less in the design of all systems and question the ever-growing demand for consumer goods. Industries favor reuse or recycling of materials.	New industries with advanced equipment and the invention of new technologies should be encouraged. All new industries must be responsible for using our resources with care.

CONTRIBUTORS TO CHAPTER 10: *John Vogler, Steven L. Lamy, and John Masker.*

Glossary

Acquiescent strategy A foreign policy that accepts, sometimes unhappily, the interests of more powerful actors in the international system.

Adaptation strategy A foreign policy based on reacting to international events and adjusting national goals to conform to the effects of events external to that state.

African Union (AU) Created in 2002 and consisting of fifty-four member states, this union was formed as a successor to the Organization of African Unity. Its goals are centered primarily on African unity and security, human rights, peace security and stability, economy, sustainable development, and equality.

Al Qaeda Most commonly associated with Osama bin Laden, "The Base" (as it means in Arabic) is a militant Islamic fundamentalist group. With the death of Osama bin Laden, Ayman al-Zawahri assumed leadership of the organization. Groups affiliated with Al Qaeda are operating in Yemen, Somalia, Syria, and Mali.

Anarchic system A realist description of the international system that suggests there is no common power or central governing structure.

Anarchy System operating in the absence of any central government. It does not imply chaos but, in realist theory, the absence of political authority.

Appeasement A policy of making concessions to a revanchist (or otherwise territorially acquisitive) state in the hope that settlement of more modest claims will assuage that state's expansionist appetites. Appeasement remains most (in)famously associated with British Prime Minister Neville Chamberlain's acquiescence to Hitler's incursions into Austria and then Czechoslovakia, culminating in the Munich Agreement of September 1938. Since then, appeasement has generally been seen as synonymous with a craven collapse before the demands of dictators—encouraging, not disarming, their aggressive designs.

Armistice A cease-fire agreement between enemies in wartime. In the case of World War I, the armistice began at 11:00 a.m. on November 11, 1918.

Arms race This is a central concept in realist thought. As states build up their military to address real or perceived threats to their national security, they may create insecurity in other states. These states, in turn, develop their military capacities and thus begin an arms race. This never-ending pursuit of security creates the condition we know as a security dilemma.

Association of Southeast Asian Nations (ASEAN) A geopolitical and economic organization of several countries located in Southeast Asia. Initially formed as a display of solidarity against communism, it has since redefined its aims and broadened to include the acceleration of economic growth and the promotion of regional peace. By 2005 the ASEAN countries had a combined GDP of about $884 billion.

Asymmetric conflict In symmetrical warfare, armies with comparable weapons, tactics, and organizational structures do battle. Wars are fought on near-equal terms. When stakes are high and those actors in conflict are not equal in terms of weapons and technology, the weaker side adopts asymmetrical tactics. These include guerrilla warfare, roadside bombs, attacks on civilians, and other terrorist tactics.

Autarchy The mercantilist recommendation that states strive for economic self-sufficiency by using trade protectionism or policies of complete isolation.

Bipolar A term to describe an international political order in which two states dominate all others. It is often used to describe the nature of the international system when the two superpowers, the USSR and the United States, were dominant powers during the Cold War.

Blitzkrieg The German term for "lightning war." This was an offensive strategy that used the combination of mechanized forces—especially tanks—and aircraft as mobile artillery to exploit breaches in an enemy's front line. The irony was that in 1940 the French army had more tanks than the German army. The French tanks, however, were spread among units along the front line, whereas the German commanders concentrated their tanks in a few units.

Bretton Woods system The name given to the three institutions that comprise the post–World War II international political economic system. It is called Bretton Woods after the hamlet in northern New Hampshire where the leaders from the

United States, the United Kingdom, and forty-two other countries met in July 1944.

Capacity building Providing the funds and technical training to allow developing countries to participate in global environmental governance.

Capitalism A system of production in which human labor and its products are commodities that are bought and sold in the marketplace.

Charter rights Civil liberties guaranteed in a written document such as a constitution.

Civil society The totality of all individuals and groups in a society who are acting neither as participants in any government institutions nor in the interests of commercial companies.

Clandestine or "sleeper" cell Usually a group of people, sent by an intelligence organization or terrorist network, that remains dormant in a target country until activated by a message to carry out a mission, which could include prearranged attacks.

Class A social group that in Marxism is identified by its relationship with the means of production and the distribution of societal resources. Thus, we have the bourgeoisie, or the owners or upper classes, and the proletariat, or workers.

Climate change A convention on climate was agreed to at the Rio Conference in 1992. Climate change represents a change in the statistical distribution of weather over periods of time that range from decades to millions of years. It can be a change in the average weather or a change in the distribution of weather events around an average (for example, greater or fewer extreme weather events). Climate change could be limited to a specific region, or it could occur across the whole earth.

Coercive diplomacy The use of diplomatic and military methods that force a state to concede to another state. These methods could include the threat of force and the actual mobilization of military forces so as to gradually "turn the screw" but exclude the actual use of force. The implication is that war is the next step if diplomacy fails.

Cold War The period from 1946 to 1991 defined by ideological conflict and rivalry between the United States and the Soviet Union. This was a global struggle for the hearts and minds of citizens around the world that was characterized by political conflict, military competition, proxy wars, and economic competition.

Collective security Refers to an arrangement where "each state in the system accepts that the security of one is the concern of all, and agrees to join in a collective response to aggression" (A. Roberts and Kingsbury 1993, 30).

Common security At times called "cooperative security," it stresses noncompetitive approaches and cooperative approaches through which states—both friends and foes—can achieve security. Sometimes expressed as "until all people are secure from threats of war, no one is secure."

Community A human association in which members share common symbols and wish to cooperate to realize common objectives.

Conditionality When regional or international lending agencies require that recipient national governments accept certain policy conditions to receive a loan or some form of economic assistance.

Constructivism An approach to international politics that concerns itself with the centrality of ideas and human consciousness. As constructivists have examined world politics they have been broadly interested in how the structure constructs the actors' identities and interests, how their interactions are organized and constrained by that structure, and how their very interaction serves to either reproduce or transform that structure.

Containment US political strategy for resisting perceived Soviet expansion, first publicly espoused by a US diplomat, George Kennan, in 1947 and aimed at limiting Soviet expansion in Europe. Containment became a powerful factor in US policy toward the Soviet Union for the next forty years and a self-image of Western policy makers. However, Kennan's view of containment did not include the aggressive militarization that brought the world closer to the brink of nuclear destruction.

Coordination A form of cooperation requiring parties to pursue a common strategy to avoid the mutually undesirable outcome arising from the pursuit of divergent strategies.

Cosmopolitan culture A pattern of relations within which people share the same goals and aspirations, generally to improve that culture for all members.

Cosmopolitan democracy A condition in which international organizations, transnational corporations, and global markets are accountable to the peoples of the world.

Critical theory Theories that are critical of the status quo and reject the idea that things can be fixed under the present system. These theories challenge core assumptions of the dominant paradigm and argue for transformation and not just reform.

Deep ecology Often identified with the Norwegian philosopher, Arne Naess, the core belief is that the living environment has a right to live and flourish. The word deep refers to the need to think deeply about the impact of human life on the environment.

Defensive realism A structural theory of realism that views states as security maximizers—more concerned with absolute power as opposed to relative power. According to this view, it is unwise for states to try to maximize their share of power and seek hegemony.

Democratic peace thesis A central plank of liberal-internationalist thought, the democratic peace thesis makes two claims: First, liberal polities exhibit restraint in their relations with other liberal polities (the so-called separate peace), but second, they are imprudent in relations with authoritarian states. The validity of the democratic peace thesis has been fiercely debated in the international relations literature.

Dependency theory The world capitalist system divides the world into core, semiperiphery, and periphery states. The core states control both the economic and the political system and exploit the people and resources in the periphery and semiperiphery. The capitalist system is seen as impossible to reform, and only by withdrawing from the system can poor states break this dependency.

Deregulation The removal of all regulation so that market forces, not government policy, control economic developments.

Desertification This is the extreme deterioration of land in arid and dry subhumid areas caused by loss of vegetation and soil moisture; desertification results chiefly from manmade activities and is influenced by climatic variations. This condition is principally caused by overgrazing, overdrafting of groundwater, and diversion of water from rivers for human consumption and industrial use—all of these processes fundamentally driven by overpopulation.

Détente Relaxation of tension between East and West; Soviet–American détente lasted from the late 1960s to the late 1970s and was characterized by negotiations and nuclear arms control agreements.

Deterrence The threat or use of force to prevent an actor from doing something the actor would otherwise do.

Development In the orthodox view, top-down; reliance on "expert knowledge," usually Western and definitely external; large capital investments in large projects; advanced technology; expansion of the private sphere. In the alternative view, bottom-up; participatory; reliance on appropriate (often local) knowledge and technology; small investments in small-scale projects; protection of the commons.

Diplomacy The process by which international actors communicate as they seek to resolve conflicts without going to war and find solutions to complex global problems.

Dollar standard By 1947, the British pound and gold could no longer serve as the world's money. The only currency strong enough to be used to meet the demands for international liquidity was the US dollar. For both political and economic reasons, the US government was willing to become the world's central bank and use dollars for the key currency in the international monetary system.

Ecocentric Having a nature or ecologically centered rather than a human centered set of values.

Ecological footprint Used to demonstrate the load placed on the earth's carrying capacity by individuals or nations. It does this by estimating the area of productive land and water system required to sustain a population at its specified standard of living.

Ecologies Communities of plants and animals in an environment that supply raw materials for all living things.

Economic base In Marxist theory, the substructure of the society is the relationship between owners and workers. Capitalists own the means of production and control technology and resources. The workers are employed by the capitalists, and they are alienated, exploited, and estranged from their work and their society.

Economic sanctions A tool of statecraft that seeks to get a state to behave by coercion of a monetary kind, for example, freeing banking assets, cutting aid programs, or banning trade.

Ecosystem A system of interdependent living organisms that share the same habitat, functioning together with all of the physical factors of the environment. Ecosystems can be permanent or temporary. The Convention on Biological Diversity (CBD)—ratified by more than 175 countries—defines the protection of ecosystems as natural habitats and the maintenance of viable populations of species in natural surroundings.

Ecotopian Someone who believes in protecting and preserving the environment and promotes progressive political goals that promote environmental sustainability, social justice, and economic well-being.

Electronic commerce The buying and selling of products and services over the telephone or Internet. eBay and Amazon are examples of leaders in this area of commerce.

Embedded liberalism A liberal international economic order based on the pursuit of free trade but allowing an appropriate role for state intervention in the market in support of national security and national and global stability.

Empire A distinct type of political entity, which might or might not be a state, possessing both a home territory and foreign territories. This could include conquered nations and colonies.

Enlightenment Associated with rationalist thinkers of the eighteenth century. Key ideas (which some would argue remain mottoes for our age) include secularism, progress, reason, science, knowledge, and freedom. The motto of the Enlightenment is *"Sapere aude!"* (Have courage to know!) (Kant 1991, 54).

Ethic of responsibility For historical realists, an ethic of responsibility represents the limits of ethics in international politics; it involves the weighing up of consequences and the realization that positive outcomes may result from amoral actions.

European Union (EU) The EU was formally created in 1992 following the signing of the Maastricht Treaty. However, the origins of the EU can be traced back to 1951 and the creation of the European Coal and Steel Community, followed in 1957 with a broader customs union (the Treaty of Rome, 1958). Originally a grouping of six countries in 1957, "Europe" grew by adding new members in 1973, 1981, and 1986. Since the fall of the planned economies in Eastern Europe in 1989, Europe has grown and now includes twenty-seven member states.

Export-led growth An outward-oriented economy that is based on exploiting its own comparative advantages, such as cheap labor or resources, to capture a share of the world market in a given industry. Many of the countries in Asia took advantage of cheap labor to gain control of industries like electronics and textiles and thereby to control most of the exports to the world.

Failed (or fragile) state A state that does not command the primary loyalty of its citizens or subjects. These states have no monopoly of force at

home and lack complete control over their own territory.

Feminism A political project to understand so as to change women's inequality, liberation, or oppression. For some, the aim is to move beyond gender, so that it no longer matters; for others, to validate women's interests, experiences, and choices; for others, to work for more equal and inclusive social relations overall. Feminist theories tend to be critical of the biases of the discipline. Many focus their research on the areas where women are excluded from the analysis of major international issues and concerns.

Foreign policy The articulation of national interests and the means chosen to secure those interests, both material and ideational, in the international arena.

Foreign policy style Often shaped by a state's political culture, history, and traditions, this describes how a country deals with other states and how it approaches any decision-making situation. For example, does it act unilaterally or multilaterally; does it seek consensus on an agreement or does it go with majority rule?

Foreign policy tradition A tradition includes national beliefs about how the world works and a list of national interests and priorities based on these beliefs. It also refers to past actions or significant historical events that act as analogs and give guidance to leaders about what strategy would best secure their national interests.

Formulation phase of policy making When government officials design the programs that will implement the foreign policy goals of their state.

Fourteen Points President Woodrow Wilson's vision of international society, first articulated in January 1918, included the principle of self-determination, the conduct of diplomacy on an open (not secret) basis, and the establishment of an association of nation-states to provide guarantees of independence and territorial integrity. Wilson's ideas exerted an important influence on the Paris Peace Conference, although the principle of self-determination was only selectively pursued when it came to American colonial interests.

Free market A market ruled by the forces of supply and demand, where buying and selling are not constrained by government regulations or interventions.

Free trade An essential element of capitalism that argues for no barriers or minimal barriers to the exchange of goods, services, and investments between states.

G-8 (Group of Eight) Established in 1975 as the G-5 (France, Germany, Japan, the United Kingdom, and the United States); subsequently expanded as the G-7 to include Canada and Italy; and since 1998 the G-8, to include the Russian Federation. The G-8 conducts semiformal collaboration on world economic problems. Government leaders meet in annual G-8 summits, and finance ministers or their leading officials periodically hold other consultations. See further www.g8online.org.

G-20 (Group of Twenty) Established in 1999, the G-20 is a major forum that promotes cooperation in economic and financial policy areas. The G-20 brings together finance ministers and central bank governors from nineteen countries: Argentina, Australia, Brazil, Canada, China, France, Germany, India, Indonesia, Italy, Japan, the Republic of Korea, Mexico, Russia, Saudi Arabia, South Africa, Turkey, the United Kingdom, and the United States of America plus the European Union, which is represented by the President of the European Council and by the head of the European Central Bank.

Game theory A branch of mathematics that explores strategic interaction.

Genocide Deliberate and systematic extermination of an ethnic, national, tribal, or religious group.

Glasnost Policy of greater openness pursued by Soviet leader Mikhail Gorbachev beginning in 1985, involving greater toleration of internal dissent and criticism.

Global capital markets These are banks, investment companies, insurance companies, trusts, hedge funds, and stock exchanges that transfer funds to industries and other commercial enterprises globally.

Global commons Areas and resources not under national sovereignty that belong to no single country and are the responsibility of the entire world. The oceans beyond the 200-mile limit, outer space, and Antarctica are global commons areas.

Global environmental governance Governance is the performance of regulative functions, often in the absence of a central government authority. Global environmental governance usually refers to the structure of international agreements and organizations but can also involve governance by the private sector or NGOs.

Global goods Products that are made for a global market and are available across the world.

Global governance Involves the regulation and coordination of transnational issue areas by nation-states, international and regional organizations, and private agencies through the establishment of international regimes. These regimes might focus on problem solving or the simple enforcement of rules and regulations.

Globalization A historical process involving a fundamental shift or transformation in the spatial scale of human social organization that links distant communities and expands the reach of power relations across regions and continents.

Global politics The politics of global social relations in which the pursuit of power, interests, order, and justice transcends regions and continents.

Global polity The collective structures and processes by which "interests are articulated and aggregated, decisions are made, values allocated and policies conducted through international or transnational political processes" (Ougaard 2004, 5).

Global sourcing Obtaining goods and services across geopolitical boundaries. Usually the goal is to find the least expensive labor and raw material costs and the lowest taxes and tariffs.

Government The people and agencies that have the power and legitimate authority to determine who gets what, when, where, and how within a given territory.

Great Depression A byword for the global economic collapse that ensued following the US Wall Street stock market crash in October 1929. Economic shockwaves soon rippled around a world already densely interconnected by webs of trade and foreign direct investment, with the result that the events of October 1929 were felt in countries as distant as Brazil and Japan.

Great power State that has the political, economic, and military resources to shape the world beyond its borders. In most cases such a state has the will and capacity to define the rules of the international system.

Greenhouse effect The trapping of the sun's warmth in the earth's lower atmosphere because of gases that act like the glass of a greenhouse.

Gross domestic product (GDP) The sum of all economic activity that takes place within a country.

Hard power The material threats and inducements leaders employ to achieve the goals of their state.

Hegemony A system regulated by a dominant leader, or political (and/or economic) domination of a region, usually by a superpower. It is also means power and control exercised by a leading state over other states.

Historical versus social scientific approaches to research Two of the methods that international relations scholars use as tools to analyze events.

Holocaust The term used to describe the attempts by the Nazis to murder the Jewish population of Europe. Some 6 million Jewish people were killed in concentration camps, along with a further 1 million that included Soviet prisoners, Roma, Poles, communists, homosexuals, and the physically or mentally disabled.

Human development The notion that it is possible to improve the lives of people. Basically, it is about increasing the number of choices people have. These might include living a long and healthy life, access to education, and a better standard of living.

Humanitarian intervention The use of military force by external actors to end a threat to people within a sovereign state.

Human security The security of people, including their physical safety, their economic and social well-being, respect for their dignity, and the protection of their human rights. Simply put, it is freedom from fear and freedom from want.

Hyperpower A term meant to describe the situation of the United States after the Cold War ended. With the Soviet Union's military might greatly diminished and China having primarily only regional power-projecting capability, the United States was unchallenged in the world.

Idealism Referred to by realists as utopianism because it underestimates the logic of power politics and the constraints this imposes on political action. Idealism as a substantive theory of international relations is generally associated with the claim that it is possible to create a world of peace. Some idealists seek to apply liberal thinking in domestic politics to international relations—in other words, to institutionalize the rule of law.

Ideational This refers to ideas like democracy, capitalism, peace, and social justice.

Ideational/ideal interest The psychological, moral, and ethical goals of a state as it sets foreign and domestic policy.

Identity The understanding of the self in relationship to an "other." Identities are social and thus always formed in relationship to others. Constructivists generally hold that identities shape interests; we cannot know what we want unless we know who we are. But because identities are social and produced through interactions, identities can change.

Imperialism The practice of foreign conquest and rule in the context of global relations of hierarchy and subordination. It can lead to the establishment of an empire.

Individual level of analysis The beliefs, personality factors, images, and perceptions that also shape how government officials make decisions.

Intellectual property rights Rules that protect the owners of content through copyright, patents, trademarks, and trade secrets. The World Intellectual Property Organization (WIPO) is the forum where states (184 members in 2010) discuss this issue.

Intercontinental ballistic missiles (ICBMs) Weapons system the United States and USSR developed to threaten each other with destruction. The thirty- to forty-minute flight times of the missiles created a situation that is sometimes called mutually assured destruction (MAD) or the balance of terror.

Interdependence A condition where states (or peoples) are affected by decisions taken by others. Interdependence can be symmetric (i.e., both sets of actors are affected equally) or it can be asymmetric, where the impact varies between actors. If political or economic costs of interdependence are high, a state is in a vulnerable position. If costs are low, it is a situation of sensitivity interdependence.

Intergovernmental organization (IGO) An organization whose members are not states, such as the United Nations, NATO, the European Union, the World Trade Organization, the International Monetary Fund, and the Arctic Council.

International Court of Justice (ICJ) The main judicial organ of the United Nations, consisting jointly of fifteen judges elected by the General Assembly and Security Council. The ICJ handles disputes between states, and although a state does not have to participate in a case, if it elects to do so it must obey the decision.

International Criminal Court (ICC) The first permanent, treaty-based, international criminal court, established to help end impunity for the perpetrators of the most serious crimes of concern to the international community.

International law The formal rules of conduct that states acknowledge or contract between themselves.

International order The normative and the institutional pattern in the relationship between states. The elements of this could be thought to include such things as sovereignty, the forms of diplomacy, international law, the role of the great powers, and the codes circumscribing the use of force. It is a shared value and condition of stability and predictability in the relations of states.

International organization Any institution with formal procedures and formal membership from three or more countries. The minimum number of countries is set at three, rather than two, because multilateral relationships have significantly greater complexity than bilateral relationships.

International relations In a traditional sense, this is the study of the interactions of states in the international system. It was initially considered a part of diplomatic history or political science. Today, departments of international relations include concentrations in international security, political economy, foreign policy, human rights, global governance, and environmental issues. The field now includes the study of other actors, including corporations and NGOs, and a wide variety of issues, such as culture, identity, and ethics.

Interparadigm debate This is the debate between the two main theoretical approaches in the field of global politics, realism versus liberalism. Some present this debate as one between neorealism and neoliberalism. Critics argue that this is no real debate because the two theoretical approaches share many assumptions.

Intervention Direct involvement within a state by an outside actor to achieve an outcome preferred by the intervening agency without the consent of the host state.

Intrafirm trade International trade from one branch of a TNC to an affiliate of the same company in a different country.

Intransigent foreign policy A foreign policy that challenges the rules established by the great powers or rule-making states.

Jihad In Arabic, *jihad* simply means "struggle." Jihad can refer to a purely internal struggle to be a better Muslim or a struggle to make society more closely align with the teachings of the Koran.

League of Nations The first permanent collective international security organization aimed at preventing future wars and resolving global problems. The League failed because of the failure of the United States to join and the inability of its members to commit to a real international community.

Legitimacy A legitimate authority is respected and recognized by those it rules and by other rulers or leaders of other states. The source of legitimacy

can be laws or a constitution and the support of the society.

Levels of analysis Analysts of global politics can examine factors at various levels—such as individual, domestic, systemic, and global—to explain actions and events. Each level provides possible explanations on a different scale.

Liberal Account of Rights The belief that humans have inherent rights that the state has a responsibility to protect.

Liberal democracy States with democratic or representative governments and capitalist economies that are promoters of multilateralism and free trade. Domestic interests, values, and institutions shape foreign policy.

Liberal feminism A position that advocates equal rights for women but also supports a more progressive policy agenda that would include social justice, peace, economic well-being, and ecological balance.

Liberal internationalism A perspective that seeks to transform international relations to emphasize peace, individual freedom, and prosperity and to replicate domestic models of liberal democracy at the international level.

Liberalism According to Michael Doyle (1997, 207), liberalism includes the following four claims. First, all citizens are juridically equal and have equal rights to education, access to a free press, and religious toleration. Second, the legislative assembly of the state possesses only the authority invested in it by the people, whose basic rights it is not permitted to abuse. Third, a key dimension of the liberty of the individual is the right to own property, including productive forces. Fourth, liberalism contends that the most effective system of economic exchange is one that is largely market driven and not subordinate to bureaucratic regulation and control.

Liberalism of privilege Developed democratic states have a responsibility to spread liberal values for the benefit of all peoples of the earth.

Liberalization Describes government policies that reduce the role of the state in the economy, such as the dismantling of trade tariffs and barriers, the deregulation and opening of the financial sector to foreign investors, and the privatization of state enterprises.

Market democracy See Liberal democracy.

Marshall Plan Officially known as the European Recovery Program, it was a program of financial and other economic aid for Europe after World War II. Proposed by Secretary of State George Marshall in 1948, it was offered to all European states, including the Soviet Union, and these funds played a critical role in European recovery.

Marxism A theory critical of the status quo or dominant paradigm. It is a critique of the capitalist political economy from the view of the revolutionary proletariat, or workers. The relations of production, or the relationship between workers and owners, is the determining factor in political relations. Marxists believe that those who own the means of production also control the political system. In capitalist systems, workers are exploited and thus alienated from both the economic and the political systems. Marxists' ideal is a stateless and classless society.

Material This refers to things that we can see, measure, consume, and use, such as military forces, oil, and currency.

Material interest The tangible physical goals of state officials as they set foreign and domestic policy.

Materialism In this context materialism means the spreading of a global consumer culture and popular-culture artifacts like music, books, and movies. Christopher Lasch called this the "ceaseless translation of luxuries into necessities." These elements are seen as undermining traditional cultural values and norms.

Middle powers These states, because of their position and past roles in international affairs, have very distinctive interests in the future order. Middle powers are activists in international and regional forums, and they are confirmed multilateralists in most issue areas. They support an equitable and pluralistic rule-based system. They are, for the most part, trading states and thus favor a relatively open and stable world market. Because stability is so important to them, most middle powers see themselves as global problem solvers, mediators, and moderators in international disputes (Holbraad 1984; Wood 1998).

Modernization theory A theory that considers development synonymous with economic growth within the context of a free market international economy.

Monopoly capitalism A term introduced by Lenin that suggested that competitive capitalism had been replaced by large corporations that control the market in specific sectors.

Most favored nation status This is the status granted to most trading partners that says trade rules with

that country will be the same as those given to a country's most favored trading partner.

Multilateralism The process by which states work together to solve a common problem.

Multinational corporation or enterprise (MNC/ MNE) A business or firm with administration, production, distribution, and marketing located in countries around the world. Such a business moves money, goods, services, and technology around the world depending on where the firm can make the most profit.

Nation A community of people who share a common sense of identity, which may be derived from language, culture, or ethnicity; this community might be a minority within a single country or live in more than one country.

National interests The combination of material and ideal goals that comprise the goals of the government of a state.

National level of analysis The attributes that comprise what is unique about a state and therefore influence decision making. These might be natural resources, economic factors, population size, or the kind of political system.

National security A fundamental value in the foreign policy of states, secured by a variety of tools of statecraft including military actions, diplomacy, economic resources, and international agreements and alliances. It also depends on a stable and productive domestic society.

Natural law The idea that humans have an essential nature, which dictates that certain kinds of human goods are always and everywhere desired; because of this, there are common moral standards that govern all human relations, and these common standards can be discerned by the application of reason to human affairs.

Neoliberalism Shaped by the ideas of commercial, republican, sociological, and institutional liberalism. Neoliberals see the international system as anarchic but believe relations can be managed by the establishment of international regimes and institutions. Neoliberals think that actors with common interests will try to maximize absolute gains.

New wars Wars of identity between different ethnic communities or nations and wars that are caused by the collapse of states or the fragmentation of multiethnic states. Most of these new wars are internal or civil wars.

Niche diplomacy Every state has its national interests and its areas of comparative advantage over other international actors. This is its area of expertise and where it has the greatest interests. Hence, this is where the state concentrates its foreign policy resources.

Noncompliance The failure of states or other actors to abide by treaties or rules supported by international regimes.

Nongovernmental organization (NGO) An organization, usually a grass-roots one, with policy goals, but not governmental in makeup. An NGO is any group of people relating to each other regularly in some formal manner and engaging in collective action, provided the activities are noncommercial and nonviolent and are not on behalf of a government.

Nonintervention The principle that external powers should not intervene in the domestic affairs of sovereign states.

Non-nuclear weapon state (NNWS) A state that is party to the Treaty on the Nonproliferation of Nuclear Weapons, meaning that it does not possess nuclear weapons.

Nonpolar world A world in which there are many power centers and many of them are not nation-states. Power is diffused and is in many hands in many policy areas.

Nonstate actor Any participant in global politics that is neither acting in the name of government nor created and served by government. NGOs, terrorist networks, global crime syndicates, and multinational corporations are examples.

Normative orientation In foreign policy this means promoting certain norms and values and being prescriptive in one's foreign policy goals.

Norms These specify general standards of behavior and identify the rights and obligations of states. Together, norms and principles define the essential character of a regime, and these cannot be changed without transforming the nature of the regime.

North Atlantic Treaty Organization (NATO) Organization established by treaty in April 1949 including twelve (later sixteen) countries from Western Europe and North America. The most important aspect of the NATO alliance was the US commitment to the defense of Western Europe. Today NATO has twenty-eight member states.

Nuclear deterrence Defined by nuclear strategists as the possession of sufficient power to inflict unacceptable damage on a potential adversary. Nuclear deterrence must involve explicit threats to effectively prevent a state from using weapons. These threats must be seen as credible and must be clearly communicated.

Nuclear terrorism The use of or threat to use nuclear weapons or nuclear materials to achieve the goals of rogue states or revolutionary or radical organizations.

Nuclear weapon state (NWS) A state that is party to the Nonproliferation Treaty and has tested a nuclear weapon or other nuclear explosive device before January 1, 1967.

Offensive realism A structural theory of realism that views states as security maximizers.

Oligarchs A term from ancient Greece to describe a political system in which a few people control a state.

Organization of African Unity (OAU) A regional organization founded in 1963 and replaced in 2002 by the African Union. The OAU had a policy of noninterference in member states, and it had no means for intervening in conflicts; as a result, this organization was only a passive bystander in many violent conflicts.

Organization of American States (OAS) A regional international organization including thirty-five member states. It is the world's oldest regional organization, founded in 1890 as the International Union of American Republics (changing its name to OAS in 1948). Its goals are to create "an order of peace and justice, to promote their solidarity; to strengthen their collaboration; and to defend their sovereignty, their territorial integrity, and their independence."

Ostpolitik The West German government's "Eastern Policy" of the mid- to late 1960s, designed to develop relations between West Germany and members of the Warsaw Pact.

Paradigm A model, or example. In the case of international relations theory, the term is a rough synonym for "academic perspective." A paradigm provides the essential basis for a theory. It presents a comprehensive framework for the identification of factors that are referenced in the construction of theory. It tells us what is real and significant in a given area. Research questions fall within the paradigm. It provides a means of selecting what will be the object of theory.

Paradox An absurd or self-contradictory statement.

Peace enforcement Designed to bring hostile parties to agreement and may occur without the consent of the parties.

Peace of Utrecht, 1713 The agreement that ended the War of the Spanish Succession and helped to consolidate the link between sovereign authority and territorial boundaries in Europe. This treaty refined the territorial scope of sovereign rights of states.

Peace of Westphalia, 1648 The treaties of Osnabrück and Münster, which together form the Peace of Westphalia, ended the Thirty Years' War and were crucial in delimiting the political rights and authority of European monarchs.

Peacekeeping The interposition of third-party military personnel to keep warring parties apart.

Peacemaking Active diplomatic efforts to seek a resolution to an international dispute that has already escalated.

Perestroika Gorbachev's policy of restructuring, pursued in tandem with glasnost, and intended to modernize the Soviet political and economic system.

Pluralism The political theory of pluralism holds that political power and influence in society do not belong just to the citizens, nor to elite groups in various sectors of society, but are distributed among a wide number of groups in the society. It can also mean a recognition of ethnic, racial, and cultural diversity.

Political-economy approach The study of the interactions between states or public actors and the market at domestic and international levels.

Positivism and postpositivism Positivists (social scientists) and postpositivists (critical and constitutive theorists) form the basis for fierce debates among scholars. At the core lies a disagreement about whether social science theory can be value free. Positivists believe we can explain the social world as effectively as natural and physical scientists explain their phenomena. Postpositivists believe we cannot possibly be objective—value free—observers because we are actively or passively a part of the events and issues unfolding before us.

Positivists Analysts who use the scientific method to structure their research.

Postconflict peace building Activities launched after a conflict has ended that seek to end the condition that caused the conflict.

Postmodern or new terrorists Groups and individuals subscribing to millennial and apocalyptic ideologies and system-level goals. Most value destruction for its own sake, unlike most terrorists in the past, who had specific goals, usually tied to a territory.

Postmodernity The postmodern international system is one where domestic and international affairs are intertwined, national borders are permeable, and states have rejected the use of force for resolving conflict. The European Union is seen as an example of the evolution of the state-centric system (R. Cooper 2003).

Post–Washington Consensus A slightly modified version of the Washington Consensus, promoting economic growth through trade liberalization coupled with pro–poor growth and poverty-reduction policies.

Poverty In the orthodox view, a situation suffered by people who do not have the *money to buy food* and satisfy other basic *material needs*. In the alternative view, a situation suffered by people who are not able to meet their *material and nonmaterial needs* through their own effort.

Power This is a contested concept. Nye (2011) states that power is the capacity to do things and, in social and political situations, to affect others to get the outcome one wants. Sources of power include material or tangible resources and control over meaning or ideas.

Preservative strategy A foreign policy that seeks to keep an existing international order in place.

Preventive diplomacy Measures that states take to keep a disagreement from escalating.

Problem-solving theory Realism and liberalism are problem-solving theories that address issues and questions within the dominant paradigm or the present system. How can we fix capitalism? How can we make a society more democratic? These are problem-solving questions that assume nothing is wrong with the core elements of the system.

Promotive foreign policy A foreign policy that promotes the values and interests of a state and seeks to create an international system based on these values.

Protectionism Not an economic policy but a variety of political actions taken to protect domestic industries from more efficient foreign producers. Usually this means the use of tariffs, non-tariff barriers, and subsidies to protect domestic interests.

Protestant Reformation A social movement in reaction to the widespread perception that the Catholic Church had become corrupt and had lost its moral compass.

Public diplomacy The use of media, the Internet, and other social culture outlets to communicate the message of a state.

Radical liberalism This is the utopian side of liberalism best exemplified by the academic community called the World Order Models Project (WOMP). These scholars advocate a world in which states promote values like social justice, economic well-being, peace, and ecological balance. Radical-liberal scholars see the liberal order as predatory and clearly in need of transformation.

Rapprochement Reestablishment of more friendly relations between the People's Republic of China and the United States in the early 1970s.

Rational choice The idea that decision makers will always act as value maximizers and thus a state's actions are based on rational calculations in which policy options are assessed and valued.

Realism The theoretical approach that analyzes all international relations as the relation of states engaged in the pursuit of power. Realists see the international system as anarchic or without a common power, and they believe conflict is endemic in the international system.

Reciprocity A form of statecraft that employs retaliatory strategy, only cooperating if others do likewise.

Regimes Sets of implicit or explicit principles, norms, rules, and decision-making procedures around which actors' expectations converge in a given area of international relations. Often simply defined as governing arrangements in a regional or global policy area.

Regional diversity Each region of the world has experienced economic development differently based on traditions, culture, historical development, and even geographic location.

Relative gains One of the factors that realists argue constrain the willingness of states to cooperate. States are less concerned about whether everyone benefits (absolute gains) and more concerned about whether someone might benefit more than someone else.

Responsibility to Protect Resolution (R2P) The 2001 final report of the International Commission on Intervention and State Sovereignty; a UN publication that asserted the moral obligation for states to intervene in a state when that state violates the human rights of people living there.

Revolution in military affairs (RMA) This is the effect generated by the marriage of advanced communications and information processing with state-of-the-art weapons and delivery systems. It is a means of overcoming the uncertainty and confusion that are part of any battle in war.

Risk culture A pattern of relations within which people share the same perils.

Security Measures taken by states to ensure the safety of their citizens, the protection of their way of life, and the survival of their nation-state. Security can also mean the ownership of property that gives an individual the ability to secure the enjoyment or enforcement of a right or a basic human need.

Security community A regional group of countries that have the same guiding philosophic ideals—usually liberal-democratic principles, norms, and ethics—and tend to have the same style of political systems.

Security dilemma In an anarchic international system, one with no common central power, when one state seeks to improve its security it creates insecurity in other states.

September 11, 2001 The day when Islamic terrorists in the United States hijacked four aircraft—two of which destroyed the World Trade Center in New York, one that partially destroyed the Pentagon, and a fourth that crash-landed in a field in Pennsylvania (also called 9/11).

Sex and gender Sex is the biological difference, born male or female; sexual difference. Gender is what it means to be male or female in a particular place or time; the social construction of sexual difference.

Skyjacking The takeover of a commercial airplane for the purpose of taking hostages and using these hostages to bargain for a particular political or economic goal.

Social movement People with a diffuse sense of collective identity, solidarity, and common purpose that usually leads to collective political behavior. The concept covers all the different NGOs and networks, plus all their members and all the other individuals who share the common value(s). Thus, the women's movement and the environmental movement are much more than the specific NGOs that provide leadership and focus the desire for social change.

Society of states An association of sovereign states based on their common interests, values, and norms.

Soft power A concept developed by Joseph Nye to describe influence and authority deriving from the attraction that a country's political, social, and economic ideas, beliefs, and practices have for people living in other countries.

Sovereign equality The idea that all countries have the same rights, including the right of noninterference in their internal affairs.

Sovereignty The condition of a state having control and authority over its own territory and being free from any higher legal authority. It is related to, but distinct from, the condition of a government being free from any external political constraints.

Standard operating procedures (SOPs) The prepared-response patterns that organizations create to react to general categories of events, crises, and actions.

Standards of civilization A nineteenth-century European discourse about which values and norms made a country "civilized" or "barbaric" and "uncivilized." The conclusion was that civilized countries should colonize barbaric regions for the latter's benefit.

State A legal territorial entity composed of a stable population and a government; it possesses a monopoly over the legitimate use of force; its sovereignty is recognized by other states in the international system.

Statecraft The methods and tools that national leaders use to achieve the national interests of a state.

State sovereignty The concept that all countries are equal under international law and that they are protected from outside interference; this is the basis on which the UN and other international and regional organizations operate.

Strategic Arms Reductions Treaty (START) Negotiations began in 1982 and progressed at a very slow pace over eight years. The United States and the USSR debated these issues in twelve rounds of formal negotiations, thirteen foreign ministers' meetings, and six summit conferences. In May 1990, George H. W. Bush and Gorbachev agreed to a framework for arms reduction. A treaty was signed in Moscow in July 1991. This treaty reversed a forty-five-year-old strategic nuclear arms race. The treaty broke new ground because it called for a reduction of nuclear arms rather than just a limit on the growth of these weapons.

Strategic Defense Initiative (SDI) A controversial strategic policy advocated by some conservative politicians and nuclear physicists, such as Edward Teller, who helped to create the hydrogen bomb. SDI was embraced by the Reagan administration. The plan called for a defensive missile shield that would make Soviet offensive missiles ineffective by destroying them in flight. This defensive posture was to replace the US strategy of mutually assured destruction. Reagan wanted to make nuclear weapons impotent and obsolete. The plan is often derisively called "Star Wars," after the movies that were popular at the time.

Summit diplomacy A direct meeting between heads of government (of the superpowers in particular) to resolve major problems. The "summit" became a regular mode of contact during the Cold War.

Superstructure In Marxist theory, this is the government or political structure that is controlled by those who own the means of production.

Supranational global organization An authoritative international organization that operates above the national state.

Supraterratoriality Social, economic, cultural, and political connections that transcend territorial geography.

Survival In this context it is the survival of the person by the provision of adequate food, clean water, clothing, shelter, medical care, and protection from violence and crime.

Sustainable development This has been defined as development that meets the needs of the present without compromising the ability of future generations to meet their own needs.

Systemic level of analysis Refers to the system created by the interactions of nation-states. Factors such as the distribution of power (e.g., bipolarity or unipolarity) and the nature of order (e.g., anarchy or regional governance) as well as treaties, obligations, and shared norms and traditions shape the international system and thus influence national decision makers.

Technology transfer The process of sharing skills, knowledge, technologies, methods of manufacturing, and facilities among governments and private actors (like corporations) to ensure that scientific and technological developments are accessible to a wider range of users for application in new products, processes, materials, or services.

Terrorism The use of violence by nonstate groups or, in some cases, states to inspire fear, by attacking civilians or symbolic targets and eliminating opposition groups. This is done for purposes such as drawing widespread attention to a grievance, provoking a severe response, or wearing down an opponent's moral resolve to effect political change.

Theocracy A state based on religion.

Theory A proposed explanation of an event or behavior of an actor in the real world. Definitions range from "an unproven assumption" to "a working hypothesis that proposes an explanation for an action or behavior." In international relations we have intuitive theories, empirical theories, and normative theories.

Third-tier states Sometimes called the "less-developed states" or the "premodern states." These countries fail to provide the basics, such as border protection, law and order, and maintenance of a functioning economy.

Thirty Years' War The last of the great wars in Europe nominally for religion. Some historians believe that political leaders cynically used religious differences as an excuse to extend their kingdoms.

Trade liberalization The removal or reduction of barriers to free trade such as tariffs or quotas on the trading of specific goods.

Transborder Economic, political, social, or cultural activities crossing borders.

Transnational actor Any nongovernmental actor, such as a multinational corporation or one country's religious humanitarian organization, that has relations with any actor from another country or with an international organization.

Transnational corporation Λ company or business that has affiliates in different countries.

Transnational nonstate actor Any nonstate or nongovernmental actor from one country that has relations with any actor from another country or with an international organization.

Treaty of Versailles, 1919 The Treaty of Versailles formally ended World War I (1914–1918). The treaty established the League of Nations, specified the rights and obligations of the victorious and defeated powers (including the notorious regime of reparations on Germany), and created the "Mandate" system under which "advanced nation-states" were given legal tutelage over colonial peoples.

Trench warfare From 1914 to 1918 the two sides in the war dug elaborate defensive fortifications in the ground. Because of the power of weapons like machine guns and rapid-fire cannons, trenches often gave the advantage in battle to the defenders.

Truman Doctrine Statement made by US President Harry Truman in March 1947 that it "must be the policy of the United States to support free people who are resisting attempted subjugation by armed minorities or by outside pressures." Intended to persuade Congress to support limited aid to Turkey and Greece, the doctrine came to underpin the policy of containment and American economic and political support for its allies.

United Nations (UN) Founded in 1945 following World War II, the United Nations is an international organization made up of 193 member states dedicated to addressing issues related to peace and security, development, human rights, humanitarian affairs, and international law.

United Nations Charter (1945) The charter of the United Nations is the legal regime that created the United Nations as the world's only "supranational" organization. The charter defines the structure of the United Nations, the powers of its constitutive agencies, and the rights and obligations of sovereign states party to the charter. Among other things, the charter is the key legal document limiting the use of force to instances of self-defense and collective peace enforcement endorsed by the United Nations Security Council.

United Nations Economic and Social Council (ECOSOC) This council is intended to coordinate the economic and social work of the United Nations and the UN family of organizations. The ESOSOC has a direct link to civil society through communications with nongovernmental organizations.

United Nations General Assembly Often referred to as a "parliament of nations," the General Assembly is composed of all member states and meets to consider the world's most pressing problems. Each state has one vote, and a two-thirds majority is required for decisions on key issues. Decisions reached by the General Assembly only have the status of recommendations and are not binding decisions.

United Nations Secretariat The Secretariat carries out the administrative work of the United Nations as directed by the General Assembly, the Security Council, and other organs. The Secretariat is led by the secretary-general, who provides overall administrative guidance.

United Nations Security Council The council is made up of five permanent member states (sometimes called the P-5)—Great Britain, China, France, Russia, and the United States—and ten nonpermanent members. The P-5 all have veto power over all Security Council decisions.

United Nations Trusteeship Council On creation of the United Nations, this council was established to provide international supervision for eleven trust territories administered by seven states in an effort to prepare them for self-government or independence. By 1994, all trust territories had attained self-government or independence, and the council now meets on an ad hoc basis.

Universal Declaration of Human Rights The principal normative document on human rights, adopted by the UN General Assembly in 1948 and accepted as authoritative by most states and other international actors. It asserts that all human beings are inherently entitled to a certain set of universal rights.

Veto power The right of the five permanent members of the Security Council (United States, Russia, China, France, and Great Britain) to forbid any action by the United Nations.

Warsaw Pact The Warsaw Pact was created in May 1955 in response to West Germany's rearmament and entry into NATO. It included the USSR and seven communist states (although Albania withdrew support in 1961). The organization was officially dissolved in July 1991.

Washington Consensus The belief of key opinion-formers in Washington that global welfare would be maximized by the universal application of neoclassical economic policies that favor a minimalist state and an enhanced role for the market.

Weapons of mass destruction A category defined by the United Nations in 1948 to include "atomic explosive weapons, radioactive material weapons, lethal chemical and biological weapons, and any weapons developed in the future which have characteristics comparable in destructive effects to those of the atomic bomb or other weapons mentioned above."

Widening school of international security Sometimes called the Copenhagen School, this refers to authors who extend the definition of security to include economic, political, societal, and environmental policy areas.

World Bank Group A collection of five agencies, the first established in 1945, with head offices in Washington, DC. The WBG promotes development in medium- and low-income countries with project loans, structural-adjustment programs, and various advisory services.

World order This is a wider category of order than the "international." It takes as its units of order not states, but individual human beings, and assesses the degree of order on the basis of the delivery of certain kinds of goods (be they security, human rights, basic needs, or justice) for humanity as a whole.

World-system theory A theory emphasizing that world systems, and not individuals or states, should be the basic unit of analysis. Thus, the political and economic structure of the world shapes global politics. World system refers to the international division of labor, which divides the world into core countries, semiperiphery countries, and periphery countries. The foreign policies of these states are shaped by their position in the global system.

World Trade Organization (WTO) Established in 1995 with headquarters in Geneva. Membership (2010) of 153 states. The WTO is a permanent institution to replace the provisional GATT. It has a wider agenda, covering services, intellectual property, and investment issues as well as merchandise trade. The WTO also has greater powers of enforcement through its dispute-settlement mechanism. The organization's Trade Policy Review Body conducts surveillance of members' commercial measures.

Zero-sum game Part of game theory, a situation in which one participant's gain is equal to another's loss; thus, when the total gains are added and the total losses subtracted, the sum comes to zero. It describes a strictly competitive system.

Zero-sum world A pessimistic view of any interaction that suggests that another's gains are your losses.

References

Acharya, A. 2004. A holistic paradigm. *Security Dialogue* 35:355–56.

——. 2007. *Promoting human security: Ethical, normative and educational frameworks in south east Asia*. Paris: United Nations Scientific, Cultural and Educational Organization.

Allison, G. 1971. The impact of globalization on national and international security. In *Governance in a globalizing world*, ed. J. S. Nye and J. D. Donahue, 72–85. Washington, DC: Brookings Institution.

——. 2000. The impact of globalization on national and international security. In *Governance in a globalizing world*, ed. J. S. Nye and J. D. Donahue, 72–85. Washington, DC: Brookings Institution.

Allison, G. T. (1971) *Essence of Decision: Explaining the Cuban Missile Crisis* (Boston, MA: Little Brown).

Almasmari, H. 2012. Suspected U.S. drone strike kills civilians in Yemen, officials say—CNN.com. Cable News Network. http://www.cnn.com/2012/09/03/world/meast/yemen-drone-strike/ (accessed September 14 2012).

Armstrong, D. 1993. *Revolution and world order: The revolutionary state in international society*. Oxford, UK: Clarendon.

Axworthy, L. 2003. *Navigting a new world*. Toronto: Alfred Knopf Canada.

Barnett, M., and R. Duvall. 2005. *Power in global governance*. Cambridge, UK: Cambridge University Press.

Beitz, C. 1979. *Political theory and international relations*. Princeton, NJ: Princeton University Press.

Bellamy, A. J. 2002. *Kosovo and international society*. Basingstoke, UK: Palgrave.

Bello, W. 1994. *Dark victory: The United States, structural adjustment and global poverty*. London: Pluto.

Bennett, J., and S. George. 1987. *The hunger machine*. Cambridge, UK: Polity.

Booth, K. 1999. Three tyrannies. In *Human rights in global politics*, ed. T. Dunne and N. J. Wheeler. Cambridge, UK: Cambridge University Press.

Booth, K., and T. Dunne. 1999. Learning beyond frontiers. In *human rights in global politics*, ed. T. Dunne and N. J. Wheeler, 303–28. Cambridge, UK: Cambridge University Press.

Braun, L. 1987. *Selected writings on feminism and socialism*. Bloomington: Indiana University Press.

Brewer, A. 1990. *Marxist theories of imperialism: A critical survey*, 2nd ed. London: Routledge.

Brocklehurst, H. 2007. Children and war. In *Contemporary security studies*, ed. A. Collins, 367–82. Oxford, UK: Oxford University Press.

Brodie, B., ed. 1946. *The absolute weapon: Atomic power and world order*. New York: Harcourt Brace.

Brown, D. 2006. Study claims Iraq's "excess" death toll has reached 655,000. *Washington Post* October 11:A12.

Brown, L. R., and H. Kane. 1995. *Full house: Reassessing the earth's population carrying capacity*. London: Earthscan.

Brundtland, G. H., et al. 1987. *Our common future: Report of the world commission on environment and development*. Oxford, UK: Oxford University Press.

Bull, H. 1977. *The anarchical society: A study of order in world politics*. London: Macmillan.

Buvinic, M. 1997. Women in poverty: A new global underclass. *Foreign Policy*: 38–53.

Buzan, B. 1991. *People, states, and fear: An agenda for international security studies in the post-Cold War era*. 2nd ed. Boulder, CO: Lynne Reinner.

Cammack, P. 2002. The mother of all governments: The World Bank's matrix for global governance. In *Global governance: Critical perspectives*, ed. R. Wilkinson and S. Hughes. London: Routledge.

Carr, E. H. 1939. 1946. *The twenty years' crisis 1919–1939: An introduction to the study of international relations*. 2nd ed. London: Macmillan.

Carson, R. 1962. *Silent spring*. Harmondsworth, UK: Penguin.

Castells, M. 2005. Global governance and global politics. *PS* (January):9–16.

Chairman of the Joint Chiefs of Staff. 2006. *National military strategic plan for the war on terrorism*. Washington, DC: Joint Chiefs of Staff.

Ching, F. 1999. Social impact of the regional financial crisis. In *The Asian economic crisis: Policy choices, social consequences and the Phillipine case*, ed. L. Y. C. Lim, F. Ching, and B. M. Villegas. New York: Asia Society. http://www.asiasociety.org/publications/update_crisis_ching.html (accessed June 25, 2007).

Clark, I. 1989. *The hierarchy of states: Reform and resistance in the international order*. Cambridge, UK: Cambridge University Press.

Coglianese, C. 2000. Globalization and the design of international institutions. In *Governance in a globalizing world*, ed. J. S. Nye and J. D. Donahue, 297–318. Washington, DC: Brookings Institution Press.

Cohn, C. 1987. Sex and death in the rational world of defense intellectuals. *Signs* 12(4):687–718.

Cooper, A., R. Higgott, and K. R. Nossal. 1993. *Relocating middle powers*. Vancouver, Canada: UBC Press.

Cooper, A. F. 2007. *Celebrity diplomacy*. Boulder: Paradigm.

Cooper, R. 2003. *The breaking of nations: Order and chaos in the 21st century*. New York: Atlantic Monthly Press.

Cox, R. 1989. Middlepowermanship, Japan, and the future world order. *International Journal* 44(4):823–62.

Cronin, A. K. 2002/3. Behind the curve: Globalization and international terrorism. *International Security* 27(3):30–58.

Department for International Development. 2005. *Fighting poverty to build a safer world*. London: HMSO. http://www.dfid.gov.uk/pubs (accessed June 25, 2007).

———. 2006. *Eliminating world poverty: Making governance work for the poor*. Cm 6876. London: HMSO. http://www.dfid.gov.uk/pubs (accessed June 25, 2007).

Doyle, M. W. 1986. Liberalism and world politics. *American Political Science Review* 80(4):1151–69.

———. 1997. *Ways of war and peace: Realism, liberalism, and socialism*. New York: Norton.

Easterly, W. 2002. How did heavily indebted poor countries become heavily indebted? Reviewing two decades of debt relief. *World Development* 30(10):1677–96.

Ekins, P. 1992. *A new world order: Grassroots movements for global change*. London: Routledge.

Falk, R. 1995a. Liberalism at the global level: The last of the independent commissions. *Millennium Special Issue: The Globalization of Liberalism?* 24(3):563–76.

———. 1995b. *On humane governance: Toward a new global politics*. Cambridge, UK: Polity.

Fausto-Sterling, A. 1992. *Myths of gender: Biological theories about women and men*. New York: Basic Books.

———. 2000. *Sexing the body: Gender politics and the construction of sexuality*. New York: Basic Books.

Finnemore, M. 1996. *National interests in international society*. Ithaca, NY: Cornell University Press.

Finnemore, M., and K. Sikkink. 1998. International norm dynamics and political change. *International Organization* 52(Oct.):887–918.

Finnis, J. 1980. *Natural law and natural rights*. Oxford, UK: Clarendon.

Fox-Keller, E. 1985. *Reflections on gender and science*. New Haven, CT: Yale University Press.

Frank, A. G. 1967. *Capitalism and underdevelopment in Latin America*. New York: Monthly Review Press.

Friedersdorf, C. 2012. Obama supporters know his drone war is indefensible. *The Atlantic* June 7.

Friedman, J., ed. 2003. *Globalization, the state and violence*. Oxford, UK: AltaMira Press.

Friedman, T. 2000. *The lexus and the olive tree: Understanding globalization*. New York: Anchor Books.

Gendering human security: From marginalisation to the integration of women in peace-building. 2001. Oslo: Norwegian Institute of International Affairs and Fafo Forum on Gender Relations in Post-Conflict Transitions. http://www.fafo.no/pub/rapp/352/352 .pdf (accessed June 25, 2007).

George, A. 1991. *Forceful persuasion*. Washington, DC: USIP.

Glendon, M. A. 2002. *A world made new: Eleanor Roosevelt and the Universal Declaration of Human Rights*. New York: Random House.

Gong, G. W. 1984. *The standard of 'civilization' in international society*. Oxford, UK: Clarendon.

Goodman, D., and M. Redclift. 1991. *Refashioning nature: Food, ecology and culture*. London: Routledge.

Gottlieb, R. S., ed. 1989. *An anthology of western Marxism: From Lukacs and Gramsci to socialist-feminism*. Oxford, UK: Oxford University Press.

Gray, C. S. 1996. The second nuclear age: Insecurity, proliferation, and the control of arms. In *The Brassey's Mershon American defense annual, 1995–1996: The United States and the emerging strategic environment*, ed. W. Murray, 135–54. Washington, DC: Brassey's.

Green, D. 1995. *Silent revolution: The rise of market economics in Latin America*. London: Latin America Bureau.

Haraway, D. 1989. *Primate visions: Gender, race, and nature in the world of modern science*. New York: Routledge.

———. 1991. *Symians, cyborgs and women: The re-invention of nature*. New York: Routledge.

Harrington, M. 1989. *Socialism past and future*. New York: Arcade.

Hartsock, N. 1998. *The feminist standpoint revisited and other essays*. Boulder, CO: Westview.

Hass, R. 2008. The age of nonpolarity. *Foreign Affairs* 44–66.

Henderson J., K. Jackson, and R. Kennaway, eds. 1980. *Beyond New Zealand: The foreign policy of a small state*. Auckland, NZ: Methuen.

Hennessy, R., and C. Ingraham, eds. 1997. *Materialist feminism: A reader in class, difference, and women's lives*. London: Routledge.

Hettne, B. 1999. Globalization and the new regionalism: The second great transformation. In *Globalism and the new regionalism*, ed. B. Hettne, A. Intoai, and O. Sunkel. Basingstoke, UK: Macmillan.

Higgins, R. 1994. *Problems and process: International law and how we use it*. Oxford, UK: Oxford University Press.

Hill, C. 2003. *The changing politics of foreign policy.* Basingstoke, UK: Palgrave Macmillan.

Hobbes, T. 1651. *Leviathan or the matter, forme, and power of a common wealth ecclesiasticall and civil.* Cambridge, UK: Cambridge University Press.

Holbraad, C. 1984. *Middle powers in international politics.* London: Macmillan.

Holsti, K. 1991. *Peace and war: Armed conflicts and international order 1648–1989.* Cambridge, UK: Cambridge University Press.

Humphreys, M., and A. Varshney. 2004. Violent conflict and the millennium development: Goals: Diagnosis and recommendations. CGSD Working Paper No. 19, Center on Globalization and Sustainable Development, The Earth Institute at Columbia University, New York. http://www.earthinstitute .columbia.edu/cgsd/documents/humphreys_conflict_ and_MDG.pdf (accessed June 25, 2007).

Huntington, S. 1993. The clash of civilizations. *Foreign Affairs* 72(3):22–169.

Hurrell, A. 2002. Norms and ethics in international relations. In *Handbook of international relations,* ed. W. Carlsnaes, T. Risse, and B. A. Simmons. London: Sage.

Hurrell, A., and N. Woods. 1995. Globalization and inequality. *Millennium: Journal of International Studies* 24(3):447–70.

Ingebritsen, C., I. Neumann, S. Gstohl, and J. Beyer. 2006. *Small states in international relations.* Seattle: University of Washington Press.

Intergovernmental Panel on Climate Change. 2007. *Climate change 2007: The physical science BASIS.* Contribution of Working Group 1 to the Fourth Assessment Report of the Intergovernmental Panel on Climate Change. www.ipcc.ch.

International Commission on Peace and Food. 1994. *Uncommon opportunities: An agenda for peace and equitable development.* London: Zed.

Jolly, R., and D. B. Ray. 2006. *National human development reports and the human security framework: A review of analysis and experience.* Brighton, UK: Institute of Development Studies.

Junaid, S. 2005. *Terrorism and global power systems.* Oxford, UK: Oxford University Press.

Kaldor, M. 1999. *New and old wars: Organized violence in a global era.* Cambridge, UK: Polity.

Kant, I. (1991), *Political Writings,* Hans Reiss (ed.) (Cambridge: Cambridge University Press).

Kennedy, P. 2006. *The parliament of man: The past, present, and future of the United Nations.* New York: Random House.

Keohane, R., ed. 1989a. *International institutions and state power: Essays in international relations theory.* Boulder, CO: Westview.

——. 1989b. Theory of world politics: Structural realism and beyond. In *International institutions and state power: Essays in international relations theory,* ed. R. Keohane. Boulder, CO: Westview.

Keohane, R., and J. Nye, eds. 1972. *Transnational relations and world politics.* Cambridge, MA: Harvard University Press.

Kissinger, H. A. 1977. *American foreign policy.* 3rd ed. New York: Norton.

Koehler, S. 2007. Professor explains continuous threat from land mines. *Ozarks Local News,* February7. http://www .banminesusa.org (accessed June 25, 2007).

Laqueur, W. 1996. Post-modern terrorism. *Foreign Affairs* 75(5):24–37.

Leventhal, P., and Y. Alexander, eds. 1987. *Preventing nuclear terrorism.* Lexington, MA: Lexington Books.

Lin, P. 2011. Drone-ethics briefing: What a leading robot expert told the CIA. *The Atlantic* December 15.

Little, R. 1996. The growing relevance of pluralism? In *International theory: Positivism and beyond,* ed. S. Smith, K. Booth, and M. Zalewski, 66–86. Cambridge, UK: Cambridge University Press.

Longino, H. E. 1990. *Science as social knowledge: Values and objectivity in scientific inquiry.* Princeton, NJ: Princeton University Press.

Luard, E., ed. 1992. *Basic texts in international relations.* London: Macmillan.

MacFarlane, N., and Y. F. Khong. 2006. *Human security and the UN: A critical history.* Bloomington: Indiana University Press.

Mackinnon, C. 1993. Crimes of war, crimes of peace. In *On human rights,* ed. S. Shute and S. Hurley. New York: Basic Books.

March of the robots. 2012. *The Economist* June 2.

Marx, K. 1967. *The communist manifesto,* with an introduction by A. J. P. Taylor. Harmondsworth, UK: Penguin.

——. 1992. *Capital: Student edition,* ed. C. J. Arthur. London: Lawrence & Wishart.

Marx, K., and Engels, F. (1848), *The Communist Manifesto,* intr. by E. Hobsbawm (London: Verso, 1998).

Meadows, D. H., D. L. Meadows, and J. Randers. 1972. *The limits to growth.* London: Earth Island.

Mearsheimer, J. 2001. *The tragedy of great power politics.* New York: Norton.

Metz, S. 2004. *Armed conflict in the 21st century: The information revolution and post modern warfare.* Honolulu, HI: University Press of the Pacific.

Milner, H. V. 1988. *Resisting protectionism: Global industries and the politics of international trade.* Princeton, NJ: Princeton University Press.

Mingst, K. 2004. *Essentials of international relations.* New York: Norton.

Morgenthau, H. J. [1948] 1955, 1962, 1978. *Politics among nations: The struggle for power and peace.* 2nd ed. New York: Knopf.

——. 1960. *Politics among nations.* New York: Knopf.

——. 1985. *Politics among nations.* 6th ed. New York: McGraw-Hill.

Mousseau, F., and A. Mittal. 2006. Free market famine: Foreign policy in focus commentary. www.fpif .org/pdf/gac/0610famine.pdf (accessed June 25, 2007).

Muldoon, J. P. 2004. *The architecture of global governance: An introduction to the study of international organizations.* Boulder, CO: Westview.

Naim, Moises. (2003). "Five Wars of Globalization." *Foreign Policy.* 1 January. http://www.foreignpolicy .com/articles/2003/01/01/five_wars_of_globalization.

Nardin, T. 1983. *Law, morality and the relations of states.* Princeton, NJ: Princeton University Press.

National Counterterrorism Center. 2005. *NCTC fact sheet and observations related to 2005 terrorist incidents.* www.NCTC.gov (accessed June 25, 2007).

Nye, J. S. 2004. *Soft power.* New York: Public Affairs.

Nye, Joseph S. *The Future of Power.* 1st ed. New York: PublicAffairs, 2011.

Office of the Director of National Intelligence. 2005. Letter from Al-Zawahiri to Al-Zarqawi. October 11.

Office of the Secretary of Defense. 2008. *Annual report to Congress: Military power of the People's Republic of China, 2008.* Washington, DC: Office of the Secretary of Defense.

Ogilvie-White, T., and J. Simpson. 2003. The NPT and its prepcom session: A regime in need of intensive care. *The Nonproliferation Review* 10(1):40–58.

Olson, J. S., ed. 1988. *Dictionary of the Vietnam War.* New York: Greenwood.

Ougaard, M. 2004. *Political globalization—State, power and social forces.* London: Palgrave.

Oxfam. 2003. Boxing match in agricultural trade. Briefing Paper No. 32. www.oxfam.org (accessed June 25, 2007).

Palme Commission. 1982. *Common security: A programme for disarmament. The report of the Palme Commission.* London: Pan Books.

Panofsky, W. K. H. 1998. Dismantling the concept of "weapons of mass destruction." *Arms Control Today* 28(3):3–8.

Pastor, R. 1999. *A century's journey: How the great powers shape the world.* New York: Basic Books.

Pearson, R. 2000. Rethinking gender matters in development. In *Poverty and development into the twenty-first century,* ed. T. Allen and A. Thomas, 383–402. Oxford, UK: Oxford University Press.

Pendergrast, M. 1993. *For God, country and Coca-Cola: The unauthorized history of the great American soft drink and the company that makes it.* London: Weidenfeld & Nicolson.

Peters, J. S., and A. Wolper, eds. 1995. *Women's rights, human rights: International feminist perspectives.* New York: Routledge.

Pillar, P. 2001. *Terrorism and US foreign policy.* Washington, DC: Brookings Institution Press.

Pogge, T. 2002. *World poverty and human rights: Cosmopolitan responsibilities and reforms.* Cambridge, UK: Polity.

Price, R. 1998. Reversing the gun sights: Transnational civil society targets land mines. *International Organization* 52(3).

Pugh, M. 2001. Peacekeeping and humanitarian intervention. In *Issues in world politics,* 2nd ed., ed. B. White, R. Little, and M. Smith. London: Palgrave.

Purdy, M. 2004–2005. Countering terrorism: The missing pillar. *International Journal* 60(1).

Rapley, J. 1996. *Understanding development.* Boulder, CO: Lynne Rienner.

Rehn, E., and E. J. Sirleaf. 2002. *Women, war, peace: The independent experts' assessment on the impact of armed conflict on women and women's role in peace-building.* http://www.unifem.org/resources/ item_detail.php?ProductID=17 (accessed June 25, 2007).

Reus-Smit, C. 1999. *The moral purpose of the state.* Princeton, NJ: Princeton University Press.

——. 2001. The strange death of liberal international theory. *European Journal of International Law* 12(3):573–93.

Richardson, J. L. 1997. Contending liberalisms: Past and present. *European Journal of International Relations* 3(1):5–33.

Rischard, J. F. 2002. *High noon: Twenty global problems, twenty years to solve them.* New York: Basic Books.

Roberts, A. 1996. The United Nations: Variants of collective security. In *Explaining international relations since 1945,* ed. N. Woods, 309–36. Oxford, UK: Oxford University Press.

Roberts, A., and B. Kingsbury. 1993. Introduction: The UN's roles in international society since 1945. In *United Nations, divided world,* ed. A. Roberts and B. Kingsbury. Oxford, UK: Clarendon.

Roberts, G. 1984. *Questioning development.* London: Returned Volunteer Action.

Roche, D. 1986. Balance out of kilter in arms/society needs. *The Financial Post* January 18:8.

Rorty, R. 1993. Sentimentality and human rights. In *On human rights*, ed. S. Shute and S. Hurley. New York: Basic Books.

Rosamond, B. 2000. *Theories of European integration.* Basingstoke, UK: Macmillan.

Rosenau, J. 1981. *The study of political adaptation.* London: Pinter.

Sagan, Scott D. "Why Do States Build Nuclear Weapons? Three Models in Search of a Bomb." *New Global Dangers: Changing Dimensions of International Security.* Boston: MIT Press, 2004. 45–77.

Sagan, S. D., and K. N. Waltz. 1995. *The spread of nuclear weapons: A debate.* New York: Norton.

Sageman, M. 2004. *Understanding terror networks.* Philadelphia: University of Pennsylvania Press.

Sargent, L., ed. 1981. *Women and revolution: A discussion of the unhappy marriage of Marxism and feminism.* Boston: South End.

Schwarz, A. 1999. *A nation in waiting: Indonesia's search for stability.* Sydney: Allen & Unwin.

Sen, A. 1981. *Poverty and famines.* Oxford, UK: Clarendon.

——. 1983. The food problem: Theory and policy. In *South–south strategy*, ed. A. Gauhar. London: Zed.

——. 1999. *Development as freedom.* Oxford, UK: Oxford University Press.

Shue, H. 1996. *Basic rights.* 2nd ed. Princeton, NJ: Princeton University Press.

Simon Fraser University, Human Security Research Group (2011), *Human Security Report 2009–2010,* available online at: http://www.hsrgroup.org/human-security-reports/20092010/text.aspx, last accessed on 24 November 2012).

Singer, P. 2009. *The life you can save: Acting now to end world poverty.* New York: Random House.

——. 2012. Do drones undermine democracy? *New York Times* January 21.

Smith, K. E., and M. Light, eds. 2001. *Ethics and foreign policy.* Cambridge, UK: Cambridge University Press.

Smith, M. J. 1986. *Realist thought from Weber to Kissinger.* Baton Rouge: Louisiana State University Press.

Smith, S. 1999. The increasing insecurity of security studies: Conceptualising security in the last twenty years. *Contemporary Security Policy* 20(3).

Spivak, G. C. 1988. Can the subaltern speak? In *Marxism and the interpretation of culture*, ed. C. Nelson and L. Grossberg. Basingstoke, UK: Macmillan.

Steans, J. 1998. *Gender and international relations: An introduction.* Cambridge, UK: Polity.

Suganami, H. 1989. *The domestic analogy and world order proposals.* Cambridge, UK: Cambridge University Press.

Suhrke, A. 2004. A stalled initiative. *Security Dialogue* 35(3):365.

Taylor, A. J. P. 1961. *The origins of the second world war.* Harmondsworth, UK: Penguin.

Thomas, A., et al. 1994. *Third world atlas.* 2nd ed. Milton Keynes, UK: Open University Press.

Thomas, C. 2000. *Global governance, development and human security.* London: Pluto.

Thomas, C., and P. Wilkin. 2004. Still waiting after all these years: The third world on the periphery of international relations. *British Journal of Politics and International Relations* 6:223–40.

Thomas, T. 2004. *Dragon bytes: Chinese information-war theory and practice.* Fort Leavenworth, KS: Foreign Military Studies Office.

Thucydides. [1954] 1972. *The Peloponnesian war*, trans. R. Warner. London: Penguin.

Tickner, J. A. 1992. *Gender in international relations: Feminist perspectives on achieving global security.* New York: Columbia University Press.

Tow, W. T., and R. Trood. 2000. Linkages between traditional security and human security. In *Asia's emerging regional order*, ed. W. T. Tow, R. Thakur, and In-Taek Hyun, 14. New York: United Nations University Press.

United Nations. 2002. *Women, peace and security: Study submitted by the secretary-general pursuant to security council resolution 1325 (2000).* New York: United Nations. http://www.un.org/womenwatch/feature/wps/ (accessed June 25, 2007).

——. 2004. Report of the Secretary-General's High-level Panel on Threats, Challenges and Change (2004). *A More Secure World: Our Shared Responsibility* (N. Y.: UN Department of Publications).

——. 2005. *In larger freedom: Towards development, security and human rights for all: Report of the Secretary-General.* New York: United Nations.

——. 2011. *UN peacekeeping background note.* UN Department of Peacekeeping Operations. http://www.un.org/en/peacekeeping/documents/backgroundnote.pdf (accessed April 14, 2011).

United Nations Development Programme. 1994. *United Nations human development report.* New York: Oxford University Press.

——. 1997. *United Nations human development report 1997.* New York: United Nations Development Programme.

——. 1998. *United Nations human development report 1998.* Oxford, UK: Oxford University Press.

——. 2003. *United Nations human development report*. New York: United Nations Development Programme.

——. 2005. *Human Development report 2005: International cooperation at a crossroads*. New York: United Nations Development Programme.

——. 2011. *United Nations sustainability and equity: A better future for all*. New York: United Nations Development Programme.

United Nations General Assembly. 10 December 1948. *Universal declaration of human rights*, 217 A (III). New York: United Nations General Assembly.

United Nations Inter-Agency Committee on Women and Gender Equality. 1999. *Final communiqué, women's empowerment in the context of human security* (7–8 December 1999, ESCAP, Bangkok, Thailand). http://www.un.org/womenwatch/ianwge/collaboration/finalcomm1999.htm (accessed June 25, 2007).

University of British Columbia, Human Security Center. 2005. *Human security report 2005: War and peace in the 21st century*. New York: Oxford University Press.

——. 2006. *The human security brief 2006*. http://www.humansecuritybrief.info/ (accessed June 25, 2007).

US Campaign to Ban Landmines. *United States Campaign to Ban Landmines*. Affiliated with the International Campaign to Ban Landmines. www.uscbl.org (accessed April 4, 2013).

US Department of State. 2003. *Country reports on human rights practices, Burma*. http://www.state.gov/g/drl/rls/hrrpt/2002/18237.htm (accessed June 25, 2007).

Vincent, R. J. 1974. *Nonintervention and international order*. Princeton, NJ: Princeton University Press.

Vogel, R. J. 2011. Drone warfare and the law of armed conflict. *Denver Journal of International Law and Policy* 39(1). http://ssrn.com/abstract=1759562.

von Grebmer, K., D. Headey, T. Olofinbiyi, D. Wiesmann, H. Fritschel, S. Yin, Y. Yohannes, C. Foley, C. von Oppeln, B. Iseli, C. Béné, and L. Haddad. 2013. *2013 Global Hunger Index—The Challenge of Hunger: Building Resilience to Achieve Food and Nutrition Security*. "Global Hunger Index Scores by Severity" map. Bonn, Germany: Welthungerhilfe; Washington, DC: International Food Policy Research Institute; Dublin, Ireland: Concern Worldwide.

Wallerstein, I. 1979. *The capitalist world-economy*. Cambridge, UK: Cambridge University Press.

Waltz, K. 1959. *Man, the state and war*. New York: Columbia University Press.

——. 1979. *Theory of international politics*. Reading, MA: Addison-Wesley.

——. 1989. The origins of war in neorealist theory. In *The origin and prevention of major wars*, ed. R. I. Rotberg and T. K. Rabb, 39–52. Cambridge, UK: Cambridge University Press.

Walzer, M. 1977. *Just and unjust wars: A moral argument with historical illustration*. Harmondsworth, UK: Penguin.

——. 1994. *Thick and thin: Moral argument at home and abroad*. Notre Dame, IN: University of Notre Dame Press.

Weber, H. 2002. Global governance and poverty reduction. In *Global governance: Critical perspectives*, ed. S. Hughes and R. Wilkinson. London: Palgrave.

Weber, M. 1949. *The methodology of the social sciences*, ed. E. Shils and H. Finch. New York: Free Press.

Weiss, T. G. 2004. The sunset of humanitarian intervention? The responsibility to protect in a unipolar era. *Security Dialogue* 35(2):135–53.

Wendt, A. 1992. Anarchy is what states make of it: The social construction of power politics. *International Organisation* 46(2):391–425.

Wessel, I., and G. Wimhofer, eds. 2001. *Violence in Indonesia*. Hamburg, Germany: Abera-Verl.

Wiener, A., and T. Diez, eds. 2004. *European integration theory*. Oxford, UK: Oxford University Press.

Wilkinson, P. 2003. Implications of the attacks of 9/11 for the future of terrorism. In *Global responses to terrorism*, ed. M. Buckley and R. Fawn. London: Routledge.

Wood, B. 1998. *The middle powers and the general interest*. Ottawa, Canada: North-South Institute.

Wright, R. 1986. *Sacred rage: The wrath of militant Islam*. New York: Simon & Schuster.

Zalewski, M. 1993. Feminist standpoint theory meets international relations theory: A feminist version of David and Goliath. *Fletcher Forum of World Affairs* 17(2).

Credits

PHOTO CREDITS

Chapter 1
p. 1: AP Photo/Peng Sun, Pool; p. 4: AP Photo/Jason DeCrow; p. 5: MAXIM SHEMETOV/Reuters/Corbis; p. 7: AP Photo/Elizabeth Dalziel, File; p. 9: AP Photo/Bernat Armangue; p. 11: AP Photo/Obed Zilwa; p. 12: AP Photo/Hassan Ammar; p. 14: AP Photo/Korean Central News Agency via Korea News Service; p. 15: AP Photo/Kin Cheung, File; p. 21: © Hole-in-the-Wall Education Limited 2012; p. 23: AP Photo/Brennan Linsley; p. 25: Kyodo via AP Images; p. 26: AP Photo/Charles Platiau, Pool

Chapter 2
p. 30: AP Photo/Mohammed Asad; p. 33: AP Photo; p. 35: AP Photo; p. 37: Time & Life Pictures/Getty Images; p. 41: AP Photo; p. 43: AP Photo; p. 46: Dario Mitidieri/Contributor; p. 50: AP Photo/AU-UN IST, Stuart Price; p. 52: Color China Photo/AP Images/Hu Shanmin; p. 53: AP Photo/U.S.M.C., Sgt. Don L. Maes, File; p. 55: AP Photo/Jonathan Kalan; p. 57: AP Photo/Evan Vucci; p. 58: AP Photo/Korean Central News Agency via Korea News Service; p. 63: AP Photo/The White House, Pete Souza

Chapter 3
p. 67: AP Photo/Korea Pool; p. 71: AP Photo/Aman Sharma; p. 73: AP Photo/Jacquelyn Martin; p. 75: AP Photo/Mikhail Metzel; p. 78: WITT/SIPA/1205210421; p. 79: AP Photo/Ben Curtis; p. 81: DEA Picture Library; p. 82: AP Photo/Michel Euler; p. 84: Time & Life Pictures/Getty Images; p. 86: Photo by Bill Greene/The Boston Globe via Getty Images; p. 89: AP Photo/Hassene Dridi; p. 91: AP Photo/Herbert Knosowski; p. 94: AP Photo/Chitose Suzuki; p. 97: Press Association via AP Images; p. 98: AP Photo/Czarek Sokolowski; p. 100: AP Photo/Hassan Ammar; p. 101: AP Photo/Rafiq Maqbool

Chapter 4
p. 108: REUTERS/Kacper Pempel; p. 112: AP Photo/Yves Logghe; p. 114: AP Photo/Felipe Dana; p. 119: AP Photo/Carlos Espinoza; p. 124: AP Photo/Peter Dejong; p. 128: AP Photo/Eranga Jayawardena; p. 132: Lucile Grosjean—ACF—Philippines; p. 134: AP Photo/Lee Jin-man; p. 136: AP Photo/Jerome Delay; p. 137: AP Photo/Richard Drew, File; p. 139: European External Action Service–EEAS

Chapter 5
p. 145: AP Photo/Yves Logghe; p. 148: AP Photo/Mary Altaffer; p. 151: AP Photo/Cliff Owen; p. 154: AP Photo; p. 160: tatif55/Shutterstock ® images; p. 162: AFP/Getty Images; p. 168: AP Photo/Saurabh Das; p. 170: AP Photo/Bela Szandelszky; p. 173: AP Photo/Christian Lutz;

p. 175: Getty Images; p. 178: AP Photo/pa; p. 179: AP Photo/Cliff Owen; p. 181: AP Photo/Lennart Preiss; p. 182: Alex Masi/Corbis/APImages; p. 183: AP Photo/Gonzalez

Chapter 6
p. 188: Uriel Sinai/Getty Images; p. 191: AP Photo/Visar Kryeziu; p. 192: AP Photo/Turkish Military HO; p. 193: AP Photo/DoD photo by Master Sgt. Val Gempis, U.S. Air Force; p. 194: AP Photo/Hasan Sarbakhshian; p. 195: Ole Spata/picture-alliance/dpa/AP Images; p. 196: AP Photo/Steve Helber; p. 201: AP Photo/Ebrahim Noroozi; p. 204: AP Photo/Kim Kwang Hyon; p. 206: AP Photo/Charles Krupa; p. 208: AP Photo; p. 211: AP Photo/Keystone, Salvatore Di Nolfi; p. 212: AP Photo/Koji Sasahara; p. 218: AP Photo/Ted S. Warren; p. 219: AP Photo/Lee Jin-man

Chapter 7
p. 221: AP Photo/Sven Kaestner; p. 227: AP Photo/Alexandre Meneghini; p. 229: AP Photo/Shaam News Network; p. 233: AP Photo/Sakchai Lalit; p. 234: AP Photo/Mohammad Hannon; p. 236: AP Photo/Kathy Willens; p. 239: AP Photo/Heng Sinith; p. 240: AP Photo/Bullit Marquez; p. 243: AP Photo/Vincent Yu; p. 250: AP Photo/Desi Sari; p. 252: Associated Press via AP Photo

Chapter 8
p. 256: AP Photo/Sergei Chuzavkov; p. 260: AP Photo/Abe Fox; p. 263: FABRICE COFFRINI/AFP/Getty Images; p. 266: AP Photo/Nikolas Giakoumidis; p. 269: AP Photo/Doug Mills; p. 273: AP Photo/Koji Sasahara; p. 275: AP Photo/Jockel Finck; p. 277: Imaginechina via AP Images; p. 280: AP Photo/Rajanish Kakade

Chapter 9
p. 285: Rex Features via AP Images; p. 288: AP Photo/Mary Altaffer; p. 293: AP Photo/Al Behrman; p. 298: AP Photo/Felipe Dana; p. 301: Andreas Arnold/picture-alliance/dpa/AP Images; p. 302: AP Photo; p. 303: AP Photo/Christine Nesbitt; p. 307: AP Photo/Gregory Bull; p. 309: ROBERTO SCHMIDT/AFP/Getty Images

Chapter 10
p. 313: NASA EO/Rex Features via AP Images; p. 316: Copyright Kristian Buus/In Pictures/Corbis/APImages; p. 320: AP Photo/POLFOTO, Linda Johansen; p. 321: AP Photo/Joana Coutinho, MCRCP; p. 324: AP Photo/John McConnico; p. 329: AP Photo/Mark Baker; p. 330: Nurcholis / Rex Features via AP Images; p. 332: MCT via Getty Images; p. 334: AP Photo/NOAA; p. 337 (top): AP Photo/Marcio Jose Sanchez; p. 337 (bottom): AP Photo/Wichita Falls Times Record News, Torin Halsey; p. 338: AP Photo/Aris Messinis; p. 339: AP Photo/John McConnico

FIGURE CREDITS

Chapter 1
p. 13: Pew Global Attitudes Project, a project of the Pew Research Center

Chapter 2
p. 44: Vital Signs 2006-2007, The Worldwatch Institute

Chapter 4
p. 111: Pew Global Attitudes Project, a project of the Pew Research Center; p. 116: The Fund for Peace; p. 121: CIA World Factbook

Chapter 5
p. 155: © United Nations; p. 157: "The United Nations System" © United Nations Department of Public Information, 2007; p. 178: Union of International Associations; p. 180: 2012 Global Go To Think Tanks Report and Policy Advic. FINAL UNITED NATIONS UNIVERSITY EDITION, JANUARY 28, 2013. Think Tanks and Civil Societies Program © 2012, University of Pennsylvania, International Relations Program.

Chapter 6
p. 199: Federation of American Scientists; Nuclear Threat Initiative

Chapter 7
p. 247: Themnér, Lotta & Peter Wallensteen, 2013. "Armed Conflict, 1946–2012." Journal of Peace Research 50(4).

Chapter 8
p. 276: Word Trade in 2009/http.www.abh-ace.org/impor_en/info-center/trade-statistics/comments-mf/2009/12-months-wto-com_en.pdf/Volume of world merchandise exports, 1965–2009 (Annual % change)/World Trade Organisation-March 2010 . . . . World Trade in 2012/http://www.abh-ace.be/en/binaries/World%20Trade%202012_BD_tcm450-228713.pdf

Chapter 9
p. 289: United Nations, based on data and estimates provided by: Food and Agriculture Organization of the United Nations; Inter-Parliamentary Union; International Labour Organization; International Telecommunication Union; UNAIDS; UNESCO; UN-Habitat; UNICEF; UN Population Division; World Bank; World Health Organization—based on statistics available as of June 2013. Compiled by Statistics Division, Department of Economic and Social Affairs, United Nations; p. 297: Per capita Real GDP Growth Rates of Main Countries from "On Globalization and the World Economy in 2010–Prospects and Policy Implications to Japan–The Report of the Globalization Working Group in the Economic Outlook Committee," the Economic Council, Japan; p. 305: First and second billion: Population Reference Bureau. Third through ninth billion: United Nations, World Population Prospects: The 1998 Revision (medium scenario). See www.prb.org

Chapter 10
p. 333: Copyright Philip's; p. 335: Netherland's Environmental Assessment Agency; p. 336: Copyright Philip's

MAP CREDITS

Frontmatter
xxviii–xxix: Cartography © Philip's; xxx: Cartography © Philip's; xxxi: Cartography © Philip's; xxxii: Cartography © Philip's; xxxiii: Cartography © Philip's; xxxiv: Cartography © Philip's; xxxv: Cartography © Philip's

Chapter 2
p. 34: Cartography © Philip's; p. 41: Cartography © Philip's

Chapter 6
p. 198: Gizmodo World Conflict Map 2012, The Atlas of War and Peace, and Globalmajority.org; p. 215: National Consortium for the Study of Terrorism and Responses to Terrorism (START), 2011. Global Terrorism Database [Data file]. http://www.start.umd.edu/gtd

Chapter 7
p. 236: Freedom in the World 2013: Democratic Breakthroughs in the Balance. Selected Data from Freedom House's Annual Survey of Political Rights and Civil Liberties. Freedom House: http://www.freedomhouse.org/sites/default/files/FIW%202013%20Booklet.pdf

Chapter 9
p. 304: von Grember et al. (2013). Reprinted with permission from the International Food Policy Research Institute

Chapter 10
p. 315: © CarbonMap.org by Kiln.it

Index

Page numbers in bold indicate photos, figures, and tables.